BUDGETING

"Spending—uh—I mean speaking!"

Drawing by Alan Dunn; © 1959, The New Yorker Magazine, Inc.

BUDGETING
A Comparative Theory of Budgetary Processes

AARON WILDAVSKY
*Professor of Political Science and Dean
of the Graduate School of Public Policy,
University of California, Berkeley*

LITTLE, BROWN AND COMPANY
Boston   Toronto

Library of Congress Catalog Card No. 75–14991

SECOND PRINTING

Published simultaneously in Canada
by Little, Brown & Company (Canada) Limited

Printed in the United States of America

Chapter 3 has been adapted from Otto A. Davis, M. A. H. Dempster, and Aaron Wildavsky, "Towards a Predictive Theory of Government Expenditure: U.S. Domestic Appropriations," *British Journal of Political Science,* vol. 4 (October 1974), pp. 419–452. Published by Cambridge University Press. By permission.

Chapter 14 includes material from Aaron Wildavsky and Arthur Hammond, "Comprehensive Versus Incremental Budgeting in the Department of Agriculture," *Administrative Science Quarterly,* vol. 10, no. 3 (December 1965), pp. 321–346. By permission.

Portions of chapters 16, 17, and 18 have been taken from Aaron Wildavsky, *The Politics of the Budgetary Process,* 2nd ed. (Boston: Little, Brown, 1974), chapters 6 and 7. By permission.

For Leroy Graymer,
Associate Dean of the Graduate School of Public Policy,
without whose friendship and talent I could not have
continued in the worlds of administration and scholarship.

Contents

Preface

The purpose of this book is to collect in one place existing knowledge on budgeting. By "existing" I mean reasonably reliable accounts of how budgeting is carried on in a particular level of government. The reason the book features Britain, France, Japan, and the United States among wealthy countries, rather than Germany, Sweden, or the Soviet Union, for instance, is simply that the budgetary processes of the former countries have been studied and reported on while the latter have not yet received scholarly treatment. By "knowledge" I mean a set of true propositions or a corpus of fact which describes each budgetary process as an instance of a type with recognizable properties.

The focus of *Budgeting* is explicitly comparative. The processes studied here are classified according to the ways they exemplify the dominant variables (wealth and predictability) at work in producing their characteristic forms of budgetary behavior. This explains what might otherwise appear as a strange order of exposition. The four rich countries are followed by American cities, then poor countries, then American states, and finally deviant cases from a variety of American public organizations. I have ordered the analysis by category, not by country. The wealthy and certain (rich countries) are followed by the poor and certain (American cities), the poor and uncertain (low income countries), combinations of the others (American states), and some that deviate from all the rest because key elements (the roles of spending advocate and treasury guardian) are absent. By understanding what it takes to produce the exceptions — the virtual absence of roles or the total presence of resource constraints — we learn why everyone else follows the rules.

Seeking "ruleful" behavior (that is, knowledge) across countries and continents is no easy task. Talk about comparative analysis rarely is matched by action. My search for comparative propositions about governmental institutions, policies, or processes has proven unrewarding.[1] One may think these exist because they ought to exist, because one vaguely recalls studying them, because one hears they exist; but in fact they do not. What we do find are comparative studies of electoral arrangements[2] and of citizen or elite answers to similar questions about political subjects.[3] These studies have in common (1) data manufactured as a byproduct of the studies, i.e., proportions of votes for parties or differences in opinions among citizens, and (2) lack of concern with actual operation of government. It is not so much that attitudes set forth in these studies may not be tightly coupled to actual behavior, but rather that the subjects chosen may have little to do with anything the respondent knows or cares about or is supposed to act upon. To ask about, say, European integration or the seizure of power by force is not necessarily to receive an answer from a person who expects (or is expected by others) to act in these areas. Answers, then, are products of the interview situation rather than of close connection to the life of the respondent or of the polity. Types of electoral systems are more closely related to who occupies governmental office and, therefore, to what governments do. Whether or not political people perceive the impact of these rules the way scholars do, whether they can or do act on them to secure advantage, must remain problematical apart from investigation of purposeful social action in support of or in opposition to prevailing arrangements. Invariably, elegance of formulation, aided by restricting analyses to the formal electoral rules as they produce numerical outcomes, is sacrificed to understanding political action. My point is not that these studies are trivial, for surely they are interesting, but that they are too remote from processes of government. Comparative analysis must deal directly with the universe of governmental activity, however messy and awkward that may turn out to be. This book is such an effort.

The reasons for studying budgeting (or the expenditure process, as it is sometimes called) are many. It exists. The people involved in it care about what they do. Their actions are important to many others in or out of government. The bonds between budgeting and "politiking" are intimate. Realistic budgets are an expression of practical politics. The allocation of resources necessarily reflects the distribution of power. Budgeting is so basic it must reveal the norms by which men live in a particular political culture — for it is through the choices inherent in limited resources that consensus is established and conflict is generated. The authority of government is made manifest

---

[1] For a very recent exception see Hugh Heclo, *Modern Social Policy* (New Haven: Yale University Press, 1974).

[2] See Douglas Rae, *Political Consequences of Electoral Laws* (New Haven: Yale University Press, 1967).

[3] See Gabriel Almond and Sydney Verba, *The Civic Culture; Political Attitudes and Democracy in Five Nations* (Princeton: Princeton University Press, 1963), for citizens, and Robert Putnam, *The Beliefs of Politicians: Ideology, Conflict, Democracy in Britain and Italy* (New Haven: Yale University Press, 1973).

by its ability not only to make a budget but also to make it stick. Public policy-making in action — which programs to benefit whom will be established or maintained at what levels of support? — is epitomized through the budget. So is implementation; for, when push comes to shove, programs will not be carried out as intended (or at all) unless commitment is memorialized by money. If justice delayed is justice denied, a budget rejected is a program aborted, a fund diverted is a policy perverted. When a process involves power, authority, culture, consensus, and conflict, it captures a great deal of national political life.

The study of budgeting also conveys important methodological advantages. The budgetary process normally is well defined and is carried on in some way anywhere scarce resources are to be divided among numerous claimants, that is, virtually everywhere. Caught between crisis and constancy, between appraising governmental effectiveness by looking at infrequent major events or continuous minor modifications, the student of politics finds a reasonable compromise in budgeting: decisions of considerable importance are being made all the time. Where data exist and are reliable (and there are such places), outcomes of the processes appear in quantified form. In the United States, for instance, both inputs (requests for spending) and outputs (actual appropriations) are made public. There it is possible to test budgetary hypotheses (derived by asking people what they do and by observing how they do it) in a more rigorous form.

Still, comparison does demand a high level of generality and hence a loss of specificity. There is no instrument good for all purposes and all times. (There may be men for all seasons, but Colonel Nicholson of the *Bridge Over the River Kwai* — wonderful under some conditions, terrible under others — rather than Sir Thomas More, seems to me truer to the modern condition). Thus the reader will not find discussion of individual persons who fill the roles that will be so much talked about. Yet we all know that it does matter who (by ideology, class, party, etc.) occupies these positions. Gladstone and Disraeli were Chancellors of the Exchequer, one justly more famous than the other for guarding the Treasury. Nevertheless, I believe that knowing the *role* attached to an institutional position almost always is more helpful than any other bit of information. If one is mainly interested in figuring out the likelihood of the latest move in a specific situation involving expenditure, knowledge of the personality and predispositions of the key decision-makers is essential. If one is looking for the most powerful predictive variables over the largest number of instances, role will beat personality hands down. When this is not true, it is a sure sign that something is very much wrong with either observer or observed.

A trade-off can be made between parsimony and completeness. A full explanation of all factors bearing on the budgetary process, if such were possible, would exhaust everyone without enlightening anyone. It would look more like a laundry list (or better still, a telephone directory) than a coherent explanation. Naturally, such conditions (oil crises, inflation, strikes, internal party disputes and heaven knows what else) keep changing. What we want, really, is knowledge of the more permanent and persistent forces so we can apply it to the results of contemporary investigations. Knowledge, as Kenneth Boulding once said, involves a progressive loss of information; otherwise, one would be overwhelmed by the multitude of apparently disparate happenings.

The substantive content of budgets (so much for this program, so little for that activity, hardly anything for our favorite bureau) is not my subject. Full comprehension of how and why each budgetary decision was made and implemented would imply nearly complete understanding of government itself. No one can make such a claim. For by the time one has exhausted the implications of spending on this or that rather than on something else across the board of governmental policies, not much is left that needs explanation. This book is about budgetary processes, not about energy or welfare or defense. The units of analysis are organizations, not policies. Anyone who wishes to investigate particular areas of policy must do precisely that, taking advantage of what is known about budgeting along with many other things.

But one area of policy — policy about the desirable structure and operation of budgetary processes — is directly relevant to the concerns of this book, for if we have gained some understanding of budgeting, we should be able to apply it to the perennial problems of reform. Knowing why things work the way they do is an indispensable (though not the only) part of figuring out how to make them work better, or at least differently. Thus the last section of this book is devoted to a consideration of the leading reform of modern times — program budgeting: How has it worked? Why isn't it more successful? What other reforms might work better? I shall try to show how understanding the major variables at work in regular budgeting helps explain failures and points to avenues of success in reform.

No book that tries to cover as wide a range of phenomena as this one does — budgetary process in far-flung corners of the contemporary world — could possibly be the work of a single person. I could not and did not do it all alone. Help there has been in abundance. I have been fortunate in my collaborators. It is now (the spring of 1974) fourteen years that I have been studying budgeting. For eleven of those years, Otto Davis, Michael Dempster, and I have been working together on mathematical models of the United States Federal budgetary process. The last part of Chapter 2 and all of Chapter 3 are products of our collaboration. By the time this book appears, in the fall of 1975, we should be able to put to the test our predictions of agency requests and congressional appropriations.

I have adapted Chapters 4 and 19, on the expenditure process in Britain, from my joint effort with Hugh Heclo, *The Private Government of Public Money* (London: Macmillan; Berkeley and Los Angeles: University of California Press, 1974). Naomi Caiden and I took the material for Chapter 7 from our book on *Planning and Budgeting in Poor Countries* (New York: John

Wiley, 1974). The historical section of Chapter 13 has been done with Carolyn Webber. My "diagram doctor," Peter Sperlich, helped redraw the diagrams for that chapter with customary elegance. Chapters 14 and 15 on various budgetary experiments in the Department of Agriculture have been taken respectively from a paper I wrote with Arthur Hammond: "Comprehensive versus Incremental Budgeting in the Department of Agriculture," *Administrative Science Quarterly,* 10 (December 1965), 321–346; and a book with Jeanne Nienaber, *The Budgeting and Evaluation of Federal Recreation Programs: Or, Money Doesn't Grow on Trees* (New York: Basic Books, 1973).

Not only have I drawn freely on past collaborative work, I have also worked with others in writing several chapters. Chapter 6 on American cities is a product of both forms of collaboration. It contains a section on Oakland revised from an earlier paper with Arnold Meltsner, "Leave City Budgeting Alone! A Survey, Case History and Recommendations for Reform," in *Financing the Metropolis: The Role of Public Policy in Urban Economics,* Vol. IV, edited by John P. Crecine and Louis H. Masotti (Beverly Hills: Sage Publications, Inc., 1970), pp. 311–358; it has now been expanded through a joint effort by Alex Radian and myself. Radian also coauthored Chapter 8 on American states and Chapter 9 on deviant budgetary processes. A substantial part of Chapter 12 on "Wealth, Taxes, and Politics in Rich Countries" was written with Aidan Vining, a student at the Graduate School of Public Policy. The sections in Chapter 17 that deal with experience of cities, states, and the federal government in implementing program budgeting were written together with Brian Tannenbaum. Therefore, it is appropriate for me to use the plural "we" when discussing much of this work.

Besides working with collaborators, I have also drawn heavily for Chapter 5 (about France and Japan) on splendid work by Guy Lord, *The French Budgetary Process* (Berkeley and Los Angeles: University of California Press, 1973), and John Creighton Campbell, "Contemporary Japanese Budget Politics" (doctoral dissertation, Columbia University, 1973, soon to be published by University of California Press). Everyone who studies federal budgeting is indebted to Richard Fenno's classic, *The Power of the Purse* (Boston: Little, Brown, 1966). The chapters on program budgeting also benefited greatly from background provided by Herman von Gunsteren, *The Quest for Control* (to be published by John Wiley) and by Allen Schick in various articles and from his *Budget Innovation in the States* (Washington, D.C.: Brookings Institution, 1971). John Crecine's *Governmental Problem Solving: A Computer Simulation of Municipal Budgeting* (Chicago: Rand McNally, 1969) was invaluable in the chapter on cities. My understanding of the need for budgetary reform at the federal level in the United States has been enriched by reading several papers authored by Louis Fisher who, like Schick, is with the Congressional Research Service. My own ideas developed after extensive conversation with William A. Niskanen, who has himself contributed valuable proposals.

Although I have drawn extensively on previous work, there is also a great deal in *Budgeting* that is new. All chapters dealing explicitly with comparison are new — the first chapter, presenting the variables used for comparison; the tenth, on calculations and strategies; and the eleventh and the twelfth, on conflict. Also new are most of the chapters on cities, on PPBS around the world, and on requirements for reform. The chapters on American states and deviant cases also are new. Every chapter, moreover, has been rethought, revised, and revamped to fit into a comparative framework. The reader should be able to understand not only how budgetary processes work in various places but also to learn how and why they resemble and differ from one another. If past work survives here, it does so because I think it has present value.

Once I heard a story, possibly apocryphal, about a learned gentleman who spent his life studying the organization of post offices, first in one country, then in another. I do not intend to follow his example. Sufficient is enough. This book contains my last original research on contemporary budgetary processes. If its reception should warrant the effort, however, I would expect to bring it up to date by incorporating new work done by others.

My final effort in the field of budgeting, I hope, will be historical: Carolyn Webber and I now are studying the history of expenditure and taxation from earliest recorded times to as far as we get. Most of what has happened in budgeting, after all, is not a product of our time, or even of our century, but of the several thousand years preceding the events recorded here. Traditional subjects in budgeting — auditing, control of corruption, record keeping — are better understood in their historical context, so I will wait to deal with them. The inadequacies of this book, therefore, can conveniently be blamed on lack of historical perspective, which will (as always) be provided later.

The time has come to thank those who have helped me. I am bound to fail at this task because complete acknowledgments would have to be extended to all those who have helped me in the past fourteen years. My collaborators are acknowledged above. Here I must content myself with expressing appreciation to those who have commented upon the first draft: Eugene Bardach, John Campbell, Andrew Cowart, Hugh Heclo, Martin Landau, Arnold Meltsner, Fred Pryor, Robert Putnam, Allen Schick, Walter Weyrauch, and an anonymous reviewer for the publisher.

Alex Radian, a graduate student in the Department of Political Science, was my research assistant while I wrote this book and did his utmost to keep me from going astray. Mappie Seabury did her usual invaluable job of editing, sometimes more than once; her insistence on clear and colloquial expression has added to whatever stylistic felicity the book possesses. Florence Myer did a beautiful job typing the manuscript, including endless changes to the "final" draft. Helen Josephine checked footnotes with exactitude and, as a librarian, provided expert help in compiling the bibliography.

Aaron Wildavsky

I
Theory

1

Toward a Comparative Theory of Budgetary Processes

This book is about budgetary processes. It covers budgeting in four rich countries — Britain, France, Japan, and the United States — numerous poor ones, American cities and states, and a variety of deviant cases. Its focus is on budgeting as a political instrument. Its purpose is explicitly comparative. Before the operation of the many budgetary processes we shall consider may be understood in their full "particularity," we must understand the forces at work in their utmost "generality." In this chapter I shall define budgeting, develop a simplified model of budgetary relationships, and present a scheme for comparative analysis of budgetary processes. Why is budgeting, whatever it is, the way it is? Because, so far as I know, the variables I am about to discuss interact to make it so.

BUDGETS SERVE DIVERSE PURPOSES

Budgeting is translating financial resources into human purposes. Behind currencies stand human limitations; unless one lives on an everlasting lake of oil or possesses an alchemist's stone for turning base metals into gold, resources are limited. But human desires are not. Hence some way must be found to apportion available funds among competing people and purposes. Behind every government budget, then — which necessarily takes revenues from some citizens and distributes them to others — lies conflict. Invariably, there are more wants than money. Given the infinite variety of human desires, the budget of a collectivity (like a government) can never be just one thing but must be many.

A budget is a record of the past. Victories and defeats, bargains, and compromises over past allocations are reflected in the items included and (by inference) those left out. A budget also is a statement about the future; it attempts to link proposed expenditures with desirable future events. Budgets, therefore, must be plans; they try to determine future states of affairs through a series of current actions. Hence budgets also are predictions. They try to specify connections between words and numbers on the budget documents and future human behavior. Whether or not the behavior intended by the authors of a budget actually takes place, however, is a matter of empirical observation rather than of definitional postulation.

Since funds are limited, a budget becomes a mechanism for allocating resources. If receiving the largest returns for a given sum of money is stressed, or if the push is toward obtaining desired objectives at the lowest cost, a budget may become an instrument for pursuing efficiency. When efforts are made to make money grow, as it were, by considering spending a form of investment, budgets become means for securing economic growth. Expenditures are economically rational insofar as they add to (rather than detract from) a nation's wealth. To the extent that governments take money from some people in the form of taxes and give it to others who benefit from the expenditures, budgets becomes engines of income distribution. Of course, it is imperative to assess the direction of the distribution: does the money go from the rich to the poor or vice versa?

If organizations are seen as political coalitions, budgets are mechanisms through which subunits bargain over conflicting goals, make side-payments, and try to motivate one another to accomplish their objectives. A budget may represent an organization's expectations; it may contain the amounts the organization expects to spend. A budget may also reflect organizational aspirations; it may contain figures the organization hopes to receive under favorable conditions; since amounts requested for one purpose rather than for another often affect amounts received, budget proposals often are strategies. The total amount of money and its distribution among various activities may be designed to support an organization's goals. When a budget is used to keep spending within set bounds and to fixed purposes, it becomes a device through which some actors try to control the behavior of others. Then budgets may become forms of power.

Budgets are signals. As each participant acts on the budget, he receives information on the preferences of others and communicates his own desires through the choices he makes. Here a budget is a network of communications in which information is being continuously generated and fed back to the participants. Once enacted, a budget becomes a precedent; the fact that something has been done before vastly increases the chances that it will be done again. Should the document lack predictive value, however, should actual expenditures not flow from inclusion within it, a budget cannot act as a compass. No one can take his bearings from it. Then one must look elsewhere for the real mechanisms of resource allocation.

Budgets with predictive value may be seen as expressing the part played by government in national life, as the most operational expression of national priorities in the public sector. Compared to party platforms and most legislative laws, inclusion in the budget carries a higher probability of concrete action. Little can be done without money, and what will be tried is embedded in the budget. If one asks "Who gets what the government has to give?" then the answers for a specific moment in time are recorded in the budget. If politics is regarded as conflict over whose preferences are to prevail in the determination of policy, then the budget records the outcomes of this struggle. Let us, then, conceive of budgets as *attempts to allocate financial resources through political processes to serve differing human purposes.*

A Simplified Model of Budgetary Relationships

To define is not necessarily to establish a fact. Should we treat budgets as hypotheses — if the funds requested be granted, then they will be spent as promised — it remains to be seen whether and to what degree testing will validate them. It will prove useful to start by outlining a simplified model of budgeting apart from any particular environment or specific conditions other than scarcity, societal complexity, and (at least partially) conflicting preferences for expenditures. There is never enough money, people disagree on how to spend it, and they cannot fully understand the consequences of their actions. But they do have some discretion; their actions are not totally determined by others. In this way I shall set out the terms for future discussion.

Making decisions depends on calculating which alternatives to consider and to choose. Calculation involves determining how problems are identified, get broken down into manageable dimensions, and are related to one another; how choices are made as to what is relevant and who shall be taken into account. A major clue to understanding budgeting is the extraordinary complexity of the calculations involved. In any large organization, a huge number of items must be considered, many of which are of considerable technical difficulty. Yet in most areas of policy there is little or no theory which would let practitioners predict the consequences of alternative moves and the probability of their occurring. Man operates according to the principle of "bounded rationality." He sees "through a glass darkly." His ability to calculate is severely limited; time is always in short supply, and the number of matters that can be encompassed in one mind at the same time is quite small. Nor has anyone solved the imposing problem of the interpersonal comparison of utilities: outside of the political process, there is no agreed-on way to compare and evaluate the merits of different programs for different people whose preferences vary in kind and in intensity.

Those who budget deal with their overwhelming burdens by adopting heuristic aids to calculation. They simplify in order to get by. They make small moves, let experience accumulate, and use the feedback from their decisions to gauge consequences. They use actions on simpler matters (which they do understand) as indices to complex concerns. They try to judge the capacity of the men in charge of programs even if they cannot appraise the policies directly. They may institute across-the-board cuts to reduce spending, relying on outcries from affected agencies and interest groups to let them know if they have gone too far.

By far the most important aid to calculation is the incremental approach. Budgets are almost never actively reviewed as a whole, in the sense of considering at one time the value of all existing programs compared to all possible alternatives. Instead, this year's budget is based on last year's budget, with special attention given to a narrow range of increases or decreases. The greatest part of any budget is a product of previous decisions. Long-range commitments have been made. There are mandatory programs whose expenses must be met. Powerful political support makes the inclusion of other activities inevitable. Consequently, officials concerned with budgeting restrict their attention to items and programs they can do something about — a few new programs and possible cuts in old ones.

Incremental calculations, then, proceed from an existing base. By "base" I refer to commonly held expectations among participants in budgeting that programs will be carried out at close to the going level of expenditures. The base of a budget, therefore, refers to accepted parts of programs that will not normally be subjected to intensive scrutiny. By encapsulating the past in the present through the base, budgeters limit future disputes. Since many organizational units compete for funds, there is a tendency for the central authority to include all of them in benefits or deprivations to be distributed. Budgeters often refer to expectations regarding their *fair share* of increases and decreases. The widespread sharing of deeply held expectations concerning the organization's base and its fair share of funds provides a powerful (although informal) means of coordination and stability in budgetary systems.

The lack of an accepted base wreaks havoc with common calculations. Spending agencies do not know how much they will need; reviewing bodies do not know how much they should allocate. Requests for spending and actual appropriations fluctuate wildly. Both supplemental appropriations, when the initial amounts are too low, and underspending, when the agency cannot spend what it has, become commonplace. New agencies and new programs frequently encounter these difficulties because they necessarily lack a historical pattern of requests, allocations, and actual expenditures from which everyone can take their bearings, or, when, for any number of reasons — from lack of trust among the main participants to changes in demand for agency services to alterations of the party in power — past allocations are no longer good guides to future ones. Relationships between budgetary actors have shifted; there is a break with prior patterns; budgeting becomes non-incremental. Over a period of years, however, a new budgetary base is negotiated as the spending agencies and reviewing organs seek stability, the one in expenditure flows, the other in disbursements. The sources of this strain toward predictability lie in the differing but complementary roles assumed by the participants in the process of budgeting.

Roles (the expectations of behavior attached to institutional positions) are parts of the division of labor. Administrative agencies act as advocates of increased expenditure, and central control organs function as guardians of the treasury. Each expects the other to do its job; agencies can advocate, knowing the center will impose limits, and the center can exert control, knowing that agencies will push expenditures as hard as they can. Thus roles serve as calculating mechanisms. The interaction between spending and cutting roles makes up the component elements of budgetary systems. Why do the main actors — advocates and guardians — behave as they do?

Wherever one unit depends on another for its income, the same kind of situation will arise: each considers its own expenditure increases to be too small to affect the total; it feels free, then, to aggrandize itself without considering the effect of that action on the nation's financial position. Nor does it see revenues as fixed. Agencies have seen totals altered so often they come to regard them as a kind of sleight of hand — now you see it, now you don't. Let somebody else worry about what it all adds up to.

Every agency wants more money; the urge to survive and expand is built in. Clientele groups, on whom an agency depends for support, judge the agency by how much it does for them. The more clients receive, the larger they grow, the more they can help the agency. Resource allocation within an agency, moreover, is much easier with a rising level of appropriations. The prestige of the chief within his agency depends on being able to meet, to some extent, employee demands for higher salaries, amenities, and programs, all of which mean additional funds. Rather than cutting some to increase others, he can mitigate internal criticism by doing better for all or at least not doing worse for anyone. His advantage lies in making such "Pareto optimal" decisions within his agency.

There is also the problem of relative prestige among agencies. Chiefs who can get more than their previous share of the total for new or expanded programs believe themselves (and are believed by others) to be more powerful. Since their reputations become identified with the budgetary success of their agencies, chiefs come to believe that financial growth is the road to fortune; self-interest, joined with the demands of organizational life, reinforces the tendency to overemphasize the importance of one's own unit. They all want more. Thus agencies are advocates of their own expenditures, not guardians of the nation's purse.

And the job of a finance ministry (as central control organs will now be called) is to see that they don't get it — not everyone, and not all. It is not merely cynicism or even a widespread belief that the center alone sees the whole picture. It is more that incentives for the finance ministry all lie in expenditure limitation. People do not complain about a surplus, but if there is a large deficit leading to increased taxes or inflation, the ministry of finance will take the blame. Finance usually is entrusted with administering the tax process so that there is money on hand to meet pressing obligations. Its power motive can rarely be satisfied by advocating more expenditure — spending agencies take care of that. Setting priorities is done more easily by cutting at the margins than by taking over the entire work of the agencies. To exercise leadership demands a balance of sanctions and rewards, not elimination of those who are to be led.

Guardians and advocates play in a mixed motive game. Though they conflict, they must also cooperate. Both require trust. Each role implies its opposite; guardianship expects advocacy to provide a choice among items to cut, and advocacy needs guardianship to supply at least tacit limits within which to maneuver. Resources, after all, cannot be allocated without either proposals for spending or boundaries within which to fit them. The classic strategies participants use to improve their position — asking for more than they expect to get and making percentage cuts across the board — depend on keeping within accepted limits so that budgets have meaning.

Meaningful budgets, then, depend on trust and calculability, which in turn are related to each other. A finance ministry that cannot figure out how much money it has on hand cannot determine what is available for spending agencies. Either it will give them too much in the budget, so that the money has to be reclaimed later despite the earlier commitment, or it will provide too little, so that agencies run out of funds before the end of the fiscal year. Agencies that do not know about how much they can spend will ask either for too much (leaving money idle), or for too little (resulting in emergency requests at unpredictable intervals). Any of these patterns of behavior necessarily reduce trust as the participants learn they cannot rely on one another or on the budget. Without trust, guardians must impose the strictest controls; these lead to evasive action by the overly constrained advocates. Without trust, advocates are tempted to engage in gross deception or to go outside the central budget altogether; guardians then impose further restraints, until no one can count on anyone and all learn to disregard the formal budget.

Permanent organizational interests dominate temporary policy preferences. Agencies try to protect their existing spending levels (and hence their employees and their status) and to increase them year by year to make organizational life easier. This interest is compatible with many different arrays of policy preferences. One policy may be sacrificed for another or, despite defects, promoted in order to gain support for other purposes.

Finance ministries try to keep spending totals within a zone of acceptability. Pushing programs may be a way to increase expenditures, or an impediment if they are unpopular. Opposing programs may or may not be a way to keep expenditures down, depending on whether the subsequent unpopularity might damage the ability of finance to hold the line elsewhere. The point is that policies are bargainable. Guardians and advocates trade on policies, therefore, with the perspectives that define their roles in commanding positions. Knowledge of how they will act on a policy such as welfare or transportation calls for detailed comprehension of situational factors. Knowledge of their behavior in general may be deduced from the roles they play under a variety of conditions. These environmental conditions — economic wealth, financial predictability, social norms, political structure — are the major dimensions of the comparative analysis that follows.

COMPARING BUDGETARY PROCESSES

The lament of the poor working girl — "It's the same the whole world over" — sounds a responsive note in regard to budgeting. Familiar behavior appears wherever one goes. Yet between cities, states, and the federal government in the United States; between England, France, Japan, and America; among rich and poor countries; dramatic differences do appear. My task is to account for both similarities and differences.

First the similarities. There are constants in budgeting, no matter where practised, that lead to regular patterns of behavior. Everywhere there are spenders and savers. Those in charge of the great purposes of government naturally tend to identify their fortunes with the interests entrusted to their care. So they defend against cuts and seek increases whenever they can. Relating expenditure to income is likewise an essential state function. Guardians of the treasury will not do well if they are forced into inflationary measures or constantly have to raise taxes because they cannot control spending. So they cut and trim and otherwise try to keep spending within hailing distance of revenues.

Beyond this elemental division of budgetary roles, all participants in budgeting are overwhelmed by its complexity. None can relate the myriad factors to one another simultaneously so as simply to achieve desired allocations. Complexity appears to be a threshold variable; once the number of factors involved has grown considerably beyond the capacity of the human mind, it does not seem to matter how much more it grows. Decision-makers in a city, who are overwhelmed by 86 variables, do not appear to behave that much differently than those in a state, who cannot manage 860, or in a nation that finds 8600 too much. All adopt aids to calculation. All simplify the task of decision by proceeding from a historical base, largely accepting what has gone before, in order to concentrate on proposed new increments. Given teams of spenders and savers operating in a world none can quite comprehend, the same practices — padding, across-the-board cuts, increased spending at the end of the fiscal year, and refusal to release a proportion of budgeted funds during the year — are found wherever one cares to look. At a sufficiently remote level of observation, to be sure, all objects begin to look alike. Closer inspection is in order.

Now for the differences. The most important stem from wealth, predictability, political institutions, elite values, and size. It is convenient to begin with the last. Size alone can alter relationships in the budgetary process. Although city, state, and federal budgetary practices in the United States may be described as incremental, for instance, the base from which increments proceed differs enormously. The national budget is larger by several orders of magnitude than any city or state budget. The salary for a janitor or the rental of a Xerox machine, for example, is about the same for governments of all sizes, but the expenditure represents a vastly different percentage of the total for each. Although absolute costs increase arithmetically when moving from city to state to federal levels, relative costs decrease in more like a geometric direction. With a total budget of some $60 million a year, for instance, a decision to innovate with one-tenth of one percent of a city's income would involve $60,000 — enough, perhaps, to hire two or three people with an office and a secretary. A state spending $6 billion a year would end up with $600,000 — sufficient, perhaps, to support a small research program. A similar decision at the federal level, where spending approximates $300 billion a year, would involve $300 million, enough to fund a host of programs. A federal decision on how to spend that money might actually involve several decisions with composite alternatives. The state decision would be just that: a single decision. The city decision might look more like a reflex action than a considered choice. Scale profoundly changes the practical importance of making decisions by increments. To no one's surprise, how much there is to spend makes a great difference not merely in how much is spent but in the mechanisms for making the expenditure.

The poor and the rich budget in dramatically different ways. Their distinctive features can be traced to two variables: wealth and predictability. Wealth refers to gross disparities in per capita gross national product (above $2000, below $1000) that can be mobilized, and predictability to degrees of certainty or uncertainty regarding available resources versus likely demands for spending. Budgetary poverty, accordingly, means inability to mobilize sufficient resources (because they are lacking or for some other reason) or to control expenditures or (usually) both. Budgetary uncertainty means inability to calculate the flow of expenditures, revenues, or both in the immediate past and to project them into the near future. Budgetary riches and certainty stipulate precisely the opposite conditions.

The combination of certainty and largesse among the rich produces budgeting by increments. Past decisions determine most future expenditures, as commitments are kept, so present choice focuses on adding or subtracting a small percentage (the increment) over the existing base. It is not the increment, however, but the base that is crucial, for it signifies acceptance of the past. Old quarrels will not be argued again.

In American cities, where rich people may live but which are in a poor resource position because balanced budgets are required and revenues are inelastic, we find an almost whole control-orientation, less strategic maneuver than among the rich, and generally little scope for decision. Budgeting becomes a form of revenue behavior; income determines outgo. City officials know where they are, but they cannot go very far. In poor countries we find repetitive budgeting under which budgets are made and remade throughout the year amid endless strategic byplay. Poverty leads them to delay lest they run out of money; uncertainty leads them to reprogram funds repeatedly to adjust to the rapidly changing scene. Poor countries do not know where they are now, and the budget does not help them learn where they will be next year. Most in need of stable budgets, they are least able to secure them. Poor countries lack the redundancy that wealth makes possible — the duplication that provides a margin of safety to cope with emergencies, the overlap to compensate for imperfect arrangements — and that is essential for reliable performance. The combination of poverty and uncertainty is devastating; these countries have little to spend because they are poor, and they find it hard to spend wisely because they are uncertain.

Wealth and predictability control all other variables. Poverty homogenizes behavior. When nations are extremely poor and woefully uncertain, the consequences are so pervasive and profound as to determine almost all budgetary behavior. The rulers, so long as they are in power, may decide who gets what the government has to give, but the formal budget is unlikely to be a good guide to what will happen.

Rich and certain nations produce budgets with predictive value — most things supposed to happen during the year will happen. The redundancy created by wealth absorbs uncertainty to create the minimum stability necessary for annual budgets to be meaningful instruments of resource allocation. The formal budget and the informal understanding among the participants flash readable signals. By and large the numbers and words in the budget document refer to real events that will probably occur; roughly the specified amounts of money will be spent for something like the designated purposes. The ability to make a meaningful budget is a prerequisite for concern over the distributive consequences (the "who gets what") of that budget.

My hypothesis about budgeting in environments that are rich but administratively uncertain is that, when such environments are discovered, they will be found to engage in supplemental budgeting — treating each expenditure request and grant as if it were a supplement due to unexpected circumstances. The spending agency would wait until its funds ran out, because it could not estimate what it would need or actually be able to spend; and the finance ministry would reconsider its allotments, because it was not at all certain of how much revenue it could raise or had on hand. Budgetary processes falling in the rich and uncertain box will not be discussed in detail here because I have not been able to find accounts of contemporary governments with these characteristics. The Third and Fourth French Republics, however, did combine considerable wealth with even greater political instability. One result was the famous practice of voting "twelfths" (one month's appropriations) to pay for government services while the politicians were unable to agree on the budget. Thus the French experienced alternating incremental and repetitive budgeting depending on the political situation.

Using the two leading variables — wealth and predictability — to create a fourfold table, I have classified the budgetary processes under consideration so far (see Figure 1.1). Rich and certain environments lead to incremental budgeting; poverty and predictability generate revenue budgeting; unpredictability combined with poverty generates repetitive budgeting; and riches plus uncertainty produce alternating incremental and repetitive budgeting.

When budgetary processes operate in environments that may be characterized as poor but certain, we see the syndrome characteristic of American cities; when environments are poor and uncertain, the characteristic conditions of budgeting in poor countries appear. Following this procedure, we find that the United States, Japan, Great Britain, and France all seem to belong in the same rich and certain box. Although it is true that their budgetary behaviors

Figure 1.1.   FIVE BUDGETARY PROCESSES

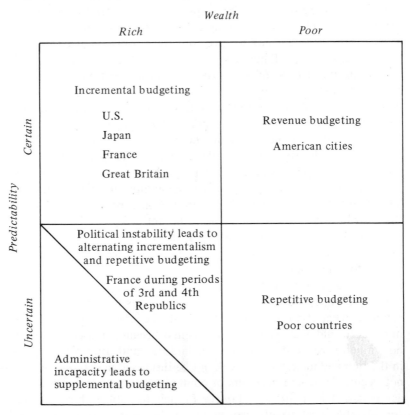

are more like one another's than like those of nations in other boxes, there are differences among them. How can we identify and account for the differences?

Clearly, to compare and contrast budgetary processes in societies that are relatively wealthy and predictable calls for a more refined analysis than to distinguish among those without these dominant traits. One aspect is the dissimilarity of powerful political institutions. Only Japan has an electoral party (the Liberal Democratic Party) that plays a regular part in budgeting; only France has a combined presidential-parliamentary regime; only the United States possesses a legislature, independent of the executive, with significant influence over the budget; and only Britain has a cabinet that actually makes important decisions. Ways must be found, evidently, to compare the contributions of these singular institutions. Because these nations are all relatively rich, however, distinctions of degree among them must be introduced to permit contrast; unless degrees of wealth are accounted for, it will not be possible to assess the varying contributions of different political arrangements. Dissimilarities in budgeting between Britain and Japan, for example, may relate more to the large gap in growth rates than to differences in political institutions or cultural values.

Absolute wealth matters in politics, but so does rate of growth. It is much easier politically to support spending out of growth, without increasing tax rates, than to take a larger share of income from those accustomed to holding on to what they have. The four richer countries that we shall examine differ substantially in their absolute wealth and relative rates of growth and hence in the severity of the problems posed for each in resource allocation.

To compare budgeting among rich countries it is necessary to connect wealth, taxes, and politics. The idea is to gauge the political difficulties posed for the respective governments by the increases in taxes necessary to support spending as compared with the ability of their budgetary processes to handle the conflict generated. Thus I shall rank these nations on the degrees to which their tax rates and composition provide more or less support for spending. How well these nations handle the resulting conflicts over resource allocation depends on their political structure (relationship among institutions) and elite culture (norms regulating behavior). Political structures for processing the budget differ both in the absolute number of institutions significantly involved and in their relative power. Budgetary relationships are regulated by the number of levels required to interact and by the formal authority of each.

The elites manning these political institutions are part of an orderly social scene. Interpersonal relationships are mediated by prevailing norms of desirable conduct. The norms affecting budgeting most are: the degree of personal trust among the higher civil service and politicians; preferences for face-to-face versus formal, legal, courtroom-like modes of resolving disputes; and the extent to which decisions are made on proportional grounds — that is, on the basis of treating the competing units in a uniform and equitable way — rather than by deciding each case on the merits.

Norms of conduct are intertwined with forms of institutions. For one thing, the norms of governing elites may shape institutional forms — the less they trust one another, I hypothesize, the more levels of decisions may be needed to contain their conflicts. For another, the institutions through which they must work may shape their norms; loyalty to the chief executive cannot quite be the same where an independent legislature exercises the power of the purse as where a civil service is tightly knit.

By combining the number of institutional levels with prevalent elite values we can identify distinct political styles of handling conflict which percolate up through the budgetary process. The diversionary style practiced in the United States combines a large number of levels with extensive use of all three norms — proportionality, arbitration, and trust. Conflict is not so much resolved as confused, diverted, and sidetracked. The containment (or fortress or even "Maginot line") style practised in France is an attempt to keep conflict within bounds by arbitrating disputes at many levels up the hierarchy. The Japanese, whose smaller number of levels is accompanied by an emphasis on proportionality, have a style based on avoidance. No one has to be told he is wrong. All share equally in the benefits or the misery because proportional rewards (usually, comparable increases) are granted at each level. The British style is one of absorption. Working with a high degree of trust and a few levels of decision, the British accommodate conflict through anticipatory adjustment. No one is expected to deny differences, but these are carried on within the overall expectation that each actor will work out his position so as to take account of the vital interests of others. That they should be able to settle is usually more important than the substance of the agreement. That is what it means to carry on Her Majesty's Government.

There is, of course, more under the sun than is dreamed of in this small sample. Its range of institutional variation is woefully restricted. Because the poor and uncertain are compelled to act in similar ways, it obviously is not possible to show how their varied political institutions and norms governing elite relationships lead to differences in behavior. Theoretical effort is better spent in attempting to show why their vast differences still lead to similar budgetary processes. The wealthy, as everyone knows, enjoy more liberty; they are not so deeply constrained. Their differences are worth looking at. But they do not always arrange their political lives to help students of comparative politics. Our four rich countries do not vary on all the relevant institutional features, or differ when it would suit our purposes. How can we discern the general effects of partisanship when all four rich governments rank high on that dimension? How can we establish conditions for legislative effectiveness with only the United States federal government to rely upon? How can we speak about roles, apart from the authority that goes with institutional positions?

An increase in the number of budgetary processes that include the desired institutional characteristics would certainly be helpful, even if that means taking account of subnational units of government. Consider partisanship. American cities are useful because they are similar in wealth (which they lack) and predictability (which they have) while differing in partisanship. Thus it becomes possible to see that partisanship increases both the scope of the alternatives considered in budgeting and the disposition of municipal legislatures to act contrary to the wishes of the executive. The existence of parties creates the need for some sort of program, and the organization of the legislature on a partisan basis increases its cohesion. The weakness of most municipal legislatures may be traced to nonpartisan organization, part-time service, low salaries, and lack of staff support, all of which inhibit the growth of specialization, expertise, and cohesion necessary to counter the executive.

To look at American state governments is even more instructive because they differ on dimensions of special interest to us. Some combine the relative poverty and certainty of cities, while others resemble rich governments in their largesses and certitude. Yet their budgetary institutions vary greatly in authority. Thus it becomes possible to observe how the role of the legislature and governor changes from guardian to advocate when specific institutional provisions — an item veto for the governor, a balanced budget requirement for the legislature — alter the incentives, calling forth different roles under various financial conditions. A legislature that knows that a governor has an item veto and the state a surplus, for example, is tempted to vote more funds and leave the executive with the onus of reducing them. If a legislative majority and the executive come from different parties, the legislative urge toward advocacy is enhanced.

One essential type of variation still has not been covered — budgetary processes that are unlike the others in essential respects. Everything said thus far is based on the assumptions of scarcity and discretion. Without scarcity there is no need to choose and without discretion there is no possibility of choice. Hence the fundamental distribution of roles between spenders and savers breaks down. What happens when there are no guardians or no advocates or neither? That depends. If resource scarcity does not exist, as two of our deviant cases show, everyone gets along quite well. There is no need to budget when there is no need to budget. If scarcity is there but the participants refuse to recognize it, or if discretion is absent, as the other two cases suggest, bad things happen. Governments run out of money when no one plays guardian; vital operations run down when no one plays advocate. These deviant cases should enable us to understand better the rationales behind the more normal operations of budgetary processes.

The theoretical framework I propose for understanding normal budgeting begins with two constants: scarcity and complexity. Unlike desires, resources always are limited and knowledge of the causes and consequences of the choices that go into making a budget always is incomplete. Scarcity creates the ubiquitous division of roles between advocates and guardians; from complexity comes the use of aids to calculation. To make a meaningful budget within these constraints — to relate revenue and expenditure to each other and to choose wisely within these limits — is *the problem*.

Within these fixed bounds, the major variables affecting budgeting are (1) economic wealth, (2) financial predictability, (3) spending size, (4) political structure, and (5) elite culture. Economic wealth has been decomposed, first, by a dichotomy between rich and poor governments, and second, by distinguishing among the relatively rich and more or less rapidly growing in wealth. Financial predictability has been measured in terms of the ability to anticipate flows of available resources in relation to spending commitments. Political instability aggravates fiscal uncertainty, for not only *what* must be decided but *who* is to decide is in flux. Certainty may be imposed from outside by predetermining how much revenue can be raised or how much money can be spent. The capacity of one governmental unit to impose expenditure and revenue limitations evidently determines what the subordinate unit can do. Size, through its threshold effect, separates small from large spending units, so that the importance of incremental decision-making grows as the expenditure base increases.

To make political structures comparable I have ranked them by the number of levels that make decisions effectively allocating resources. Elite norms are compared on three dimensions: trust, proportionality, and arbitration. All budgetary processes, so far as I know, contain elements of these three norms. The question is one of degree: are all three used about equally, or is one dominant? Then I have combined the number of levels and elite norms to postulate political styles for managing conflict.

Up to this point, I have presented the explanatory factors — the so-called independent variables that, in various combinations, are supposed to answer questions about budgeting. But what exactly are these questions, the dependent variables, which my analysis is supposed to answer?

The dependent variables are, of course, various kinds of budgetary behavior, especially the behavior of organized units that do budgeting. Spending units make requests and authorizing units grant appropriations. When both sets of figures are available for periods of time, as in the United States Federal Government, it is possible to provide quantitative tests for the verbal arguments in this book. Since comparable data for other nations are not available, the dependent variables for comparative purposes must be more general.

At the most general levels, I have tried to account for the characteristic patterns of budgetary behavior previously defined in "shorthand" as incremental, repetitive, revenue, and alternating incremental and repetitive budgeting. Why and where is budgeting carried on in these distinctively different ways?

Descending from these overarching patterns to a middle level, from "macro" to "micro" activity, I shall try to explain everyday patterns of behavior in budgeting, the calculations and strategies used by participants. The patterns of budgetary action that require explanation may be identified most parsimoniously by the strategic behavior of the institutional participants and by the calculations they use to make their tasks more manageable.

How actors try to get their way — their strategies — depends on the connections they make between their ability to articulate budgetary preferences and the opportunities and constraints their environment offers for realizing them. Their attempts to exercise power in budgeting reveals their institutional differences. The British interest group, for instance, is unlikely to appeal to Parliament as the American does to Congress, and neither is as likely as the Japanese to consider the political parties outside their respective legislatures.

How budgetary actors decide what moves to make — their calculations — depends on how they cope with complexity — the large number of items, the even larger number of interactions, and the uncertainties surrounding them. The search by budgetary actors for means to make their choices more rational is a reaction to complexity; so, in the rich countries, is their abandonment of this rationality for simplicity as shown by the way they institutionalize incrementalism. Their convergence on similar devices to increase certainty tells us much about their response to the common complexity of modern life. The far different aids to calculation used by the poor countries pose a question whose answer is sought in their special environmental conditions.

The ability to ask questions and to find answers about budgetary behavior should extend to attempts to change existing practices as well as to explain why they are there in the first place. Reform is a good testing ground for social science. Reforms necessarily assume an "if-then" posture; if the recommended changes are introduced, certain consequences (hopefully desirable) will ensue. Dependent variables become efforts at reform; the test is whether independent variables can explain patterns of failure and give at least some indication of the factors behind that single success, the Public Expenditure Survey Committee in Britain.

Now all of this — questions asked, patterns to be explained — is within the realm of budgeting. It would be interesting also to use budgetary processes as independent variables explaining other phenomena. I have chosen conflict (the resolution or worsening of differences in government) to get at the links between budgeting and politics. Questions about conflict are as hard to frame as they are to answer. It is hard to say exactly how much conflict there is and how intense it has become. It is not easy to say precisely how much budget practices are geared to conflict resolution vis-à-vis other purposes. Nevertheless, it is clear that budgetary processes are (and must be) geared to handling conflict. Budgetary calculations are not merely ways of figuring out what to do but also means for structuring conflict. How problems are broken down affects who will confront them, the extent of their differences, and the possibilities of reconciliation. A large number of small problems may be easier to accommodate than a small number of larger ones. Strategies are not only means of achieving financial objectives but also ways to present demands and provide support. The relative power of the institutions that participate in budgeting, their relationships to one another, and the values of the elites who man them evidently are important in determining not only who will win and lose, but how they feel about the outcomes. If budgeting can be connected to political styles, and these to handling conflict, budgeting at last will become a fully political subject by demonstration as well as by definition.

I would like to end with predictions, at least for the United States. The test of a model is explanation; did the budgetary process act as if it followed the rules (derived from studying behavior) embodied in symbolic form as equations? The power of a theory is prediction: do the models generate requests and appropriations for agencies similar to those that will take place one, two, and even five years in the future? The test of explanation is met, I believe, on the basis of the data presented; and the test of prediction is partially satisfied, pending further elaboration of the research presented in this volume. To stress what is important for present purposes: the mathematical models show that the basic conceptions used in this book — roles, calculations, and strategies of institutional participants — make sense in terms of their interaction in the systemic whole we call the process of budgeting.

For the rest, I am willing to be held to account to the extent that organizations operating under conditions meeting the assumptions and independent variables specified here should produce the kinds of budgeting expected of them. The Soviet Union, for example, though its political institutions differ from the rich countries in our sample, all of which rely on electoral competition, nevertheless should engage in incremental budgeting. Though its priorities may differ, wealth and predictability ought to determine the main features of its budgetary process.[1] Even such unanticipated events as the oil crisis should be assimilable in terms of our theoretical categories. Britain, France, and Japan, according to the degrees they are affected, should begin to look more like poor countries as they rearrange their budget during the year to take account of sudden decreases in income. Poor countries without oil will become still poorer; they will look as they always did, only more so.

In the present state of research, with only four rich countries available for study, tests of budgetary theory are limited by the absence of contemporary national governments that are rich but uncertain due to political in-

---

[1] Literature on Soviet industrial firms, which are part of governmental budgeting, provide some clues. There is a great deal of bargaining over production targets and the resources for achieving them. Through numerous iterations the participants hover about a fixed point, based on past negotiations, from which they make small yearly departures. See Joseph Berliner, *Factory and Manager in the USSR*, Russian Research Studies, 27 (Cambridge: Harvard University Press, 1957); and David Granick, *Management of the Industrial Firm in the USSR, a Study in Soviet Economic Planning*, Studies of the Russian Institute, Columbia University (New York: Columbia University Press, 1959). For what it is worth at so long a distance, my guess is that China can usually be characterized by revenue behavior (poverty plus certainty) but moves into repetitive budgeting (poverty plus uncertainty) during periods of internal political instability.

stability or administrative incapacity. I suspect the world is about to make up for this lack. In the meantime, we need something more than passing reference to the bad old days in France to keep us going. This is why I have introduced sub-national levels of government, which do have the necessary characteristics. This is also why I have sought to ring as many changes on wealth and predictability as current experience allows.

The arrangement of chapters in this book might be described as arithmetical — addition, subtraction, multiplication, and division. I begin by *adding* wealth and predictability to order the budgetary processes for which there are reasonably complete reports. Chapters 2 through 5 cover the rich and certain countries. Then comes *subtraction;* wealth is taken away in Chapter 6, leaving us with budgetary processes in American cities that are certain but poor. Next goes predictability. By subtracting both riches and certainty in Chapter 7, we are left with countries that are poor and uncertain.

At this point, in order to increase the variety of budgetary processes, multiplication and division enter into the scheme. Chapter 8 *multiplies* the number of processes by bringing in American state governments and then *divides* them by wealth and institutional characteristics to permit more detailed observation of the effect of political structure. Chapter 9 might be thought of almost like negative numbers that enter the analysis on a different plane. The situations discussed there are considered deviant precisely because they differ in critical respects from the others. Strategies and calculations in all these budgetary processes are compared in the tenth chapter. The eleventh and twelfth chapters use budgetary theory to study the exacerbation or mitigation of conflict over resource mobilization and allocation. Chapter 13 changes direction by considering requirements for reform of budgeting. Having tried to discover why budgetary processes operate as they do, we turn this material around in Chapters 14 through 19 by asking what our theory has to tell us about failure and success in sponsoring change. If the earlier chapters were largely concerned with how budgetary institutions seek to maintain stability, the later ones are concerned with their acceptance or rejection of change. The final chapter tries to show how knowledge gained from studying both stability and change can be used to guide budget reform.

II
Experience

2
The Wealthy and the Predictable: Budgeting in the United States Federal Government

The United States is larger than life. It is not only the richest large country, but also the most visible. Because its political processes are more open (and hence amenable to study) than those of any other important nation, more is known about the operation (and hence the defects) of its budgetary process. Its accessibility is accentuated by the presence of a unique feature possessed by no other nation available for scrutiny — a relatively independent legislature that actually exercises a significant degree of power over appropriations. Congressional hearings consequently assume considerable importance, a circumstance that leads both to more public efforts to use budgetary strategies and to a convenient record of these happenings through verbatim transcripts of the testimony. The drama (not all, perhaps, but enough) is there for anyone to see; they may not like what they see, but they know what is there.

I shall take advantage of the well-known properties of federal budgeting by transmuting the usual verbal account into mathematical symbols in order to test the validity of the main propositions in a more formal manner. The availability not merely of budget enactments but of agency requests lets us decide whether the relationship between what agencies ask for and what they get is consonant with the verbal model of the budgetary process I am about to present. This chapter contains the basic explanatory models in qualitative, then in quantitative form; and the next, several efforts at prediction.[1] Let us start, as is only proper, with the advocates.

[1] The qualitative theory is taken from my *Politics of the Budgetary Process* (Boston: Little, Brown, 2nd ed., 1974), from joint work with Otto Davis of Carnegie Mellon University and Michael Dempster of Balliol College, Oxford, and from Richard F. Fenno, Jr., *The Power of the Purse* (Boston: Little, Brown, 1966).

ADVOCATES AND GUARDIANS

With their great expertise and large numbers, working in close proximity to their policy problems and clientele groups, and eager to expand their horizons, administrative agencies generate action through advocacy. But how much shall they ask for? Life would be simple if they could just total the costs of their ever-expanding needs and submit it as their request. But if they ask for amounts much larger than the appropriating bodies believe is reasonable, their credibility will suffer a drastic decline. In such circumstances, the reviewing organs are likely to apply a "measure of unrealism" with the result that the agency ends up with much less than it might have obtained with a more moderate request. So the first decision rule for agencies is: do not come in too high. Yet agencies must not come in too low, either, for the assumption is that if the agency advocates do not ask for funds they do not need them. Since the budgetary situation is always tight — terribly tight, or impossibly tight — reviewing bodies are likely just to accept a low request with thanks and not inquire too closely into its rationale. Given the distribution of roles, cuts must be expected and taken into account. Thus the agency decision rule might read: come in a little high (padding), but not too high (loss of confidence). But how high is too high? What agency heads usually do is to evaluate signals from the environment — last year's experience, legislative votes, executive policy statements, actions of clientele groups, reports from the field — and come up with an asking price somewhat higher than they expect to get.

Having decided how much to ask for, agencies engage in strategic planning. (Strategies are the links between the goals of the agencies and their perceptions of the kinds of action their political environment will make efficacious.) Budget officers in American national government uniformly act on the belief that being a good politician — cultivating an active clientele, developing confidence by other officials (particularly the appropriations subcommittees), and skillfully following strategies that exploit opportunities — is more important in obtaining funds than demonstrating efficiency. Top agency officials soon learn that appropriations committees are very powerful; Congress accepts committee recommendations approximately 90 percent of the time. Since budgetary calculations are so complex, legislators must take a good deal on faith; thus they need agency budget officers who demonstrate a high degree of integrity. If appropriations committees believe that an agency officer has misled them, they can do grave damage to his career and to the prospects of his agency. Doing a decent job may be a necessary condition for the agency's success in securing funds; having clientele and the confidence of legislators is so important that all agencies employ these strategies.

In addition, there are contingent strategies, which depend on time, circumstance, and place. To defend the base, for example, cuts may be made in the most popular programs; but a public outcry can result in restoration of the funds. The base may be increased within existing programs by shifting funds between categories. Substantial additions to the base may come about through proposing new programs to meet crises and through campaigns involving large doses of advertising and salesmanship. The dependence of these strategies on the incremental, increase-decrease type of budgetary calculation is evident. The Office of Management and Budget (OMB) in the United States has the assigned role of helping the president realize his goals (when it can discover what they are supposed to be). This role is biased toward cutting, however, simply because agencies normally push so hard in making requests for funds. The OMB helps the president by making his preferences more widely known within the executive branch so that those who want to go along have a chance to find out what they should do. Since Congress usually cuts the president's budget, OMB figures tend to be the most that agencies can get, especially when the items are not important enough to justify intensive scrutiny by Congress. Yet the power of the purse remains actively with Congress. If the OMB continually recommended figures that were blatantly disregarded by Congress, agencies would soon learn to pay less and less attention to the president's budget. As a result, the OMB follows consistent congressional action.

In deciding how much money to recommend for specific purposes, the House Appropriations Committee is broken down into largely autonomous subcommittees in which the norm of reciprocity is carefully followed. Specialization is carried further as subcommittee members develop limited areas of competence and jurisdiction. Budgeting is both incremental and fragmented as the committees deal with adjustments to the historical base of each agency. Sequential decision-making is the rule; problems are first attacked in the subcommittee jurisdiction in which they appear and then followed step by step as they show themselves elsewhere. Subcommittee members treat budgeting as a process of making marginal monetary adjustments to existing programs rather than as a mechanism for reconsidering basic policy choices every year. Fragmentation and specialization are further increased through the appeals function of the Senate Appropriations Committee, which deals with what has become (through House action) a fragment of a fragment. When the actions of subcommittees conflict, the difficulties are met by repeated attacks on the problem or through reference to the House and Senate as a whole.

The members of the United States House Appropriations Committee consider themselves guardians of the Treasury who take pride in their frequent reductions in estimates. They reconcile this role with their role as representatives of constituency interests by cutting esimates to satisfy one role, and generally increasing amounts over the previous year to satisfy the other. As guardians of the public purse, committee members are expected to cast a skeptical eye on the blandishments of a bureaucracy ever anxious to increase its dominion by raising its appropriations.

Tough as they may be in cutting budgets, appropriations committee members, once having made their decision, generally defend their agencies against further cuts on the floor. This action is in part self-interest. The power of the appropriations subcommittees would be diminished if their recommendations were successfully challenged very often. Members believe that the House would "run wild" if "orderly procedure" — that is, acceptance of committee recommendations — were not followed. The role of defender also has its roots in the respect for expertise and specialization in Congress, and the concomitant belief that members who have not studied the subject should not exercise a deciding voice without the presence of overriding considerations.

A member of the Senate Appropriations Committee is likely to conceive of his proper role as the responsible legislator who will not let the irrepressible lower House do too much damage either to constituency or to national interests. The senators are rather painfully aware of the House committee's preeminence in the field of appropriations. They know they cannot hope to match the time and thoroughness that the House body devotes to screening requests. For this reason, the Senate committee puts a high value on having agencies carry appeals to it. Senators value their right to disagree on disputed items as a way to hold on to influence in crucial areas while putting the least possible strain on their time and energy. The Senate role of responsible appeals court depends, of course, on agency advocacy and House committee guardianship.

CALCULATION AND COORDINATION

The budgeting process is incremental, built on a historical base and operating on accepted notions of fair shares, in which decisions are fragmented, made in sequence by specialized bodies, and coordinated through repeated attacks on problems and through multiple feedback mechanisms. The very terms I have used to describe budgetary practices — specialized, incremental, fragmented, sequential, nonprogrammatic — imply that at no one time is the budget effectively considered as a whole so as to systematically relate its component parts to one another. As long as lack of coordination results from ignorance of other people's activities or the complexity of organization, there is a good chance of overcoming it by dedicated staff work or some formal coordinating mechanism. But often lack of coordination comes from conflicting views about policy held by men and agencies with independent bases of influence in society and in Congress. The only way to secure coordination here is for one side to convince or coerce or bargain with the other. If coordination means mutual awareness of each other's activities, then they have it; if coordination means that one side gives in to the other, they may not. When it is understood that "coordination" is often just another word for "coercion," the full magnitude of the problem becomes apparent. For there is no one, the president and congressional leaders included, who is charged with the task of dealing with the "budget as a whole" and able to enforce his preferences. To vest formal power for coordinating the budget effectively would be tantamount to a radical change in the national political system, involving the abolition of the separation of powers and a federally controlled party system, among other things.

Is there anything to say about coordination, then, if we take the existing political system as not subject to drastic change? We can come up with an obvious answer by taking as our standard of coordination the existence of a formal structure charged with the task and able to execute it. There is very little coordination now, beyond what the president can manage through the OMB. But by accepting the possibility of informal coordination, of participants who take into account what others are doing, we can say there is a great deal of coordination that has escaped notice.

Let us pose the following question: how does an appropriations subcommittee know when things are not working out in other areas affected by its actions? Are its budgetary decisions coordinated with decisions made by other subcommittees? Part of the answer comes from a committee member who commented that "People can't be too badly off if they don't complain." (If they don't complain because they are not effectively represented in the political process, the system will not work for them; that is why faults in budgeting have to be corrected through political as well as budgetary changes.) Subcommittees do not consider themselves to be the only participants in budgeting. In accordance with sequential decision-making, they expect committees and organizations in the affected areas to take corrective action. When an agency shouts more loudly than usual; when an interest group mounts a campaign; when other congressmen begin to complain; subcommittee members have a pretty good idea that something is wrong. If their perceptions of the array of political forces lead them astray, the appropriations subcommittees can be brought back into line by a rebellion within the full committee or by an adverse vote on the floor. Unless members have an exceedingly intense preference, they will try to come up with appropriations that will not be reversed on the floor; to do otherwise would be to risk losing the great prestige the committee enjoys. The subcommitee may be thought of as exercising discretion over a zone of indifference, within which others are not aware enough or concerned enough to challenge them, but beyond which others will begin to mobilize against them. In this way, a semblance of coordination is maintained. No one has to check up on everyone; it is sufficient that occasional marked departures from commonly held notions of fair shares would generate opposition.

Indeed, these informal procedures can be powerful coordinating mechanisms: when one thinks of all the participants who are continuously engaged in interpreting the wishes of others, who try to feel the pulse of Congress, the president, interest groups, and special publics, it is clear that a great many adjustments are made in anticipation of what other participants are likely to do. As far as I can see, this is just another term for coordination, unless one insists that coordination be redefined to call for conscious control by a single individual or group.

Interaction between appropriations committees and administrative agencies includes at least seven modes of coordination:

1. Laws commanding specific actions
2. Committee reports demanding specific action on (implicit) pain of future penalties
3. Exchange of indulgences
4. Taking each other's preferences into account without direct contact
5. Accommodations to prior actions of the other without consultation
6. Argument in which one side convinces the other
7. Granting of side payments by one participant in return for action by the other

The most powerful coordinating mechanisms in budgeting undoubtedly are the various roles adopted by major participants in the budgetary process. Because the roles fit in with one another and set up a stable pattern of mutual expectations, they do a great deal to reduce the burden of calculations for individual participants. Agencies need not consider in great detail how their requests will affect the president's overall program; they know that such criteria will be introduced in the OMB. The appropriations committees and the OMB know that the agencies are likely to put forth all the programs for which there is prospect of support and can concentrate on fitting them into the president's program or on paring them down. The Senate committee operates on the assumption that if important items are left out through House action the agency will carry an appeal. If the agencies suddenly reversed roles and sold themselves short, the entire pattern of mutual expectations might be upset, leaving participants without a firm anchor in a sea of complexity. If the agency were to refuse the role of advocate, it would increase the burden on congressmen; they would not only have to choose with some fervor among desirable items placed before them, but also would have to discover what these items might be. This task is ordinarily far beyond the limited time, energy, information, and competence of most congressmen.

The roles appear "natural" to the occupants of these institutional positions. A man who has spent many years working in, say, natural resources can be expected to believe that his programs are immensely worthy of support. (He may try to eliminate programs he deems unworthy, but there are always others to take their place.) Indeed, he would hardly be worth having as a governmental employee if he did not feel this way in his position.

The House Appropriations Committee's role of guarding the Treasury, with its emphasis on reducing requests, makes sense in the context of agency advocacy. If congressmen can be reasonably certain that the agency has put its best foot forward, then their decisions may be viewed as choices along the margins of the top percentage of expenditures advocated by the agencies. The role of guardianship provides congressmen with reasonably clear instructions — cut the estimates — while keeping the area within which they must focus their attention (the largest increases) manageable in terms of their limited time and ability to calculate.

CONGRESSIONAL POWER

Guardianship is exercised through detailed scrutiny of budget requests, which of course involves interference with administration. To demand that congressmen not interfere so much in details of administraton would be to consign them to impotence. Grand policy decisions come few and far between. Most policy is made through interpretation of statutes by administrators or through a succession of marginal adjustments in the form of legislative amendments. To keep Congress from handling the details is to keep it out of power. I agree so completely with the position taken by Richard Fenno that I would like to quote his comments at some length.

> To relegate Congress to the making of broad policy decisions and to oversight in terms of broad program management is to prescribe precisely those tasks which Congress is least capable of performing. To criticize Congress for intervening in a specific and detailed fashion is to attack it for doing the only thing it can do to effectively assert its influence. Specifics and details are the indispensable handles which Congressmen use to work inductively toward broader kinds of oversight judgments. Specifics and details are what concern the constituents on whose behalf Congressmen must intervene with the bureaucracy. Specific and detailed requests from an interested Congressman to a bureau head or division chief do more to "galvanize the internal disciplines of administration" (Arthur Macmahon's phrase) than any broad statement of policy. The profusion of committees and subcommittees make possible a degree of specialization which gives to Congressmen the detailed and specific information they find most useful in influencing executive behavior.
>   ... The legislator ought not to be criticized for using those controls which are available to him and which his experience tells him bring the greatest influence over executive activity. If we do not recognize this, we will continue to prescribe impossible control tasks. . . .[2]

The power of Congress to control budgetary decisions depends on the strength of its appropriation committees. For no large assembly of men can

[2] Richard F. Fenno, Jr., review of *Congressional Control of Administration* by Joseph P. Harris, in *American Political Science Review*, 58 (September 1964), 674.

develop the expertise, self-direction, cohesiveness, and dispatch necessary for the large volume of budgetary business. A good index of the power of any legislature is whether it develops and follows committees of experts in specific areas of decisions. Where such committees are absent, as in Great Britain, the power of Parliament becomes a fiction. (A common definition of a Cabinet is a committee which permits no rivals.) The appropriation committees measure up exceedingly well when we consider that their recommendations are adopted by the houses of Congress approximately 90 percent of the time. Although one might contemplate with equanimity some reduction in this record of success, a drop below, say, 75 percent would seriously compromise the appropriations committees with the president and the agencies. A great deal of the ability to have agencies follow congressional will, after all, is dependent on the knowledge that the appropriations committees are watching and that to a high degree of certainty their actions will be upheld. If the power were transferred to Congress as a whole, its exercise would become so uncertain and diffuse that no one could count on it. Congressmen simply do not have the time and the knowledge to debate a very large number of appropriations with sense and then follow through. Most congressmen do well to keep the appropriations committees in line with an occasional defeat on the floor to remind them to whom they are ultimately beholden.

The great power of the appropriations committees consists in the extent to which agencies and the OMB systematically take account of their preferences. Anyone who has seen budget offices in operation knows that the unseen hand of Congress is never far from the surface. The agency practice of holding mock hearings in which some officials are assigned the role of appropriations committee members is a vivid illustration of how Congress makes its will felt indirectly.

In the past decade the budgetary process just described has undergone considerable strain. Pressures for vastly increased spending have proved irresistible, but not enduringly attractive. As a result, congressmen have begun to lose confidence in their appropriations committees and concomitantly in their own budgetary activities. Year by year they have withdrawn spending from the purview of the appropriations committees until only about 44 percent of the total remains. The level of conflict between legislative committees and appropriations committees has risen, as evidenced by the sharp increase in annual authorizations and the frequency of challenges on the floor. The role of guardianship declined as the appropriations committees responded to insistent demands for expenditure. The most dramatic symptom, which brought matters to a head, was the growing presidential tendency to impound funds after they had been appropriated; for a few months President Nixon virtually assumed the right not to spend even after Congress had passed an appropriations bill over his veto. And no one knows whether this episode represents a temporary abuse of executive power or functional adaptation to a system in which congressmen prefer to take the credit for spending but wish the President to take the blame for taxing.

Perhaps the cries of outrage against impounding are merely the death rattles of a Congress inclined to self-destruction. Perhaps. But there is nothing inevitable about what is happening; all signs point to strong citizen concern over the decline of Congress. Many congressmen are at least ambivalent enough to wish it were otherwise. Most congressmen stand to lose the power that makes their job worth having; they might respond to proposals for maintaining that power. They have just created mechanisms for revamping their appropriations process.[3]

FORMAL EXPLANATION

The qualitative account of the budgetary process just summarized indicates clearly the kind of quantitative models we wish to develop. It is evident, for example, that budgetary decision-makers think in terms of percentages. Agencies talk of expanding their base by a certain percentage. The OMB is concerned about growth rates for certain agencies and programs. The House Appropriations Committee deals with percentage cuts, and the Senate Appropriations Committee with the question of whether or not to restore percentage cuts. These considerations suggest that the quantitative relationships among the decisions of the participants in the budget process are linear in form.

The attitudes and calculations of participants in budgeting seem stable over time. The prominence of the agency's "base" is a sign of stability. The roles of major participants are powerful, persistent, and strongly grounded in the expectations of others as well as in the internal requirements of the positions. Stability is suggested also by the specialization that occurs among the participants, the long service of committee members, the adoption of incremental practices such as comparisons with the previous year, the fragmentation of appropriations by program and item, the treatments of appropriations as continuously variable sums of money rather than as perpetual reconsiderations of the worth of programs, and the practice of allowing past decisions to stand (while coordinating decision-making only if difficulties arise). Since the budgetary process appears to be stable over periods of time, it is reasonable to estimate the relationships in budgeting on the basis of time series data.

Special events can and do upset the apparent stability of the budgetary process. Occasionally, world events take an unexpected turn; a new law or administrative ruling changes the structure of appropriation accounts; some agencies act with exceptional zeal, while others suffer drastic losses of con-

---

[3] See Chapter 20 for further consideration of congressional reform.

fidence on the part of the appropriations subcommittees; and so on. It seems plausible to represent such transient events as random shocks to an otherwise deterministic system. Therefore, our model is stochastic rather than deterministic. Where these shocks occur with any regularity, of course, we have included variables in an attempt to model their effects.

Various participants in budgeting use strategies — some of them quite complicated — to further their aims. However, much of the process can be explained by simpler strategies based on the relationship between agency requests for funds (through the OMB) and congressional appropriations. Because these figures are made public and are known to all participants, and because they are directly perceived and communicated without fear of information loss or bias, they are ideal for feedback purposes. True, there are other indicators — special events, crises, technological developments, actions of clientele groups — which are attended to by participants in the budgetary process. But if these indicators are to be effective, they must quickly be reflected in the formal feedback mechanisms — the actions of departments, the OMB, and Congress — to which they are directed. Some of these indicators are represented by the stochastic disturbances; others, such as war, depression, or partisan change, are incorporated as specific variables into the extended models in the later part of the analysis. Nonetheless, the formal indicators are more precise, more simple, more available, more easily interpreted than the others. They are therefore likely to be used by participants in the budgetary process year in and year out. Present decisions are based largely on past experience, and this lore is encapsulated in the amounts which the agencies receive as they go through the steps in the budgetary cycle.

For all the reasons discussed in this section, our basic models of the budgetary process are linear, stable over periods of time, stochastic, and strategic in character. They are "as if" models: an excellent fit for a given model means only that the actual behavior of the participants has an effect equivalent to the equations of the model. The models, taken as a whole, represent a set of decision rules for Congress and the agencies.

Generally our methods follow what we conceive to be the canons of scientific procedure. The initial models are based on firsthand observation of budgetary phenomena. They are then tested on a sample of roughly half the domestic agencies. Critical comments are converted into hypotheses and tested against the same data. Two deviant cases are analyzed in order to uncover variables to improve the models. These variables are used to create new hypotheses that are tested again on more conclusive data. Corrections are then made preparatory to trying broad-ranging predictions for the future. Our extended models (in the next chapter) are aimed at prediction. They are an attempt to state conditions under which essential relationships between the executive agencies and Congress, modeled by shifts in the coefficients of the equation, will change.

THE ORIGINAL MODELS

Since agencies use various strategies and Congress may respond to them in various ways, we shall begin by proposing several alternate decision rules for both agency-OMB requests and congressional action on these requests.[4] For each series of requests or appropriations, we shall select that rule which most closely represents actual behavior. We shall use the variables

y_t the appropriation passed by Congress for any given agency in the year t. Supplemental appropriations are not included in the y_t.

x_t the appropriation requested by the OMB for any given agency for the year t. The x_t constitutes the president's budget request for an agency.

We will also introduce certain symbols representing random disturbances of each of the postulated relationships.

Equations for Agency-Budget Bureau Decision Rules

In this section we shall present three simple models of agency requests. The first states agency requests as a function of the previous year's appropriation. The second states requests as a function of the previous appropriation as well as a function of the differences between the agency request and appropriation in the previous year. The third states requests as a function of the previous year's request. In all three linear models provision is made for a random variable to take into account the special circumstances of the time.

An agency, while convinced of the worth of its programs, tends to realize that extraordinarily large or small requests probably will be viewed with suspicion by Congress; an agency does not consider it desirable to make extraordinary requests, which might precipitate unfavorable congressional reaction. Therefore, the agency usually requests a percentage (generally greater than 100 percent) of its previous year's appropriation. This percentage is not fixed: in the event of favorable circumstances, the request is a larger percentage of the previous year's appropriation than would otherwise be so; similarly, the percentage might be reduced in the event of unfavorable circumstances.

Decisions made in the manner described above may be represented by a simple equation. If we take the average of the percentages implicitly or explicitly used by budget officers, then any request can be represented by the sum of

---

[4] The following material has been adapted from Otto A. Davis, Michael A. H. Dempster, and Aaron Wildavsky, "A Theory of the Budgetary Process," *American Political Science Review*, 60 (September 1966), 529–547; and "On the Process of Budgeting II: An Empirical Study of Congressional Appropriations," *Studies in Budgeting*, ed. by Byrne, Charnes, Cooper, Davis, Gilford (Amsterdam-London: North-Holland Publishing Co., 1971), pp. 292–375.

this average percentage of the previous year's appropriation plus the increment or decrement due to the favorable or unfavorable circumstances. Thus

$$x_t = \beta_0 y_{t-1} + \xi_t \qquad (2.1)$$

The agency request (through the OMB) *for a certain year is a fixed mean percentage of the congressional appropriation for that agency in the previous year plus a random variable (normally distributed with mean zero and unknown but finite variance) for that year.*

is an equation representing this type of behavior. The average or mean percentage is represented by β_0. The increment or decrement due to circumstances is represented by ξ_t.

We have chosen to view the special events of each year for each agency as random phenomena capable of being described by a probability density or distribution. We assume here that the random variable is normally distributed with mean zero and an unknown but finite variance. Given this specification of the random variable, the agency makes its budgeting decisions as if it were operating by the postulated decision rule given by Equation 2.1.

An agency, although operating somewhat like the organizations described by Equation 2.1, may wish to take into account an additional strategic consideration: while this agency makes a request which is roughly a fixed percentage of the previous year's appropriation, it wants also to smooth out its stream of appropriations by taking into account the difference between its request and appropriation for the previous year. If there was an unusually large cut in the previous year's request, the agency submits a "padded" estimate to make up for the loss in expected funds; an unusual increase is followed by a reduced estimate to avoid unspent appropriations. This behavior may be represented by an equation or decision rule where

$$x_t = \beta_1 y_{t-1} + \beta_2 (y_{t-1} - x_{t-1}) + \xi_t \qquad (2.2)$$

The agency request (through the OMB) *for a certain year is a fixed mean percentage of the congressional appropriation for that agency in the previous year plus a fixed mean percentage of the difference between the congressional appropriation and the agency request for the previous year plus a stochastic disturbance.*

ξ_t is a stochastic disturbance, which plays the role described for the random variable in Equation 2.1, the βs are variables reflecting the aspects of the previous year's request and appropriation that an agency takes into account: β_1 represents the mean percentage of the previous year's request which is taken into account, and β_2 represents the mean percentage of the difference between the previous year's appropriation and request $(y_{t-1} - x_{t-1})$ which is taken into account.

Finally, an agency (or the president through the OMB), convinced of the worth of its programs, may decide to make requests without regard to previous congressional action. This strategy appeals especially when Congress has so much confidence in the agency that it tends to give an appropriation which is almost identical to the request. Aside from special circumstances represented by stochastic disturbances, the agency's request in any given year tends to be approximately a fixed percentage of its request for the previous year. This behavior may be represented by

$$x_t = \beta_3 x_{t-1} + \xi_t \tag{2.3}$$

The agency request (through the OMB) for a certain year is a fixed mean percentage of the agency's request for the previous year plus a random variable (stochastic disturbance).

---

where ξ_t is a stochastic disturbance and β_3 is the average percentage.

These three equations are not the only ones that could represent the actual behavior of the combined budgeting decisions of the agencies and the OMB. However, they represent the agency-OMB budgeting behavior better than all other decision rules tried.

Equations for Congressional Decision Rules

In considering congressional behavior, we shall again postulate three decision equations from which a selection must be made that best represents the behavior of Congress in regard to an agency's appropriations. Since Congress may use various strategies in determining appropriations for different agencies, different congressional decision equations may be selected as best representing congressional appropriations for each agency in our sample. Our first model states congressional appropriations as a function of the agency's request (through the OMB) to Congress. The second states appropriations as a function of the agency's request and as a function of the deviation from the usual relationship between Congress and the agency in the previous year. The third model states appropriations as a function of that segment of the agency's request which is not part of its appropriation or request for the previous year. Random variables are included to take account of special circumstances.

If Congress believes that an agency's request, after passing through the hands of the OMB, is a relatively stable index of funds needed by the agency to carry out its programs, Congress responds by appropriating a relatively fixed percentage of the agency's request. The term "relatively fixed" is used because Congress is likely to alter this percentage somewhat from year to year because of special events and circumstances relevant to particular years. As in the case of agency requests, these special circumstances may be viewed as random phenomena. One can view this behavior as if it were the result of Congress' appropriating a fixed mean percentage of the agency requests, adding to the amount so derived a sum represented by a random variable. One may represent this behavior as if Congress were following the decision rule

$$y_t = \gamma_0 x_t + \eta_t \tag{2.4}$$

The congressional appropriation for an agency in a certain year is a fixed mean percentage of the agency's request in that year plus a stochastic disturbance.

---

where γ_0 represents the fixed average percentage and η_t represents the stochastic disturbance.

Although Congress usually grants an agency a fixed percentage of its request, this request sometimes represents an extension of the agency's programs above (or below) the size desired by Congress. This can occur when the agency and the OMB follow presidential aims differing from those of Congress, or when Congress suspects the agency of padding the current year's request. In such a situation Congress usually appropriates a sum different from the usual percentage. If γ represents the mean of the usual percentages, this behavior can be represented by equation or decision rule

$$y_t = \gamma_t x_t + \xi_t$$

where ξ is a stochastic disturbance representing that part of the appropriations attributable to the special circumstances that cause Congress to deviate from a relatively fixed percentage. Therefore, when agency aims and congressional desires differ markedly (so that Congress may be said to depart from its usual rule), the stochastic disturbance takes on an unusually large positive or negative value. In order to distinguish this situation from the previous one, more must be specified about the stochastic disturbance ξ_t. In a year following one in which agency aims and congressional desires markedly differed, the agency will make a request closer to congressional desires, or Congress will shift its desires closer to those of the agency (or the president), or both will occur. In the year after a deviation, then, assume that Congress will make allowances to normalize the situation. Such behavior can be represented by an equation where η_t is a random variable and the symbol γ_t stands for the stochastic disturbance in the previous year (γ_{t-1}) as well as the new stochastic disturbance for the year involved. Thus our second congressional decision rule is

$$y_t = \gamma_t x_t + \gamma_t \xi_{t-1} + \eta_t \tag{2.5}$$

The congressional appropriation for an agency is a fixed mean percentage of the agency's request for that year plus a stochastic disturbance representing a deviation from the usual relationship between Congress and the agency in the previous year plus a random variable for the current year.

Finally, suppose that Congress knows the decision rule of a given agency, and assume that the agency's rule may be represented by one of the equations discussed above, so that Congress can take into account the (positive or negative) padding or gaming behavior of the agency, although otherwise the agency is given a certain percentage of its request. Thus

$$y_t = \gamma_3 x_t + \gamma_4 \lambda_t + \eta_t \tag{2.6}$$

is a third congressional decision rule, where λ_t is a dummy variable which in year t represents:

ξ_t	if Equation 2.1 obtains,
$\beta_2(y_{t-1} - x_{t-1}) + \xi_t$	if Equation 2.2 obtains,
ξ_t	if Equation 2.3 obtains,

depending, as indicated, upon which of the decision equations above represents the agency behavior.

The congressional appropriation for an agency is a fixed mean percentage of the agency's request for a certain year plus a fixed mean percentage of a dummy variable which represents that part of the agency's request for the year at issue which is not part of the appropriation or request of the previous year plus a random variable representing the part of the appropriation attributable to the special circumstances of the year.

The structural form of the model resulting from a combination of equations 2.1 and 2.4 can be written in standard econometric format as the vector-matrix equation:

$$(x_t y_t) \begin{bmatrix} -1 & \lambda_0 \\ 0 & -1 \end{bmatrix} + (x_{t-1} y_{t-1}) \begin{bmatrix} 0 & 0 \\ \beta_0 & 0 \end{bmatrix} + (\xi_t \eta_t) = (0\ 0) \tag{2.7}$$

which shows explicitly the dependence of the current variables x_t, y_t on their immediately previous values x_{t-1}, y_{t-1}, but subject to stochastic disturbances ξ_t, η_t. How well do these explanatory models stand up under empirical tests?

INITIAL EMPIRICAL RESULTS

Time series data for the period 1947 through 1963 were studied for all nondefense agencies of the United States government with organizational stability over the years. The requests (x_t) of these agencies were taken to be the amounts presented to Congress in the president's budget. In all instances the congressional decision variable (y_t) was taken to be the final appropriation before any supplemental additions.

The principal selection criterion we used originally was that of maximum (adjusted) correlation coefficient (R). For a given dependent variable this criterion leads one to select from alternative specifications of the explanatory variables that specification which leads to the highest sample correlation coefficient.

The empirical results (see Table 2.1) support the hypothesis that, up to a random error of reasonable magnitude, the budgetary process of the United States government is equivalent to a set of temporally stable linear decision rules. Estimated correlation coefficients for the best specifications of each agency are generally high.[5] But the table shows also that the fits between the decision rules and the time series data for the congressional decision equations are, in general, better than those for the agency-OMB equations, a finding that also recurs in future work.

Table 2.2 presents a summary of the combinations of the agency-OMB and congressional decision equations. For those agencies studied, the most popular combinations of behavior are the simple ones represented by Equa-

Table 2.1. BEST SPECIFICATIONS FOR EACH AGENCY ARE HIGH

Frequencies of Correlational Coefficients

	1–.995	.995–.99	.99–.98	.98–.97	.97–.96	.96–.95
Congressional	55	5	21	9	1	5
Agency	10	2	9	17	6	10

	.95–.94	.94–.93	.93–.90	.90–.85	.85–0
Congressional	4	1	4	4	7
Agency	6	7	8	14	27

[5] For more detailed information on how the tables in this section were compiled, see Davis, Dempster, Wildavsky, "On the Process of Budgeting II."

tions 2.1 and 2.4 respectively. When Congress uses a sophisticated "gaming" strategy such as Equation 2.6, the corresponding agency-OMB decision equation is the relatively simple Equation 2.1. And, when Congress grants exactly or almost exactly the amount requested by an agency, the agency tends to use decision Equation 2.3.

Our discussion thus far has assumed fixed values for the coefficients (parameters) of the equations we are using to explain the behavior underlying the budgetary process. In the light of the many important events occurring in the period from 1946 to 1963, however, it seemed reasonable to suppose that the appropriations structure of many government agencies was altered. If this is correct, the coefficients of the equations — literally, in this context, the values represented by the on-the-average percentages requested by the agencies and granted by Congress — should change from one period of time to the next. The equations would then be stable for a period, but not forever.

The year when the coefficient of an equation changes from one value to another is termed the *shift point*. The time series we are using are so short that it is possible to find only one meaningful shift point in each of the two equations that describes the budget request and appropriation best fitting an agency. We therefore broke each time series into two parts and used Chow's F-statistic[6] to determine temporal stability by testing the null hypothesis that the underlying coefficients did not shift (against all alternatives) for the individual equations. Since most of the coefficients did shift, it is evident that although the process is temporally stable for short periods, usually it is not stable for the whole period.

Table 2.3 presents, for both congressional and agency-OMB decision equations, frequencies of the shift points for those agencies for which the decision rules of the participants appeared to change. It turns out that most

Table 2.2. Budgetary Behavior Is Simple

Summary of Decision Equations[a]

Congress		2.4	2.5	2.6
	2.1	53	6	9
Agency	2.2	10	2	3
	2.3	27	5	1

[a] Including eight subagencies from the National Institutes of Health.

[6] G. C. Chow, "Tests of Equality between Sets of Coefficients in Two Linear Regressions," *Econometrica*, 28 (July 1960), 591–605, and the appendix to Davis, Dempster, Wildavsky, "On the Process of Budgeting II."

Table 2.3. LIKELY SHIFT POINTS ARE CONCENTRATED IN THE FIRST YEARS OF THE EISENHOWER ADMINISTRATION

Frequencies of Shift Points

	1948	1949	1950	1951	1952	1953	1954	1955	1956	1957	1958	1959	1960	1961	1962	1963
Congressional	1	2	3	2	0	6	21	31	6	3	4	4	4	2	2	3
Agency/Bureau	1	2	4	1	5	6	20	16	5	1	5	5	4	3	3	6

shifts are discovered during the first two budgets of the Eisenhower administration (1954–1955). Party variables clearly have a place in a budgetary theory.

Although the original empirical evidence indicated that our models describe the budgetary process of the United States government, we are well aware of certain deficiencies in our work. Our models so far are not predictive but explanatory. The alternate decision equations can be tried and the most appropriate one used when data on requests and appropriations are available. The appropriate equation explains the data in that, given a good fit, the process behaves "as if" the data were generated according to the equation. Thus our explanatory models are backward looking: given a history of requests and appropriations, the data appear as if they were produced by the proposed and appropriately selected scheme.

The models are not predictive because the budget process is temporally stable only for short periods. We have found cases in which the coefficients of the equations change, i.e., those in which there are alterations in the realized behavior of the processes. We have so far no a priori theory to predict the occurrence of these changes, but merely our ad hoc observation that most of them took place during Eisenhower's first term. Predictions must be based upon estimated values of the coefficients and on statistical properties of the stochastic disturbance (sometimes called the error term). Without a scientific method of predicting the shift points in our model, we cannot scientifically say that a request or an appropriation for some future year will fall within a prescribed range with a given level of confidence. We can predict only when the process remains stable in time. If the decision rules of participants have changed, our predictions may be worthless.

It is possible, of course, to make conditional predictions by taking the estimated coefficients from the last shift point and assuming that no shift will occur. Limited predictions as to the next year's requests and appropriations could be made and might turn out to be reasonably accurate. However, scholarly efforts would be better directed toward knowledge of why, where, and when changes in the process occur so that accurate predictions might be made. And this is what we shall now try to do through an analysis of deviant cases.

DEVIANT CASES

Although we argue that the results support the claim that the budgetary process behaves "as if" the data were generated according to the specified equations of these models, we do not claim that the models have predictive power in the usual statistical meaning of the term, in which a prediction is bounded by confidence intervals. The results indicate that, at least for some agencies, budgetary behavior does change. Since the models do not yet contain provisions enabling one to predict a priori when, say, a structural coefficient might shift, confidence limits on predictions lose their traditional meaning.

If one assumes that it is desirable to develop the basis for such a predictive theory, then there may be merit in intensively studying the record, for select agencies, during those years in which behavior did appear to change. One purpose of such an intensive study would be to determine whether reasonable explanations were apparent for observed changes. Another would be to uncover new variables that should be included in any attempt to construct a predictive theory.

The rest of this chapter reports such an extensive study.[7] We will not pretend that the conclusions are definitive or the methods anything but rough and ready. Although the mode of identifying a shift point is reasonably accurate within bounds, our determination of the explanation for it is largely judgmental. From the set of agencies previously studied, 53 were selected for intensive study by beginning with the entire set classified as unstable, eliminating the Eisenhower years (1953–1955), and arbitrarily stopping due to rapidly diminishing returns, because no new explanatory variables turned up.

The classification adopted for causes of shift points is one of convenience and utility. The number of categories was kept down to facilitate analysis. Nothing would be gained by proliferating categories when the total number of cases was reasonably small and we did not have the extraordinary amount of time it would require to develop complete and objective histories of the cases. We also looked for categories which, though justified in the data, would help determine whether new variables might be devised for the development of predictive theory. Thus, though accounting changes may loom large but be trivial as an explanatory category, partisan controversy is both suggestive for future work and significant as a manifestation of the interaction between the budgetary process and the electorate. Each category is described below with appropriate examples.

Classification of Causes of Shift Points

ACCOUNTING.   Variations in the dollar amounts caused primarily by changes in the procedure for billing accounts, or of type of appropriation, were categorized as caused by changes in accounting. These are "paper," rather than actual, changes. They involve how monies are accounted for rather than the actual size or use of the appropriation. The Southeastern Power Administration, for example, changed from gross to net billing of accounts. This caused its appropriation to drop from $1,939,000 to $735,000. The Bureau of Employee Compensation changed from a regular to an indefinite appropriation in 1952 and then back to a regular appropriation in 1953. Indefinite appropriations are carried in the reports in brackets, but are not included in the total

---

[7] We are indebted to Rose M. Kelly, a graduate student in the Department of Political Science at Berkeley, for the research on which this account is based.

for the agency. This change caused the bureau's appropriation to jump from $3 million in 1952 to $63 million in 1953 and then back from $63 million to $3 million in 1962.

CONGRESSIONAL SUPERVISION.   If the Appropriations Committees feel that an agency is wasting the taxpayers' money, they may refuse to fund the wasteful activity or place restrictions on it. The committees felt, for example, that the Bureau of Internal Revenue was spending too much money on paperwork and in collecting small accounts. The Senate Appropriations Committee Report stated: "The committee approves the House allowance of $266,000,000 for the Bureau of Internal Revenue, which is $6,500,000 below the 1954 budget estimate. The reductions will be applied to areas concerned with revision of procedures to eliminate unnecessary notices and reports and to avoid spending more in the collection of small deficiencies than is actually recovered." (Report 373, 83rd Cong., 1st Sess., p. 6.)

REORGANIZATION.   Shifts caused by legislative or administrative transfer of activities from one agency to another are categorized as reorganization if this transfer involves more than a change in accounting. The House Appropriations Committee, for example, decided to consolidate the appropriations for all soil and water conservation activities in the appropriations for fiscal year 1958. The House Committee Report stated that one of the purposes of this action was to produce economy of operation "by bringing together for the first time the administrative costs for soil and water conservation." The change was, then, clearly aimed at more than a mere transfer of activities.

EXTERNAL VARIABLE.   Some shifts are caused by a change in demand for a government service due to alteration in some external variable. These shifts are, of course, different from changes in policy because they are not controlled by the agency. Thus a drop in demand for coins caused the appropriation for the Bureau of the Mint to decrease. When Alaska and Hawaii became states, the appropriations of the Office of Territories were reduced. And when the Bureau of Accounts completed the liquidation of several wartime agencies, its appropriation level also decreased.

NEW LAW.   This category includes shifts that were caused either by new legislative programs or by amendments to existing legislation. The increase in the 1957 appropriation for the Farmers' Home Administration, for example, was caused by extension of the Farm Housing Act and by several amendments to the Bankhead-Jones Farm Tenant Act that increased the limits on various types of farm credit. The Bureau of Accounts jumped from approximately $13 million to $17 million in 1955 because of the increase in social security check issues resulting from the Social Security Amendments of 1955.

CHANGE IN APPROPRIATIONS POLICY.   When a shift resulted from a change in policy that did not require new substantive legislation, it was placed in this category. A good example is the Women's Bureau of the Department of Labor. In fiscal 1949, Congress deleted the appropriation for the field service of the bureau. And in 1951, Congress reversed this policy and allowed an appropriation to reestablish the field service. This policy change produced a large enough change in the money variables to cause a shift in both the Budget Bureau (now the OMB) equation (1952) and the congressional equation (1951).

A relevant question at this point is what criteria were used to determine whether a shift should be categorized as a change in policy or as partisan controversy. For the cause of a shift to be categorized as a policy change, it had to:

1. involve a specific policy, rather than just an "across-the-board" change (e.g., "cut federal spending");
2. have a duration longer or shorter than could be attributed to change in partisan control.

The Bonneville, Southeastern, and Southwestern Power Administrations can be used to contrast shifts due to changes in policy and shifts due to changes in partisan control. Here there was a fairly well defined issue: whether publicly owned power companies should build their own facilities and transmission lines. The decision was that they should purchase additional power needed from private companies and transmit power over privately owned lines. The duration of this policy change was much longer than could be attributed to partisan control. After the policy was changed, there was no appropriation for construction of facilities during the remaining portion of the time series.

PARTISAN CONTROVERSY.   These shifts are caused by a change in the partisan composition of Congress or of the presidency. Shifts due to partisan controversy differ from the changes in legislative policy in that (1) their duration is about the same as the duration of the partisan change; (2) they are oriented toward implementation of party ideology, rather than changing specific policies; and (3) they involve sharp differences in treatment of agencies by Democrats and Republicans.

One would, for instance, expect shifts to occur when the predominantly Republican and very conservative 83rd Congress took office. If these shifts extended for about the duration of Republican control of the Congress, if most Republicans favored deep cuts and most Democrats were opposed, and investigation showed them to involve ideological bias (i.e., let free enterprise do it), it would be included in the category of shifts due to partisan controversy. Republican ideology is visible in the House Appropriations Committee Report for 1954 explaining a $95 million cut in the Public Health Service. "The major part of the reduction has been made in grants to states and technical assistance to states. Funds for grants to states were requested under ten different appropriations totaling about $130,000,000. . . . It is the belief of this committee that much of the grant funds go to provide services that are strictly a state and local responsibility, and that action should be taken during the next few years to return financial responsibilities to states and localities." (House Report 426, 83rd Cong., 1st Sess., p. 10.) Similarly, the Bureau of

Reclamation was denied $85 million because "in applying the reductions which the committee has made for the various projects in construction and rehabilitation, the general policy of not appropriating for things that industry can do for themselves has been followed. . . ." (House Report 314, 83rd Cong., 2nd Sess., p. 14.)

NOT IDENTIFIED. The only agency for which we could not identify a cause of shift was the Fish and Wildlife Service.

Table 2.4 shows that partisan controversy is indisputably the largest single cause of shifts in relationship between the agencies and Congress.

Does this intensive study of select shift points help identify variables that might be included in an expanded and predictive theory? The answer is both yes and no. Partisan controversy clearly is important but it is hard to imagine the kind of variable, available yearly from 1947 to the present, that would predict the policy matters resolved by reorganization rather than in other ways. The same comment applies to special congressional supervision of agencies.

The remaining fourteen cases concern public policy. The variety of these policies and the likelihood that they stem from widely divergent causes does not create optimism that simple explanatory variables are close at hand. Consider some of the cases under the new law category. Amendments concerning unemployment compensation raise appropriations for the Bureau of Employment Security. Passage of the Taft-Hartley Act increases funds for the National Labor Relations Board. The Extension Service gets $5 million to provide the employers' contribution in a new law setting up a retirement fund for extension agents. The Bankhead-Jones Act eases farm credit leading to larger expenditures by the Farmers' Home Administration. A change in the formula for loans enables the Rural Electrification Administration to expand

Table 2.4. PARTISAN CONTROVERSY IS THE SINGLE LARGEST CAUSE OF IDENTIFIED SHIFTS

Categories of shift point cause	Number of shift points	Percentage
Accounting	5	9
Congressional supervision	3	6
Reorganization	4	8
External variable	6	11
New law	10	19
Appropriations policy	9	17
Partisan controversy	15	28
Not identified	1	2
Total	53	100

Note: Included are categories of shift point cause for 39 temporally unstable cases (FY 1949–1963) and 14 temporarily unstable cases (FY 1948–1952 and 1956–1963).

its services and hence its administrative costs. Extending coverage of the Social Security Act means that the Bureau of Accounts needs more money to write checks. A legislative decision to revise the Consumer Price Index brings several million dollars to the Bureau of Labor Statistics.

A few examples from the next largest category, appropriations policy, just add to the diversity of situations. After years of reluctance to provide funds for repair and replacement of facilities, the appropriations committees relented in 1956, thus leading to a shift for the Federal Prison System. Between 1950 and 1951 Congress enabled the Women's Bureau to reestablish its field service on a modified basis. The Geologic Survey got new money to do more mineral surveys, expand its water resources investigations, and construct a new office building. The Agricultural Marketing Service had its entire appropriation for marketing services cut out because of a dispute over poultry inspection. The Bonneville and Southeast Power Administrations were consistently denied funds for construction of new facilities but their appropriations began to rise again after 1956 when they agreed to purchase private power.

None of the above examples suggest a general class of widely available variables which might be included to provide automatic indications of shift points and behavioral changes. It may be, however, that some of the other policy changes respond to broad movements in the economy. Questions of farm credit, labor relations, electric power, social security, consumer prices, and so on may reflect changes in economic life. And we can use commonly available time series (prices, employments, population, etc.) in an attempt to capture them. Then we can begin the work of prediction.

3
Toward a Predictive Theory of United States Domestic Appropriations

We are interested in predicting government expenditures in total and by bureau not only to increase understanding of the United States federal budget process, but also with a view to closing United States national econometric models. Estimates of likely spending using standard econometric techniques are poor, both in absolute terms and in comparison with our own work. Management of the economy should be improved by using predictors based on the view of budgeting as a political process responsive to economic and social conditions. Use of mathematical models in the social sciences should be furthered, not by arguing their hypothetical utility, but by demonstrating that they work. The proof is in the prediction.

For each of the two equations best specifying an agency's request and appropriation, we tested the hypothesis of no shift in the underlying relationship against the occurrence of a single shift. Shift points were found to cluster in years of partisan political change — the Republican 80th Congress and the early years of the Eisenhower and Kennedy presidencies — and the obvious conclusion was drawn that a truly predictive theory should take account of the political party controlling the presidency and Congress. Next we took a sample of 52 shift points in both request and appropriation relationships (in which points in the years F1953 to F1955 were excluded) and analyzed them in detail. Again, we discovered that political variables were important. We also found that demands for governmental services altered due to changes in identifiable external variables outside the formal budgetary process. An analysis of deviant cases gave us some hope that by including exogenous political, economic, and social variables into the basic system (Equation 2.7) its explanatory and predictive power would improve.

THE EXTENDED MODEL

Using clues provided by our deviant-case analyses, standard economic series, and a few social indicators, we chose a set of 18 exogenous variables for possible inclusion in the extended version of the model. Table 3.1 lists all the explanatory variables considered for the two equations of the extended system. The process variables are those of the simplest equations (the leading variables) plus the variable found in the agency equation representing the difference between the previous appropriation and request. Sources and construction details for the political, administrative, economic and social exogenous variables are listed elsewhere.[1] Here only a few comments are in order.

Consider first the political variables. Party control of the Senate and presidency and the year prior to a presidential election are treated as binary dummy variables taking the value 1 in a year in which the named event occurs and 0 otherwise. There are, however, 4 such variables representing party

Table 3.1. EXPLANATORY VARIABLES IN THE EXTENDED MODEL

Process

LV	Leading variable	Either agency request (estimate in president's budget message) x_t (endogenous), or final appropriation in previous year y_{t-1} (predetermined).
$(y-x)_{t-1}$	. . .	Difference between request and appropriation in the previous fiscal year.

Political

HND	House non-Southern Democrats	Non-Southern (including Western) Democrats hold between 100 and 150 seats in the House of Representatives.
HLND	House large non-Southern Democrats	Non-Southern Democrats hold over 150 seats in the House.
HDM	House Democratic majority	Democrats hold between 217 and 250 seats in the House.
HLDM	House large Democratic majority	Democrats hold over 250 seats in the House.

[1] See O. A. Davis, M. A. H. Dempster, and A. Wildavsky, "Toward a Predictive Theory of the Federal Budgetary Process," delivered at the Annual Meeting of the American Political Science Association, September 1973. (Mimeographed.)

Table 3.1. (continued)

SDM	Senate Democratic majority	Democrats hold 50 or more seats in the Senate.
RP	Republican president	. . .
PRE-EL	Pre-election year	Fiscal year of presidential election (dated one year subsequent to election year).

Administrative

B.DEF$_{-1}$	Budget deficit in previous fiscal year	Previous fiscal year estimated in surplus (0) or deficit (1) by the Council of Economic Advisors as announced in the current president's budget message in January.
PBRR	Projected budget receipts ratio	Estimate of administrative budget receipts for the coming fiscal year divided by the estimate for the previous fiscal year at the time of the six-month review in December.

Economic

EC.REC.	Economic recession	Fiscal year judged a recession year by Council in a *subsequent* budget message.
UER	Unemployment rate	5 percent is 1.00.
RNNP	Real net national product	Net national product deflated by the private price index per head of adult population. F1971 is 1.00.
GNPD	GNP deflator	F1958 is 1.00.
FPPR	Federal/private price ratio	Ratio of federal government to private price index.

Social

WAR	. . .	Nation at war (declared or de facto).
AFO	Armed forces overseas	A two-year (t and $t + 1$) moving average of armed forces overseas *per head* of adult population $\times$ 10^2.
YPR	Young population ratio	Ratio of young to adult population.
ADP	Adult population	F1971 is 1.00.

control of the House of Representatives. It is an axiom of American politics that the elements of the Democratic coalition have widely different goals on many issues. Hence two variables were included to represent non-Southern Democratic seats in the House. For both the non-Southern and total Democratic seats, one might expect that changes of a few seats are unlikely to have much effect on the composition or mood of House Appropriations Subcommittees. On the other hand, a change in large numbers of non-Southern or total Democratic seats is likely to have a substantial effect. Although threshold levels are to some extent arbitrary, the 2 dummy variables for each of these variables is meant to reflect such considerations.

The two variables listed as "Administrative" — budget deficit in previous year and projected budget receipts ratio — are known, as estimates, to both the executive (demand) and congressional (supply) side of the appropriations process during the annual budget cycle. Although "we are all Keynesians now," the fact of a continuing deficit or surplus undoubtedly weighs on the minds of both president and congressional appropriations subcommittee members as political animals (although perhaps in different ways). We decided therefore to represent the estimate of surplus or deficit in the previous fiscal year as a binary dummy variable. Since the magnitude and even the direction of the president's estimate of surplus or deficit is often wildly in error,[2] and in any event is political as well as statistical, it is reasonable that participants on both sides of the process consider the best estimate of revenues (i.e., administrative receipts) independently of requests or appropriations. To smooth out fluctuations this estimate is likely to be compared to the current estimate of revenue for the preceding fiscal year. The latest real data are used as a hedge against a future estimate. Our second administrative variable is therefore a ratio of these two estimates; a ratio is used to generate a variable near one for numerical stability in estimating the extended model.

The exogenous economic variables are a standard set of economic climate, output, and price variables. The exogenous social variables represent military preparedness and population. The first is a binary dummy variable representing the state of war. The second gives an average measure of overseas military presence in per capita terms. Although it may be argued that these are policy rather than exogenous social variables, there is less exception to taking them as exogenous to the domestic budget. A ratio of young to adult population as well as a normalized adult population variable was used in an attempt to reflect the differing social needs and wants of a young population and the differing political priorities of the generations over the past two decades.

Consider now the problem of incorporating these exogenous variables $z_1, \ldots, z_m$ into the basic system (Equation 2.7) describing the formation of

[2] See W. Niskanen, "Controllability of the Fiscal Variables," Evaluation Division Report, Office of Management and Budget, 1971.

an agency's annual appropriations. We want variables that influence coefficients over a number of years, not variables that affect a single agency for a single year, so we can interpret the beta coefficients as a basic change in relationships. In order to retain the behavioral significance of the estimated coefficients, they must, therefore, be entered multiplicatively into both equations of the system. By using the combination of binary variables, representing discrete party political and major economic and social events, we model the abrupt changes in behavior in response to exogenous forces discovered in our previous work; by using the continuous administrative, economic and social variables we hope to model the incremental dynamics of the system more closely.[3]

Evidently we have sacrificed information by treating some continuous variables as binary. The reason for this choice goes to the heart of our method: the budgetary process shows evidence of being subject to discrete shocks — war, depression, party alternation — and we must use discrete binary (0–1) variables to model those shocks.

Variables originally were entered into the model in sets of a few at a time. At no time were more than ten explanatory variables included in a model estimated. We were interested in comparing the results of the algebraic or curve-fitting criterion $t > 1$, which maximizes the sample multiple correlation coefficient corrected for degrees of freedom, and the (frequentist) statistical criterion t, significant at the 5 percent level. Although the statistical selection criterion appeared marginally superior in prediction due to the elimination of a few apparently spurious influences, results for both criteria will be reported in the next two sections.

Empirical Results of the Extended Model

How does the extended model, with its exogenous variables, compare with the original model, which incorporates only factors internal to the budgetary process? The obvious way to begin is to see which set of models better fits the requests and appropriations data. Then we can determine whether the ways in which the exogenous data enter the agency and congressional equations fit roughly with expectations based on knowledge of American political life. The acid test, of course, is whether we can do some real prediction with the extended model.

Table 3.2 reports goodness-of-fit for the original models, and the extended models with both the 10 binary dummy variables and the full set of 18 exogenous variables. The histograms show the percentage of the agencies, on their request and appropriation sides separately, whose goodness-of-fit measure $\bar{R}^2$ fell within the indicated intervals. Although the fits were good for our original, they are even better for the extended versions of these models. Note

---

[3] For discussion of estimation problems, see Davis, Dempster, and Wildavsky, "Toward a Predictive Theory of the Federal Budgetary Process."

Table 3.2. EXTENDED MODEL FITS BETTER THAN ORIGINAL MODEL

Goodness-of-fit histograms

Request (x)	1–.99	.99–.98	.98–.96	.96–.94	.94–.92	.92–.90	.90–.88	.88–.86	.86–.81	.81–.72	.72–0
Original	.08	.00	.06	.11	.09	.04	.08	.08	.08	.15	.25
Extended (10)	.08	.09	.13	.19	.06	.04	.06	.00	.08	.11	.17
Extended (18)	.08	.08	.15	.17	.09	.04	.06	.08	.08	.02	.17
Appropriation (y)	**1–.99**	**.99–.98**	**.98–.96**	**.96–.94**	**.94–.92**	**.92–.90**	**.90–.88**	**.88–.86**	**.86–.81**	**.81–.72**	**.72–0**
Original	.43	.15	.13	.06	.02	.00	.06	.02	.08	.00	.06
Extended (10)	.38	.28	.11	.02	.04	.00	.00	.00	.06	.06	.06
Extended (18)	.54	.15	.08	.06	.06	.02	.00	.02	.04	.04	.00

Note: Goodness-of-fit histograms used here are $\bar{R}^2$ for fifty-three selected agencies.

especially the percentage increases of those agencies whose $\bar{R}^2$ falls within the very high end of the scale. Also notice that fits for the congressional side of the process are much better than those for the agencies and that this conclusion obtains for both the extended and the original models. Thus, introducing more traditional political variables does not alter the conclusion that the congressional side of the process is more amenable to explanation by behavioral models. It is possible that by treating each agency individually — in isolation from other agencies in the same department or with similar programs or functions — we are ignoring important marginal corrections to internally desired request levels imposed on the agency by bureaucratic constraints such as those discussed under the heading of "fair shares." [4]

The hypothesis underlying the extended model is that temporal instability is caused by misspecification — by not including the effects of important events in the equations. Omission of these variables then causes what appears to be shifts in the underlying relationships. The question is whether and to what degree we now have included some of the missing variables.

Testing the Extended Model against the Original

Our principal aim in proposing the extended model (Equation 2.7) of the previous section is to explain observed temporal instabilities in process terms. Therefore a significant improvement in fit over the original models during the estimation period is not sufficient to demonstrate increased explanatory power due to the exogenous variables. A better fit tells us only that, for some unknown reasons, the explanatory power of the original models has been improved without our learning precisely which outside influences are responsible for the change. Indeed, the estimated external influences might be either spurious or nonrecurring. Further, significant (even major) influences on a given agency's appropriation may be missing from our set of exogenous variables.

It would be easy enough to find variables that would explain behavior in an individual agency. But we are looking for general variables, which influence a number of agencies, not variables specific to a particular agency.[5] We therefore determined to test the increased explanatory power of the extended model by ex post predictions over the five-year post estimation period F1964–1968.[6]

---

[4] See A. Wildavsky, *The Politics of the Budgetary Process* (Boston: Little, Brown, 2nd ed., 1974), pp. 16, 154 for discussion of fair shares.

[5] In some cases, however, the estimation bias of known once-for-all events, e.g., Sputnik, has been removed by adding a binary dummy variable to our set for potentially affected agencies, e.g., NASA, NSF, AEC, etc.

[6] Of course not all exogenous binary dummy variables which changed over the estimation period did so over the prediction period, so they cannot be used to test the increased explanatory power of the extended model. Changes took place in 3 (HDM), 4 (HLDM), 7 (PRE-EL), 10 (EC. REC.), and 15 (WAR).

This test must rest on successfully capturing shifts in the underlying coefficients of the basic model over the prediction period with exogenous variables that affect a series of agencies.

The problem of evaluating the predictive performance of the extended model over a sample of agencies whose appropriations exhibit widely varying behavior is nontrivial. Econometricians have recently given some attention to evaluating and comparing econometric models from their prediction and forecasting performance.[7] However, this attention has not been focused on the problem at hand, namely, tests for the successful structural modeling of systems subject to discrete exogenous shocks. The most common measure of predictive performance is the *mean square error* (MSE) of model predictions over the prediction period.

But we are interested in the absolute forecasting performance of the extended model. We require a measure of performance that considers prediction error relative to variability in the predicted variable. This is achieved by considering variance in prediction error relative to the variance in the differences between the old and new series as smoothed by using moving averages. The procedure is embodied in the statistic MANMSE (Moving Average Normalized Mean Square Error).

The first step in evaluating the increase in explanatory power of the extended system (Table 3.1) for the 52 agencies in our sample (3 were disbanded or amalgamated with others during the period) is to compare its predictive ability over the postestimation period F1964–1968 to that of the basic systems. A computer program COMPARE was written to compare the MSE of system predictions of each agency's appropriation (y) generated by 4 possible systems. The 4 systems are formed by the 4 possible combinations of best specifications of the 2 equations by the basic and extended models.

Table 3.3 shows the basic results of choices made by COMPARE for the extended model specifications selected from the 10 binary dummy exogenous variables (z_1 to z_8, z_{10} and z_{15} in Table 3.1) according to both the algebraic criterion (individual t-statistics exceed 1) and the statistical criterion (individual t-statistics significant at the 5 percent level). Also it shows comparable results for extended model specifications selected from the full set of 18 exogenous variables according to the statistical criterion. Results for three situations are not markedly different. MSE is reduced in around 25 percent. Analogous to the situation in which fit is improved over the estimation period, the exogenous variables tend to be roughly twice as effective in reducing prediction error on the congressional side of the process as they are on the executive side. In

[7] See, e.g., P. J. Dhrymes, E. P. Howrey, S. H. Hymans, et al., "Criteria for Evaluation of Econometric Models," *Annals of Economic and Social Measurement*, 1 (1972), 291–324; and E. P. Howrey, L. R. Klein, and M. D. McCarthy, "Notes on Testing the Predictive Performance of Econometric Models," Discussion Paper No. 173, Wharton School, Department of Economics, University of Pennsylvania, 1970.

Table 3.3. THE EXTENDED MODEL SPECIFICATION LEADS TO LOWER SYSTEM MSE IN ABOUT 25 PERCENT OF THE 104 EQUATION CASES

| | 10 Exogenous variables | | | | | | 18 Exogenous variables | | |
| | Algebraic criterion (t > 1) | | | Statistical criterion (t sig. 5%) | | | Statistical criterion (t sig. 5%) | | |
	Extended y eqn.	Basic y eqn.	Total x eqn.	Extended y eqn.	Basic y eqn.	Total x eqn.	Extended y eqn.	Basic y eqn.	Total x eqn.
Extended x eqn.	6	4	10	2	6	8	2	2	4
Basic x eqn.	12	30	42	17	27	44	15	33	48
Total y eqn.	18	34	52	19	33	52	17	35	52

terms of explaining temporal instabilities with the extended model, however, our results in Table 3.4 are conservative. We are justified in considering as *better explained* by the extended model, systems for which COMPARE chose a basic equation but we had in a previous study[8] found this equation to be temporally unstable. Table 3.4 classifies systems as better explained or not improved in a comparable manner to Table 3.3. More than half the cases are better explained by the extended model.

Let us now examine the relationship between better explanation as exhibited in Table 3.4 and satisfactory equation prediction. For this purpose we shall consider an agency's requests or appropriations predicted over the post-estimation period F1963–1968 if the appropriate NMSE is less than 1, i.e., if (approximately) some proportion of the variance of the predicted variable over the period is explained.

The overall figures for equation prediction show that the better fits for both original and extended appropriation equations over the estimation period are reflected in superior prediction of appropriations over the prediction period — 39 instances of appropriation prediction versus 26 instances of request prediction. Wherever the request was predicted (see Table 3.5), so was the appropriation; a good specification of the agency equation is the key to good system prediction.

Yet Another Effort to Analyze Deviant Cases

In an attempt to discover possible general influences missing from our set of 18 exogenous variables, we computed the prediction error in each year of the prediction period F1964–1968 for each equation and the system across the 50 agencies for which we have a complete record. The results are seen in Table 3.6, which shows a marked jump in prediction errors in F1966 and F1967 as measured by the square roots of NMSE for the 3 types of predictions.

An analysis of the signs and magnitudes of prediction error in these years revealed evenhanded behavior across agencies. It therefore seems likely that rather than being due to the omission of exogenous variables for which a suitable time series is available, the disturbances to the normal situation are due to exceptional, probably nonrecurring, events. By the relative sizes of the jump in prediction error, it is clear also that the disturbances to previous behavior originated on the executive side of the process.

What did in fact happen? After the November 1964 election, the 89th Congress reflected a large Democratic swing in the composition of the House of Representatives from an already clear Democratic majority in the previous Congress. A large Democratic swing in seats in the House occurred twice previously in the postwar period: in the year of Truman's surprise victory, 1948, and in the 1958 midterm elections during Eisenhower's second term.

---

[8] Davis, Dempster, and Wildavsky, "On the Process of Budgeting II."

Table 3.4. The Extended Model Specification Better Explains Over Half the 104 Equation Cases

	10 Exogenous variables						18 Exogenous variables		
	Algebraic criterion (t > 1)			Statistical criterion (t sig. 5%)			Statistical criterion		
	y Eqn. better explained	y Eqn. not improved	Total x eqn.	y Eqn. better explained	y Eqn. not improved	Total x eqn.	y Eqn. better explained	y Eqn. not improved	Total x eqn.
x Eqn. better explained	16	12	28	17	10	27	13	9	22
x Eqn. not improved	11	13	24	12	13	25	12	18	30
Total y eqn.	27	25	52	29	23	52	25	27	52

Table 3.5. THE BEST SPECIFICATION LEADS TO A HIGH INCIDENCE OF APPROPRIATION EQUATION PREDICTION

	10 Exogenous variables						18 Exogenous variables		
	Algebraic criterion ($t > 1$)			Statistical criterion (t sig. 5%)			Statistical criterion (t sig. 5%)		
	y Predicted	y Not pre-dicted	Total x	y Predicted	y Not pre-dicted	Total x	y Predicted	y Not pre-dicted	Total x
x Predicted	25	0	25	26	0	26	24	2	26
x Not predicted	12	15	27	13	12	26	13	13	26
Total y	37	15	52	39	13	52	37	15	52

Table 3.6. THE EFFECTS OF THE GREAT SOCIETY AND THE VIETNAM WAR

Cross-sectional prediction error: 50 agencies

	1964	1965	1966	1967	1968
$RNMSE_x^e$	.76	.71	1.36	1.28	.33
$RNMSE_y^e$	.07	.09	.15	.13	.14
$RNMSE_y^s$	.77	.73	.98	.94	.39

We therefore constructed a binary dummy variable for the extended model which took the value 1 in F1950 and F1960 in an attempt to predict the effects of the swing in the 1964 election on the F1966 budget presented to the new Congress. This variable was found to be significant only for the extended appropriation equations of a couple of agencies — hardly enough effect to pick up the jump in prediction error. We therefore turn to nonrecurring events.

The F1966 budget was prepared by the Johnson Administration under the assumption that the incumbent would win the 1964 election — with this assumption verified, the Great Society was launched in the president's message to Congress in January 1965. July 1965 saw the Gulf of Tonkin Resolution and intensification of the war in Vietnam. Thus the jump in agency equation prediction error in F1966 is due to Great Society programs, and in F1967 to a combination of these and the war. Ultimately, our models must account for these periods of change as well as for years of greater stability.

In the previous section we were concerned with ex post prediction for its value in comparing the explanatory power of extended and original models. In this section we wish to evaluate the explanatory power of our models by studying their predictive capability vis-à-vis a number of naive predictors. It is only by demonstrating superior predictive power over alternative theories that validation of our models can proceed. A minimal requirement is to demonstrate a higher level of prediction on average than the alternatives. The term "on average" here refers to the sample of our 55 agencies which has been deliberately selected to include a higher proportion of agencies not satisfactorily fitted by the original models than the proportion reported for the 116 agency sample. Few structural econometric models have so far passed the test of superior predictive power to (statistically sophisticated) naive predictors.[9]

Consider first six-month prediction of agency appropriations when estimates (requests) in the president's budget are known. This is the forecasting period relevant to the macroeconomic calculations of the Council of Economic Advisors which assume that the president's "estimates," i.e., requests x, will

---

[9] Howrey, Klein, McCarthy, "Notes on Testing the Predictive Performance of Econometric Models."

be appropriated unchanged by Congress. An obvious test of this assumption results from treating each agency's request x as a predictor of its appropriation y. A similar naive predictor over the annual forecasting period required for internal and private forecasts of government expenditure results from assuming an agency's appropriation y remains the same as the previous year's appropriation y_{-1}. We shall see that for both, the naive predictors do poorly in absolute terms and in relation to our own work.

Up to this point we have considered only summary statistics based on our sample — agencies have been cases of occurrence of this or that event. It is high time we looked at the ex post predictive performance of our models across a section of named agencies. Actual and predicted appropriations for an individual agency over the 21-year postwar period F1947–1968 are reviewed in Figures 3.1 through 3.7. Predictions are by the extended appropriation equation over the regression period F1947–1963 and by the best specification of the system chosen by COMPARE predicting 1 year ahead over the 5-year prediction period F1963–1968.

Figure 3.1 shows the time series for the Wage and Hour Division (WHD) of the Department of Labor. Its appropriations settled down over the prediction period to a linear trend after considerable earlier variability. Here the basic

Figure 3.1. WHD: TEN-VARIABLE EXTENDED MODEL
(appropriation in thousands of dollars)

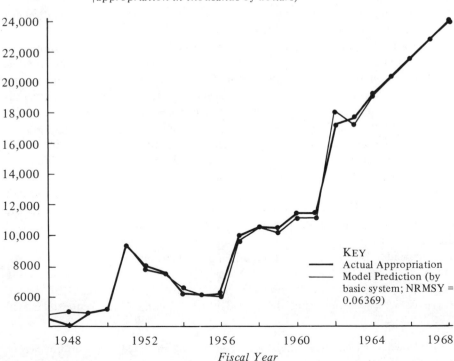

KEY
—— Actual Appropriation
—— Model Prediction (by basic system; NRMSY = 0.06369)

Fiscal Year

Figure 3.2. POD: TEN-VARIABLE EXTENDED MODEL
(appropriation in tens of thousands of dollars)

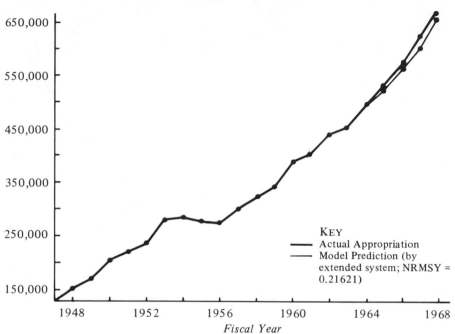

KEY
—— Actual Appropriation
—— Model Prediction (by
extended system; NRMSY =
0.21621)

Fiscal Year

system (Equation 2.7) predicts very well (NMSE$_y^s$ = 0.004, MANMSE$_y^s$ = 0.216), better in fact than either the appropriation equation or any of the naive predictors.

The time series for the Post Office Department Total (see Figure 3.2) exhibits similar behavior to those for WHD. Here system prediction with an extended system in which all House and Senate variables enter the appropriation equation negatively is good (NMSE$_y^s$ = 0.047, MANMSE$_y^s$ = 4.12), but the best predictor is the auto-regressive scheme which specifies a 6.4 percent increase per annum (NMSE$_y^a$ = 0.024).

Figure 3.3 shows the time series for the Public Health Service which exhibits a sharply rising trend over the period. In spite of this, although the request is a better six-month predictor (NMSE$_y^x$ = 0.023) than the appropriation equation, system prediction is good (NMSE$_y^s$ = 0.095, MANMSE$_y^s$ = 0.122) and the best annual predictor. The system has an extended request equation in which a Republican president has a negative influence.

Figures 3.1, 3.2, and 3.3 deal with a (relatively) small, large, and medium-sized agency respectively, all of which provide population services and are therefore likely to exhibit an upward trend which we could expect to be well predicted by our models. The next two figures depict agencies whose political fortunes have been more controversial; although the appropriation equation

Figure 3.3. PHS: TEN-VARIABLE EXTENDED MODEL
(appropriation in tens of thousands of dollars)

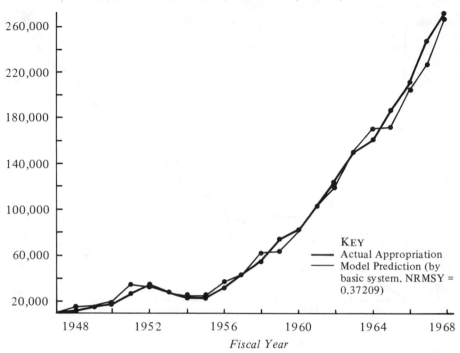

KEY
—— Actual Appropriation
—— Model Prediction (by
basic system. NRMSY =
0.37209)

Fiscal Year

predicts well, the request equation does not. Figure 3.4 shows the fluctuating time series for the Army Corps of Engineers. Although the appropriation equation is the best six-month predictor ($NMSE^e_y = 0.115$) and the basic system (Equation 2.7) is the best annual predictor ($NMSE^s_y = 1.14$ MANMSE^s_y = 10.95) the request equation makes it unsatisfactory. Figure 3.5 reveals the erratic time series of the Atomic Energy Commission. Again the extended appropriation equation, in which a Democratic majority in the Senate has a positive influence, is the best six-month predictor ($NMSE^e_y = 0.019$); but the request equation makes the system overpredict in 4 of the 5 years of the prediction period so that the previous appropriation is the best annual predictor ($NMSE^{y-1}_y = 1.40$, MANMSE$^{y-1}_y = 9.23$).

The last two agencies we shall consider are caveats to the econometrician, who must base forecasts on the assumption that history will repeat itself. Figure 3.6 shows the time series for the Bureau of Land Management. The Korean War had a depressing effect on that bureau's appropriations in Congress. At the start of the Vietnam war in F1966, the prediction for this equation was depressed when in fact an increased request got through Congress; economic recession in F1968 (first two quarters 1967) pulled the equation back on track.

Figure 3.4. ARMY ENG.: TEN-VARIABLE EXTENDED MODEL
(appropriation in tens of thousands of dollars)

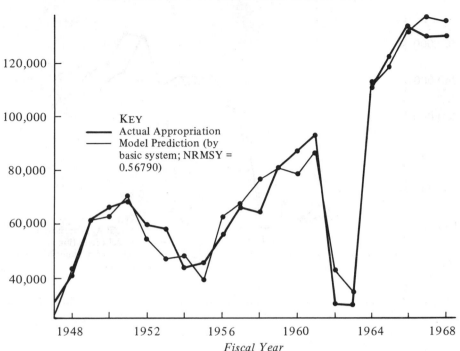

KEY
—— Actual Appropriation
— Model Prediction (by
basic system; NRMSY =
0.56790)

Fiscal Year

Figure 3.7 depicts the rise and fall of NASA, the National Aeronautics and Space Administration. The extended appropriation equation — in which war and large numbers of non-Southern Democrats in the House have a negative influence, and preelection years have a positive influence — follows closely the exponential growth of space appropriations over the regression period. The damping of space activity over the prediction period leads to wild overprediction by the extended system. Notice, however, the effect of the war variable and that if we were to allow ourselves adjustments to constants — what Professor Klein calls "tender loving care" — the system tracks the process again in the last three years of the prediction period after the turning point.

Next let us compare the overall predictive performance of our models relative to that of the naive predictors introduced above. For the six-month period, the request predicted (i.e., $\text{NMSE}^x_y < 1$) in 42 of the 52 cases. The record for the previous appropriation y_1 was not so good. But the overall results in Table 3.7 show that our models are superior to known alternatives.

Because none of the usual standard tricks to improve forecasting performance (such as reestimation after each observation, constant adjustment, etc.) are employed, the results in Table 3.7 are encouraging from the viewpoint of validation of our behavioral models and of the possibilities for genuine

Figure 3.5. AEC: TEN-VARIABLE EXTENDED MODEL
(appropriation in tens of thousands of dollars)

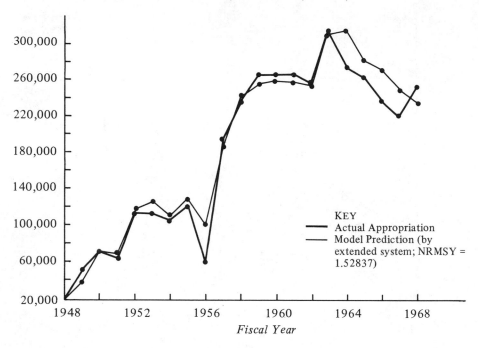

forecasting.[10] In future work we hope to make an even more convincing case; therefore, we must learn more about how and why our outside variables did or did not enter the equations for each agency.

Table 3.7. OUR MODELS ARE THE BEST PREDICTORS OF THOSE CONSIDERED

Best six-month prediction

	Eqn.	System	Request	Auto-reg.	y_{-1}	Total
All agencies	18	8	23	2	3	54
$\text{NMSE}_y < 1$						
Agencies	16	6	20	2	0	44

Best annual prediction

	System	Auto-reg.	y_{t-1}	Total
All agencies	23	12	19	54
$\text{NMSE}_y < 1$				
Agencies	16	12	2	3

[10] For efforts to predict expenditures see H. Galper and H. F. Wendell, "Progress in Forecasting the Federal Budget," *Proceedings of the Economics and Business Section of the American Statistical Association,* 1968, pp. 86–98.

Figure 3.6. BLM: TEN-VARIABLE EXTENDED MODEL
(appropriation in thousands of dollars)

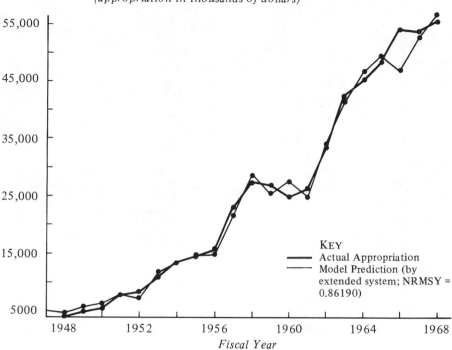

KEY
—— Actual Appropriation
—— Model Prediction (by extended system; NRMSY = 0.86190)

Fiscal Year

EXPLORING ENVIRONMENTAL INFLUENCES ON AGENCIES

Our objective in this section is to delineate those exogenous variables which significantly affect the 52 agencies in our sample, in respect to both the agency request and the congressional appropriation.[11] We are trying to find out if any agency or group of agencies is particularly susceptible to these environmental influences, and if so, what influences affect which agencies. So as not to be deluded by possible spurious influences improving the fit over the regression period F1947–1963, we shall consider only those exogenous variables (of our full set of 18) which entered equations (chosen by COMPARE) as best predictors over the prediction period F1964–1968. What type of agency, we asked, is affected by these variables? Which agencies are most highly influenced? What type of influence usually affects agencies? Do certain variables cluster together when they affect agencies? Let us look at these questions in turn.

---

[11] Aidan Vining, a student at the Graduate School of Public Policy in Berkeley, helped prepare this section.

Figure 3.7. NASA: TEN-VARIABLE EXTENDED MODEL
(appropriation in hundreds of thousands of dollars)

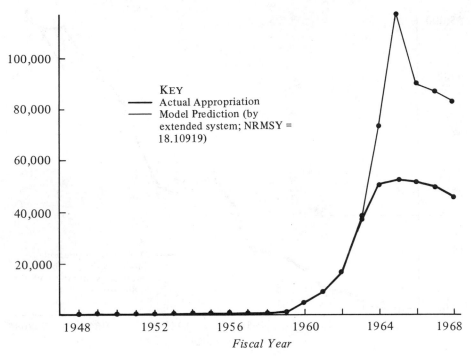

What kind of agency is affected by our exogenous variables? In order to examine what kind of agency is subject to environmental influence, we devised a six-fold classification of the 52 agencies in our sample. The six functional categories settled upon were:

1. Labor, Welfare, Health, Urban-areas (Housing), Education, Veterans, Indian Affairs
2. Natural Resources
3. Agriculture and Agricultural Services
4. Regulation, Transportation, and Commerce
5. General Services to the National Administration and Population
6. Space

Of 17 agencies influenced by outside variables,[12] 12 fell within the General

---

[12] The seventeen agencies are: ICC, Interstate Commerce Commission; TVA, Tennessee Valley Authority; EOP, Executive Office of the President; AEC, Atomic Energy Commission; GSA, General Services Administration; POO, Post Office Operations; POD, Post Office Department Total; OOVR, Office of Vocational Rehabilitation; OOT, Office of Territories; BOLM, Bureau of Land Management; CGS, Coastal and Geodetic Survey; BOMT, Bureau of the Mint; FWS, Fish and Wildlife Service; FHAL, Farmers' Home Administration (Loans); ARS Agricultural Research Service; NASA, National Aeronautics and Space Administration; and BON, Bureau of Narcotics.

Services to the National Administration and Population and Natural Resources categories. Not only were there few agencies that fell within the other three categories (5 out of the 17), but with the exception of NASA these tended also to be agencies that experienced minimal environmental influence (usually they were affected by just one exogenous variable). The two categories chosen — services and resources — appear to include the agencies that would normally be considered either highly political or very little affected by politics. Thus the Bureau of the Mint and the General Services Administration are usually not politically controversial, while TVA and the Bureau of Land Management have generated considerable conflict. Agencies in these two categories also experience the greatest number of environmental influences.

Our next question, then, is what particular type of environmental influence affects these agencies. Dividing the 18 exogenous variables into 4 functional categories — political (7), economic (5), social (4), and administrative (2), we found that no one group affected the agencies to the exclusion of the others. There could hardly be a more even distribution among political, social, and economic categories. The only functional group that occurs less frequently is administrative; this is about what we might expect, since there were only 2 variables in this category.

Another way to look at the political variables is to ask which occur most frequently and whether their influence is usually positive or negative. In our sample, Senate Democratic majority and non-Southern Democrats holding over 150 votes in the House occur most frequently. As we might have expected, the influence of these variables is usually positive (6 out of 7); this is generally true for all the political variables: in 11 out of 16 instances there is an increase. As 5 out of 7 political variables represent various forms of Democratic dominance in the legislature, it would seem to confirm the hypothesis that Democratic legislators tend to be "spenders" rather than "cutters." There is one exception to this general pattern of increases — the Post Office. Its budget tends to be cut by Democratically controlled Houses and only occasionally restored by the Senate. In all 4 cases where this variable is significant, there is a negative influence, only once offset by a positive influence in the Senate. This result seems a little surprising given the political muscle of postal unions and will require further examination. It does seem apparent, however, that the political process is important — including who is president, which party controls Congress, and the size of its majority.

Our second functional group of variables is economic. They are, as we have seen, as important as political variables. Again, the General Services category is by far the most important, while Natural Resources does not appear to be too important here. Changes in economic conditions, then, are taken out on routine, noncontroversial activities.

The most influential economic variables are the GNP deflator (number 13) which affects 6 out of the 17 agencies, the unemployment rate (number 11), and the federal/private price ratio (number 14), each of which affects

3 out of the 17 agencies. In contrast to political variables, however, economic variables are as likely to have a negative as a positive influence — 9 and 7 instances respectively. There are too few examples of economic variable influence for us to draw conclusions concerning the countercyclical effects of the budget process; this is another area that will require further examination.

By way of summary, an examination of exogenous variables shows that when they do exert an influence, it is over the most vulnerable agencies. Outside influences affect an agency when it performs a routine service (easily pushed forward or held back as circumstances suggest) or when it is an object of dispute, so that its fortunes depend on the growth of friends or the decline of foes. For the most part, however, our agencies live in worlds of their own, worlds fully comprehensible to them but not yet to us. When and if we can better model the executive side of the budgetary process, we shall have largely solved the problem of prediction. Even so, we have demonstrated that our models now predict better than known alternatives. On that judgment this chapter rests.

4
Budgeting as Trust:
The British Expenditure Process

Political institutions must be described one at a time; yet political life at the center of British government is a highly interrelated whole. To preserve this systematic quality we use concepts that retain at least some flavor of the essential unity amid diversity. We are speaking of people whose common kinship and culture separates them from outsiders. Coherence among British political administrators is expressed through exclusiveness, with their interactions sequestered within the executive. Apart from the final decisions reached, their behavior is neither known nor intended to be known beyond government circles. Insiders are overwhelming; outsiders are overwhelmed. In a word, governing public money is a private affair.

This privacy at the political center can best be introduced in terms of three central features in British government: mutual trust, common calculations, and political climate. None is absolutely unique to Britain, but there are probably few nations in which all three can be found to the same extent or in such powerful combination. Mutual trust is a pervasive bond for dealing with members of one's own group and, by extension, strangers. Common calculations help political administrators deal with a complex world, but their misunderstanding of governmental problem-solving also separates them from the layman, who finds it difficult to see why government cannot simply decide on the right policy and execute it. Political winds often gather force outside government, but blow this way or that largely because of insiders' concentration on their own reactions and assessments. Confidence, calculations, and climate, then, are variations on the theme of a shared, exclusive group life inside the British government community.

Adapted from Hugh Heclo and Aaron Wildavsky, *The Private Government of Public Money: Community and Policy Inside British Political Administration* (Berkeley: University of California Press; and London: Macmillan, 1974). By permission.

MUTUAL TRUST

Imagine the top layers of the executive arm of British government as a system of reputations. The elements of the system are the holders of top official positions; counters by which reputations are measured and traded are units of esteem. These counters can be used to help obtain faster promotion or better positions or quicker action or indulgence of policy preferences. Esteem is measured in terms of intellect (Is he bright?), influence (Can he carry along his colleagues and masters?), and especially in terms of trust (Is he reliable?). All three factors combine to affect the participants' sense of mutual confidence.

Few people are directly involved. When we speak of political administrators in British central government, we mean that assemblage of ministers and senior civil servants who preside over the work of Cabinets and departments. At the margins of government are important backbench MPs, journalists, and interest group leaders. The number of people involved is at most a few hundred, and they change but slowly. They all know or know about each other, and they all enjoy rating one another. Ministers are likely to be aware, not only of each other's political performance, but also of the exact university degree (first, second, or third) that colleagues won and where. There is no permanent secretary not prepared to rate the leadership abilities of ministers under whom he has served. No Treasury official of any experience hesitates to judge the incisiveness and reliability of his opposite numbers in the departments. No departmental finance officer worth his salt is unaware of the extent to which Treasury supply officials know the substantive merits of proposals he sends them.

The bedrock of British political administration is the vital importance placed on personal trust for each other. By trust one means personal dependability, "soundness," a feeling that here is a person in whom one can reliably place confidence and confidences. Mutual trust is considered paramount by officials who know they will have to continue doing business with each other year after year on issue after issue; they believe that if professionalism means anything it means knowing how to treat members of one's own group. Trust also is vital between ministers and civil servants — each of whom must fight the other's battles, one behind Cabinet doors and in the public arena, the other among the mass of departmental expertise and official encounters. Mutual reliance is important, though (as we shall see) less operational, among ministers of the government who survive by hanging together against the other party's crowd and an intractable world. Since everyone's prospects for power over policy and authority over decisions depend on the judgment of colleagues, reputation in general is always likely to be more important to participants than is any particular issue.

British central government recognizes mutual dependence even — indeed, especially — in the midst of conflict. Treasury–spending department relations are a superb expression of the networks of reciprocal trust. What is at stake goes well beyond mutual pleasantness. It is a question of building and using personal working relationships. "I try to create an atmosphere so they'll tell me things they shouldn't," a Treasury supply officer observed. "And I do the same, sometimes sending [the department finance officer] a copy of a paper I have done for my masters. You can't expect to get something for nothing." Men know they are assessed on their ability to establish confidential relationships. Another Treasury man put it bluntly: "I think you're judged on how far you manage to get inside the other department. I should have enough contacts to know how things are going. Even if the department's minister wouldn't agree and his civil servants shouldn't say, you should know it." Departments operate on the same imperatives. Civil servants there unanimously agreed that when they had the confidence of Treasury people, they could do things that would be otherwise difficult if not impossible.

Trust, particularly at higher levels, is created not only by talk but by action. A Treasury man wants to know whether the department official can keep his side of the bargain. When the two agree that "as between ourselves, this is the line we will take with our ministers," the Treasury man expects the minister to be briefed accordingly, with a straight face and with noticeable effect. Or as one Treasury undersecretary put it, "Can my opposite number deliver his master or not?"

Trust is more than a question of frankness, consultation, and internal controls. Treasury people also want to trust men who are able. Getting competent work done in departments is one way to protect reputations and learn whom to trust. Since they cannot observe the work directly, they must take the department official's ability to discuss and defend it as a surrogate of his competence.

CALCULATIONS

The entire Treasury sector, which oversees public spending, includes only 28 people above the level of principal; this makes it easy for Treasury people to get to know each other, but difficult to probe all bids for spending. If a certain Treasury undersecretary devoted every minute of every working day for a full year simply to reviewing existing government expenditure, he would be able to give perhaps 35 seconds to every £100,000 spent.

To make their jobs manageable, the men responsible for making public expenditure decisions use certain shortcuts or rules-of-thumb. Personal trust, for instance, is one invaluable aid to calculation. With such trust, each sum need not be redone, many details can be confidently overlooked, advance warnings can reduce uncertainty, informal chats will distinguish the real fire from smokescreen issues, and political administrators more confidently can bypass most of what goes on.

Probably the most widespread and frequently used aid to calculation is concentration on expenditure changes at the margins. Nowhere do the constraints imposed by the past on the future stand out more starkly than in the annual allocation of government spending. How much leeway, then, do departments and their ministers actually have in altering expenditures during a single year? Something between 1.5 and 2.5 percent. Our argument is not merely that some expenses are so committed as to permit only marginal change; it is that virtually all expenditure decision-making concentrates instinctively at these margins. Incrementalism in spending is understood and taken for granted by all British political administrators. They know it, live with it, and use it in their daily work.

CLIMATE

Despite networks of trust and aids to calculation, the operating environment of expenditure decision-making is ambiguity. Political administrators learn to assess the climate before determining spending strategy because to misjudge it may mean suffering a surprising reverse — perhaps embarrassment or, possibly worse, the loss of reputation for trustworthiness itself. Normally climate can be judged only intuitively. Ministers and officials grow up in a political environment and learn to be sensitive to the expenditure implications of events; such sensitivity is one aspect of that vague but vital factor which political administrators invariably refer to as "experience."

One climatic feature is so prevalent as to be almost a constant: Britain, unlike the United States and some other industrial nations, has no thick cushion of economic plenty from which to draw and, if necessary, fall back on when international payments accounts turn sour. With one-fourth the U.S. population, Britain must get by with something like one-tenth the U.S. economic product. Although Britain historically has survived on narrow margins, exporting and investing abroad to pay its import bill, the precariousness of its economic position has been borne home with a vengeance in a series of postwar balance-of-payments and currency crises.

Economic crises and emergency cuts in government spending have recurred so often as to be a normal part of the contemporary British expenditure process. These exercises usually have followed a deteriorating balance-of-payments situation, speculation against the pound, and international creditor pressure to "hold back" public expenditures. Similarly, when for purposes of economic management the government deliberately embarks on policies of reflation or deflation, the changing mood is picked up quickly by officials who have spent years developing a fine sensitivity to ministerial nuances.

Often there is no formal decision to cut or increase spending but a series of decisions shows that ministerial attitudes are changing. The new climate alters subtly, as officials switch on their well-trained sensors. Messages and moods gradually filter down. Treasury people are always hearing from their elders and betters what has been picked up at meetings. Most senior officials are also in a position to read in the official minutes the points made during Cabinet debate.

What do people in the Treasury talk about when they meet each other? Like everybody else, they talk shop. They cheerfully report the latest horror stories; they discuss new personalities and evidence concerning judgments made about old ones. They mention a department man who has done a brilliant analysis or who has gotten away with an extremely shrewd maneuver. They pass on a tip about mechanisms out of control that may prove useful elsewhere. They warn each other about events and people.

One could commit no greater error than to think that this village gossip, because it is sometimes frivolous and haphazard, therefore is unimportant. It lies at the center of Treasury effectiveness. Coordination in the Treasury is based above all on a never-ending round of personal contacts among people who know each other and who have a strong professional interest in talking about their work. No formal method of communication would be so effective.

In all corners of British central government, climate is assessed also by that pervasive aid to calculation: marginal rates of change. Everyone knows that everyone else plays this game, and anticipated reactions are a vital climatic barometer. Percentage changes in individual expenditure blocs are typical signals of opportunity or vulnerability. By the same token, an area with a lagging record of increases eventually arouses claims for compensatory fair play. Often classes of expenditure suddenly move ahead when it becomes apparent they have been overlooked, as a neglected boulder might become the cornerstone of the house.

THE TREASURY

At the vortex of all the confidences, calculations, and climatic assessments involved in doing this job stands the Treasury. It is the great communication net (some would say knot) of the spending process, the vantage point from which to observe all that happens elsewhere. As political administrators know, and academics learn, understanding the expenditure process begins at the Treasury.

Justification by faith alone is not a Treasury doctrine; good works also are required. Trust depends in part on competence — or at least the appearance thereof — and yet spending issues are vast in number, complex in their interrelationships, and uncertain in their ramifications. How then can anyone make competent decisions about what should be spent on the vast range of government activities? Over the years Treasury has developed norms that help in this task.

One of the first and most obvious things learned is that the Treasury's business is to save money, not spend it. A Treasury man who comes up with ideas for how a department can spend more, albeit in a good cause, is likely to be told that it is not his business to think about spending money. Departments will do that on their own. In this sense, the Treasury is inherently reactive.

A second lesson is that the Treasury is not an original research organization. Since there are less than 30 expenditure controllers above the level of principal, ultimately they must learn to leave actual research work to the administrative organizations directly concerned. The Treasury's task is not to do that work itself but to see that the department does what it should.

The culture of the Treasury calls for a role somewhat more active than mere skepticism, that is, to be energetically critical. Those at the Treasury learn to pride themselves on seeing through arguments misjudged by others.

Playing the spending game involves never saying "yes" right away. You must ask most thorough questions. You must go through the questioning process in order to see if the proposer is serious; he can't want it seriously unless he pushes for it and stands up to questioning. Also you want to delay and question to see if he has inflated the figures.

Above all, tough Treasury probing is a norm valued for its indirect effect. Treasury men believe that departments will restrain their spending plans in anticipation of Treasury reactions.

These relentless inquiries must usually remain haphazard sampling, but some also are motivated by well-established principles — which some respondents in the institution called "Treasury dogma." Violations of these are like red flags to the bull-like Treasury man. There is therefore a certain slant to his critical skepticism; he learns not so much what to look for as what to look out for. It may be described generally as hostility to hidden or built-in spending escalators. Here we will mention five common types.

1. Watch out for the thin wedge of expenditures to see that items which may become large in the future do not slip through simply because they seem small in early years.

2. Oppose open-ended commitments. Treasury men will resist programs they otherwise might approve, because they do not believe the administrative arrangements are stringent enough to prevent totals from rising astronomically.

3. Avoid precedent-setting behavior. This does not mean what it might mean in a department, i.e., sticking closely to past lines of action, but rather, avoiding settlements with one department that will have the effect of raising expenditure in others.

4. Oppose public commitment to specific rates of economic growth. The Treasury as an institution never has believed in the philosophy of economic growth. Its officials may not be against growth as such, but they are vehemently against committing resources on the basis of what one deputy secretary called "a hoped-for, phoney paper growth rate, which only leads to false expectations,

disappointments, cuts, and further disillusionment." They want to see the color of the money first. Otherwise, people will only be encouraged to spend more, and then it will be the Treasury's task, and an unpopular one, to find the money. The staple of Treasury doctrine is not growth, but the limit on national resources.

5. Resist disguised expenditures, which cannot be controlled if they are not identified. The Treasury likes subsidies clearly tagged as such so that, for example, a loan at an artifically low rate of interest is likely to be opposed.

To summarize, Treasury norms include:

1. Decide by reacting.
2. Let others do the technical work.
3. You know as much as anybody and more than most.
4. Above all, be skeptical — especially of enthusiasts.
5. Probe, delay, and question again.
6. As a rule, cut by bargaining rather than by absolute no's.
7. Earn a reputation for toughness that inhibits would-be spenders.
8. Be on guard against built-in expenditure escalators.

The Treasury's supreme talent lies in its sensitivity to others. It rules indirectly by trying to shape others' assumptions, expectations, and mental sets. But it is always up to someone else to take the cue. There is therefore something unreal about the Treasury considered in isolation. We must now turn to the most common expression of ambivalence in British central government — relations between Treasury officials, who live to control, and departmental operators, who love to spend.

DEPARTMENT-TREASURY BARGAINING

The Treasury is responsible for managing the economy, departments for managing their subject matter. Since the Second World War, this theoretical distinction has been increasingly accepted by both sides and has contributed much to the improved spirit of cooperation between Treasury and spending departments. Yet relationships between the two also constitute a mixed-motive game. Each can both help and harm the other immeasurably; they need each other but they need, too, to get around one another.

Departmental views of the Treasury are suffused with ambivalence. They admire but fear it. The more droll are likely to refer half-seriously to the Treasury as "a necessary evil — necessary *and* evil." They know someone has to guard the purse and manage the economy but wish they did not have to suffer for it. They hope the Treasury will avoid concentrating on minute details, but are unhappy when it delves into major policies. All Treasury people care about is totals, departmental people complain, in the same breath muttering that Treasury men think they know the department's business better than those who are entrusted with it. Department people like to feel protected in general but free in particulars. They want Treasury men to understand them but not to interfere. They want the Treasury to be powerful except when department and Treasury differ, cynical except when a department needs trust, and benevolent except when other departments are depriving them of a fair share of funds.

The Treasury expects spending departments to want more money. That is their job, and no one is penalized for doing it well. But the Treasury hates what is called *the theory of the bounce*. The bounce, in American parlance, is very like playing someone "for a sucker" and is, at its extreme, a contradiction of the norm of trustful dealing. When "bouncing" the Treasury, a department deliberately withholds nasty news while gaining an initial Treasury commitment. Waiting until it is up against a deadline — such as a contract running out or an international conference — the department then returns repeatedly to the Treasury, crying that more money is essential and a response is needed quickly. Here it is not simply a question of the thin end of the wedge, which Treasury men eagerly blunt, but of a programed baiting of the expenditure hook.

The bounce is anathema to the Treasury; it will do anything to punish a department that tries this too often. But it would be misleading to suggest that bouncing the Treasury is in any way a common strategy. The preponderance of departmental opinion is that sharp practice is unwise.

The following summary list of suggested practices for getting along with the Treasury, provided by several officials, would be accepted by most of their breed:

1. Consult early and thoroughly. Do not give the Treasury a proposal at the last minute and say that it has no consequences if it does.
2. Rather than trying to hide them, give the costs (in a sufficient depth of years) to show if there really is going to be a large charge.
3. Clear the line beforehand with other departments; i.e., show your awareness of the sideways effect of the proposal. When more staffing is required you'll look good to the Treasury if you show them you have cleared it with the Civil Service Department.
4. In trying to get more, preserve your credibility by dealing in reasonable negotiating margins.
5. When in doubt, send more, rather than less, information to the Treasury.

No department official can be as effective in his own cause as his own Treasury watchdog can be for him. His Treasury man cannot, however, give special preference to all programs under his jurisdiction because that sector would then be getting more than its share of the total. Advocate of a departmental program he may be some of the time; guardian of the Treasury he must be all the time. Department officials know they can sometimes convert their Treasury counterpart, but they know also that in return they may have to give him a greater say in determining department policies. That watchdog, who negotiates between them and the Treasury, is the Principal Finance Officer.

The department's Principal Finance Officer (PFO) really is less a Treasury outpost than the man in the middle. His effectiveness within his own department depends on establishing confidential relationships within the Treasury. He cannot serve his departmental colleagues or his minister if the Treasury does not trust him. Should he fail to achieve this trust, his fellow officials and minister will consider him incompetent, for it will become evident that he cannot gain approval for the simplest things without going through a tortuous review process. Yet even if he is on the closest terms with his Treasury counterparts, all the obvious advantages may be dispelled by a feeling from below that he has sold out the operating divisions in order to get on with the controllers. The minister, if he is aggressive and demanding, may want what he wants when he wants it. He may suggest tactics that will prove effective in the short run but would undermine the possibility of good relations with the Treasury in the long run. For its part, the Treasury expects the PFO to keep it fully informed on what is *really* going on, to honor his bargains, and to help out in times of distress — even if this means violating expectations of department officials. The finance officer is a cross-pressured man. His life is never easy.

The wise PFO stresses his scrupulous honesty. He reveals weaknesses in his case before Treasury people find out about them. He wants to create the impression that he is, if anything, more zealous than they are to see that money is well spent. With a reserve of credibility firmly established the finance officer can cash it in at the Treasury when he most needs to, providing he does not go to the bank too often.

There does come a time when the PFO must stand and fight. Long identification with a department may make him a convinced advocate of a particular program. His standing with his minister and his departmental colleagues may depend on doing something dramatic to obtain funds. Therefore, he may occasionally become emotional and get "bloody-minded." He will try every trick of salesmanship he knows. He will produce figures, charts, elaborate graphs, all of which will show that there is a convincing need for some particular expenditure. The cost of being able to act this way at the most critical junctures is a self-denying ordinance prohibiting the PFO from doing anything like it most of the time. Department officials who think the PFO should go all out for them on every conceivable occasion, no matter how unproductive this might be, are the bane of his existence.

The critical skill of a finance officer, if he has it, lies in being able to determine how far up he can push department expenditures without courting grave difficulties that will rebound against the institution he represents and himself personally. He is constantly balancing internal demands against external conditions. To the extent that he can improve the external situation, that is, take advantage of its strategic opportunities, he can make his internal bargaining much easier. To the extent that he can convince his own department to mitigate its demands, his external relationships are improved. In all this he is on his own. Only rarely will he get help from other departments.

Active departmental alliances, which are otherwise rare, can materialize if departments find a common interest in assaulting Treasury rules that will affect them all adversely. One Treasury device, which departments initially disliked in concert, is the *relative price effect* (RPE). The Treasury, bolstered by its small corps of economists, has argued that the public sector will tend to take an increasing proportion of national income as a natural consequence of government's labor-intensive activity. Experience rather than theory tells the Treasury that if public expenditures and the economy grow at the same rate for five years, the tax burden will be greater at the end than the beginning because prices will have risen faster in the public than in the private sector. Although some Treasury people, like the spending departments, do not find the reasoning wholly convincing, they would rather be safe than sorry.

It did not take long, however, for departments to discover a silver lining, for the cloud was only relatively dark. In the beginning, departments worried that RPE adjustments would make their programs look more costly. Since then, however, departments have discovered small advantages in having two ways of expressing their programs. Should Education wish to show that it is doing more, for example, it will likely include the price adjustment; should it wish to show how little is being spent, the department will concentrate on volume rather than relative costs by omitting or cutting down RPE. Maybe the lesson for the day is that budgetary strategies rarely are static because the kind of thinking men you want in the bureaucracy will find ways to get around last year's bright idea.

To say that there are few active alliances among departments against the Treasury is not to say that departments do not act in unison. Quite the opposite. Alliances among departments are omnipresent, but they take the passive form of never cutting each other down in front of the Treasury. Just as a Treasury norm is to avoid doing the departments' work, so the departments give no gratuitous aid to the Treasury by knocking each other.

We have tried to show how the vast bulk of expenditure business is conducted between Treasury and department officials who are familiar with each other and each others' strategies. Over most of this bargaining, ministers serve as ex officio presiding officers. To say this is not to advance any general theory of bureaucratic conspiracy. Ministers' limited involvement in the spending process is an inevitable fact of life given restrictions in their time, interests, and tenure in office. A minister (at least on the average in the last fifteen years) can count on only about two years in the same job. They have insufficient time to take a continuing part in the public expenditure process.

But there is more to it than this. Ministers fail to become more involved also because civil servants prefer it this way. And officials do so with the best intentions in the world. One man's "decision preemption" is another man's "conflict resolution." Top civil servants often regard ministers as an unreliable breed, long on haphazard arrangements and short on appreciation for the department's continuing needs. Even when officials do not have this attitude, their innate preference is for cooperation rather than conflict. Inside the department, officials will have done their best to hammer out an agreed view to present to the minister; his brief is likely to be a monolithic department tract in which the most vital differences are airbrushed into a light fuzz.

Outside their departments, civil servants can also be found trying to mute the natural differences that spring up between their organizations. To do so they may "coordinate" advice to be given ministers. They will sometimes allow feuds to smolder for years rather than "cause the minister trouble." They will interpret the political will of their masters in a politic way. In Cabinet official committees, at working parties, over lunch in Cabinet Office mess, civil servants can be found searching for a common solution to recommend to their political masters.

This creative official role stops well short of any deliberate strategy to deny power to ministers. Civil servants have their own trade-offs to make. For men whose forte is mutual trust and embarrassment-avoidance, there is no worse position than to be caught out with an agreement the minister will not back. Officials know they must balance arrangements among themselves with a fine sensitivity to ministerial interests. The means for doing so consist of what is almost a normal body-function for top civil servants: intense, incessant, incurable minister-watching.

"Knowing the minister's mind," as the phrase goes, allows the civil servant to map boundaries beyond which he will not take it upon himself to negotiate expenditure bargains. If the minister has pet issues, and nearly all do, decision on these matters usually will be reserved for him. Ministers' influence is thus indirectly increased by officials' anticipations of ministerial reactions. Politicians often "decide" unknowingly by virtue of the anticipations they have created in officials. However close his relationship with civil servants, at the day's end only the minister can fight for his department's position against other ministers. Only he can argue for that supreme guideline coveted by all civil servants — a favorable Cabinet decision.

The minister's indispensability for interministerial bargaining explains the universal observation of officials and ex-ministers: civil servants invariably prefer a strong to a weak minister. Margins in expenditure decision-making may be small, but everyone wants his share of the bit that is going. Given a choice between someone who passively accepts advice and someone who can effectively protect and advance departmental interests, officials in Treasury and spending departments would unanimously choose the stronger character. In part this preference stems from the officials' need to make accurate anticipations; the strong minister who knows his own mind gives clear signals which others can safely interpret. He is predictable.

An equally fundamental reason behind officials' desire for strong ministers is departmental advantage. As Baroness Sharpe emphasized, "The thing you ask of your Minister is that he should be able to get his way in Cabinet." An ex-minister summed up the situation: "Civil servants hate a weak minister. He reflects badly on the department. If he waffles in debate or is getting kicked about by his colleagues it affects the department. His permanent secretary, when he goes to the Reform Club, will be embarrassed and pitied by other permanent secretaries."

But what does it take to be considered "strong" or "weak"? How do ministers struggle for money and how does this interaction produce one allocation among the virtually illimitable purposes for which public money might be spent? In short, what part does the Cabinet government play in the expenditure process? For answers to these questions we must turn to the major ministerial protagonists — the spending and Treasury ministers.

Spending Ministers: Fighting Your Corner

Spending ministers did not acquire the name for nothing. They head departments that spend most of the funds consumed by the national government. Apart from two Treasury ministers, several nondepartmental members (e.g., Duchy of Lancaster), and a few very small spending departments (e.g., Foreign Office), the bulk of any Cabinet is made up of major spending ministers. The money they spend and the increases they seek mean a great deal to many people.

Whether one calls it the Collectivist Age, Welfare State, or positive government, a general consensus has grown up in postwar Britain that the political bouquets go to spenders. There may be times when the prime minister and his Cabinet desire action requiring the minister to incur the enmity of large sectors of society. Spreading unpopularity, however, can never be the norm but only an exception in a democratic government, which must appeal periodically to the electorate. The minister who undertakes to deprive citizens of their customary indulgences can expect few rewards. The officials below view him, if not with distaste, then at least with despair. They expect him to support the large objectives with which their lives are identified. And the minister himself after an initial period, during which he may revise policy made by his predecessors, easily identifies with his department. Ministerial responsibility means that the department's successes and failures are also his own. The normal way to gain respect and advance himself is to enhance some of the great purposes of his department. And great purposes usually cost money.

This rule of ministerial advocacy knows no party boundaries. How else is the spending minister to answer the question of what he did when he was in office? Few objective measures exist for judging a minister, but ability to hold his own (and perhaps do better than his colleagues) in gaining funds is one of the most well-worn touchstones in Whitehall, in Cabinet, and in the outside public.

From our variety of sources one can piece together the following "identikit" picture of the successful minister in the contemporary expenditure process. First, he is supremely well informed in presenting his own case. The strong minister realizes that Cabinet and Treasury ministers are quick to discount anyone who is confused and tentative. Colleagues will respect a minister's plea only if he is obviously knowledgeable about what matters to him and can defend his position. Second, the successful spending minister can talk beyond his own brief and knows how to mobilize political arguments. He can drive home the political consequences of proposed actions by showing, for instance, the loss of public sympathy in instituting fees on a certain group while other groups not overly warm toward the party continue to be heavily subsidized; by recalling that a particular service was conceived by the party and is now "regarded as our baby"; by discussing the loss of seats in local elections; and by arguing that a delay in something already programed will leave it to the tender mercies, or electoral credit, of the next government. Above all, the successful spending minister is a fighter — tough, persistent, formidable. Political associates know how such a minister wants something only by seeing how hard he fights for it.

If spending ministers won all the time, however, public expenditure would know no bounds. This cannot be; limits must be set and Treasury ministers must be supported in keeping to them. Prime ministers and their colleagues know that inherent in the structure of British Cabinet government is the fact that only exceptionally and on small issues can they take sides against Treasury ministers. To do so regularly on major spending issues is an operational definition of a government crisis. Consequently, most spending ministers at most times are forced to funnel demands through Treasury ministers. To these powerful politicians we must now turn.

A full account of the British expenditure process would include elaborate discussion of the Chief Secretary of the Treasury, who has taken over most of the Chancellor of the Exchequer's detailed negotiations with spending ministers. Acknowledging his importance, this summary account must essentially treat him as a Treasury minister without specifying what he does or how he relates to the chancellor except to say they work closely together.

Chancellor of the Exchequer:
Victim or Victimizer of Spending Ministers?

The chancellor's lot is rarely a happy one. In the economic sphere his every move is watched by critical eyes. He is second-guessed on all sides:

within the Treasury, by ministerial colleagues, by financial interests, and by a gaggle of reporters specially assigned to the job.

Public preoccupation with the chancellor as manager of the economy suggests an important truth to which inadequate attention has been paid. Chancellors basically are not interested in expenditures; they are interested in the economy: productivity, employment, interest rates, money supply, exports, balance of payments — anything and everything but spending. The result is that spending limits are part of their economic policy rather than an end in themselves or a means of allocating resources in a better way.

Behind all the discussions that Treasury officialdom has with departments, and all the negotiations Treasury ministers undertake with spending colleagues, lies the Treasury's and chancellor's overriding interest in taxation. This, indeed, is the substance of British constitutional practice: a balance between spending and saving, to be maintained not by some abstract formula but by giving specific individuals, standing at the head of concrete institutions, an interest in promoting these rival claims.

Every chancellor knows that the climate in which negotiations are conducted also has an enormous effect on their outcome. His task is to depress expectations by creating an overwhelming atmosphere of stringency. Experience has taught all chancellors that the easier the economic situation, the more abundant the resources, the more difficult it is to convince spending ministers they must do with less. Once storm clouds gather, the chancellor can rise to his full height and prevail by saying that the economy demands restrictive measures to prevent flood and famine in the country or an intolerable increase in taxation, or both.

Two estimates prepared by Treasury officials bring the expenditure process to a head each year. One is an economic forecast, which projects likely trends for investment, private consumption, employment, the balance of payments, and other economic indicators. The second is the Public Expenditure Survey Committee (PESC) report, which projects the level of spending for the next several years on the assumption that existing policies will be maintained. In the background is a third element to come before the Cabinet, a list of "bids" from spending ministers for any new money available. In considering these three statements, what is the Cabinet actually deciding about?

In essence, the Cabinet has before it a projection of the cost of existing policies and a Treasury judgment as to whether this is too large or there is room for growth. In the normal course of events, the total considered allowable by the Treasury is almost always less than the collective demands of spending ministers for more money. To cut it down is the problem for Treasury ministers and officials.

The Treasury has no automatic equation or fixed numerical relationship to determine the allowable size of total public expenditure. It does have economic forecasts (or as some in the Treasury prefer to call them, economic assumptions) on the expected expansion of the economy, balance of payments, inflation, and employment. Its expenditure judgment is (and can be no more than) a compound of knowledge, hunch, and intuition.

The most important factor to have developed over the last ten years is the Treasury assessment of the rate of growth in "productive potential." This is less a forecast than a historically derived average (going back approximately ten years) showing the growth in economic output if demand were held level at full employment. Neither the exact economic calculation of this figure nor its validity need concern us here; what does concern us is that by laying the growth in productive potential alongside the proposed growth rate in public expenditure, the Treasury has an important standard for saying how much is allowable.

Whatever the uncertainties, the official Treasury expenditure judgment is almost inevitably taken as the point of departure for what the Cabinet considers its own range of decision-making. Let us be clear; we are not saying that the Treasury sets out to dictate to and overrule a democratically elected government. But the Treasury expenditure judgment *is* the center around which official and ministerial bargaining takes place. Modified, increased, or decreased, the Treasury economic view is the assumption worked upon.

To support their bruising economic argument, Treasury ministers are outfitted with two big sticks. The first, sequencing, is a strategic option which not all chancellors have used but which appears, through hard experience, to have become the norm. Before 1968 the desirable spending total was debated alongside individual items. Arguing the general against the particular is never easy and is now recognized as a poor strategic choice for Treasury ministers. The sequence was changed. The chancellor first puts in his paper saying expenditure is X, will be Y, and asking for cutbacks to allow a certain growth rate. Once the Cabinet has this basic figure, or some variant of it, the chancellor begins bilateral bargaining with spending ministers. His hand is immeasurably strengthened by this sequence. With the total figure agreed upon, everyone can be made to feel they must do their own bit.

The other club behind the Treasury's expenditure judgment, taxing, goes much farther back than sequencing, but by no means has cracked with age. Taxes are the favorite weapon of Treasury ministers. If the Cabinet does not hold down spending, Treasury threatens the members with having to put up taxes.

The force of the Treasury tax weapon lies not merely in the threat of having to increase taxes but also of having to overturn another sophisticated and independently arrived at economic assessment. In its postwar role as navigator of the economy, the Treasury acknowledges taxation and public expenditure to be two sides of the same coin; the cutting edge where they meet is economic management. If spending plans are too large and taxes not increased, the economy (assuming full employment) will allegedly be overheated. Thus the Treasury weapon, and also Cabinet choice on total spending, becomes three-pronged: reduce expenditure projections, raise taxes, or destabilize the economy.

Backed by a generally agreed limit on spending growth rates, an advance influence on expenditure bids, the chancellor's status as a major politician and sole interpreter of economic needs, the ability to sequence strategic decisions, and a predetermined revenue standard, Treasury ministers and officials can feel sure that their preparations have not been in vain. Yet security in setting the boundaries scarcely means that the political battle is over. Though the major economic guideline is likely to go by default to Treasury ministers, spending ministers still want their share of whatever is going.

Now is the hour for the prime minister to bring the sensitivity of his own political judgment to bear on expenditures. Certain items, he suggests privately to the chancellor, will not be stomached by the Cabinet and should be taken off the table. Occasionally the prime minister will suggest compromises on other items, such as going for a reduction of £7 million rather than £10 million. On a few issues the prime minister probably will have his own sense of government priorities and personal preferences; on these he will refuse to go along with the chancellor. "For the rest," the prime minister says — and must say, for the chancellor to retain credibility — "I'll back you." Thus, well before the Cabinet meeting, the chancellor has a good idea of where he will be backed and where let down, where to push and where to give up regretfully but gracefully.

Whatever their formal names, there will usually be regular Cabinet committees in the areas of defense, agriculture, economic policy, and domestic affairs. Collective government means that each minister has a right, though he will not always choose to exercise it, to ask for the full Cabinet's judgment. Of course he may be better off accepting less in committee than suffering a resounding defeat in Cabinet. Prudence also suggests that he save his appeals in Cabinet for the most critical issues and accommodate himself to committee views on lesser matters. Cabinet committees are useful to the prime minister and chancellor, not because they settle everything, but because enough is settled there to bring into bold relief questions that the Cabinet alone can answer.

Major disputes float up to Cabinet, but much bargaining on expenditures is sectionalized among the half dozen or so Cabinet committees. The Treasury judgment on the total, now usually agreed beforehand, typically is broken down by departments, each with a rate for "natural" and "improvement" increases, or what one minister called "bargaining counters to play with." Departments take these away to their committees, there to begin thrashing out an accommodation among themselves and the chief secretary. One committee dealing with social services and another with industrial policy will have almost no contact with each other. Each has its own budget to discuss among its own members. In the normal course of events, therefore, hospitals will confront schools and not industrial subsidies or agricultural payments. There is no established capacity for one committee to argue its expenditures against another.

Disheartening though this sectionalism may be for those seeking a more comprehensive allocation, it has advantages. Departments know that they will be bargaining with others sufficiently close in subject matter for there to be some sympathetic understanding. Full Cabinets have notoriously little interest in department details; one spending minister was typical in being able to recall only two semi-knowledgeable Cabinet discussions about substantive issues of a major department during his three years as its minister. In the committees, however, departments can be sure of at least some empathy with the cherished purposes of each other's spending. At the same time the Treasury is interested in holding down Cabinet conflict and knows that while departments' spending bids can still be played off against each other, conflicts based on ignorance and misunderstandings will be minimized. If bargaining occurs across groups, where there is less sympathy for each other's purposes, conflicts will proliferate.

Surely, some men have reasoned, there must be a better way. After all it is not just the chancellor but the government as a collectivity which is responsible for controlling expenditures. Cannot a Cabinet committee of senior ministers — ministers without departmental spending axes to grind — look dispassionately at major spending proposals and consider each against the other in the context of limited total resources? This was in fact one of the major ideas proposed by the blue-ribbon Plowden Committee in 1961. Two little-known experiments in Cabinet government, one in the early 1960s under Conservatives and the other later under Labour, can add much to our understanding.

On these occasions, the Plowden idea, with Treasury support, became translated into a committee of nonspending ministers who were presumed to be more objective because they had no departmental responsibilities or their departments did not spend a great deal. The committee was composed of the Treasury minister, the chancellor of the Duchy of Lancaster, the leader of the House of Commons, and a few other ministers without departmental responsibility or, like the Foreign Secretary, with only a minimum amount of spending. Such ministers have always sat and provided a measure of disinterest on standard Cabinet committees. Now they were to be assembled into one committee able to give objective judgments on the relations among whole and parts. All participants — officials originally in favor and those opposed, Labour and Conservative ministers — agree that this commonsensical experiment was a failure.

The expenditure committee of nonspending ministers failed for three interrelated reasons, none of which by now should come as a surprise to the reader. First, and least important, there were not enough ministers with time to do the work. It turned out that nonspending ministers were too busy and few in number and the committee, therefore, had to include "little spending" ministers. Hence there was trouble in dealing with the expenditures (however small) of their departments within the committee.

The second reason for failure goes to the heart of the Cabinet government. To say the least, nonspending ministers were reluctant to create difficulties for themselves by telling one minister he was getting too much and another he was not getting enough. What was in it for them?

When the committee did manage to bring forth its "objective" view of an allocation, it only fired resentment among the spending ministers in Cabinet. This third reason for failure reflects the quintessence of decision-making on expenditures. The political reputation of a minister depends on how successful he is at fighting for his department. He can't allow others to deprive him of a chance to fight. "My whole authority with the [policy interests of his ministry] world," as one put it, "depends on fighting hard for expenditures. You are fighting for interests including your own." Multiply this minister by a half dozen or more and the failure of the committee of nonspending ministers becomes wholly explicable. As unhappiness accumulated and passions rose, the spending ministers called on their ancient prerogative — a jury of their Cabinet peers. They still may have to admit defeat; but they will be damn well certain they fall in complete battle regalia, in open field and in full view of the assembled hosts.

THE CABINET MEETING

The tendency of Cabinet meetings to confound losers and confuse winners, including those who firmly believe they understand Cabinet best, suggests the advisability of starting with the end results. Except in the rarest circumstances, what definitely will *not* emerge from Cabinet is a comprehensive consideration of overall priorities within the total spending figure. The intention that the Cabinet as a whole should take such decisions under the current PESC system — which might be thought to distinguish earlier Cabinets from later ones — has not impressed most ministers that way. Though each bit may be related to total spending, only rarely will one set of expenditures be weighed against another. To understand the British expenditure process, it is essential to know why this is so.

Despite recent talk about priorities, strategies, and rational allocation, the British Cabinet is unable to consider and decide upon any clear overall allocation of expenditure resources. Why?

Taking all outstanding issues together is a Herculean task and no one knows how to manage the calculations involved. Simultaneous consideration of spending bids is difficult, moreover, when they do not occur at the same time. Overarching all other barriers to weighing expenditures against each other are the behavioral norms against mutual attack. Sectionalism among Cabinet committees reflects and reinforces such norms, but far more important is the political-administrative culture itself. "Greasings" by civil service society will already have muted most interdepartmental squeaks before Cabinet meetings. Department briefings may prepare the minister for protecting his own position but offer little scope for analyzing others' claims. Reciprocity in ministerial discussions (you leave my programs alone and I'll leave yours alone) is the counterpart of reciprocal neutrality among civil servants in relation to each other's spending. Spending ministers' reluctance to criticize each other's proposals is a standing guarantee that the sequence of decisions usually will not be disturbed by explicit trade-offs or cross references.

Our listing of barriers to comprehensive Cabinet allocation is necessarily an abstraction from the complex interactions of real life. Important Cabinet operations are easily obscured by making the deliberations seem less messy than they in fact are. There is some value, then, in looking more closely at the details of Cabinet bargaining. The fact that a spending total is apparently agreed on by the Cabinet does not mean that the expenditure pattern has been accepted or that the programs within the total are consistent with one another. The existence of a coordinating figure no more means that coordination has been achieved than does the mere existence of a prime minister signify that leadership is being effectively exercised. Following discussion and agreement on the Treasury expenditure judgment and on individual Cabinet committee reports, the Cabinet will move through the departments one by one and consider the outstanding individual expenditure disputes. The Treasury, under PESC procedures, has agreed to so much for each department and they, in turn, have expressed certain disagreements. The unagreed margin between the Treasury figure and the departmental proposals forms the focal point of initial Cabinet discussions. The chief secretary or, if necessary, the chancellor argues that the department must cut and, with the briefing of his civil service divisions, proposes items. The spending minister, in substance, says "over my dead body."

Settling the allocation is not the work of an afternoon around the Cabinet table. Cabinet decisions on expenditure are an endless iteration resembling the labors of Sisyphus more than the thunderbolts of Zeus. Choices are not taken at once but through a series of meetings, some informal and others in the Cabinet itself; decisions are made, remade, postponed, and brought up again until exhaustion sets in and an end is reached. Unless the chancellor were to announce all decisions at once, and permit no alteration, hardly credible in collective rule, there is no way of avoiding sequential decision-making.

Several weeks are likely to elapse between Cabinet meetings. Time is needed to heal wounds, to permit the chancellor to hold discussions with aggrieved ministers, and to help ministers get used to the prospect of having less to spend than they would like. Tension is high and all hope that the passage of time will work a soothing influence. Often the two Treasury ministers will have agreed that the chief secretary should go all out in arguing the Treasury case at the first several meetings. Although the chancellor will support his colleague against the spending minister, this division of labor means the chancellor is also in a position to propose a compromise at a later date without loss of face.

Agreements in Cabinet are easiest to reach when they are made across the board: every department either increased or cut by roughly the same proportions. Sacrifices are (or appear to be) equally shared. There is more grumbling when reductions have to be absorbed, but they are easier to take when all ministers suffer equally and none can claim that he did better than the other. The problem with so-called equality of sacrifice is that not all programs and departments are in fact equal. Some are better able to absorb cuts than others. And needless to say, some policy areas also figure more prominently in election pledges and are dearer to the hearts of party members. If politics inside the Cabinet suggest that equal treatment will make life easier, politics outside the Cabinet imply the reverse. So, though easy, across-the-board, flat-rate cuts remain a rare strategic move in Cabinet, resorted to "only with reluctance" and in the direst economic emergency.

It is more usual to find everybody achieving marginal increases over past allowance with some doing better than others. Disagreement over purposes and rivalries among ministers still may combine to ensure heated discussion and bruised egos. Yet, when each minister can tell his clientele that he has done better for them than before, though never as much as he hoped, the worst conflicts are mitigated. No one has lost out entirely and everyone has got something. Members realize that their party has a policy (and should have if it does not) and this means that some programs will be favored over others.

The most difficult Cabinet meetings — those which remain in ministerial memory as bitter and unmercifully long — invariably involve deep cuts, applied unequally, in which most ministers lose and only a few can win. Ministers whose programs have been favored at the expense of others become targets of envy if not outright hostility. Did they make secret arrangements with the chancellor to sell out their colleagues? Are they being groomed for advancement to which other ministers believe themselves better entitled? On these occasions the dividing line between paranoia and politics may be exceedingly fine.

Ministers do have second thoughts. They wonder whether there might not be some better way to allocate resources. They will play the game to the hilt although they are not always sure that it is the right game.

Attempts to respond to such second thoughts and to embody answers in institutional form have been made in recent years. The essential purpose of the PESC procedure is to provide information on likely levels of government expenditure over the next five years to get a general idea of total commitments and available margins for new expenditure. The PAR process (Program Analysis and Review) is supposed to select major issues in both new and old spending programs for sustained analysis so that choices within the available margins can be made in a more intelligent way. The Central Policy Review

Staff is designed to supplement these procedures by providing Cabinet members with independent nondepartmental analyses of major issues. No one with the experience of the Cabinet committee of nonspending ministers in mind should underestimate the difficulties in making these innovations work. Implicated are not merely alterations in expenditure procedure but also major changes in relationships among political administrators and hence the entire spirit of Cabinet government under the British model. Later on (see Chapters 16 and 19), when we turn to efforts to reform budgetary practices, we shall take a closer look at how and why PESC succeeded when efforts to sponsor change in other countries have failed.

We close our account by considering briefly why Parliament is not an important arena for influencing expenditure decisions. We have been able to bypass traditional maxims concerning Parliament's power over the purse for one straightforward reason: Parliament plays little direct part in expenditure decision-making. Supply estimates are considered and approved almost automatically. In the modern era of party discipline, any other outcome would be considered by the Government as cause for resignation. So automatic has this approval become that even the fiction of Supply Days for approving departmental estimates has been dropped and renamed Opposition Days to signify the set-piece partisan debates between Government and Opposition on general policy rather than on finances.

Any part played by Parliament is at least once or twice removed from the legislature itself. Ministers and civil servants trying to assess the expenditure climate frequently will use their reading of parliamentary opinion as one barometer. Political climate in Great Britain refers mostly to predispositions within government and, unable to get a grasp of what the public at large may think, officials occasionally use members of Parliament as an acceptable surrogate.

Parliament is used to help weigh people as well as issues in public spending. The "standing" of department ministers, and thus an important part of their weight in the bargaining process, reverberates within the House. In part, the assurance of the minister in debate and his avoidance of embarrassment under questioning is the obvious testing ground. Equally (if not more) important is the less-structured gossip which washes throughout the Palace of Westminster concerning ministerial performances inside government. X is making his name at the Department of Environment; Y is as dismal as expected; but, isn't Z doing surprisingly well at Employment? With political life so close in London, it is not surprising that opinion in the House is sometimes regarded as public opinion itself.

One of Parliament's most important contributions to the spending process is essentially passive. Trust, we have observed, is crucial in the interactions of those making expenditure decisions inside the government. Parliament, as the ever-present outsider, provides a vital political counterweight to sustain the reality of trustful behavior within the various parts of the executive. By knowing what is not and will not be told to Parliament, political administrators know that they can confide in each other. Official advice to ministers is held confidential; Cabinet official committees and working parties do not exist; the deals, bargaining, and conflict of the expenditure process are interdicted subject matter for legislative scrutiny. The doctrine of ministerial responsibility — the idea that the political minister, and only he, is responsible for all the actions of his department — is hoary but nonetheless potent in dealing with parliamentary "snooping." The doctrine of collective responsibility holds that all members of the government publicly abide by, support, or fall together in the decisions of Cabinet. Only the minister and government as a whole are answerable to the House of Commons. The reciprocal of this situation is that the executive remains largely impenetrable, without handles or edges for its legislature to use as leverage.

Our account would be totally misleading, however, if it implied that the executive has been a fatal constraint either on the Expenditure Committee's work or on PESC debate in Parliament. The fundamental limitation on parliamentary expenditure reform stems not from executive secrecy, but from the members of Parliament themselves. Most do not care. One of the founding members of the Expenditure Committee summed up his experience after two years' service. "The chief enemy of our work has been that the majority of Members don't want it or are ambivalent."

Service on parliamentary committees is not the way in which MPs consider their careers to be advanced. A U.S. congressman can reasonably hope to rise to positions of power through work on legislative committees, but he cannot reasonably hope to gain access to positions of executive power. Not so the British MP. Parliament and local constituency eminence may be the end of his ambition. Those seeking further advancement know their chances depend upon becoming apprentices to the executive. And there is a wealth of such patronage at the prime minister's disposal. In 1970 there were no less than 79 paid posts and another 32 Parliamentary Private Secretary posts availble for appointments from within Parliament; with almost a third of MPs in any majority party bound to be appointed to some post in the government, the attractions of the executive are obvious and alluring.

But there is more to parliamentary indifference than alternative career routes. Most members of Parliament do not seem to see their jobs in terms of the policy-making. When members think of participating in Parliament, they generally think of maintaining the running political battle between Government and Opposition. Through constant teasing, chiding, and searching out the chinks through which to stab home some political embarrassment, each side tries to demonstrate its own competence and the other's incompetence. For the Opposition, the aim is not to become involved but to take over the full range of executive power after the next election.

The circularity is obvious. Members are not interested in hard policy analysis because they do not have the means to play a part; they do not have the means because they are not interested.

In one respect, Parliament is to the executive as the Treasury is to spending departments: it must depend on others to do most of the work and provide most of the information it needs. But unlike department dependence on the Treasury, no one needs Parliament's active aid and participation in order to spend money. Nor is anyone in the executive likely to as long as most members see themselves almost exclusively as disciplined partisans in the perpetual election campaign of parliamentary politics.

I have gone into British budgeting at length for two reasons; one is because the Public Expenditure Survey (see Chapter 19) is the most important and impressive budgetary reform of our time and it needs to be considered against a fairly full background; the other concerns the representativeness of the findings. For the most part the budgetary process in Britain is similar to those in France and Japan. The various Treasury dogmas and norms in Britain have their near counterparts in the other countries. The accounts of budgeting in France and Japan are shorter because I have concentrated on what makes them different.

5
Arbitration and Balance: Budgeting in France and Japan

FRANCE: BUDGETING AS SUCCESSIVE
COURTS OF APPEAL

During the nineteenth century France would have been in greater contrast to the rich countries of today because it insisted on balanced budgets (*le principe de l'équilibre budgétaire*). To achieve this end — in other than extraordinary periods such as war — parliaments voted expenditure before taxation. After it was clear how much was going to be spent, *Parlement* proceeded to adjust revenues. The rule of *l'antériorité des dépenses sur les recettes* has, of course, been reversed in the twentieth century since the notion of a balanced budget also has fallen into disuse.[1]

Contrasts between France and other parliamentary regimes would have been heightened under the Third and Fourth Republics because legislative committees exercised real power. Not for nothing was the Finances Committee called "the committee of successors." As heterogeneous majority governments collapsed from lack of cohesion within, and more unified minority governments were overturned from without, the budget process was rather more tumultuous than it is today. Factions in Parlement could afford to bargain more directly over shares in the budget and, when they could not agree, the

---

In preparing this chapter I have drawn heavily on two sources. The account of the French system is adapted entirely from Guy Lord, *The French Budgetary Process* (Berkeley: University of California Press, 1973). The account of budgeting in Japan is taken entirely from John Creighton Campbell, "Japanese Balanced Budgeting" (prepared for the Research Conference on Japanese Organization and Decision-Making, Maui, Hawaii, Jan. 5–10, 1973), and from Campbell's doctoral dissertation, "Contemporary Japanese Budget Politics" (Columbia University, 1973), by permission.

[1] Ibid., pp. 8–9. See also Rene Stourm, *The Budget* (New York: Appleton, 1971) trans. by Thaddeus Plazinski from the 7th ed. (Paris, 1913).

practice grew up of voting "twelfths," that is, of continuing governmental spending at existing levels for one month at a time. Thus for a time the lack of consensus at the top of French political life produced an approximation of the characteristic condition of poor countries — repetitive budgeting.[2]

But only for a time. During the Fourth Republic French politicians learned to embrace the inevitable to protect the nation from these small perturbations. Though it appeared that the entire budget was under review, practice had long since abandoned that fiction; serious discussions concentrated on changes from the existing base. Lord relates that

> In 1955, when it became obvious that Parlement would not have the time to vote the 1956 budget before the election, the government asked Parlement to adopt the measures which had already been approved in the 1955 budget, and kept for further discussion after the elections those which were being proposed for the first time. The procedure worked well, and the authors of the 1956 budgetary reform institutionalized it.
>
> They divided each chapter into two categories of measure: all those approved by Parlement in the previous years, called *services votés* and translated here as *continuing items*, and *mesures nouvelles* (new measures).
>
> The continuing items "represent the minimal funds which the government considers indispensable to carrying out the public services under the terms approved by Parlement the previous year. . . ." [3]

As is now done under the British Public Expenditure Survey (and no doubt with the same infighting), continuing items represent the cost of existing policy if no changes are to be made. After de Gaulle assumed power, the authors of a budgetary reform in 1959 stipulated that Parlement, in a single vote, would endorse all the continuing items, reserving separate votes for new measures. This procedure has gone so far now that the vote on continuing items is not considered an appropriation, but merely a confirmation that the expenditure has been approved as a result of earlier decisions. At first, members of Parlement thought that they could not challenge past decisions at all. This is not correct. What they must do, however, is propose as new measures cuts in old ones. But we need go no further, for Parlement is as unable to gain its will on new-new measures as it is to change new-old ones. Indeed, governments under the Fifth Republic can and do use a procedure for a package vote that enables bills for entire ministries or parts thereof to be approved in their entirety without having to consider messy subclauses which might cause political difficulty. Here we find a rather more flexible (though no less debilitating)

---

[2] See Philip Williams, *Crisis and Compromise: Politics in the Fourth Republic,* 3d ed., previous edition published as *Politics in Post War France* (Hamden, Conn.: Anchor Books, 1964).

[3] From Guy Lord, *The French Budgetary Process* (Berkeley: Univ. of California Press, 1973), 30. Originally published by the University of California Press; reprinted by permission of the Regents of the University of California.

procedure for turning ordinary bills into votes of confidence, a device much used in the Fourth Republic in an unsuccessful effort to shore up weak governments.

What, then, is different about French budgeting? As usual there are advocates, the spending ministries, and guardians, the Finances ministry; budgets are considered in increments with usually little more than 10 percent available for new measures. Differences occur in the way conflict is fragmented through serial reduction into manageable bits, and resolved through multiple levels of appeal, at least until the next year. Just as in other aspects of French social life, personal relationships appear relatively distant, formal, structured, and mediated at the end by essentially legal modes of conflict resolution.

Whereas British government could accurately be described as a federation of departments, France more precisely could be called a confederation of bureaus and divisions verging on the American model. Civil servants are divided not only into black and white (Ministry of Finances and spending ministries), but also into many small "ethnic groups" of each race (bureaus, divisions, ministries, and overhead agencies) which have considerable autonomy and conflict with each other. Because of the absence of an arbitrator at the administrative level (such as the British Permanent Secretary), conflicts between groups of civil servants are appealed to higher political levels for settlement. Hence the court system. There are basically three levels: from the lower district courts (individual ministers), through courts of appeal (the prime minister), to the supreme court (the president). Each court arbitrates conflicts at its own level between divisions of ministries and the Bureau of Budget in each ministry; between the Minister of Finances and the spending minister; and between the prime minister and other Cabinet members. Conflict is not so much resolved as dissipated.

Fearing that they will become victim of the dead hand of the past, which vastly restricts their room for financial maneuver, and the quarrelsome voices of the present, which risk submerging them in endless squabbles, the men at the top — the Minister of Finances, the prime minister, the president, and their staff assistants — have tried to enlarge their area of discretion. They have tried to reserve for themselves what are called *grandes options,* such as the total level of spending, the proportions allocated between military and domestic purposes, and the amount of borrowing for capital projects. They then try to make their further interventions effective by concentrating on proposals for new expenditures. They try also to create mechanisms for slowing down the rise in the cost of existing programs because it is the growth of these recurrent expenditures which reduces the financial margin available to them or faces them with the unpopular task of increasing taxes. Although these men wish to increase their ability to control events in general, they often diverge on how this should be done in particular. They cannot all have the same pet programs, nor do they all face the same risks. And, squeezing spending ministers in unison, though it has appealing aspects, is not without its unpleasantness. Before we go further in exploring budgetary process in France, we must know more about the major participants and their relationships with one another.

Ministries are composed of relatively autonomous units called divisions which, in turn, are made up of relatively autonomous subunits called bureaus. Needless to say, each bureau, division, and ministry wants more money for its own purposes and is suspicious of the others. Each has not only its own policy preferences but wishes also to protect its main lines of access to the Ministry of Finances, dispenser of such largesse as is to be had, against all comers. Each level attempts to accumulate some degree of slack — resources in excess of immediate operating expenses — to provide flexibility, a hedge against uncertainty, and an entering wedge for new projects. One unit's slack, however, is another's unit's opportunity; slack in bureaus may become the surplus of divisions, and the flexibility of divisions may be converted into the new initiatives of the minister. If it is not exactly a war of all against all, neither is it precisely the peace that passeth all understanding. Communications are rarely horizontal; bureaus see little reason to consult or cooperate with their competitors for divisional support, a condition that also prevails at divisional and ministerial levels. It is to the Ministry of Finances that all look with intermingled hope and despair.

The Finances ministry generally is powerful, as is true in most countries around the world. But the scope of its power and its relative priorities must clearly be understood. Even more so than the Treasury in England, the French Ministry of Finances is concerned primarily with economic management and taxation. The rate of taxation is important, both as a major instrument of macroeconomic policy and as a decision with deep political repercussions, especially for the Ministry of Finances; total expenditures rather than specific items within it are of major interest. Finances is more likely to object to proposals with built-in spending increases, or that use earmarked taxes, or that otherwise reduce the future flexibility of the institution, than it is to have strong substantive interests of its own.

Control of spending is in the hands of the budget division of the Ministry of Finances. Like its counterparts elsewhere, it learns to be chronically suspicious of the importunings of spending departments who always want more and never less. "Aware of the intentions, selfish motives, and even ruses of the spenders," as Lord puts it, "they tend to consider them with mistrust and to approach the budgetary discussions with a rather unsympathetic and cynical view of their counterparts." [4] Those in the budget division justify their role, just as those in other central budget agencies do, by saying that they are

[4] Ibid., p. 131.

in a position to view the total picture. They claim to be unselfish and serve the national interest while spenders are in the grip of special interests and concerned only about their own narrow corner. So far as one can tell, in what must be essentially a qualitative judgment, their animus toward spenders and their belief in their mission to set things straight is rather greater than it is elsewhere. So, accordingly, is the anger directed at Finances by spending agencies for callous disregard of their own needs. Advocates and guardians, then, may use attitudes and behaviors of the others as justification for reinforcing their own perspective.

Spending departments may be experts in their own activities; the Minister of Finances can claim to be expert on the entire economy. When he claims that the economic situation demands a certain limit on expenditure, it is very hard for others to argue with him. He can threaten the prime minister with dire forebodings or a costly resignation. His task is to make ministers work within a given total (however arbitrary it may in fact be) that he has imposed. The job for spending ministers is first and foremost to persuade him; failing that, to appeal to the prime minister; and, if necessary or possible, to the president. It would do ministers little good to gang up on the Minister of Finances because, to say the least, they lack the necessary collective spirit; moreover, his position is not at all that dependent on theirs.

So far we have only talked about the causes of antagonism, and not about vehicles of collaboration. If all that went on consisted of furious snipings (as important a feature of the French budgetary process as that may be), it would be difficult to agree on an annual budget or to keep ministers together in the same government for very long. There have to be, and there are, emollient influences. Some men within the system must know and respect one another. It is necessary for participants to be able to express their grievances and have them adjudicated, in order minimally to permit their continuance in the government. The web of personal relationships, so far as it exists in French government, is provided by the *grand corps* of the civil service.

The prestige corps of civil servants — the General Inspectorate of Finances, the Court of Accounts, and the *Conseil d'Etat* — provide the glue. Theirs is the task of coordination, not in the hopeless sense of providing a unified and coherent overview to which everyone submits, but in the sense of knowing what is going on in the most important places and communicating it to each other. One reason ministerial bureaus of the budget are not important is that their chiefs rank below the grand corps and a representative of the Ministry of Finances (called the Grand Controller) is placed in every ministry, where he exercises a priori financial control or, as the French put it, *le contrôle de l'engagement des dépenses.* Furthermore, a member of the grand corps concerned with resource allocation will take his place as part of the cabinet surrounding each minister. In the president's office, the Finances ministry, and the ministerial cabinets; in the parliamentary Finances committee (where civil servants are allowed to serve as deputies), in the main over-head branches of government concerned with budgeting, and through all important ministerial committees, members of the *grand corps* proliferate their influence. Wherever it matters, they are there. When it comes time for ministers within spending departments to arbitrate among the divisions; when the Finances minister is trying to determine spending totals, or give an opinion on the largest items of expenditure; when the president is deciding whether to intervene to secure a higher level of funding for a particular project, members of the grand corps are present. They know what goes on because they are Johnny-on-the-spot where it is happening. Fortunate is the minister with a bright and dedicated young man in his cabinet who has originally come from the Inspectorate of Finances and who knows his classmates and their friends in the cabinets of the Minister of Finances, the prime minister, and the president. These higher civil servants are supposed to be the best. Sometimes they may know best; but, and most importantly, they know each other and therefore what others who matter consider best.

Disagreements between bureaus often are not settled at the divisional level, but are carried forward to ministers and their cabinets who also adjudicate between one division and another. The minister's job, at least as far as spending agencies and associated interest groups are concerned, is to get more money. No minister is likely to make a reputation by doing less than his predecessors. Spending agencies are fond of ministers who admire their pet programs. Better still, they like ministers who are effective in getting funds for them from Finances. The weak minister is likely to be an object of contempt and a cause of much hand wringing.

According to the organic law, the budget is prepared under the authority of the prime minister. He has options, however: to choose delegation of these powers largely to the Finances minister, to keep a few key areas to himself, or to deal almost entirely with disputes referred to him when spending ministers in Finances cannot agree. More often than not, he is likely to be an arbitrator. Even here, he may be a passive arbitrator — in the sense of dealing largely with disputes referred up to him from the numerous interministerial committees — or he may (more actively) call up the kinds of differences with which he wishes to deal. His cabinet undoubtedly will wish to settle a number of points with their counterparts elsewhere, or refer them back to committees for resolution. But in the end, on the most important matters, the spending ministers involved and the Minister of Finances will appear before the prime minister, make their case, and receive his decision.

The key role in the prime minister's office is played by his budgetary adviser. He is the man who maintains continuous contact with the Ministry of Finances, spending ministries, and the president's office. By the network of contacts he has established through service in one of the grands corps and through those who have worked with him in previous positions, he is in a strong position to structure the issues and advice that come to the prime minister. When it comes time to meet with ministerial committees or to engage in the various *arbitrages,* the budget adviser is always at the prime minister's side. His voice is important also when the president, prime minister, and finance minister meet early in the game to work out the various limits, levels, and proportions in the global budget.

Up to this point the part played by the president in budgeting has necessarily remained sketchy. He helps set global margins at the beginning and may arbitrate disputes near the end. But what, if anything, does he do in the middle? That depends on him. Although the prime minister ostensibly has formal power over the budget, nothing in the constitution or organic laws prohibits the president from intervening. And since prime ministers are appointed by presidents, it is presumably wise for the subordinate to listen to the superior. Since in addition they are mutually dependent, a fair degree of collaboration would seem in order. Whatever their relationship, the existence of two levels of potential authority over the budget makes for interesting strategic opportunities and pitfalls. Foiled by a prime minister, any minister (including the Minister of Finances) may appeal to the president. No doubt it is unwise to appeal any but the very most important matters on which a particular president might be deemed sympathetic. A minister does not serve his own cause by being considered a time waster and petty nuisance. But the president can — as the original model for the office, General de Gaulle, undoubtedly would have wished — avoid implication in all but those areas of major interest to him. Thus prime ministers can choose between leaving such areas for presidential discretion or being, on occasion, rudely surprised. Perhaps the most likely source of difficulty comes when the president wishes to pursue some great purpose, such as increases in family allowances, which have such large expenditure implications that they severely constrain what the prime minister and his Minister of Finances can do in other areas. Yet the situation is not entirely without advantage to the prime minister. Because he is not the court of last resort, he can use the president as a double buffer: he would love to do certain things but the president will not let him because he has a definite personal view; or, the matter at issue can be resolved only by the president. One hears of prime ministers deliberately referring differences between ministers to the president. With presidential responsibility, therefore, comes a share of the blame.

For those brought up on the notion of parliamentary regimes following the British model, it may seem strange that the cabinet, the Council of Ministers, has not been mentioned so far. This is not because its formal authority is meager — far from it. Its members go through a series of meetings in which spending limits and governmental priorities are decided. The real decisions are normally made elsewhere, however, so that the Council becomes the forum in which they are registered and announced. As a civil servant told Guy Lord:

On budgetary matters the Council of Ministers ratifies. There is no discussion. Everything is discussed beforehand between the Prime Minister, the Minister of Finances, and, sometimes, the President. Even under the Fourth Republic the budget was not the cause of much discussion at the meetings of the council, except when a parliamentary group was threatening to resign from the government if satisfaction was not given on a particular matter. Generally, it was a question of obtaining more in order to please an interest group.[5]

Disagreements, which in Britain would be settled in Cabinet, are in France decided in bilateral negotiations between each spending minister and the Finances minister, the prime minister, or president.

In order for the Council of Ministers to confirm prior decisions, there must be previous agreements for them to register. The important thing is that differences between the Minister of Finances, and the prime minister as advised by the president, be ironed out in advance. An important mechanism for accomplishing this purpose is the interministerial economic committee including not only the Minister of Finances and the prime minister, but also the Minister of State for the Budget, the economic adviser to the president, the General Commissioner of the Plan, and the usual accompaniment of personal cabinet surrounding these important officials. Spending ministers ordinarily do not attend. Here participants go over the draft budget proposed by the Ministry of Finances as it concerns the division between recurrent and capital expenditures, investments indicated by the plan, and sectors which are to receive greater or lesser priorities. Here is the prime minister's opportunity, if he wishes to exercise it, for displaying his views in the budget. This is the place where planners swim or sink, usually the latter,[6] in their efforts to make what the government will actually do correspond to what the plan once said it ought to be doing. Here, too, the Minister of Finances takes one of his final stands as he tries to keep the budget within a size appropriate for his management of the economy and his stewardship of tax rates.

What about spending ministers? Surely they cannot be terribly pleased at being left out of the most important phases of budget making. When their protest reached a crescendo in 1961, an effort of a kind was made to bring them in on preparation of the global budget. It took the form, appealing to finance ministries, of having them participate in setting ceilings on their own spending as had been true before only in regard to the Ministry of Defense. The advantage of this approach presumably was that they could then be freer to set their own priorities within that total. The story Lord tells about what

---

[5] Ibid., p. 85. By permission.
[6] See Stephen Cohen, *Modern Capitalistic Planning; the French Model* (Cambridge: Harvard University Press, 1969).

happened gives as good a picture of power relations in French budgeting as one is likely to get:

> But the spending ministers soon found that the Minister of Finances was using this procedure to force them to make extremely difficult and unpopular decisions, if only as the result of its own rigor in distributing the credits and setting up priorities. Furthermore, during the detailed preparation of the budget, the budget division kept challenging and opposing items of expenditure which were the automatic results of the previously approved ceilings and which should not have been questioned at that stage. So, instead of being subject to one series of controls, the ministers were subject to two successive series of controls. Their position, thus, had not improved. The procedure was further modified for the 1963 budget in a way which, again, did not help the spending ministers. Indeed, the Minister of Finances decided that spending ministers would have to prepare their budgets in accordance not only with ceilings, but also with principles set up beforehand by himself and his administration.
>
> Of course, these principles would be submitted to the interministerial economic committee and discussed in the Council of Ministers, but not directly between the Minister of Finances and the spending ministers. This again reduced the margin of discussion left for each minister and consequently shortened the period of budgetary meetings between ministers. The only way spending ministers could influence these options was — and still is — through good personal relations with the Minister of Finances and his administration or through the Prime Minister and the Elysée.[7]

Notice what we have observed about the handling of conflict in the French budgetary process. Bureaus do not confront one another; they meet individually with divisional and ministerial heads. The same is true at the divisional level; ministers and their personal cabinets arbitrate among the divisions. Spending ministers do not meet together to bargain out their differences. Each meets separately with the Minister of Finances and, if that is insufficient, possibly with the prime minister and the president. Only the Minister of Finances, the prime minister, and the president need confront one another directly. By that time, however, they would not have to deal with anything like the entire range of budgetary decisions. Each confrontation would be about a matter that has been refined in successive negotiations and could be taken in the context of other decisions already made. There is no way totally to avoid face-to-face conflict over a small number of decisions, but if there is a way to reduce these personal hostilities to the absolute minimum (outside of giving total power to a single official), that way is found in France.

---

[7] Lord, *French Budgetary Process*, pp. 161–162. By permission.

THE JAPANESE WAY: CONVERTING VALUES
TO FACTS BY MAXIMIZING FAIR SHARES
TO MINIMIZE CONFLICT

Similarities in budgeting come from the universal requirements it imposes: allocating limited resources to maintain political support and enhance economic viability. If financial resources were unlimited, there would be no problem of choice, and everyone could get what he wanted. If political support were guaranteed, there would be no need to consider the effects of different allocations on the stability of the regime. All nations face the problem of making budgetary decisions manageable and securing the legitimacy of the governing organs by ordering conflict. The main differences in budgeting stem from variants in poverty and uncertainty reflected in the distance between insistent social demands and available political and economic resources. Among the four rich countries we are studying, that gap is smallest in Japan, which combines the highest rate of economic growth with the least apparent demand for military and welfare spending. These "given" conditions might be enough in themselves to give Japanese budgeting a special cast. But Japan is reputed also to be singular in another respect. Its cultural norms, that is, its uniquely national components, are said to be especially important (or at least visible), and have caused much comment. Examination of Japanese budgeting permits at least a limited exploration of whether and how specific cultural features affect the budgetary process.

The norms that concern us in budgeting are those relating to the behavior of organizations or to individuals as members of organized bodies. It is customary in Japan for individuals, whether in business or government, to spend their lifetimes working within a single organization and rarely to leave it. Loyalty to that organization is expected, and its leaders in turn are expected to behave paternally to them. Within the constituent elements of government — essentially the ministry, perhaps an important bureau — internal decisions are supposed to be made through adjustments (*chōsei*) of the desires of those affected by the decisions. Harmony is the ideal, and if that means compromise or even ignoring controversy, so be it. According to Nakane Chie, the criterion for judgment is that "any decision should be made on the basis of a consensus which includes those located lower in the hierarchy. . . . It should leave no one frustrated or dissatisfied. . . ." [8] Translated into budgetary terms, these norms would imply relative equality in losses and gains. Whether

---

[8] Nakane Chie, *Japanese Society* (Berkeley: University of California Press, 1970), pp. 144–145, as quoted by Campbell, "Japanese Balanced Budgeting," p. 43. See also Ronald P. Dore, ed., *Aspects of Social Change in Modern Japan* (Princeton: Princeton University Press, 1967); and Nathaniel B. Thayer, *How the Conservatives Rule in Japan* (Princeton: Princeton University Press, 1969).

rewards or punishments, increases or decreases are to be allocated, no one wins or loses all. Everyone can say that he got something out of it or that he was treated no worse than others. At the ministerial level, the norm of fair shares means treating subunits in a comparable way. For the Ministry of Finance, fair shares must translate itself into some equitable way of treating spending ministries so that none are left empty-handed. To the political party leadership, including the prime minister, falls the task of fairly adjusting differences among the Ministry of Finance, the spending ministries, and various subgroups in the ruling party. If rules permitting winner to take all are prohibited, how is it possible for all to play poker (or make a budget) and leave the game with more than they put in? How can budgeting be made into a positive sum game? The Japanese may not succeed entirely, but they come close.

It is easy to understand how conflict is regulated within a single ministry. Consider the prestigious and influential Ministry of Finance; entry typically comes with graduation from Tokyo University Law School. Early retirement at age 55 is followed by a second career as a representative of the Liberal Democratic Party (LDP) in the Diet, or on the board of a major corporation. This pattern of lifetime employment contracts ensures that relationships are stable over the length of a career, while the controlled access ensures a shared set of values. The pattern of relationships is so stable, especially considering the importance of patron-client relationships between seniors and juniors, that they change only with the movement of generations. Mitigation of conflicts within a ministry might be secured, however, at the price of increased conflict among ministries. Organizational loyalty might become the fuel for governmental conflagration. After all, latent possibilities for budgetary conflict between advocates and guardians, and between one advocate and another are ever-present. Additional norms and practices are required, therefore, in order to regulate interorganizational hostilities. There are; and they do.

Ministries can practice avoidance. They can sidestep outright conflict by rarely dealing directly with one another. Communications within government, as might be expected, run vertically within ministries and hardly ever laterally across them. Avoidance may account for the use of newspapers and reporters to carry messages from one ministry to another — communications that are at once public and depersonalized because no one has sent word directly to any other. Contact between spending ministries and the Ministry of Finance is unavoidable, however, unless the opening bid is also to be the final result. Since that cannot be, what is to be done?

The most acute form of this problem surfaces in relationships between examiners of the Bureau of the Budget in the Ministry of Finance and the Director of the Ministerial Accounting Division who has the burden of defending ministerial requests. Efforts are made and sanctions are available for maintaining mutual trust. Confidence is enhanced by each participant's accepting a norm of candor called *shojiki,* a combination of being honest and trustworthy with all cards on the table and no deviousness or trickery. "If you cheat," a director told Campbell, "you can do it only once; if you make them understand, you will continue to prosper." [9]

But the interests of the two organizations do differ; one must be concerned with furthering the programs dear to its heart and the other with imposing some limits on them. They have chosen, as we shall see, to get around this potential conflict by adopting the norm of reciprocity in which each accepts an appropriate sphere for its activities. These potential antagonists cannot wholly avoid one another, but they can accept the other's sphere of influence — one side understanding that the total must be limited, and the other allowing discretion in how it is spent. They coordinate their activities by reducing the scope for decision and then by dividing the remainder into spheres of reasonably independent responsibility. Either they deemphasize policy components of expenditure decisions or they divide the spheres according to their interests and capabilities. How all this is worked out, how resources are allocated to accord with special Japanese characteristics while performing necessary tasks, is well exemplified by the characteristic features of the Japanese budgetary process. The Japanese have, in effect, institutionalized incrementalism by the formal requirement that no ministry submit a budget larger than 125 percent of the past year's. When one considers that under Japanese conditions some 10 percent to 15 percent of last year's budget would be taken up by advances in the cost of living or mandatory expansion of services, participants are left with no more than half of the 25 percent to negotiate.

But this ceiling is only a beginning. In the 1930s and again in the 1950s the Ministry of Finance tried to work with a Standard Budget, which was supposed to include expenses that did not vary much and that could be resolved by technical discussion at the staff level. The Standard Budget fell into disuse, however, apparently because it covered too small a proportion of the total. So the finance ministry began using more powerful methods of elimination. It now begins its First Expenditure Estimate essentially by taking for granted the budget of the previous year. Added to this is the Natural Expenditure Increase made up of mandatory items required by law or based on the cost of living. Nothing if not sophisticated, the Ministry of Finance adds yet another amount for what are called "seminatural increases" — expenditures such as public works that everyone knows will have to be made whether or not the law says so. Although one is tempted to follow this vocabulary in suggesting that the remainder must somehow be made up of "unnatural" increases, in fact they are called by the more acceptable title of "policy expenditures." By the time the Ministry of Finance has finished its own calculations, the total left for programs which can reasonably be expected to change is probably no

---

[9] Campbell, "Contemporary Japanese Budget Politics," Chap. iii, p. 44.

more than 5 percent of the amount Finance has independently estimated should be the spending limit on the basis of economic and tax considerations. In order to firm up its expenditure estimates, which have been kept secret for fear of stirring up unwanted pressure for increases, Finance holds another round of internal discussions on Important Items in order to gather the latest information, receive recommendations from its own examiners, and give them an idea of the limits within which they can move. By this time, Finance knows a lot more about what ministries will request and what it will give. Having gotten over the Second Expenditure Estimates, the Ministry of Finance is now ready to reveal its draft to the ministries concerned.

But hold on. Ministries whose requests are turned down may think themselves disadvantaged. Interests surrounding them might feel their needs have not been taken into account. Although participants already are dealing with the margin of a margin, they may still be marginally dissatisfied. And this will not do in Japan. So, two additional measures increase the sense of being treated fairly; one of these — balance — is designed to be an embodiment of equity; the other, which we shall deal with first, has been devised to channel the competitive spirit while letting everybody do somewhat better than on the first time around.

Roughly equivalent, perhaps, to the *repêchage* (in which all crews that have lost in previous races are given a second chance to win a berth for the finals) but to no budgetary procedure of which I am aware, ministries that have had cuts in their requests are given a crack at some 3 percent of the total put aside for that very purpose by the Ministry of Finance. Appropriately called "resurrection" or "revival" negotiations (since requests previously denied are figuratively brought back from the dead) these appeals go on for about a week. During this time the Bureau of the Budget and the ministry divide up bits and pieces in seesaw negotiations. Ministries, as we shall see, work through the policy divisions of the Liberal Democratic Party which goes back in its turn to Finance. Ultimately, the half-dozen or so items that may have remained unresolved — involving a modest proportion of the 3 percent or so up for grabs — are disposed of as political questions between the LDP and the Ministry of Finance. The colorful aspects of the revival negotiations — mass demonstrations, public appeals by interest groups, reports of devious maneuvers — lend an air of public participation to proceedings that have actually become successively refined and routinized between the chief official participants.

For the most basic norm of Japanese budgeting, *baransū* (or balance) is used to see that everyone gets a fair share of what there is to give. Increases in comparable activities are made proportionally. Insofar as possible, every activity, program, or ministry is balanced by being brought along at roughly the same level. Naturally participants can and do disagree about the appropriate level of comparison: whether, for example, public works should be balanced from one ministry to another or from one purpose to another or whether indeed Japan might not properly be compared to some other nations that invariably do more. For its part, the Ministry of Finance will seek the lower order of comparison. One way to get at the notion of balance is to say, as Campbell does, what it is not: "It is not setting budgets competitively by assessing merits of a particular item compared with those of similar or related items. Rather, for balance, two or more items are seen as requiring the same expenditure because they are similar or related." [10] Thus balance serves not only as a norm in its own right, but also as an aid to calculation enabling many expenditure items to be set merely by reference to others that are already known. Specifically, as Campbell relates,

> At the most straightforward level, programs which are very similar in objectives and target groups will be balanced almost automatically. There are a variety of government-financed health insurance plans, and when benefits for one are raised, the Ministry of Welfare will not have a difficult time in appealing that the others also receive increases. Similarly, increased support for national universities will bring a call for raising the government's contribution to private universities. The demand for balance becomes a little more tenuous, but maintains persuasiveness, when extended a little further: it will be argued that if college-level support is increased, that for secondary schools should also be (or vice versa), or that hikes in health insurance subsidies should be matched by increases in other welfare programs like unemployment and life support.[11]

Although balance does not solve everything, it does resolve many questions, thus further reducing the scope for disagreement. And, as we now know, those who feel they have not been adequately balanced will be revived and adjusted.

Yet one major source of potential divisiveness remains. Spending ministries in countries the world over, and Japan is no exception, like to think of themselves as experts in their own fields. They naturally tend to regard control organs, such as a finance ministry, as interlopers who act without full understanding or appreciation of their difficulties and needs. But finance ministries function without claiming to know what is going on. If they do not have some special form of expertise, there would be no rationale for their intervention. This source of cleavage has not been entirely eliminated in Japan, but it has been narrowed, reduced, and whittled down.

Like all other central control organs, the Bureau of the Budget in Japan believes it has a special duty to protect the nation against dissipating its wealth through ruinous inflation or unnecessary spending. If other ministries were left to themselves, they would push the budget beyond reasonable bounds. The task of the Budget Bureau in the Ministry of Finance is to keep spending down. Its first instinct is to say "No!" Proposals for new spending are almost automatically turned down for inclusion in the draft budget and appear only

[10] Campbell, "Japanese Balanced Budgeting," p. 6.
[11] Ibid., p. 10.

later as a result of the revival negotiations. By turning them down the first time around, the Budget Bureau can find out whether ministries are serious by watching for the proposal to be put forward again. Since some new proposals are inevitable, the Budget Bureau can simultaneously avoid responsibility for them and be in a position to help choose among the most desirable ones. Only when the Ministry of Finance fears that a program has become so popular that its momentum will cause increases in other programs too will it intervene to announce a favorable decision early, thus holding down its losses. If it fears being caught in a vortex of irresistible pressures, Finance is not above putting trial balloons in newspapers to determine whether it should submit gracefully in advance or fight into the later stages of the process. Earmarked revenue of all sorts is suspect by the Budget Bureau in Japan, as by colleagues around the world, because it provides a way around the normal budgetary process. For similar reasons, Finance is opposed to planning or, more accurately, to the determination of spending projects long into the future by inclusion in The Plan. If spending ministries can get their bids incorporated for five years at a time, they not only will have to devote less energy to this purpose each year but can also use the approved figure as the starting point and concentrate their attenion on attaining increases. The Budget Bureau tries to see that planning works just the other way around. It does not accept planning figures as a mandate to spend but rather as an outside limit, subject to being cut in the ordinary expenditure process.

By and large, however, relations between spending ministries and the Bureau of the Budget are friendly and cooperative. Each needs the other and each recognizes the other's competent professionalism. With perhaps the highest status of all governmental organizations (all but one chief examiner had graduated in Law at Tokyo University from 1947 to 1950, and that man was an engineering graduate who dealt with scientific subjects), the Budget Bureau staff of some three hundred are known as "bureaucrat's bureaucrats" or, in more military terms, the *"samurai* of the Japanese government." [12] No one would wish to get into unnecessary struggles with them. Not only are they strong; they are also reliable. The budget examiner takes great pains to be considered trustworthy by meeting his commitments. During the one time after the Second World War when the LDP suggested a cut in the draft budget, the Ministry of Finance replied stiffly that it did not go back on its word. When the Director of the Accounting Division and the Chief Examiner, who deals with him, make a verbal agreement, this mutual understanding is considered final. Everyone gains by good personal relationships. As a ministerial budget officer told Campbell, "The man with the money tends to play hard to get and won't give up easily, but if he has confidence in you, you are more likely to receive what you want." And the lower down you go, the more important

---

[12] Campbell, "Contemporary Japanese Budget Politics," Chap. ii, p. 16.

confidence becomes because the norm of balance is less likely to predetermine results. Although each ministry can expect to be treated in roughly the same way, subunits have fewer guarantees and will want to strengthen their personal contacts. Advocates and controllers may be good people (trustworthy, loyal, honorable, and brave) but if their institutions have a great deal to argue about, relationships still may be difficult. People whose roles compel them to differ on a continuing basis may well develop a hostile stance. But this has not happened in Japan.

Spenders and savers in Japan have fixed on a division of labor that keeps them out of each other's way. The Ministry of Finance is largely concerned with managing the economy and taxation, so that it concentrates almost entirely on limiting the total of expenditures. Within these highly aggregated amounts, Finance allows departments to have the largest voice in determining priorities. Thus the work of budget bureau examiners is vastly simplified. Technicians can agree on the cost of standard and repetitive activities. Spending ministries and the budget bureau need not agree on the nation's approach to the balance of payments or supply of money. Where they might disagree, on domestic policy matters such as the type of welfare programs, the substance of the issue is left largely to ministries, with the Bureau of the Budget coming in chiefly where the various alternatives imply future spending. Conflict has not disappeared entirely, but it has been splintered into its thinnest pieces. Disagreements over amounts of money — conceived as a continuous sum which can be divided in all sorts of ways — are much more easily resolved than disputes over who is right or what philosophy should govern social policy.

A number of actions the Ministry of Finance has taken in recent years have worked well with this concentration on macro- rather than microeconomics. For example, imposing the 125 percent ceiling has by that very fact transferred more setting of priorities from the budget bureau to the spending ministry. Now the Bureau of the Budget need only trim a few percent. Abandonment of secrecy over the amount available during revival negotiations, and substituting openness also reduce conflict. For then it becomes possible for the Ministry of Finance essentially to turn over certain portions of these marginal amounts for "secretariat adjusment expenses" to allocate among the programs of each ministry and a larger amount to the party leadership for "policy adjustment expenses." Evidently the Ministry of Finance has chosen to withdraw from areas in which it had previously exercised at least some small discretion in favor of turning them over to the LDP or the spending ministries, or both.

In making this strategic choice, the Ministry of Finance may have been motivated by the great popularity and essential simplicity of Keynesian economics. This is not to say that the economy is simple, but that the Keynesian-like rules the Japanese have adopted for dealing with it are few and easily understood at the top levels. In a period during which national income and expenditure have been rising by leaps and bounds, and there is a tendency to get bogged down in discussing innumerable social policy questions, concentration on managing the economy undoubtedly has its attractions. Also it is an area in which the Ministry of Finance is unlikely to be challenged, providing it does not make too many enemies on other grounds.

If the Ministry of Finance in Japan fears anyone, it is the Liberal Democratic Party. Campbell explains that there is

> a deep-seated concern among MOF officials about LDP intrusions into their own internal processes and decisions. Although the Finance bureaucrats had always remained more aloof from the Party than those in the line ministries, the influence of politically active Finance Ministers, the numbers of MOF alumnae among LDP Dietmen and the more general trend toward close government-Party relations all tended to threaten MOF autonomy. So long as the MOF made choices that politicians saw as important, politicians would seek to bring their influence to bear. This is more a problem of microbudgeting decisions on individual programs, which interest Dietmen the most, than of macrobudgeting processes, which take place on a higher level under different ground rules. It seems at least plausible therefore that in 1968, the MOF explicitly passed much of the responsibility for making these smaller choices over to the ministries, to decide both while making up their requests and as a final marginal allocation of remaining funds. In any case, it is clear that this reform would not diminish LDP inputs into such choices, since LDP penetration of the other ministries was far more extensive than of the MOF. The shift did reduce the incentive for politicians to involve themselves in MOF decision making. As a journalist pointed out in an interview, "under the new system, when a Budget Examiner is asked a favor by a Dietman during appeals negotiations, he can now simply tell him to go over and talk to the ministry secretariat.[13]

It is apparent that in order to understand what happens in Japanese government, most certainly including its budgeting, we can no longer delay consideration of the role played by the LDP.

The Liberal Democratic Party

Although there are free elections in which the proportions of parties in the Diet vary somewhat, for our purposes we may consider Japan to have a dominant party linked with the top levels of the ministries and business interests. Since 1955 there has been no alternation of parties controlling the Diet. Pressures from interest groups and receipt of financial support are filtered largely through trade associations. Trade unions, primarily affiliated with the Socialist Party, are effectively blocked from access to the inner circle. The important interest groups owe their origins not to citizen action but to the inspiration of governmental agencies. Thus many interest groups have their organizational shape determined by the boundaries of a single ministry.

---

[13] Ibid., Chap. vi, p. 75.

When officials retire from the ministry and become officers of an interest group within their former jurisdiction, as often happens, it is hard to say whether the interest group is colonizing the ministry or vice versa. Controlling the interest groups that might want to control them is a major agency objective. Since the LDP has been in power for so long, most interest groups outside the trade unions are affiliated with the dominant party. It is not the struggle between parties that concerns interest groups, therefore, but the conflicts between ministries which show up in differences among factions within the LDP.

The dominant party in Japan is of special interest to us because, alone among western nations, it plays a recognized part in the budgetary process. Although it might be said that the United States Congress occasionally picks up a plank from a party platform or that British governments reflect in their expenditures the effects of resolutions adopted at party congresses, the parties neither attempt to form a budget nor to make specific recommendations on a wide range of items. In Japan the LDP does exactly this. The LDP's official Budget Compilation Program is prepared through the divisional structure of the Policy Affairs Research Council (PARC) which corresponds to ministerial spheres of responsibility. As Campbell says,

> In many senses, it is fruitful to regard the LDP organization as the real legislature of Japan; from this point of view, the PARC Divisions can be seen as equivalent to American legislative (not appropriations) committees. They are intimately concerned with the affairs of their corresponding ministries and support their interests, inside and outside the Party, against the competing claims of other agencies.[14]

Because ministries can help a member of the Diet in his constituency by favoring pet projects, because civil servants need LDP contact for their future careers, because there are so many ex-ministerial officials in the Diet, relationships between the PARC Divisions and the ministries are exceptionally close.

One reason the LDP has stayed in power so long is that it explicitly recognizes the need to spread material benefits around so that a heterogeneous and far-flung party will be able to withstand the ordinary vicissitudes of political life. In American terms, and with no bones made about it, the budget is viewed as a source of pork-barrel projects. "With the Upper House election coming up next spring," Campbell quotes then PARC Chairman Tanaka in 1961, "at least $100,000,000,000 of new funds in the 1962 budget is needed to settle the intra-party situation." [15] Terms in common use — "pocket money" and "intra-party adjustment funds" — suggest the omnipresence of the practice.

At the same time, the LDP cannot escape from its responsibility as the ruling party. It cannot act as if it were up to someone else to make the final

---

[14] Campbell, "Japanese Balanced Budgeting," p. 17.
[15] Campbell, "Contemporary Japanese Budget Politics," Chap. v, p. 56.

disposition. Its leader is also the prime minister, and the government is also its government. Thus the LDP, to some extent, must help the finance ministry keep expenditures within bounds by resisting programs that would lead to unpopular tax increases. When party leadership participates in sessions on large issues such as the total size of the budget; or when the PARC Divisions review ministerial requests in late summer; or even when the party participates less formally, as Dietmen seek projects for their constituents or Dietmen's Leagues seek preference for the interest groups that sponsor them, the LDP cannot quite make believe that it is not responsible for the outcome.

Why, then, hasn't the party made its budget the government budget? In the Japanese context, it would not have been unthinkable to do so. Indeed, several times the LDP has tried to do just that. Its failures are instructive to students of budgeting.

The party might have tried to make its own detailed budget, or it could have confined itself to the less exhausting task of making major decisions and setting out main priorities among new expenditures, leaving the details to Finance. But it has not been able to do either. Making a budget demands at least a minimal level of policy expertise, both in respect to what policies are preferable and to what their financial implications should be in the budget. The LDP never saw fit to equip itself with this minimum expertise. Though it might control Cabinet and Diet, the LDP was not itself the body of spending ministries or their financial controllers, and did not have adequate replacements for these men. But the essential difficulty went much deeper and was far more interesting than a mere lack of expertise.

To make a budget means to aggregate preferences across the broadest front of governmental activity. Since spending ministries always want more, the budget maker has to say how much shall be cut from this and that request and (only occasionally) how much will be added to another. To the budget maker belongs not merely the spoils, but the blame incurred from those disappointed. The LDP could not, or at least would not, incur that penalty. Policy leadership means political enmity. Choice is angular, uneven, an expression of preference — qualities far from the balance, adjustment, and harmony in which the leadership specializes. Every time the LDP tried, it got caught between the demands of its local and sectional partisans and its promises to the finance ministry not to raise the level of the budget too high. The LDP ended up breaking its promises to the Ministry of Finance as it poured in additional billions of yen for the usual intra-party adjustment expenses.

What the party has done is to issue an official budget policy statement called the Budget Compilation Program which gives everyone everything in general terms but does not tie the party (and therefore the government) to any specific list of priorities. Satisfied with the symbolism of making a general budget, the LDP actually confines itself to particular recommendations for specific projects, usually in the context of the revival negotiations. The party's influence may be seen in the extensive support given to business and agriculture — where reside its financial and electoral support — and in the frequency with which last-minute requests are made for politically important programs during the revival negotiations. As a budget examiner once said in the distinctive Japanese mode, "In the evening, you think you hear a distant bird singing, and then when the New Year dawns, it comes swooping down." [16] And who is to say that the appearance in the final budget of innumerable little projects dear to the heart of the LDP's constituency has not, in some small way, proven advantageous in a country whose infrastructure is said to lag far behind its industrial development?

If the dominant party does not make the budget, and if the spending ministries cannot always be expected to quite agree with the Ministry of Finance, how does the budget actually materialize? Perhaps the prime minister asserts his authority in the final measure? On occasion, perhaps; but, in keeping with the Japanese way, it happens seldom. Disputes may be referred up to him and he will exercise whatever mediating and soothing influence he can. By the time a matter reaches him, it has been refined down to a margin of an increment, and even then he will try to get the parties to agree rather than have to impose a solution. According to Campbell, "The Prime Minister does not develop a unified set of priorities to be implemented through the budget, and does not review expenditure allocations. It is even rarer for him to identify personally with specific proposals at all. Officials and Dietmen do, of course, seek his approval for their programs, as they do with all influential politicians, but usually he will give a sympathetic but non-committal answer." [17] Like the LDP of which he is head, the prime minister must be concerned with the stability of the government and balance his intervention between the needs of the spending ministries and their associated interests, and the requirements of the Minister of Finance. But the finance minister usually is more critical for the government. Consequently, prime ministers will be heard echoing the traditional line of finance ministers about how poor the financial picture is and how difficult it will be to increase expenditures. If anyone has final authority, it is the Ministry of Finance, but it exercises this largely, as we have seen, by shifting responsibility for most controversial decisions to the spending ministries.

Who has the power? In a system with the highest possible degree of reciprocal interaction, in which each participant anticipates the actions of the other, no one, not even those directly involved, can say who determines decisions. The spending ministries have increasingly more to say about allocation to specific activities of funds they do get. Finance controls economic management and perhaps the sequence in timing of a few new programs. Although it lacks the political strength that American presidents can lend to the Office

[16] Ibid., Chap. ii, p. 49.
[17] Ibid., Chap. v, p. 62.

of Management and Budget, it is not so often as OMB in the position of having to make room for large initiatives from the executive. The prime minister may be a court of last resort, but almost everything must have been resolved for him to be effective in dealing with the remainder. The LDP has much to say about public works and a few pet programs, but it is so large and heterogeneous that it neither can nor will impose its preferences along the widest range of governmental programs. All participants are swept along by the rising tide of national income; and all must bow to the norms that regulate conflict in Japanese society. Perhaps the most that can be said is that Japanese budgeting is very much a game of insiders in which the official participants — spending ministries, finance ministry, and party officials — resolve their differences by following mutually accepted norms.

Of certain romantic revolutionary movements it used to be said that they try to convert every question of fact into one of value. The Japanese budgetary process does exactly the reverse; it tries to convert almost all questions of value into ones of fact. Like the American expenditure process, only more so, the Japanese one functions through a sequential reduction in which larger problems are subdivided into smaller ones, and further fragmented in order to be increasingly manageable. Under current Japanese conditions, it is agreed that there always will be increases. The question is, how much? No spending ministry is allowed to ask for more than 25 percent over the previous year. Within that it is understood that there will be substantial increases over the previous year. The Ministry of Finance itself calculates the cost of standard and miscellaneous items, and for natural and seminatural increases. By this time not only the base but most of the allowable increase has been taken care of. Adjustments are then made along the margins so that similar activities, according to the norm of balance, receive comparable rates of increase. To make sure no one is left out entirely, the finance ministry puts a few percent away for the revival negotiations. Most of this is immediately factored out to salary and policy adjustments that are given on the basis of "he who has gets." It remains only to compensate the few who have lost a little and to consider which of the new items can be allowed under the ceiling. From first to last, party considerations are taken into account so that funds are left over for wide distribution among small public works, and party leadership has a chance to reconcile any emerging differences. The finance ministry has to be responsive to the party, but it is also true that the party must show awareness of financial limits on behalf of Finance. By the time the prime minister and his advisers must act, it can hardly make more than a hair's breadth difference one way or the other.

Programatic and policy considerations are deemphasized from first to last. Spending limits may be a function of economic management and taxation, but there is little scope for consideration of which spending policies are more or less desirable. Finance automatically rejects new proposals for its draft, and lets spending ministries determine priorities within their allotment. They may have to choose between projects but the finance ministry does not. The goal appears to be a budget which, if not exactly untouched by human hands, is a product of seemingly neutral rules that work automatically for the vast bulk of resources.

The achievement of the Japanese budgetary process is a high degree of stability and, hence, predictability. Past commitments in Japan are the firmest sort of guarantees for future spending. Each actor knows what to expect of the other and can use the budget as an accurate signal for future intentions. The obvious problem is how to accommodate change so that some notion of merit in expenditure (apart from maintaining harmony) is allowed to make itself felt.

That is why in recent years the Japanese have become fascinated with program budgeting. Campbell reports that the Japanese vocabulary surrounding PPBS dwells largely on its purported "scientific" qualities. For if there were some way to determine priorities among expenditures that could be characterized as "scientific," they would undoubtedly be accepted by the participants, thus adding merit while leaving harmony intact. The scientific enterprise connotes not only objective verifiability but also common acceptance of results stemming from approved procedures. It sounds (and it is) too good to be true. Even the Japanese, whose extraordinary capacities after all still fall somewhat short of the miraculous, could not make program budgeting work. They could not figure out how to make the required calculations nor how to get others to accept them.

An intriguing question remains: Will candor, balance, and harmony remain viable in bad times as in good? One way to answer this question would be to see how Japanese budgeting operated in the 1920s and 1930s. Another is to wait and see what happens when the rate of growth slows down so that the finance ministry has to impose actual cuts, and not merely turn over to spending ministries the distribution of rather large increases. But for the time being, at least, the principal actors have found a way to produce a long-running play with a happy ending.

6

The Poor and Certain: Budgeting in Cities

American cities and rich countries represent one of the polar ends of the predictability continuum. In both, certainty is high. But rich countries do not operate under tight revenue constraints; cities do. What is budgeting like under conditions of poverty and certainty, when participants know ahead of time just about how much income they will have and be allowed to spend in the next year or so? What calculations and strategies would they use, knowing that, no matter what they do, revenues determine expenditures? Would budgeting lose significance and become the exclusive domain of accountants? If not, what purpose would it serve?

To answer these questions, we turn to municipal budgeting in the United States. American cities are poor. Their expenditures are rising fast — at an average rate of 12.5 percent (a total of 60.3 in the five years leading up to 1973) — while revenues are lagging behind — increasing at an average rate of 11.5 percent (a total of 55.1 percent increase in the last five years).[1] They are confronted with a chorus of demands to solve urban problems — more police protection, better schools, a cleaner environment, to name just a few — but their capacity for mobilizing resources in pursuit of these aims is severely limited.

A MODEL OF MUNICIPAL BUDGETING

In an original empirical study of resource allocation, conducted in three large metropolitan governments — Pittsburgh, Detroit, and Cleveland —

---

[1] Stanley M. Wolfson, "Economic Characteristics and Trends in Municipal Finance," *The Municipal Year Book, 1973* (Washington, D.C.: International City Management Association, 1973), pp. 91–106.

Crecine[2] developed a computer simulation model of the municipal operating budgetary process. He recreated the central steps and calculations in the process in order to generate the outcomes. The key feature of municipal budgeting, he found, is that the budget must be balanced to meet an independent revenue constraint. Revenues must be equal to or greater than expenditures. Since operating deficits are forbidden, the budget must either provide for a surplus or be balanced.[3] This revenue constraint governs the behavior of participants in the budgetary process.

Crecine divides budgetary behavior into three submodels: (1) Departmental Request, (2) Mayor's Budget Recommendation, and (3) Council Appropriation. The model begins with the department's receipt of the mayor's budgetary guidance letter. Departments do not compete with each other for funds. Budgetary requests are based on last year's appropriation plus an increment whose size depends on the department head's calculations of "what will go" and on the tone of the mayor's budgetary letter. In the Crecine model, departments follow the mayor's instructions. His decisions are accepted and rarely challenged; it is considered politically unwise to go over his head. As one department head said, "We . . . *never* go over the mayor's head to council. It just wouldn't pay to undermine a relationship with the mayor and his staff for the sake of one 'break' in our budget for one year." [4] The mayor's submodel is crucial because the budget, by legal requirement, must be balanced at this stage in the process. As Crecine says, "The mayor's problem is largely one of recommending a budget that (1) is balanced, (2) at least maintains existing service levels, (3) provides for increases in city employee wages if at all possible, and (4) avoids tax increases." [5]

Departments, in preparing their requests, assume they will continue to receive what they already have and will get a fair share of any potential budget increase. The council, which is expected to review the mayor's budget proposal, usually rubber-stamps it. The budget's complexity and the balancing requirement, on one hand, and the council's lack of full-time status and of appropriate staff, on the other hand, leave councilmen with limited options.[6]

Simple decision rules are employed to solve these problems. Increases should be no greater than a certain percentage of last year's appropriation. The mayor makes minor adjustments to last year's budget or "governs by precedent." Crecine's model of incremental line-item budgeting emphasizes *continuity* of existing policies. It does not focus on programs or policies. City decision-makers are insulated from short-term environmental forces. The environment may influence what a department head worries about, but it does not

[2] John P. Crecine, *Governmental Problem Solving: A Computer Simulation of Municipal Budgeting* (Chicago: Rand McNally, 1969).
[3] Ibid., pp. 32–39, 179–184.
[4] Ibid., p. 38.
[5] Ibid., p. 39.
[6] Ibid.

influence the department's total budgetary level. Crecine reports some pressure to keep property tax rates constant, but he finds no direct connection between political pressure and departmental budget totals. Expenditure levels tend to "drift" over time until the decision system responds to some change in the revenue situation. The environment does not correct budgetary drift by directly changing specific expenditures. Budgetary change is more likely to be "filtered through the revenue constraint." [7]

Crecine notes several important limitations to his model. The model lacks a realistic priority scheme for treating departmental deficits and surpluses: departments are treated by account number and not in terms of individual characteristics. The model excludes capital and nongeneral fund expenditures. Political scientists may object to the lack of attention Crecine pays to environmental forces or constituency pressures. But we feel that Crecine's work adequately reflects political reality. The operating budget is insulated from the environment. There are undoubtedly occasions when political pressure results in specific expenditures, but these are likely to be infrequent.

OAKLAND: THE ALL-AMERICAN CITY

In order to penetrate the skin of general budgetary relationships, it will be helpful to look at a single city in some detail.[8] Because Oakland, California, is like Cleveland, Detroit, and Pittsburgh in budgetary essentials, we will understand all of them better by observing how Oakland carries out its budgettary process.

The local chamber of commerce usually describes Oakland as the "All-American" city, and in one sense this is not an exaggeration since it does exemplify the many dilemmas of central cities. The elements of the urban crisis are all there: racial conflict, high unemployment rate, substandard housing, poor educational achievement, and low family income.

Oakland is poor. It has far more than its share of poor people who need services they do not get. Oakland is also very short in the human resources available to work on its problems. Although the city has many intelligent and devoted men on its payroll, few have been trained to evaluate the effectiveness of existing policies or to devise new alternatives. The city has no policy analysts and few economists who could serve in that capacity. It lacks the analytical capability to make effective use of outside consultants. With little talent

---

[7] Ibid., pp. 167–168.

[8] The original version of this discussion appeared under the title "Leave City Budgeting Alone! A Survey, Case Study, and Recommendations for Reform," by A. J. Meltsner and A. Wildavsky; Chap. 12 from *Financing the Metropolis* (Vol. 4, *Urban Affairs Annual Review*), edited by J. P. Crecine, © 1970; and is reprinted by permission of the publisher, Sage Publications, Inc.

and less opportunity to analyze policies (in view of the lack of money), top city officials are forced to see the budget as a servant of lower taxation and administrative control. The budget does keep expenditures down and provide information useful in keeping tabs on departmental activities.

The main annual problem for city officials is to find sufficient revenue to maintain their current payroll. Their problem is that the city's budget demands increase faster than the tax base. Fiscal atrophy is the city's chronic malady. The city manager put it this way to the city council in a report on the fiscal potential of Oakland: "Simply stated, the disquieting fact is that under existing policies and within the constraints of the financial structure, the City of Oakland's expenditure requirements will soon exceed its income." The manager based his projection on the fact that in the 1956–1966 decade, the city budget had risen 86 percent while the property tax assessed valuation had gone up only 36 percent. Even with revenue sharing, things are pretty much the same now in 1974. The atrophy of Oakland's tax resources has limited the city simply to maintaining itself rather than trying to cope with larger social problems.

Oakland's tax problems are compounded by its land usage and by heavy migration of business and population to surrounding communities. The city has no more land to annex; it is boxed in within its 53 square miles of land. One cause of tax base erosion is that not all property within Oakland's area is included on the tax rolls. Much of the excluded real property is occupied by governmental utilities, public institutions, streets and freeways, or is merely vacant. The city's finance director has estimated that over 40 percent of Oakland's real property is tax exempt.

The city budget has expanded to meet increased operating costs, not the needs of Oakland's deprived population, and it is an operating budget: 70 percent of the total is for personnel-related costs. Oakland is not an example of expanding bureaucracy; between 1960 and 1968, budgeted full-time personnel positions rose only about 1 percent a year. But the costs of personnel have gone up every year, with built-in merit raises and rising expenditures for retirement plans. Thus it is easy to see that with the possibility of a 2–3 percent price increase for nonpersonnel costs, with standard salary increases of 4–5 percent, with slight increases in number of personnel, and with no increase in productivity, Oakland could have an 8 percent growth rate in city expenditures each year without a marked increase in the level of service.

Oakland is living with a fiscal crisis. The local property tax, main source of revenue for cities, is exhausted in a political, if not an economic, sense. The common perception among officials is that "we cannot raise the property tax rate." Taxpayers complain that the rate is too high. There is some justification for this, since Oakland has one of the highest municipal tax rates in the state of California. In fact, it was *the* highest during 12 of the past 17 years. City officials believe that raising the property tax significantly, rather than in dribs and drabs, too small to cause an outcry, would be an act of political suicide.[9]

Officials believe also that voters will be hostile to all bond proposals, and find it increasingly difficult to acquire revenue sources that will be politically feasible and have a worthwhile yield. As its costs go up, the city finds minor sources of revenue, augmenting the property tax each year by adopting a stop-gap measure such as a tax on cigarettes or hotel rooms. Since it is difficult to discover painless methods of raising money, top officials have every incentive to hold down expenditures. Their motivation is clear: the more they can cut, the less they have to worry about finding new sources of revenue.

For the past decade, the annual budget guidance to department heads has included some phrase like "hold the line"; every year the financial constraint on the city is apparent. The city manager has often said, "I don't know why we spend so much time on budgeting. After all, it shouldn't make any difference — we won't have any more money." Yet the city manager and his small finance staff spend days and weeks worrying about the budget.

To what extent, we ask, is this activity a meaningless ritual that might be of more interest to an anthropologist than to a student of public policy? How may the budget process in Oakland be considered important? Is Oakland a city where revenue constraints drive out policy considerations so that the emphasis is on cutting the budget rather than meeting community needs for services? A short answer is: "No," budgeting is not meaningless; "yes," it has important uses; but "no," it does not serve to allocate resources according to any well defined notion of public policy other than keeping down the property tax.

Control versus Steering

Control and steering are of central importance to students of public policy. Steering (or strategic planning, or policy-making) determines the goals and direction of a public organization. Control connects means and ends by ensuring that long-term goals are approached and, perhaps, reached. Since Oakland's budgeting reflects the acceptance of premises of the past as goals for the future, public officials gloss over steering and emphasize control.

The concept of control has many meanings when applied to budgetary behavior. It can mean cut the estimates because there is no money, reduce estimated expenditures in the process of budget execution, or implement the policy preferences of the person who hands out the salary raises. The city manager and his finance staff have a single motivation, however, which underlies these objectives of budgetary control: they want to balance the budget by controlling uncertainty. Once officials used budgetary control to keep people

---

[9] For a detailed analysis of the revenue question, see Arnold J. Meltsner, *The Politics of City Revenue* (Berkeley: University of California Press, 1971), pp. 311–358.

honest; now it is used mainly as a short-term hedge against unanticipated events. Balancing the budget means the city always has at least a slight surplus on hand.

We shall begin our discussion of budgeting for control, therefore, by pointing out that the goal is to create a surplus. We shall go on to show that the problem of control stems from the familiar conflict between budget spenders and budget cutters and is exacerbated by the city's overall revenue constraint.

The Goal: Create a Surplus

City officials aim to have a little more to spend than they need. This creation of slack (excess resources) essentially leaves them some discretion for adapting to unforeseen events. The first decision rule officials adopt, therefore, is always to estimate revenue lower than they actually expect it to be. The conservative bias in revenue-estimating is cumulative. At every level, supervisors reviewing the estimates tend to lower them. For example, when the city was installing an urban transit system in the downtown area, there was considerable uncertainty as to the effect this construction would have on retail sales. The revenue analyst had taken this into account in lowering his sales tax estimate, but his estimates were reduced at each stage as they went up the line. Thus, since the actual sales tax revenue was much higher than had been anticipated, the city had the unusual and pleasant task of disposing of a surplus.

The second rule for increasing slack is to estimate spending higher than one expects it to be. In this way, the finance director tries to reduce departmental surpluses and to create a financial surplus for the city manager to use. Each level of government tries to increase its available money, guard it against those above, and squeeze it out for its own use from those below. An estimate of expenditures higher and revenues lower than they really will be certainly will create a surplus for someone which can be used to finance future programs.

Allen Schick has observed that budget people in Oakland should not be called "revenue maximizers" but rather "surplus protectors." It is true that they do not try to raise all the money they conceivably could if they viewed the world differently. They attempt to maximize revenue within the constraints of the system as they understand it. Under those constraints they might first be described as "surplus producers" and then, in their budget behavior, as "surplus protectors."

To make sure that his office controls as much slack as possible, the city manager tries to protect the general fund. This fund is his, subject to his ability to convince the city council. Therefore, he is constantly looking for ways to charge special funds for costs that are currently being incurred under the general fund or to move items from the general fund to special funds.

The Problem: Revenue and Expenditure Conflict

For the city manager and his finance staff, as we have pointed out, the purpose of budgeting is not to allocate resources but to meet the revenue constraint. Indeed, the link of revenue to budgetary behavior is obscured if one sees budgeting only as a resource-allocation device. For the most part, Oakland's resources were allocated years ago when the present governmental structure was established. Previous decisions determine present allocations. The decision to have a manager-council form of government, the decision to have a free library, and the decision on the fire insurance rating of the city all were made by other participants, but they govern today's actions. If one allows for slight increases in the cost of Oakland's employees and expenses, then last year's budget is this year's budget. Although participants will argue for marginal increases, no one expects there to be enough money for a dramatic change in any particular budget. The acceptance of the "no-money" premise by most participants reinforces Oakland's incremental budgetary behavior.

The city charter forces Oakland to balance its budget. Custom dictates that money be on hand to pay all bills. Every year the city manager, his finance director, and the budget officer face the problem of cutting the budget to match the city's revenue constraint; the total amount requested is usually about 10 percent more than estimated revenues. Cutting is an intrinsic part of any budget process; what is unique to smaller governments such as Oakland is that the people who do the cutting are the city's revenue maximizers. Cutting the budget is a form of revenue behavior.

When one examines the influence of revenue on the budgetary process, the city bureaucracy appears to be dichotomized into budget-spenders (the departments) and budget-cutters (the manager and his finance staff). The latent conflict between these two sets of officials is related to functional differences: throughout the budgetary process the revenue- or resource-maintenance function of the cutters conflicts with the service-performance function of the spending departments. This conflict is particularly evident when one examines the guidance part of the process. In the fall, the Budget and Finance Department issues instructions to departments for budget preparation. One of these instructions is the manager's guidance letter, which states his assessment of the city's probable fiscal condition for the upcoming budget year. How do budget-spenders respond to the guidance of the budget-cutters? They completely ignore it, since for them the manager's letter contains nonoperational guidance. Because everybody knows there is no money, the letter expresses nothing new. A city official complains that for 20 years he has listened to the same old story from a variety of managers and budget officers: there is not enough money and the budget must be cut. City officials have cried wolf too often.

An examination of guidance letters since 1957 reveals two themes. The first states that the city has financial problems, but that the answer is to work together to cut costs and be efficient. This "efficiency" theme appeals to the conscience of the department head to give the taxpayer the most for his money. If departments can be efficient, then the city can avoid revenue increases. The second theme is more dismal; it stresses the revenue-expenditure gap. It states the no-money premise and emphasizes that services cannot be expanded. The cutters expect departments to submit expenditure requests similar to current funding levels. Taken together the two themes state: (1) you must be efficient because (2) there is no money. In Oakland, it is not a question of pulling in the belt one year and then next year things will be better. Department heads soon get cynical and adopt the stance that they have nothing to lose by asking.

In a situation of continuous fiscal deprivation, to be told to cut costs and not ask for more has no significance. Furthermore, this guidance is ambiguous:

> *Fiscal Year 1968/69.* As you begin the preparation of your departmental budget request, I would ask that you bear in mind that the City of Oakland continues to face a difficult and debilitating financial problem. The economic condition of the community is such that we as professional administrators must be constantly aware of the fiscal limitations within which we must function.

The department head who got this instruction from his manager can say, "I am aware, but so what?" Without specific instructions, department heads are free to interpret the guidance according to their own spending inclinations. Oakland does not make use of ceilings or acceptable percentage levels of deviation. Since cutters do not quantify the instruction to hold the line, spenders see the guidance more as a request than an order. Ambiguity provides room for maneuver.

The hope of getting additional funds is not the only explanation for the failure of most departments to follow guidance. The typical department head explains his response as: I am a professional; no one, not even the manager, can understand this job unless he sits here; I know our needs, and I would not be doing my job unless I expressed them. These department heads use the budgetary process for communication: it puts the problem where the money is. Often the department head is like a doctor ordering medicine for a miserly patient; his professional responsibility stops when he writes the prescription. Similarly, the city engineer states that a path needs a railing or someone might be hurt; the fire chief feels the level of protection is in jeopardy because the city should have a new pumper; and the recreation superintendent believes the golf course should be reseeded as the city is competing with other courses. Department heads feel they have done their jobs and relieve their anxiety merely by expressing their needs. Not only do they satisfy their own professional norms, but, by putting the monkey on the backs of the manager and council, they abate pressure from their employee and community constituents.

Since noncompliance is widespread, it is accepted as part of life and it carries no penalties. Departmental estimates are insulated from the city's revenue constraint and cease being fiscally realistic. Spenders ignore the revenue constraint and concentrate on their service-performance function. Budget-cutters also would like to ignore the revenue constraint, but they have no choice. They know that it is hard to get new revenue sources, so they must control the budget by cutting — an activity facilitated by the cutters' minimal service- and program-orientation. The revenue constraint thus creates two disjunctions in the budgetary process: (1) spenders ignore revenue limitations in formulating their programs, and (2) cutters ignore program and service considerations in balancing the budget.

Tools of Control: Budget Review
by the Budget and Finance Department

Most budgetary control is a matter of paring a department's request down to last year's base — getting rid of extra requests and refusing to make major reallocations of resources. Oakland's line-item budget facilitates cutting. One does not have to worry about the effects on service when cutting out small items.

Budget officers usually worry about their analysts becoming advocates for the department to which they are assigned, but this is not a problem in Oakland because the analysts do not stay long enough. The Budget and Finance Department is relatively small. Each analyst is assigned three or four departments and, given the workload during the rest of the year, it is unlikely that he will have time to learn much about any one of them. The few experienced analysts in the office have left for other jobs, and the considerable turnover has reinforced this problem of lack of experience.

The analyst does not have to reckon with the effect of his acts on service or on policy and can be quite ruthless in identifying issues on which the city manager must make "final" decisions. But the more experienced he becomes, the more knowledgeable he is about the effect of cutting on his departments, and the more reluctant he will be to make rash suggestions.

The very fact of revenue constraint makes it easier to cut. One does not have to be convinced to chop out certain items when there is no choice. Amounts requested by departments for expenditure are not realistic in the face of revenue constraints and must therefore be reduced.

How does an inexperienced budget analyst (who knows little about the department he is reviewing) cut that department's budget? Inexperience itself forces the use of certain rules of thumb common among people engaged at all levels in budgeting. The budget analyst looks at last year's appropriation to see if there has been any marked change. If not, he approves the item; if so, he is likely to reject it. Personnel needs make up the main costs of the budget. Normally, departments will come in with yearly requests that total over a hundred additional people. Given the belief that for every person added, a fixed permanent cost is incurred (because once somebody is hired he cannot be fired), the standing rule is to kill requests for additional personnel.

Expensive capital items requested will probably be cut out. A lot depends on who is doing the submitting. If a department head has a good reputation with the budget office, there will be a tendency to investigate further. On the other hand, if the department head has a reputation of always submitting certain items and never getting them, these items are automatically cut out.

Up to this point procedures are standard. The following list of observed criteria may be used by a budget analyst in reviewing a department.[10]

1. Compare request with actual spending — adherence to base.
2. Allow 3 percent for inflation.
3. A capital outlay item is not urgently needed. It would be better to delay a decision on expenditure until more study can be done.
4. There was an arithmetic error in the budget request.
5. A facility is being used more and so should get more money.
6. Recommend repair rather than replacement, unless replacement is obviously preferable.
7. Don't put money into something when you are uncertain about its future.
8. The expenditure would produce income.
9. Cut out department contingency reserves.
10. High cost, but low returns. A facility cost the city $33,000 and netted $300 revenue. Therefore, the city should consider disposing of the property.
11. Compliance with respected advice — estimation of needs by an administrator.
12. We were hard on them in this last category last year. Allow a little increase.

The analyst approves estimates the same as last year's and allows 2–3 percent for cost of living. He cuts out personnel increases and most capital items. But there are always a few borderline items.

The budget analysts generally will look to see if it is possible to trade off machines for people because of the high personnel costs in the city, but this type of review usually results in a deferral of the requests for personnel or equipment because of the need for "further study." He tries to postpone any cost that can be deferred. Equipment and buildings are repaired rather than replaced. No thought is given to the increase in maintenance costs as far as trade-offs could be concerned. The only rule that tends to interfere with the deferral policy is one that depends on the analyst's notion of safety or health. When a basement in the fire department needed shoring up because

---

[10] Observation criteria compiled by Ken Platt, graduate student in public administration, Department of Political Science, University of California, Berkeley.

heavy fire trucks driving over the basement ceiling caused the foundation to shake, the analyst went to the scene, observed the shaking, and decided that this was indeed a health and safety hazard. On the other hand, when a department requested that new restrooms be built in the park, the analyst examined the old ones and decided that they could be renovated.

Because of their inexperience, budget analysts tend to cut from the bottom of a departmental priority listing. Department heads anticipate this and often will rearrange things so that important items appear near the bottom. Through this device, they hope to confound the inexperienced analyst and thus influence him toward making no cuts at all. More experienced analysts are naturally suspicious about such rankings. This is particularly true of the city manager, who does not use the submitted lists but rather looks at the items themselves and determines what he thinks the priority should be.

The more experienced analyst (defined operationally as a person who has been in the job for more than two years) develops a conception of his role. One analyst expresses his role as that of "a voice in the court," a buffer between the department and the manager. He feels that his relations depend very much on establishing confidence with the department. Another analyst feels that his actions are mainly attempts to bring realism into the budget process, to give the department some idea of what the traffic will bear. The less experienced analysts, however, do not have a well defined conception of their role, and they operate primarily on the basis of the following decision rules.

1. Cut all increases in personnel.
2. Cut all equipment items that appear to be luxuries.
3. Use precedent; cut items that have been cut before.
4. Recommend repairing and renovation rather than replacing of facilities.
5. Recommend study as a means of deferring major costs.
6. Cut all nonitem operating costs by a fixed percentage (such as 10 percent.
7. Do not cut when safety or health of staff or public is obviously involved.
8. Cut departments with "bad" reputations.
9. Identify dubious items for the manager's action.
10. When in doubt, ask another analyst what to do.

When the budget analyst cuts out an item, it does not necessarily mean that it is forever barred from consideration. Cutting, at this level, is merely identification of a decision that has to be made by some higher authority. Oakland's budgetary process contains numerous levels of review and appeal. In theory, if a department head had a point of disagreement with an analyst, he could appeal to the budget officer, then to the finance director, the manager, and the council. With so many levels of appeal, one might expect that if a department head were persistent enough he should be able to eke out a slightly more favorable compromise at each level. The result would be that the analyst's original recommendations might bear little resemblance to the final outcome. But this does not happen. An important thing to understand about the process of appeals is that there is a strong built-in bias dictating that superiors will hesitate to overrule decisions of their subordinates. They know the review procedure would be undermined if decisions at lower echelons were not respected most of the time; the system would be swamped by appeals. The finance director and manager still reserve the right to make further cuts and, now and then, to restore part of the requests. The outcome is that a great many of the analysts' decisions prove to be final, but departments cannot be certain that an appeal is hopeless.

Tools of Control:
Budget Review by the City Manager

During our research in Oakland, we were fortunate to be working in a city in bureaucratic transition as a result of the recent appointment of a new city manager. One would think that in an old city like Oakland rules would be well defined, role expectations would be fixed, and the system of budgeting behavior would be established. Considerable evidence, however, indicates that the locus of budget decision shifts with the occupant of the city manager role.

In a movement toward reform, Oakland installed the city manager type of government in 1931. At the same time it voted a charter, which establishes independent boards, an independent auditor, and generally creates an environment of fragmented government. With a mayor who enjoys little formal authority, the city manager is relatively free to define his own role. Under the former administration, the budget was mainly handled by the finance director. He was Mr. Budget. He presented the budget to the city council; he was the one who negotiated with departments, and a great many decisions were made at his level. When the former manager's budget was presented to the council, his formal recommendations often were overturned. The council was a source of appeal by commissions and departments, and it did make changes in budgets. The new city manager, however, works quite closely with the budget subcommittee of the council to develop support for his budget. By the time the budget is discussed by the full council, no actions are taken to countermand the manager's recommendations.

The new manager makes budgeting decisions in the context of his definition of the total job. Since he is trying to centralize administration in the city, he uses the budget to find out whether department heads are fulfilling programs about which they previously informed him. It provides him a great deal of information, not so much because of the direct form of its submission, but in its function as a stimulus to further inquiry into the status of various projects.

Another element of the control orientation is indicated by the manager's desire for almost complete secrecy with respect to budget actions. He does not want the budget analysts to tell departments what he is considering. In review sessions with department heads, he asks questions about their operations but does not tell them where he is going to cut. In this way, he makes sure that when he submits the budget to the council, it is indeed *his* budget.

The city manager does not rely on budget submissions alone. In addition, he asks budget analysts to prepare a set of ancillary data for council consideration, which includes detailed analyses of personnel requests, overtime, and travel. He has a simple three-stage process of examining the budget. First, he sees whether the revenue estimate is as pessimistic as his own expectations. Then he asks that those fixed costs about which he can do nothing (such as built-in pay raises, under a city formula) be subtracted from the budget. And finally, he gets down to looking, as he says, "at the nitty gritty details."

Although the manager claims he does not want to get involved in details, he continually does so because ability to use the budget for control lies in small things. When submissions reach him, issues for decision have already been identified. The original budget submitted by the department is there, however, and he will often thumb through page by page to pick up a particular item. His review does not involve any type of meat-axe cutting — no 10 percent here or 5 percent there. It is strictly a line-item deletion governed by his own set of preferences.

No item is too small for the manager's attention. It is not true that he pays attention just to the lumpy or big dollar items. An item must be significant for him because it requires some kind of action, but amounts are only one index of saliency. For example, the city manager made considerable effort to reduce the mayor-council appropriation in order to cut down the expenditures for business cards and some minor operating costs. He did this not primarily because of the money involved but to symbolize the need for economy.

His general rule is to be less generous to a department which has gotten more than the other departments the previous year. Once, the budget analyst had cut back a submitted budget request to the previous year's level. When it got to the manager he felt that the total budget had not been cut back enough, because he remembered that the department in the previous year had won a much greater share than usual of available resources.

An ancillary decision rule followed by the manager is that he should not give resources to departments that have had insufficient time to absorb what they have already been allocated. It is the manager's prerogative to determine how much a department actually can use. An incremental approach to budgeting usually is described by a short time perspective and, essentially, as a maintenance of the basic budget. But holding the line does not always mean keeping expenditures at the same level as last year, especially when that level may have been high.

No doubt the manager's review shows a greater concern with program than the somewhat blind cutting of Budget and Finance. But because of the lack of information, the time constraint, and the volume of minor cuts, it is not usually possible to trace the effect of a particular cut on a department's output. The manager does not like to perceive the budget job merely as cutting. Because he wants to be able to reallocate but often feels that he does not have sufficient information, he continually emphasizes the need for detailed study of department operations. However, lack of skilled staff usually prevents carrying out such studies. Hence, most of the manager's activity is involved simply in cutting with insufficient information on program implications.

Because the city manager is only one man, a great deal slips by in the budget review process. In no sense can we say that the basic budget is intensively reviewed. But many items within the basic budget and incremental to it are reviewed if they are given sufficient visibility. The budget officer can spot certain issues for decision; dollar amounts focus others. But a more important source of visibility is the manager's own experience in operating city government. His expectations about what things ought to cost or what departments ought to do show up when he is looking at the budget. Similarly, his preferences about what is a reasonable program are revealed. When he was reviewing the police department budget, for instance, his predispositions about civil defense resulted in a reduction of uniformed personnel for that activity. The language of social psychology — selective perception, provision of cues — seems to describe the kind of decision process operating during the city manager review.

In his desire to gain control, the city manager has insisted that departmental requests do not show in his submission to the council. He wants the budget to appear to be his own and not to create any cause for controversy by showing the requests of the departments. For the city manager, the budget's form is almost as important as its substance.

Much of his activity goes into preparing the budget for presentation to the city council, especially to its budget subcommittee. The manager operates essentially as a gatekeeper for fiscal policy issues with respect to this subcommittee, describing what he considers to be key issues. Meetings with the subcommittee have certain mutual advantages to both participants. The city manager feels out what the council might accept, and at the same time the council is more confident that the manager is taking care of running the city efficiently, so that they do not have to worry about it. If the budget subcommittee goes along with the manager, they operate as a fairly strong lever with the council.

The manager knows that councilmen do not have time to pay attention to the whole budget, that they have "pet projects," and that he must pay attention to these. He learned in his previous assignment that, as a former councilman told him, "You've got to give the man a bone to play with, and then the rest of it goes by without review." Thus the manager simply recommends a total for such activity and allows the budget subcommittee to allocate within this total.

Councilmen generally do not want to reduce the number of city employees and, in order to counteract this reluctance, the manager goes to some length to prepare an analysis showing that a majority of the city employees do not live in the city and therefore are not voters! Another device that he uses with the council budget subcommittee is to make comparisons with other cities, such as San Diego, Sacramento, or San Jose, to show Oakland is in bad shape, either in terms of a low level of service or a high level of cost.

We can now understand that, although the city manager may claim that he should not spend much time on budgeting because there are no extra resources to distribute, he actually spends a great deal of time. He is the key figure in making most decisions. After the budget and finance people review submissions from departments and focus on some issues for decision, the city manager reviews all the budgets and, for the most part, makes the decisions. He guides the city council in its consideration; he feels that it is his budget; and he uses it to make his influence felt throughout city government.

ARE OTHER CITIES LIKE OAKLAND?

The four most important characteristics of budgeting in Oakland are revenue behavior, executive dominance, council acquiescence, and utopian departmental requests. Revenue behavior results from financial constraints — the balanced budget requirement, paucity of revenues, and uncontrollable nature of the expenditures. The executive is dominant since he is responsible for balancing the budget and since he alone has the staff aids to carry out his duties. Similarly, the structure of the city council explains its acquiescent behavior. Councilmen work part-time and lack staff aids and budgetary expertise. Elected at large in nonpartisan elections, they have no distinct constituency or political support. Confronted by a highly complex budget, they can only endorse the executive's proposals. Finally, departments advance uptopian requests since they know that regardless how much they ask for they will get only as much as is available, at best a slight increase over last year's budget. This is the only significant difference between Oakland and Crecine's three cities. Crecine found that departments in Pittsburgh, Cleveland, and Detroit follow the mayor's instruction in preparing their budget.

Similarity in the other three characteristics is overwhelming. Budgeting is revenue constrained as it is in Oakland. Mayors in the three cities are the unchallenged protagonists of the budgetary process. They make most of the important decisions and their word is final; neither departments nor councils challenge them.

Can we assert that such features characterize municipal budgeting, or are Pittsburgh, Detroit, Cleveland, and Oakland unique? No, they are not unique. To support this contention, we must compare the Oakland model with literature on municipal budgeting. Unfortunately, this literature is rich on the normative and aggregate statistical facets, but woefully poor on the descriptive side. We do not have enough detailed accounts of how cities budget, but the few that are available represent a broad range of city governments — metropolitan governments, medium- and small-size cities, manager-council and mayor-council cities, and assembly type governments. Despite this great diversity in size, geographical location, and form of government, budgetary behavior overwhelmingly is similar to the Oakland model.

Paucity of city revenues is universal. As Table 6.1 indicates, expenditures exceed revenues. Most, though not all, United States cities are in deficit.

The other financial constraints — the balanced budget requirement and the uncontrollable nature of expenditures — seem to be equally universal.[11] The result, as Anton describes it in his study of three cities in Illinois, is similar to conditions in the Oakland model.

> Revenue estimates form the theoretical upper limit of the expenditures which can be made in the next fiscal year. In each of the cities, agency heads are instructed by the manager, clerk, or finance committee chairman to base their spending requests on the estimated availability of revenue. Normally this means that agency heads are instructed to ask for no more than their current appropriation, since revenues to finance additional programs, or enlargement of existing programs are seldom, if ever, foreseen. Thus the first step in each of the cities is to determine how much money will be available, rather than how much will have to be spent. In effect, this forces local officials to think of their "budgets" as nothing more than a representation of "what we did last year" or "what we are now doing." [12]

Table 6.1. CITY EXPENDITURES ARE HIGHER THAN REVENUES
(dollar amounts in millions)

	1970–71	1969–70	1968–69	1967–68	1966–67
Revenues	37,367	32,704	29,673	26,521	24,096
Expenditures	39,061	34,173	30,451	27,007	24,375
Deficit	1,694	1,469	0,778	0,486	0,279

Source: U.S. Bureau of the Census, Governments Division, *City Government Finances, 1970–71* (Washington, D.C.: U.S. Government Printing Offices, 1971).

[11] Thomas J. Anton, *Budgeting in Three Illinois Cities* (Urbana: Institute of Government and Public Affairs, University of Illinois, 1964), p. 18.

[12] Ibid., p. 8.

The deviations that we can expect to find are in institutional characteristics and in allocation of formal powers. Executive dominance seems to be quite as common as financial constraints. Thomas W. Kressbach, in his study of 51 Michigan municipalities, notes that 80 percent of Michigan managers indicated that they have complete responsibility and concomitant authority with regard to budget matters.[13] A similar pattern is found in Lillian Ross' account of budget making in New York.[14] One of her dominant themes is the degree to which the mayor took personal responsibility for budgeting.

Though council acquiescence usually accompanies executive dominance, the literature shows some deviations. In his study of large council-manager cities in Iowa, Wright found that councils sometimes challenge the manager's proposals and conduct intensive probes into specific programs.[15] This mode of behavior was found where some of the variables which account for the Oakland City Council's acquiescence were absent. Remember, councilmen in Oakland are elected in nonpartisan elections. Since they do not represent nor benefit from the support of any specific population groups, they have little incentive to intervene in budget making. They serve their own interest best by helping the manager try to control expenditures so as to postpone imminent tax increases. If partisanship is introduced, however, things can be different. Councilmen may come under pressure from their constituencies and must assume a guardianship or advocacy role depending on the manager's initiative. Wright claims that "partisanship affects municipal budgets. . . . The more partisan the environment, the greater the tendency to probe the manager's proposals and perhaps raise policy questions." [16] With parties come, however vaguely, party programs and party promises. With partisan elections, awareness of party affiliations, and party endorsement of council candidates, the manager's discretion over the budget is restricted. The council tends to be more probing in its review of budget proposals. It holds hearings in which department heads provide testimony and it demands that the manager's budget proposal include the original departmental request.

Anton describes in some detail what is likely to happen when the chief executive's power of control is diminished and the council assumes a more active role. Powerful departments get their way; the weaker are pushed aside. He describes a police department which managed to get an increase when no other department did, by mobilizing public opinion and exerting pressure on a number of city aldermen. The police department got the increase, not be-

[13] Thomas J. Kressbach, *The Michigan City Manager in Budgetary Proceedings* (Ann Arbor: The Michigan Municipal League, 1962), p. 4.

[14] Lillian Ross, "$1,031,961,754.73," *The New Yorker,* 28 (July 12, 1947), 27–36.

[15] Deil S. Wright, "The Dynamics of Budgeting — Large Council Manager Cities," unpublished draft (Department of Political Science, Institute for Research in Social Science, University of North Carolina, 1969).

[16] Ibid., p. 25.

cause it needed the money more desperately than the other departments, but because of its strategic position in the community. In Anton's words,

> What is most significant here is the demonstration that in the absence of detailed information on the part of the council and in the absence of strong central control over the various departments, each department is relatively free to seek improvement in its financial position by putting pressure on the council. Clearly, in such a system, the advantage lies with the strong.[17]

Another way to put this is that partisanship (and the political mobilization it engenders) matters in resource allocation. The relationships found in Oakland are neither accidental nor arbitrary. City councils are fifth wheels because they are not equipped to be anything else. In Crecine's view, councils are acquiescent

> because of the complexity and detail in the mayor's budget and the lack of council staff.... The requirement of a balanced budget means that a change in one expenditure category, for instance, implies a change in other categories and for other administrative units or a change on the reverse side of the bill — i.e., one change in the budget (by council) implies many changes which the council has neither time nor staff to consider.[18]

With few exceptions, councilmen are part-time legislators. High turnover and a limited division of labor prevent most of them from acquiring the expertise required for finding one's way through the budget maze. Under these conditions it is difficult for them to challenge the mayor's recommendations, much less to make the critical decision themselves.

Though cities vary in size, form of government, and socioeconomic conditions they all share a number of constraints which homogenize budgetary behavior. The balanced budget requirement, the short supply of money in relation to rapidly increasing demands for spending, and the equally universal weakness of city councils produce similar budgetary procedures. With minor variations, most cities seem to budget the way Oakland does.

SUMMARY AND COMPARISON

The critical feature of city budgeting is that the budget must be balanced. This means that revenue controls expenditure. Since state governments control the taxes available to cities, leaving them with inelastic sources, cities find it difficult to raise revenue faster than the pace of inflation. Relying essentially on a property tax, whose income changes slowly and whose incidence is highly visible to homeowners, cities encounter heavy political liabilities by raising the rate. Few strategic choices are available to municipal

---

[17] Anton, *Budgeting in Three Illinois Cities*, p. 17.
[18] Crecine, *Governmental Problem Solving*, p. 39.

officials because spending always leans right up against the politically feasible or constitutionally permissible rate of taxation. Little attention goes to alternative allocation of resources because there are so few resources to allocate. Unless a city can afford a very large capital budget (and New York City must be considered exceptional because of its extraordinary size) budgetary activity serves largely to control bureaucratic behavior or to facilitate tax policy. Rather than using the budget process for purposes of steering, that is, to determine new directions for city operations, budgeting becomes largely a maintenance activity. Its essential purpose is to keep expenditures within legal limits by assuring that administrators carry out past policies within acceptable boundaries.

A tight revenue constraint, typical of city budgeting, would have profound effects at the federal level. To use the language of game theory, budgeting would have been converted from a variable-sum game, the way it is now in the federal government, to a constant-sum game, the way it is played in American cities. A significant increase for one city agency has a markedly unfavorable effect on the likelihood of increases for other agencies because the size of the budget pie is fixed. When expanded revenues do become available, increases are likely to be made across the board. If this were not the expectation of agency heads, the mayor, and the council, the budgetary process on the municipal level might well degenerate to a war of all against all.

At the federal level, however, revenue constraints are not nearly as stringent. An increase for one department or set of programs does not foreclose the possibility of increases in other departments. Instead of having to exhaust a narrow tax base, national spending comes from variable and elastic revenues. No departments, except occasionally the very largest, need feel that their advantage is automatically someone else's disadvantage.

At the same time, the national budget is larger than any city budget by several orders of magnitude. Increments mean less because they amount to less than at the municipal level.

Another major difference between city and national budgeting, one that goes far toward explaining the variance between the two levels in terms of overt political actions, is that the federal budget, at its level, is all-encompassing. Depending on how one treats trust funds, all expenses made by the federal government are included. This is not true in city budgeting, even assuming a separate capital budget. The Board of Education, Housing Authority, Redevelopment Agency, the Office of Economic Opportunity, Model Cities, and various county services have expenditures that are not directly under the control of the city and do not appear in the municipal budget. Not only do a sizeable proportion of city resources come from funds under the control of outsiders, but often they must surpass city budgets. Yet it is these so-called outside activities which are usually the controversial ones and where much of the political argument is concentrated. It makes some sense, therefore, to look on the city budget as an operating budget made up of expenditures which are given from year to year, which change little, but which are necessary to keep the government operating. This kind of budget is perfect for routine decision-making and makes the complex play of interests in the federal budgetary process superfluous.

These considerations result also in a difference in the outputs produced by city and national financial resource allocation. A considerable part of national spending involves income redistribution — welfare, medical care for the aged, etc. — but city governments are largely service-oriented — police, fire, water, garbage collection, and so on. One consequence of this division of labor is that a higher percentage of the city budget is fixed by a combination of uncuttable salaries and essential services. Eighty percent or more of municipal expenditures may be in salaries. Although one might say in regard to both levels of government that a high proportion is not within anyone's control, the percentage would be something like 95 for cities and 80 for federal government. Confronted with many departmental requirements, limited revenue, and the need to balance the budget, the fundamental job of the mayor or the city manager is not to think about how to allocate resources effectively among competing uses but how to meet the next payroll so that he does not unbalance the budget. Put another way, budget behavior in the federal government is demand-centered, whereas local governments are supply-oriented. Since the federal government's elastic source of revenue allows deficit spending, demand may exceed supply to a considerable degree. And it is difficult to justify cutting any one budget request on the basis of a limited supply of revenue. Just the opposite is true at the local level; most estimates have to be cut because supply dominates demand.

Congress has the power to create and manipulate public debt; thus federal revenue and expenditure can vary independently of each other, but they must go together at the municipal level — making last year's city budget a far more important determinant for next year's. Because revenue supply is relatively fixed at the local level, creating stable financial environments, the dominant actors are those persons responsible for a balanced budget. This dominance supports a fairly rigid hierarchical decision framework in which the executive predominates.

Consider the subordinate position of city councils. One of the most significant differences between city and national budgeting concerns the structural locus of the "guardianship" function. At the national level, both the OMB and the Appropriations Committee of the House cut and alter budget requests by agencies. In both of these bodies political factors play an important role in the reshaping of agency budgeting; the OMB tries to color the budget according to the president's preferences and priorities, while the House makes sure that interests of certain clientele groups and constituencies are not ignored. City councils, however, do not and cannot attempt to scrutinize budget requests in such a manner as to let them actively reshape the budget. At best, they serve as appeals courts much as does the Senate. Why?

In cities the legislative body usually is a council of part-time members who receive little or no remuneration, have no staff, and are frequently chosen in nonpartisan elections. The city councilmen therefore are at the mercy of the chief executive officer, be he mayor or city manager. Councilmen lack the time, the expertise, and the partisan political base to challenge the executive.

Compared to their federal counterparts, municipal executives have greater control over detailed expenditures by virtue of the smaller size of their jurisdictions, the routine nature of activity, and the lesser capacity for maneuvering available to potential competitors. But, though the executive may have a large degree of control over details, he has little power to direct the external forces that determine how far he can go. Levels of taxation and employee income, as well as demands on the city, are products of largely external forces beyond his control. In contrast, at the federal level, the presence of a larger budget, many more actors, and a strong legislature, make for greater fluidity in the total system. Whereas the federal executive may feel that he has a chance to do something but cannot control what goes on, the local executive wonders whether the control he exercises is actually worth having.

The distribution of city services is affected also by its subordinate position in the federal structure. In an attempt to circumvent a binding revenue constraint and expand the total resources available to agencies, for instance, cities often take part in projects, which present the possibility of sharing costs with other bodies, private or governmental, but which otherwise would not have such high priority. Officials may engage cities in programs for which little rationale exists other than that they provide a source of income. Where sharing of costs is involved, revenue constraints may translate into the norm of "those that have, get" since private developers and business groups are those most likely to be able to share costs. Urban outcomes, therefore, may be less the result of conscious choices by city officials than of their desperate need to maximize revenue wherever that may lead them.[19]

The relative poverty of cities has much to do with their apparent stability. Required to balance their budget, unable to raise revenues quickly, they may have many difficulties, but ability to determine where they are or are likely to be in the near future is not one of them. They know what expenditures and revenue have been and can expect they will be quite similar in the next year or two. When these expectations break down, when city costs rise drastically, and city revenues decline or fail to keep pace, then cities move to the category of the poor and uncertain, and begin to display forms of behavior characteristic of the so-called developing countries — nations that we classify as poor and uncertain.

---

[19] See Frank Levy, Arnold Meltsner, and Aaron Wildavsky, *Urban Outcomes* (Berkeley and Los Angeles: University of California Press, 1974), for specific examples.

To better understand the situation facing city governments, try to imagine that a constitutional amendment has been adopted forcing Congress to pass a balanced budget. Imagine also that the United Nations received and spent the revenue from income taxes and that the United States government could tax only property and sales. Imagine, finally, an economy move that would eliminate congressional salaries and staff. The federal government — in such an unlikely situation — would be in much the same straitened condition as are city governments. So would other governments in rich countries. And if we took away not only their wealth but also their predictability, they would budget like the low-income countries.

7

The Poor and the Uncertain: Budgeting in the Low-Income Countries

Scarce resources and pressing needs would seem to make budgeting a most apposite concept. As we have seen, budgeting aims at economy and the best use of resources. It plans ahead so that funds are available to fulfill needs as these arise. Budgeting provides an accounting for past expenditures and revenues, controls current spending and revenues, and forecasts those of the future. It helps determine the effectiveness of expenditures, and allocates resources accordingly. Through its budget, a government may understand its financial position, fix its best course of action, and implement public policy.

Good budgeting practices would therefore appear essential for the 60 or so countries whose major feature is lack of resources. These countries, containing almost three-quarters of the world's population, differ widely from one another — in geographical and population size, in ethnic homogeneity, cultural type, and national cohesiveness. They differ also in political experience, kind of regime, and length of national history. They share in common the poverty which afflicts most of their inhabitants, and which permeates the life of their society. Much argument has gone on about how to express this poverty and how valid are the various scales for measuring it. For convenience, poor countries are defined here as those with per capita income of less than $900 a year. The defects of this standard, or any standard at all, have not passed unnoticed; but our concern is less with establishing exactitude and more with conveying a general picture of lack of resources relative to acute needs. In this context differ-

This chapter has been adapted from Naomi Caiden and Aaron Wildavsky, *Planning and Budgeting in Poor Countries* (New York: Wiley, 1973). Copyright © 1974 by John Wiley and Sons. Like the book on which it is based, the chapter does not cover the central command economies, so that the issue of private markets versus administered prices does not get in the way of appreciating problems of poverty.

ences of emphasis and detail separating poor countries are much less important than the striking similarity in their common patterns of dealing with the paucity of resources at their disposal.

Another feature delineating poor countries is their effort to become richer, a feature that has been responsible for the euphemistic (now becoming unfashionable) label of "developing." All poor countries are under pressure — internal or external — to develop. Many have elaborate development plans and planning organizations; most have accepted loans of one kind or another from international agencies. Not a few employ foreign experts and support dramatic projects designed to push them into an age of prosperity and modernity. One effect of the development effort is to underline the importance of budgeting; funds must be accounted for, spent on the purposes for which they were allocated, programed to avoid bottlenecks, and forecast to facilitate maximum use and distribution. The government's heavy role in the development effort only emphasizes the crucial need for good budgeting.

But before unhesitatingly prescribing the budgeting procedures of rich countries for poor ones it might be well to bear in mind the obstinate waywardness often displayed by institutions when transplanted from their native habitat. Their effectiveness all too often turns out to have depended upon specific features of the original environment, without which they fail to flourish, prove useless, or undergo unexpected transformation. It is valid to inquire whether, in rich countries, good budgeting is responsible for prosperity, or whether instead the converse is true. In other words, what conditions allow a rational model of budgeting (such as outlined at the beginning of this chapter) to fulfill its purpose?

It should be admitted at the outset that no budgeting system is likely to perform consistently to perfection. The "pure" model of budgeting, in which all is accounted for, controlled, and forecast (let alone the aim of ensuring maximum effectiveness for every unit of expenditure) probably exists only in the imagination. The reason is not hard to see. The ability to forecast future revenues and expenditures with accuracy depends on the future resembling the past. This does not mean assuming that the future will remain identical with the past or even the present, but that a stable relationship should exist between them. Government policies, for example, should not exhibit sudden changes, particularly in the middle of the financial year. Participants in the budget process should play their roles consistently so that they may be relied on to behave in a preconceived manner. Prices and wages should remain stable, or rise within previously known limits. Established procedures should continue to yield familiar results. The perfect budget depends on maintaining stable relationships, based on knowledge and trust.

These conditions have rarely if ever been met. Except in a period of total stagnation, we live in an uncertain world. Uncertainties stem from a variety of causes. It is often difficult even to find out exactly what has happened in the past year and to evaluate it or assess the value of information received (even if it is forthcoming). Often, knowledge of current processes is even more sketchy, so that a valid basis for prediction is by no means assured. Add to this the problems connected with costing future activities — in conditions where prices cannot be accurately estimated, and in new activities whose costs are unknown — and it seems clear that effective budgeting must find some way of compensating for the lack of omniscience.

This is in fact what happens in countries with effective budgeting processes. These countries enjoy enough surplus resources to allow for mistakes — under- and overestimating, and taking risks without disastrous consequences. This is the essence of being rich. Rich countries usually enjoy a surplus; they do not need to consume all they produce to live comfortably. Not only does this surplus enable them to maintain a high rate of investment; in the form of what might be called a "functional redundancy" it contributes to the smooth workings of society.

"Redundancy is said to exist," Landau writes in his seminal work, "whenever there is an excess or superfluity of anything." [1] It is most often used to express a negative judgment as if it were synonymous with "wasteful." The presence of overlap and duplication is often regarded as a sign of inefficiency; the existence of competing mechanisms for performing the same tasks may suggest that they could be performed at lower cost. But reliability, the probability that a given function will be performed, depends on a certain amount of redundancy. If there is only one existing mechanism, the first breakdown will result in failure to finish the job.

In terms of budgeting, the redundancy enjoyed by rich countries is crucial. Particularly during innovation — whether technical, policy, or organizational — redundancy compensates for uncertainty. In place of economy and rationalization, the budget system incorporates duplication, competition, and back-up systems. Instead of attempting comprehensiveness and maximum accountability, it relies on spot checks, continuous feedback, and trust. It stresses reliability instead of, and sometimes at the cost of, efficiency. The built-in feature of redundancy allows experimentation and failure on the way; the process does not have to be right the first time — indeed errors are expected. Risks are spread so that should one line of policy turn out to be wrong, not only is the financial loss within acceptable limits but other alternatives have not been sacrificed in the process. [2]

It might be fair then to summarize prevailing budgetary strategies in rich countries as resting on two principles. In stable areas with adequate administrative resources, the rational budgeting model may predominate, even if it is

[1] See Martin Landau, "Redundancy, Rationality and the Problem of Overlap and Duplication," *Public Administration Review,* 29 (July/August 1969), 346.

[2] The best example of the "redundancy model" of budgeting is to be found in Harvey M. Sapolsky, *The Polaris System Development; Bureaucratic and Pragmatic Success in Government* (Cambridge: Harvard University Press, 1972), Chapter 3, where it is explicitly compared with the "rational model" in the form of PPBS.

not perfect. In areas of uncertainty, particularly those of continuous innovation, elements of redundancy are called into play to offset lack of knowledge, complexity, unknown costs, and unforeseen events. The ability to do this calls for resources — and not merely financial resources — over and above the exact amount which turn out to have been needed for the purpose. Now we have to ask what kind of budgeting will come out of a situation fraught with grave and multiple uncertainties where such redundancy is not available to compensate for them (i.e., in poor countries). Before we look at budgeting patterns in these countries, the major topic of this chapter, let us first see in what sense they suffer from uncertainty.

UNCERTAINTY IN POOR COUNTRIES

First, uncertainty is a greater problem for decision-makers in poor countries because uncertainty matters more there. A rich country — with its greater capacity to absorb and overcome uncertainties — can afford to live with them far better than a poor one. It is costly to maintain reserves, but it costs far more to be without them. Expensive expedients may have to be adopted when essential services are disrupted. Maintenance long deferred is often the most expensive kind. When funds run out it may be necessary to borrow at high rates of interest or do without.

Second, poor countries are more likely to face an intersection of uncertainties than are rich nations. A combination of uncertainties vastly multiplies difficulties, for each makes the other more difficult to calculate. Because no participant can figure out where he is or what to do next, he exacerbates the decisional problems of those who must adjust their actions to his. Instead of each level in the governmental organization absorbing uncertainty for the others, its own uncertainties pour out to engulf them.

Third, uncertainties are more intense among poor nations. In designing and carrying out projects, for example, it is often hard to know whether they will add to or detract from national income. Information about the economy may be inadequate and prices may be badly skewed so that they do not reflect the factors of production that go into them. Trained people to conduct project analysis are scarce. Funds may be cut off at any time in view of precarious financial situations. Capable construction teams are rare, and delays result from slow communications and even slower administrative action. In the meantime, original calculations are thrown off because the constellation of prices affecting the project has changed. When construction is finished, good management is likely to be scarce, sales personnel and cost accountants even scarcer. Moreover, the predicted markets may collapse because internal demand has been overestimated and international relationships beyond anyone's control have changed significantly. At each hurdle, the uncertainties and the total effects on the projects are more extreme in poor countries.

This all presses hard on budgeters in poor countries. In assessing revenues and spending (the uncertainties with which we are most concerned) they face not merely the uncertainties of the future but also those of the past. Often they don't know where they stand with respect to the basic features of national financial life; their estimates of income may be way off, their estimates of expenditure even more inaccurate. It may take two years or more before they know (within a reasonable margin of error) even how much their government has spent. They have no firm base from which to predict changes in the amount of funds available for public purposes. Fluctuations in external trade, foreign aid, and foreign currency reserves make it hazardous to predict revenues even over a short period.

A major uncertainty lies in the value of money. Inflation wreaks havoc with budgetary calculations. No one can tell at the beginning of the year how much the funds authorized will be worth during the rest of the year. This means that promises made in the budget may not be kept. Or, there may be no real budget at all. Before President Suharto enforced a balanced budget in Indonesia, a participant told us,

> it used to be that budgets were not completed until the end of the year to which they applied — nobody knew how much money was being spent and it did not much matter, the way inflation was going. Inflation actually made it impossible for us to work out any kind of budget that would be meaningful in advance. If we budgeted for a new school at the beginning of the year, by the end of the year the value of the money would be such that we could not even build a toilet. This was a tremendous disincentive to anybody working on the budget and many units wound up not submitting one at all.

Nor are government policies fixed in advance and strictly adhered to. Even in peacetime the military maintains constant pressure for funds which in time of internal disorder or apparent external threat may become irresistible. The governmental response to these demands or other political exigencies — strikes, elections, vocal pressure groups, foreign commercial interests — will depend on its current feelings of security. Inability to withstand pressure in almost any area makes its actions unpredictable.

Lack of resources both causes this situation and makes it hard to deal with. The time lags and information deficiencies which plague budgeters in all countries are acute in poor nations. Their leaders need up-to-date information on which to base decisions. But the delay involved in the process of preparing and approving estimates of proposed expenditures prevents them getting it. Preparation begins a year or eighteen months in advance; then the onerous task of approving all estimates takes a good six months. Thus, information in the budget for the coming year is at least one year (maybe two) old. This time lag matters less in stable countries where factors affecting budgetary decisions change more slowly. But in the fast-changing financial conditions of low-income countries, it can make a normal budgetary procedure impossible to follow.

Leaders are understandably reluctant to base decisions on old information, woefully incomplete even for its time. Yet the present is almost as murky to them as was the past; hence their pervasive tendency to delay acting until the last possible moment, which in turn increases uncertainty for the spending ministries.

Characteristic of this turbulent financial environment are the many changes that take place after the budget has been approved. Every government must work out some method of making supplementary appropriations and arranging transfers among categories of expenditure. No one can perfectly foresee spending patterns so as to obviate the necessity for changes during the year. Rich countries normally get by with relatively few changes, however, but poor ones face the necessity of constant alterations. The words of a Chilean official — "the budget is a series of patches" — echo a universal complaint.

Superimposed on governmental vulnerability and the uncertainties of the budget process is the development effort. Institutionally, it finds expression in the demands of planning authorities for resources, their efforts to create a long-term perspective in the programing of funds, and their pressures on government agencies to initiate projects with the assistance of foreign aid. In practice the effects of the development effort cannot be disentangled from current problems of governmental budgeting. Conceptually, however, it may be held that the impetus to develop adds a further dimension to the budgeting paradox in which the attempts to economize, and program resources, are sabotaged precisely by the same lack of funds.

In the face of acute uncertainties, while undertaking innovative activities, governments cannot rely on redundancy to compensate for budgetary inaccuracy. Participants in the budgetary process therefore adopt their own strategies to cope with the situation as each sees it. The emerging pattern might be called the "revolving constraint" model of budgeting, as participants pass on to others constraints they cannot handle. Let us now return to our previous question: What kind of budgeting will result from a situation fraught with grave and multiple uncertainties and without compensatory redundancy?

We may divide the constraints operating on participants in the budgetary process into revenue constraints and expenditure constraints. In practice these form parts of the same picture, but for purposes of analysis it is more convenient at this point to keep them distinct. All participants are concerned with the constraint on resources and make efforts either to enlarge it or to tailor expenditures to fit financial limits, but it is usually the Ministry of Finance of each country which is charged with worrying about where the money is to come from. To make its job easier, Finance adopts a variety of strategies, particularly conservative estimating procedures and repetitive budgeting (which we shall examine in the next section). By these means it attempts to pass on the revenue constraints to the spending agencies of government, which respond in their turn with strategies of their own — padding estimates, transferring funds, and finding their own sources of revenue, independent of Finance. These strategies reflect not only their own uncertainties — in not knowing how much they have or are spending or will need — but also those created by the behavior of the Ministry of Finance. The latter, in turn, is affected by departmental strategies, which cut down the revenues at its disposal and make harder its task of knowing what is really going on.

What we have broadly labeled the "development effort" complicates the picture even further. Here the major constraint and uncertainty is the size of the recurrent budget expenditures, such as teacher salaries, that come up every year and tend to swallow up any surplus money. Hence planners' attempts to capture a capital or development budget, which would help solve their own uncertainties — once again at the cost of the Ministry of Finance, which fights back for more funds with which to maneuver. An exacerbating factor is the uncertainty as to priorities, made worse by the number and instability of claimants — legislatures and their client pressures, foreign governments, political interests of the chief executive, parties that need to be held together, government employees who want benefits — mediated through governmental spending agencies.

Within this broad picture of conflicting and impinging interests, uniformities and consistent behavior emerge. Participants, in the light of previous experience, tend to learn how others will respond. Appraising this experience, the rater should realize that even if each participant, in trying to control its immediate environment, is acting rationally according to its own interests, the results of their interactions need not be socially rational.

Having witnessed the unfortunate consequences of risking too much, financial leaders in poor countries are likely to adopt strategies designed to make manageable the vast elements of uncertainty in their affairs. Finance ministries adopt drastic measures to make sure they will not run out of cash; operating departments seek special funds of their own; interests thwarted by the hit-and-run tactics of the finance ministry try to set up autonomous organizations with some independence from the government. Each participant is rational in his own terms, taking actions to help make its immediate environment more secure. It all adds up, however, to future financial problems for successive governments, because each party can increase its own security only by passing on uncertainties to someone else.

REVENUE CONSTRAINTS:
THE ROLE OF THE MINISTRY OF FINANCE

The great passion of Finance is to get and hang on to a surplus. This means that the finance minister must always be able to lay his hands on enough money to meet the most pressing needs as defined by his colleagues in the cabinet (or by whoever exercises political power). His job is to guard the treasury. Emblazoned on its doors, engraved on its innermost consciousness, the Ministry of Finance subscribes to this creed: That There Shall be Money on Hand to Pay the Bills. The task of Treasury is to have money available; if it runs out, Finance gets the blame. If money is left over, no one will say mismanagement has occurred. When faced with inexorable requirements to bring budgets closer into balance, therefore, finance ministries in poor countries try to estimate revenue low and expenditure high, thus increasing the likelihood of a surplus. Should the unexpected occur, their conservative estimating techniques protect these governments against running out of funds. Of various ways of hedging against uncertainty, the Ministry of Finance finds this practice the most certain, for Finance is directly in charge of taxation, but it must rely to some extent on spending ministries for estimates of spending (especially when accounting for previous years' figures is sure to be late and likely to be inaccurate). Although Finance does try to estimate expenditures on the high side, it is often overtaken by events beyond its control, and thus spending ends up underestimated, but hopefully by less than otherwise it would have been.

Low revenue estimates are likely to be cumulative, in the sense that each person making them feels a need to come in on the low side. In Argentina, a participant explained,

> The figures we use to estimate total revenues for the coming year are biased towards the conservative. It is not a question of our coming up with a figure that we feel is an accurate estimation of the total revenues in the year to come, and then watching the budget office cut that figure by some global amount to give them a margin of error. What we do is to take a conservative estimation in each series of calculations. If prices are estimated to go up by 10 percent, we work with a figure of 12 percent.

As the budget is gone over by successive officials, each more responsible for balancing it, or with the most discretion in using surplus funds, the tendency is to underestimate forthcoming revenue — a process reversing the famous one in which a general orders troops to be on parade at twelve o'clock and each officer in the chain of command hedges by about fifteen minutes, so that the corporal has the men lining up at nine o'clock in the morning.

No matter how hard nations try to be conservative in under-underestimating revenues, life may outwit them. Experience suggests that in a world full of surprises it is inadvisable to rely on just one precaution. Redundancy again! Too many things can happen, from discovering that a critical tax account was depleted eighteen months ago, to realizing that bills on a project included in the budget four years ago have accumulated and just now fall due for payment. At any moment the ground he thought firm will shift beneath the budgeter's feet, and he needs a technique for remaking decisions with the latest possible information.

REPETITIVE BUDGETING

Finance ministries in almost all low-income countries faced with extreme uncertainty have come to practice basically the same method: they give pro forma approval to budgetary estimates but then, when time comes to dispense funds, insist on detailed scrutiny of the actual right to spend. The twin mottoes are "delay" and "control." The longer Finance waits to make the actual decision, the better is its information on funds available and on government preferences. The more control it exercises at the last minute, the better it is able to appraise the desirability of expenditures in the light of the pressing circumstances of the moment.

According to formal statements of budgetary procedure, departments prepare careful estimates of needs and present them by a certain date to a central authority, which reviews their requests in the light of competing claims for limited funds, and finally arrives at a rational (or at least a fixed) distribution of resources issued in the form of a budget. This neat and tidy procedure is far from what actually happens in poor countries where in fact continuous expenditure control is practiced. An item appearing in the approved budget for a ministry does not ensure that money is available and may be spent; it is necessary first to get one or more detailed sanctions of expenditure from the Ministry of Finance.

The budget is not made once and for all when estimates are submitted and approved; rather, as the process of budgeting is repeated it is made and remade over the course of the year. We call this phenomenon *repetitive budgeting*. Instead of supplemental appropriations being relatively infrequent, as in the United States, the entire budget is treated as if each item were a supplemental, subject to renegotiation at the last minute. The budget is, in effect, being made all during the year. Repetitive budgeting is found in most poor countries. Its most extreme manifestation is as cash-flow budgeting where changes may be made from day to day or even from one hour to the next.

Poor nations, like many a beleaguered family, often lack funds for immediate purposes. Their ability to pay may be determined by the flow of income into the treasury, so they hold back on paying bills. To make sure the government has enough cash on hand to pay its most pressing bills, finance ministries adopt strong measures. They cut funds that are authorized or hold them back from agencies until late in the year; they postpone paying bills, or pay them piecemeal. Suppose a ministry owes a bill for the paper it uses. The company supplying the paper receives a voucher entitling it to payment from the treasury — if and when it can get the money. The mechanism for dispensing funds in Argentina works in a similar way to those of other countries that engage in cash-flow budgeting:

> We work with a payment plan every day. Every morning we receive
> word from the national bank of the financial condition of the country. The

accounts are current up to the closing of the books the previous day. This information tells us how much we can pay every day.

Our main problems occur in the beginning of the month, when we have to pay salaries. Salaries always receive top priority in our payment schedule. Many other bills have to be prorated, since we can't let one voucher exhaust our funds for the day.

We maintain a list of how much we owe to each organism, and to each private party. We determine how much we have to distribute, and give part of it to those creditors who come right here to Finance to collect. Downstairs they set limits on the maximum amount each party can collect, in order to try to spread it around. If a contractor needs money to pay his workers who are threatening to go on strike, we try to give him preference, so things don't run to a halt.

The evil results of repetitive budgeting have often been stressed and, for the spending agencies of government, it is a major source of uncertainties. But for a hard-pressed Ministry of Finance, the practice has considerable advantages. The delay that infuriates others lets Finance know whether it really has money at hand, whether political conditions have changed so that one department's projects should be preferred over another's, and whether important interests really want what they say they want. To force spending ministries to pile up one project after another, not only from the current year but also from previous years, makes them assess priorities as no simple pleas could. When Finance says there is a certain amount of money available and the spending department can have it if it can make up its mind, the Finance ministry can be reasonably certain it will get the top priority project. In the absence of repetitive budgeting and the consequent stacking of projects, Finance would be in danger of discovering that the highest priority projects at the time of funding were not the ones it had originally approved. For "priority" means not only an economist's idea of what will add to national income — a subject on which there can be endless debate — but also a political leader's specification of what is most important to him at the moment. And that moment is *the* moment, not some other moment in the past with a different set of priorities.

Reducing uncertainty at the level of the finance ministry is achieved at the price of vastly increasing it at the level of the spending departments. They never know what they have. In other words the Ministry of Finance deals with the uncertainties and constraints of revenue estimating by passing them on to others.

EXPENDITURE CONSTRAINTS: THE ROLE OF SPENDING AGENCIES

Revenue constraints are of course only one side of the picture. Money received by governments is there to be spent — wisely if possible, and preferably in a smooth and economical sequence, without bottlenecks and according to set priorities. To be avoided are excess spending in specific and possibly nonessential areas simply because there is cash on hand at that moment and buildup of unspent funds in one area while urgent needs are unmet somewhere else. But, in submitting estimates and trying to accomplish objectives during the financial year, departments face the uncertainties that have been passed on to them by the Ministry of Finance.

Foremost are the problems caused by repetitive budgeting. First, the whole process leads to inordinate delay. Vouchers may be held up for years. Those who supply the government soon learn to gear their work according to their paymaster. If it does not pay them to work on credit, they may simply wait for cash.

Second, this system of using vouchers may create a huge floating debt inside a country. After a time, no one may know how large it is or when it will be paid. And vouchers are handled at a discount, raising costs for the government as well as impugning its credit.

Third, the criteria for approving expenditure become more overtly political because Finance officials ask, in effect, "How badly does X ministry and its supporters want project Y?" In Burma, Walinsky informs us, the finance ministry would allow requests to gather dust because they reasoned "that if a proposed expenditure were really important, the department and the administrative ministry concerned would prod the finance ministry for action. If these agencies did not do so, the request remained part of an ever-growing pile of pending requests." [3]

Fourth, investments suffer because they can be postponed. When the problem of cash flow is acute, recurrent expenditures (including salaries) are given first claim on government revenue and capital projects get only what is left over. "The net effect of this," says a Philippine official, "is that an increasingly larger share of actual expenditures go into consumption rather than capital payments."

Fifth, instead of lobbying once for funds, departments maneuver continuously. If funds can be taken away for any number of reasons, departments must fight constantly to hang on to them.

Sixth, repetitive budgeting results in careless estimating by departments because no one takes the original budget seriously. Waterston points out that in Pakistan including a project in the budget provided no assurance that funds to carry it out would be made available by the finance ministry. "Consequently, operating bodies made little effort to submit accurate budget requirements when the budget was being prepared and generally made exaggerated demands for

[3] Louis J. Walinsky, *Economic Development in Burma, 1951–60* (New York: Twentieth Century Fund, 1962), p. 439.

funds. This led, in turn, to indiscriminate budget cutting by the finance ministry. . . ." [4]

If spending ministries submitted better estimates, the Ministry of Finance might be less inclined to cut them as a matter of course. But the nature of the budgetary process, including repetitive budgeting, discourages carefully prepared estimates. If Finance is skeptical about getting reasonable and well-argued estimates, spending ministries surely have no incentive to provide them. Their usual hasty compilations show only increased disrespect of the finance ministry. Since everyone knows the initial estimates don't mean much, no one is too concerned about them. Finance cuts and the struggle begins. Departments do not take long to figure out strategies to outwit predictable cuts. They ask for more than they expect to get so that after Finance makes its expected cut they will be closer to where they wish to be.

The ritualistic cycle of padding and cuts breaks down unless both sides play by the rules. Departments must try to estimate their possibilities of being cut. When departments normally request not just a little more than they expect but several times more, as was true in Korea for a long time, it's a sure sign they have lost influence over their budgets. For then the real allocations must be made at the top with little consideration for departmental requests.

The apparent opposite of padding — asking for much less than one needs — is also a favorite strategy. In America it is called "the camel's nose." By beginning small, a department hopes to get a project accepted so that when expenses (inevitably) rise the government will be committed to finishing what has been started. Emergency funds come in handy for a similar purpose. They can be used to begin projects outside the normal pattern of scrutiny by the finance ministry.

A key variable in obtaining departmental requests is the amount of available foreign exchange. Those who can get a piece of this action early enough are more likely to get a project started. It does not matter if costs are systematically underestimated because, once begun, the doctrine of sunk costs suggests that projects started are likely to be completed. Should foreign exchange have run out by that time, it matters little to the agency in question because the country is likely to go ahead with its own resources. The process we have just described is one way in which strategies used by individual departments cause low-income countries to become overcommitted in attempting to bolster their economies.

Each unit in the organizational hierarchy tries to keep a surplus for itself and to cut down the amount available to its competitors. Each participant tries to squeeze out the slack (resources in excess of those necessary for current

---

[4] Albert Waterston, *Planning in Pakistan; Organization and Implementation* (Baltimore: Johns Hopkins Press, 1963), p. 52.

operations) available to the unit over which it presumably exercises hierarchical authority, and to protect its own slack from units higher up. The interest of units down the line, therefore, is to use up their resources so fast they cannot be reclaimed by those above them. Department budget personnel report that they "fight with everybody in this secretariat, send them communiqués trying to get them to spend more." They spend in order to keep the money for themselves. Their urge to spend and spend and spend at the end of the fiscal year is due to the fact that they cannot carry over funds but will lose those not used. "When Finance found out that we were not taking advantage they took it away from us." This is the eternal voice of departmental experience.

Not only will the department lose money during the year the surplus is discovered, but the finance ministry will try to slash it back to that level the following year. The typical experience is reported from Argentina: "There is a representative of the Ministry of Finance keeping an eye on our ability to spend. You might call him a spy; I call him an agent from Interpol. He knew that we had extra money at our disposal because of an increase of rates put through last year. Accordingly, our new works program was not paid for by government grants as it should have been, but out of current revenues that are supposed to go to current expenses."

Faced with the difficulties of dealing with the Ministry of Finance, departments may try to create their own certainty by capturing sources of finance lying outside their control. This practice is extremely widespread in poor countries. The budget is not the only budget. Far from it. It may not even be the most important budget. In all countries there are special funds that do not show up in the national budget; in many poor countries they form an exceedingly large proportion of governmental resources.

Special funds exist to guarantee income to services because the treasury cannot do so, but their existence depletes the treasury still further. Thus there is a self-perpetuating, mutually reinforcing relationship between special funds and repetitive budgeting. The larger the proportion of national income which goes into special funds, the more Finance must worry about running out of funds. It is then less able to meet prior commitments, more likely to delay decisions and to reconsider the budget every month. The more difficult the finance ministry becomes about holding back or recapturing funds, the more inclined spending ministers are to look elsewhere for resources. Hence anywhere from 20 percent to 60 percent of a nation's revenue may not be under the direct control of its treasury.

The structure of autonomous agencies with their own resources merges into another activity with basically the same causes and effects. This is earmarking revenues so that they can be used only for specified purposes. These funds may belong to an autonomous agency or to a regular government department.

In attempting to compensate for uncertainties, departments have to find an alternative to the redundancy which they do not possess. Their strategies may gain some relief for them, but at a price. Uncertainties the Ministry of Finance has passed over to departments often are passed right back in a different form. For example, delay in payment often makes it hard for agencies to spend, by the end of the year, all funds eventually allocated. Unspent money may then be held as accounts payable to keep them from reverting to the central treasury. In the Philippines, as elsewhere, these obligations represent a reservoir of claims against the national government's cash assets outside the control of the budget commission. "Consequently," we were told, "fiscal policy as implemented in the budget releases may be defeated by expenditure decisions in the operating departments. From the point of view of financial management in the treasury, such a reservoir of claims presently constitutes a high degree of uncertainty in projections of the outflow of funds."

The problem of departments holding on to unspent balances is closely linked with that of underspending, the paradox of public finance in poor countries. Although they suffer from inadequate resources, departments often find difficulty in spending the funds allocated to them. An outside observer might see no problem; all the department has to do is spend the money on hand. But this is easier said than done. The department that spends most of its money early in the year will find itself desperate in an emergency situation. It must hold on to enough to deal with the unexpected. The plight of an Argentine department — "we don't know how much we have spent with any degree of accuracy" — is experienced by poor countries the world over.

A good half of the capital or development budget is spent on construction. With a few notable exceptions, poor countries have trouble getting the work done. Projects may be delayed because the weather is bad, because necessary materials have not arrived from abroad, because plans were improperly drawn, because contractors have difficulty getting paid, because skilled labor cannot be found, because of excessive paper work, and for a hundred other reasons. A report from one African country epitomizes the problem of delay:

> A serious problem for the ministry is a budget surplus at year end; this is not overestimating. Rather, it results from delays in construction work and subsequent delays in the release of capital funds. A warrant, or certificate, has to be signed by the section engineer in public works in order for a contractor to be paid for a certain portion of construction work completed. It is then sent to the planning unit in the ministry which, in turn, passes it on to the treasury to obtain fund release. Several sets of interrelated problems here account for unspent allocations. First, construction projects are delayed, most often because of a poor credit rating with foreign suppliers of imported construction materials. A second delay comes in the slowdown and backlog in the paper work between the contractor, public works, spending ministry, and finance. The long-term effect for the ministry budget is that estimates are swelled the next year by requests for money to do work which should have been done and paid for last year. This could jeopardize some new projects, as a general government policy at the moment is to give priority

to projects for which some money has already been spent. Another depressive factor is the slowness of cash releases for capital projects and the fact that only the Minister of Finance himself can authorize funds; if he is absent — for personal reasons or because of travel — no one is deputized to act in his behalf.

Poverty, therefore, means more than just not having money. Although it may seem odd at first, many poor countries not only lack enough money for investment, they also are unable to spend what they do have. (Notice that we do not say "spend wisely.") Questions of efficiency and productivity are relevant only if a government has proved that it actually can use funds it has allocated for certain purposes. If information on how much has been spent on each project during the year is nonexistent, it will be impossible to shift funds from those who cannot use them to those who can. If it takes a long time to get hold of funds already promised, projects will be delayed and expenditures not made. Underspending, idle money in the midst of poverty, is a major problem in low-income countries.

Similarly, the advantages of special funds in one area may be canceled out by their repercussions on the general scene. They aid government officials who do not have to consider the entire realm of funding but can concentrate on calculations of those funds that in a sense belong to them. It is probably true that useful expenditures, which never would have survived the ordinary budgetary process, get started by means of a special fund. Since no one is certain what the best investment policy is and there are extraordinary delays involved in the regular process of repetitive budgeting, it may well be that some action is better than none.

But these are short-term gains for a government. Spending from secret accounts and deficits from autonomous agencies may lead to unplanned national deficits. Foreign exchange reserves may be depleted and the country's credit standing impaired. It may be easier to concentrate on a limited sphere of activities in the short run, but it will be frustrating if this means very little can be achieved later on. Priorities set within the budget may amount to nothing if they can be undone by the use of funds outside central control. Arbitrary spending patterns are likely to develop because these funds pose the question not of desirable expenditure, but of who has the right to spend what is left in a specified account. Money may get spent just because it is in one pocket rather than another. But the usefulness of special funds to circumvent the usual bureaucratic routine depends on their being exceptions to the rule. The more often they are used, the greater their total impact, the more they cause financial stringency, the less useful they become.

The Ministry of Finance therefore may as the result of all these strategies find its area of certainty greatly diminished. It cannot rely on the information it receives from departments, as to the relative effectiveness of expenditures or even as to their pace. Their inability to program resources forces decisions back to the Ministry of Finance, whose own lack of information and knowledge may lead to enforced distortion of priorities. As a statement of income and outflow, the government budget in most low-income countries is woefully inadequate. It must compete with many other funds and budgets, all of which detract from the amounts available to the Ministry of Finance and which might enable it to employ some redundancy of its own.

Up to now we have paid no attention to the fact that poor countries are also developing countries. The development effort — in the shape of foreign loans, special projects, outside advisers and new demands — and its consequences — new spending power, new vested interests, expansion of the public sector, increased urbanization, pressure on food supplies, bottlenecks in transportation, and so on — create fresh uncertainties for both departments and financial authorities.

BUDGETING AND DEVELOPMENT

The preoccupation of planners and planning commissions with the budget is not hard to understand. A basic reason for the poverty of poor countries is that after current consumption they have very little money left over to invest for future return. Except in periods of revolutionary upheaval, most governmental expenditures necessarily are taken up with things done before. The best predictor of this year's spending is that of last year and the year before that. Essential services must go on. Past expenditures represent the outcomes of conflicts among contending interests, which are not likely to be set aside unless the government is willing to risk a continuously high level of conflict. The dead hand of the past controls much of what might otherwise be available to spend in the future. Recurrent spending overwhelms new investments.

Even when increased revenue becomes available, it often falls victim to the demands and priorities of prior decisions. Schools need teachers; hospitals need doctors and nurses. In a way, therefore, the task of allocating expenditure in poor countries has been made to appear more difficult than it really is. Why should the problem be so difficult when there is so little to spend? Unless there is a sudden windfall — such as a drastic increase in the price of commodities the nation produces or in foreign aid — there is unlikely to be a vast difference in the monies available from one year to the next. Taxes may be raised, but only slowly. Before worrying about what they might do with new investments, officials in poor countries would do better to watch over recurrent expenditures. If not, they will rise so quickly that they will rule out entirely any prospects for additional investment. Investments tend to increase future requirements for recurrent expenditures and thus to reduce amounts available for investment in the near future.

Fear of taking on too much recurrent expenditure explains why finance ministers are sometimes reluctant to authorize spending available funds for investments. This Chilean example could be repeated many times:

> A law may say, for example, that all factories producing pharmaceutical supplies or medicines must donate a portion of their sales to the construction of hospitals in two poorer municipalities. We know that these funds belong to the service, but we do not let it use them. Why? Because it is not convenient for us to do. If hospitals are built in these cities, then we will have to pay for the upkeep and personnel costs out of the regular budget.
> One hospital might cost 1,000,000 but the particular tax may provide only 20,000 each year. If we allowed the service to start building the hospital, we would have to bear the brunt not only of finishing the commenced work, but also the current expenses.

Planners, on the other hand, want to break the chains of the past. To do this they must rescue a portion of expenditures from the hungry and bottomless well of recurrent expenditures and direct it into capital-development projects which they hope will generate future income and prosperity.

Planners seldom have extended their ambitions to the whole budgeting function — concentrating instead on a more limited and practical perspective, public sector capital investment, which is often equated with the general development effort of a country. Calculations of economists focus on it; the public works it represents — projects such as roads, schools, airports — provide visible evidence of achievement; and it is the area most likely to receive foreign aid. Hypothetically, capital investment represents uncommitted funds, and thus is the object of fierce political battles as politicians, administrators, and various other interests vie to establish commitments within it. If they are to acquire any influence within the system, planners too must compete in the arena of capital expenditures.

As it happens, there is an admirable mechanism at hand for planners. Many poor countries have capital budgets. Identifying the capital budget with the investment portion of a nation's effort (namely, those expenditures defined as contributing most to the nation's economic growth) may easily turn it into the development budget. Here then is the portion of the nation's expenditure that belongs properly to planners, whose task is development. Whether the planning commission ends up with this bundle all to itself or whether it has to share with the finance ministry, planners have staked out their own claim to bridge the gap between plan and budget; the planning commission has gotten its own form of special funding, just like everyone else.

Capital budgeting (like Scandinavian double budgets[5] and the British dis-

[5] See Matti Leppo, "The Double Budget in the Scandinavian Countries," *Public Finance,* 5 (1950), 137–147.

tinction between expenditures above and below the line[6]) is a method for avoiding the appearance of deficit spending by giving the amount borrowed in any year a name that suggests it is an investment. Applied to the United States, for example, the ideological emphasis on the size of the deficit means that introducing a capital budget would permit substantially larger expenditures (apparently deficits) to be seen as formal surpluses. There have been many attempts to distinguish between capital assets with future returns, and ordinary expenditures which presumably do not have any, but the distinction lacks an economic rationale. Governments do not depreciate assets. Any distinction that remains soon breaks down when, under the pressure of avoiding tax increases, a nation borrows for items that appear to be quite ordinary (such as salaries of school teachers) by calling them capital expenditures.

It would be nice if the major claim made on behalf of capital budgeting were correct, namely, that it ensures that investments are not diverted to current expenditures, and safeguards such expenditure against periodic fluctuations in current revenue. Practice with capital budgeting suggests, however, that the opposite is true. Once the capital budget is established, you never know what is in it. What does matter is that often the capital budget is run by a separate agency, such as a planning commission, with ideas of its own on desirable public spending.

Capital budgets add to the problem of the disappearing budget by entrusting part of it to a separate organization. The confusion encountered thus far, however, is as nothing compared to that engendered by the further division between development and nondevelopmental expenditures. When development expenditures are equated (fully, partially, episodically) with capital expenditures the muddle is well nigh hopeless.

One Man's Development Is Another Man's Power

Development is a golden word. Everyone is for it, no one is against it. The development budget is the golden budget; everything in it is touched by the shimmering wand of the future. By definition everything in the development budget is of highest priority and the operating budget is of a much lower order of importance. It is as if one budget was identified with higher, more spiritual functions of mankind while the other was crudely identified with lower and more vulgar bodily functions; one is essential for life, but it exists for the other.

No one should believe, however, that the development budget defines what is most important. That would be reversing the order of causality. It would be more correct to say that those who are important determine what

---

[6] See Herbert Brittain, *The British Budgetary System* (New York: Macmillan Co., 1959).

should be included in the development budget. Since no one can say for certain just what does or does not contribute to development, anyone may make the claim for his own preferred expenditures over another's. Who are we to argue with those who say the army ought to be included in the development budget; or, that clerks in the planning office don't contribute more to the economic growth of their country than the poor teacher on a rural education program, who is consigned to the ordinary expenditures?

Doubts may be stilled by giving the disputed actions a beneficent label. If one is not certain whether specific actions will achieve a desired objective, or whether the objective one has in mind is in fact desirable, a proper label can quiet the doubts. The great question in budgeting is to know which expenditures are more desirable than the others. Since almost all national elites wish to develop in some sense, they can agree that development is desirable precisely because they agree neither on what it is nor on how to achieve it. Truly, a budget by any other name, a budget of retrogression or self-sacrifice, would not sound nearly so good.

The rationale behind creating a separate development budget is roughly similar to that for capital budgeting. Identifying capital with developmental expenditure, although not hard to understand, nevertheless misses the whole point. As Waterston put it, "capital expenditures may be non-developmental, and current expenditures may be developmental." [7] In a series of brilliant studies of planning and budgeting in Singapore, Ethiopia, Sudan, Ghana, Nigeria, and other poor countries, Waterston shows the reasons for his concern. Each of these countries insists on placing what he considers nondevelopmental items (parks, police stations, meteorological stations, museums, public buildings) in the development budget because they are large capital items. In the meantime, what Waterston considers to be developmental expenditures (for research and training, agriculture extension, education, and so on) are excluded from the developmental budget because they appear to be smaller by comparison or to involve expenditures for personnel. Since these distinctions are essentially judgmental and difficult to apply, more operational criteria are in fact used. It turns out that there is a tendency to equate developmental expenditures with large ones and ordinary expenditures with small ones. The development budget in the Sudan, for instance, includes any items expected to cost at least 5,000 units of currency regardless of purpose, except for the defense establishment, which had its own budget. (The ordinary budget simply included any item that cost less than 5,000.)

Two major institutions with claims on the budget immediately create problems of power; both cannot get their way. More for one means less for the

---

[7] Albert Waterston, *Practical Program of Planning for Ghana,* mimeographed (Washington, D.C.: International Bank for Reconstruction and Development, 1968), p. 7.

other. There may be talk about increasing the size of the pie in the future so that both regular and developmental expenditures can grow apace but at any one time there is only so much to go around. This last statement is incorrect, however, if it suggests that total expenditure is fixed independently of the desires of the participants. The major item of controversy is likely to be the size of the total budget, because that helps determine how much is available for investment.

The struggle to control the budget would be less severe if participants shared the same perspectives, but often they do not. Finance must make sure everything comes out to a hundred so that there will be no need for sharp increases in taxation or for the deficit financing which leads to unacceptable inflation. On the contrary, the role of the planning commission is to make everything add up to more than a hundred so there will be greater national income in the future. If that means taxes have to be raised or various groups will be deprived of customary benefits from government, others must deal with the consequences. The development budget not only takes away money from the current budget, but also creates substantial future recurrent expenditures. Investments deprive the finance ministry of resources not only in the present, but in the future. The reverse is true also; current spending eats up funds available for investment. The less invested now, the less will be available (in the form of increased national income) later. Balancing these competing claims is not easy. Profound differences in role and task reinforce the struggle for power between Finance and Planning.

This conflict is further reinforced by attitudinal differences, which stem from variations in the kind of personnel recruited for the two institutions. The finance ministry is likely to get accountants, lawyers, and low-level technicians on their way up through the bureaucracy. The planning commission is likely to include economists and other men with advanced degrees, whose identification with the bureaucracy is more tenuous. Planners are given to talk in terms of public interest and comprehensive approaches while bureaucrats speak of political necessity and administrative convenience. Bureaucrats probably have been educated at home, planners abroad. Each side is likely to accuse the other of being unrealistic in terms of its own values and modes of thought.

In budget conflicts, the Ministry of Finance is likely to be in an extremely strong position. Although little has been written on the subject, everything we know suggests that finance ministries often are the most powerful governmental institutions in their country. The occasional man who has worked in both planning and finance notices immediately that power differentials are reflected in the ability to gain information. "When I worked in the planning organization, we met no success when we asked for information. But when I ask for this type of information from my place in Finance, we get the information we want."

The finance ministry, with its control of the treasury, is likely to prevail over planners who, in Nepal, complain, "We make the plan and somebody else holds the purse." When compelled to choose, ministries will go where the money is, as a candid Thai official recognizes:

> The NEDB [National Economic Development Board] does not have power. We cannot really put our future in the hands of NEDB officials. Even if the NEDB approves our projects we may still not get money for them. This is a very crucial problem which undermines the NEDB since we are rather reluctant even to ask the NEDB to help clear the passage for our important projects. Since we know that the NEDB is not powerful in terms of allocating money, we often fall into the habit of overlooking NEDB policies and recommendations. We know that what counts in getting money lies in our dealing with the BB [Budget Bureau].

The finance ministry has the resources to reassert its power. Finance controls the level of taxation and spending that determines whether there will be a surplus for investment; it determines individual ministry spending, thus choosing the projects that can be supported; usually it controls the foreign exchange that regulates other spending.

One way to avoid conflict between planners and finance personnel is for them to treat the "development" and "ordinary" budgets as mutually exclusive preserves. But economic life is indivisible. A project may require not only large construction and initial start-up costs but also substantial maintenance and operating expenditures. Looking at the problem the other way around, spending may be encouraged because there is a surplus one year in the development account and a deficit in ordinary expenditures, or vice versa. One time buildings go up without people to put in them, and another time people are hired without any place to work. The research of Albert Waterston in low-income countries around the world amply illustrates this dilemma.

Almost all ministries of finance instinctively recognize the unity of the budget. A strong finance ministry, trying to keep the country solvent, will fight to keep its hold over the budget; it will try to make sure this year's development expenditures are not the kind that will swallow up both development and recurrent funds for several years ahead.

A strong finance ministry therefore will mean a lesser role for planners: they will have trouble gaining authority over funds. Yet one should not assume that a planning organization is well served by a weak Ministry of Finance. Without a meaningful budget there can be no meaningful plan, for such a ministry will not simply be weak in relation to planners, it will be unable also to stand up to other pressures such as maintaining control over the budget during the year, so that budgeted funds are in fact used for purposes for which they are allocated.

The relationship between Planning and Finance is generally somewhat one-sided: Finance usually holds most of the cards. It will allow Planning influence up to the point of actual decision, but will keep for itself as far as possible the prerogative of responding to exigencies and the power to make decisions regarding overall distribution of resources. Its emphasis on flexibility is not the least of the uncertainties facing planners, who, by their strategies, in turn create a new set of uncertainties for the Ministry of Finance.

In their efforts to increase public expenditure planners and planning commissions are not alone. They represent only the spearhead of a broad front of interests, which stand to gain, politically or financially, from the spoils of government. The political configuration of the country will determine just whom the Ministry of Finance will confront in its efforts to conserve resources as best it can.

POLITICS: FORMAL AND INFORMAL

Political outcomes — not least of which are the ultimate source and destination of public funds — depend on a number of different factors in every country. They include the level of political mobilization; the extent of corruption; the number and strength of pressure groups; and a variety of economic, political, and social conditions that do not lend themselves to easy or valid generalization. Prominent among them is the nature of the regime, and the shape of its formal institutions. Many poor countries are dictatorships, or in the hands of the military, and it is difficult to conduct research into the bargaining, politicking and rationale that underlie budgetary decisions. Other countries follow a pattern of cabinet-style government, in which the executive rules by virtue of its majority in the legislature. The ability to pass its budget in parliament is essential to its continuance, but as the legislature has no will distinct from that of the government it chooses to support, interests tend to make themselves felt directly on the executive — either by individual ministers or by officials in departments and agencies.

In one set of countries, however, it is possible to see a good deal of the play of interests in the open. In countries that follow the United States model of government, separation of powers assures the legislature an existence independent of the executive. In these countries, which include Latin America and also the Philippines, legislatures can exert considerable influence over the budget. In the debates of these legislatures it is possible to trace some of the pressures upon budgetary decisions. In addition, where legislatures do have influence over the budget they represent another factor in the mutually interacting pattern of uncertainty surrounding financial decision-making. They may pass appropriations in excess of those presented by the executive; they may cut items with which they disagree; they may alter detailed figures in favor of this department or that area.

In theory, the role of an independent legislature is to act as an additional watchdog for public monies and use its financial powers to audit expenditures, query allotments, and challenge policies. It might in this way improve the budgetary process by increasing participation, broadening the budget debate, exposing bureaucratic weaknesses, and checking extravagance. In practice, however, powerful legislatures in poor countries do not accept the norm of guarding the treasury. They do not try to limit spending, nor do appropriations committees (by whatever name they are called) adopt the norms of professionalism and hard work. On the contrary, since they need not often worry about how the revenues they distribute are raised, they may ignore their formal responsibility. Nor are they responsible for a consistent budget, since they are not saddled with the job of applying it. In other words, the major constraints faced by the Ministry of Finance do not apply. The budget passed by an independent legislature is therefore in some danger of becoming illusory — one which pays little attention to sources of revenue or to practical spending policies.

Actually, this rather alarming picture is unlikely to materialize. Among the few legislatures in poor countries that do constitute an independent force none we can find exercise substantial control over most of the budget. A few control that part of the budget devoted essentially to public works. Others can reduce spending and, in addition, distribute money among different programs so long as they do not raise the total. The basic feature of budgeting is that the legislature often appropriates far more money than the treasury can possibly raise. In fiscal years 1965 and 1966, for example, the Philippine legislature appropriated approximately three times as much money as the government had to spend. The same thing has happened in Argentina, Brazil, Peru, Chile, and other poor countries. The legislature thus simply abdicates control to the executive that is prepared to make the real decisions. Fabella concludes that "by providing the executive — through the Budget Commission — with a wide-ranging list of alternative choices on where to spend the available funds, Congress has relinquished operational control over funds disbursement" in the Philippines.[8] Since the president's approval is required for virtually all expenditures, a highly placed official told us, "access to the president is all-important."

Legislative committees do not try to examine proposed spending seriously or thoroughly. With the exception of public works, to which we shall return, they get through the formal process as quickly as they can. The best description we have come across is from Chile:

> Say I'm the congressional secretary, looking at the budget of the ministry of interior. I start reading the proposed budget, beginning with all the laws that set up the ministry. I'm interrupted by a parliamentarian who says,

[8] A. V. Fabella, *An Introduction to Economic Policy* (Manila: University of the Philippines, 1968), pp. 51–52.

"would the Honorable Secretary please not read this section and get on to the figures?" So the secretary goes down each service, reading the figures. He reads the item, and then the figures. The item, then the figures, until he gets to the end. He looks up, there is a motion for approval, and the budget is approved!

By the time the public works appropriation appears on the legislative scene, members of the appropriations committee "begin to read more carefully." Since they believe their election depends on these appropriations, they work hard to get them. The public works budget in the Philippines includes a special fund for direct distribution to congressmen. They can use the money for any public works they want, as long as the work is done by state engineers.

Some legislators are interested only in being able to announce that they have gotten a project in the appropriation, and do not care if it is actually built. Others see to it that the project is started but then lose interest in it. From Peru we learn that "the congressman who sponsored the hospital law is more than satisfied if he can return to his constituents and boast that he has served them well by providing a hospital for their community. And then he can blame the government for not carrying out its obligations." After Congress votes for public works in Chile, the executive vetoes most of the projects. "This is just a game to gather more votes," an official told us. "Normally the veto stands but the congressman can show his province that "I asked for such and such to improve the situation here."

Budget officials in poor countries realize that patronage is a part of the appropriations process everywhere in the world. But they claim that it has "reached gargantuanly intolerable proportions" in their countries. Consider how the legislator will go about securing his request. He will undoubtedly refuse to vote for the appropriation of the department concerned unless his own project is approved. He may insist that his friends and supporters get jobs on the government payroll before he will vote for an appropriation. Soon the countryside is littered with half-completed projects, buildings without a function, or stadiums far too large for the community in which they are located. "At the end of all this," a high-ranking official from Argentina asserted, "Finance is left with the reality of scarce resources, manifested in a restricted amount of money, against the onslaught of ministries which forever want more. The president finally must divide the money by relative political power."

By and large, the chief executive is most influential in determining who gets what the budget has to give. Whatever his constitutional framework, he bears the primary responsibility for a satisfactory political solution to the problem of how much shall be raised and for what it shall be spent. As is true also for the Ministry of Finance, the chief executive is bounded by the circumstance of poverty; there is not enough to go around, and the possibilities of augmenting public revenues — additional borrowing, increasing taxation, deficit spending — are fraught with eventual political dangers.

Yet unlike the situation in the Ministry of Finance, the fragility of his position demands that the chief executive find some solution to pressures for economic growth, social justice, and sectional improvement. A new leadership which follows may be able to hold the line for a year or two and place political stability above other considerations. But sooner or later comes the resurgence of interest in the budget; then the chief executive will need his political skills to shape it. One of his major constraints in so doing is administrative. The top man certainly lacks the time (and many lack the interest) to follow budgetary matters; he must delegate. Hence the Minister of Finance, who may not always see things as would his chief, may exert the most control over the budget. "Traditionally," a high official explained, "the Minister of Finance has been the most powerful figure in the government. This situation has not changed, since the president has confidence in him, and doesn't want to spend a lot of time dealing with these matters."

Seldom, however, will finance ministry decisions go unchallenged if there is serious executive disagreement. The very existence of a superior authority makes it inevitable for disputes to be submitted to it. Chief executives generally prefer to have cabinet members bargain out their differences. For one thing, prior arrangements reduce the number of decisions they have to make. For another, they can avoid blame by placing the burden on ministers.

Unless they are happy with any decision on which their colleagues can agree, however, chief executives will remove certain matters from the bargaining table. The finance minister undoubtedly will insist that the cabinet bargain within an agreed top figure.

Interminable ministerial bargaining over the budget is both a test of political strength and a way to determine if common interests can emerge out of creative juggling of resources. Foreign funds are useful because ministers can avoid for the time being the aspects of a zero-sum game, in which more for one means less for the others. Projects are subdivided, lengthened, and shortened in time to create divisible bargaining counters. Each participant can be indulged to some extent only if rewards are broken down into pieces that can be distributed among those present — easiest when there is either a very large surplus or a deficit. Then the executive can distribute good things to all or to none. This may explain the occasional preference of leaders for an evident crisis instead of the normal bad situation.

The more the president involves his power in budgeting, the more he is importuned for funds. Ministers are reluctant to believe that he cannot help them. It is hard for the chief executive to turn down leading political men; yet somehow he must limit spending. One tendency we have noted is for chief executives to promise funds early in the year and later on claim that new developments make it impossible for them to make good. Another tactic is to use a signaling system so that the supplicant is not turned down directly by the men at the top.

Politicians go directly to the president with requests for funds. The president usually reacts by preparing a note to the finance minister in which he asks him to accommodate the man. Apparently the president has an understanding with the finance minister wherein he [the president] signs his name two different ways — one meaning, give the man the money, the other meaning, turn him down. If it is a turndown, the finance minister has to explain that it is absolutely impossible for him to find additional money to meet the requester's needs, etc., etc.

The most important constraint by far on the chief executive is the nation's financial position. Past allocations leave little room for future changes. Old programs are difficult to hold down and terribly hard to eliminate. New ones must be introduced slowly and take years to mature. Fear of inflation and inability to get foreign exchange to purchase essential commodities place restraints on the total and types of expenditures that can be made.

The chief executive then is faced with the central dilemma of budgeting. Without the stability allowing him to try rational, long-term allocation of resources, he is unable to rely on redundancy as a response to the pressures upon him at any one time. He has to care where the money goes. Budgeting tells the man at the top how poor his country really is.

SUMMARY AND COMPARISON

Wealth comes first. It is, after all, budgetary processes we are analyzing. Before resources are allocated, there must be resources to allocate. By definition, being poor signifies lack of money. Poor people do not have to worry about allocating nonexistent riches. But the reason poor countries have trouble becoming rich is that they lack more than money: capable manpower, useful data, governmental ability to mobilize existing resources. Less able to cope with the unexpected, poor countries suffer more uncertainty of an extreme kind, like political instability, than do rich ones.

The reader of F. Scott Fitzgerald's novels, especially *The Great Gatsby,* knows that the rich *are* different from other people. Wealth makes a buffer against the world and its adversities which the poor must face up to personally. The rich man doesn't worry about losing his wallet; there is always more where that came from. Every bad turn in fortune upsets the poor man because he has so little in reserve. He trembles at risks because he has nothing to fall back on when he fails; if he doesn't succeed, he returns to squalor. The rich man can afford to fail. When he does gamble, he can afford to see it through; he need not leave the game at the first bad turn of the cards. The poor man must be better than the rich — more disciplined, more determined, more self-sacrificing — to do half as well.

Never knowing what will come next, fearful of depleting their meager reserves, concerned that the merely urgent will take precedence over the absolutely critical, finance ministries continually revise their expenditure priorities. Budgeting is repetitive as the need (new rulers, sudden economic changes) arises to remake budgets throughout the year. Spending departments (and their clientele) seek to escape these upsets by finding their own sources of funds, further depleting the central treasury, and leading to more restrictive practices, to new efforts at evasion, and so on.

Because no one is sure of how much he has or will get at any time, all participants engage in furious and incessant lobbying. The cumulative costs of past decisions force out new expenditures, and a chronic shortage of funds for investment exists side by side with inability to spend what is available. The budget disappears as if by magic; after autonomous agencies and special funds deplete the central treasury and recurrent expenditures drive out investments, one wonders what all the fuss was about.

Unable to collect taxes in sufficient amounts, without control over a significant proportion of the resources they do collect, governments work in a perpetual aura of financial crisis. When the moment comes to separate rhetoric from reality, the finance ministry usually bears the burden of decision. Fearful of being blamed when the money runs out, and anxious to respond to what it sees as real priorities of existing governments, Finance desperately seeks protection against the unexpected. Maintaining liquidity becomes its main motive. Under normal conditions of extreme uncertainty, this understandable desire leads to a sequence of conservative estimating devices, repetitive budgeting, delays in releasing funds, and inordinate amounts of paperwork. Such procedures accomplish their purposes at first: a surplus is protected for the time being, the finance ministry is able to adapt to changing circumstances by delaying decision, and the causes of uncertainty are pushed onto operating departments. They respond, in turn, by trying to stabilize their own environment. Departments withhold information on unexpended balances (thus increasing underspending) so they can retain some flexibility. They become more political because they must engage in ceaseless efforts to hold on to the money ostensibly allocated to them, lest the finance ministry claw it back. Ultimately they seek their own form of financing through earmarked taxes, or they break off to form autonomous organizations — a sequence of events encouraged by foreign donors seeking stability through creating recipient organizations with whom they can have more predictable relations. Because the official budget is not a reliable guide to what they actually can spend, departments are not motivated to take it seriously. Padding takes place on huge dimensions, and reinforces the tendencies of the finance ministry to mistrust departments and to put them in a variety of straitjackets.

Analysis of padding lets us better understand that the difference between poor and rich countries lies not in the existence but in the frequency and extremity of these practices. The stable environment of the rich reduces the extent to which it is necessary and profitable for departments to inflate the previous year's totals. Since they can count on receiving their budgeted allocation they do not need an extra margin of safety. Simultaneously, the central budget office knows more accurately what departments are spending and can penalize them more successfully for excessive requests. They pad, but not so much or so often. The rapidly shifting environment of poor countries means less certain expectation of what they can get away with, so they compensate by asking for more. Never knowing whether the finance ministry will attempt to recapture their funds, departments in poor countries do more padding to take into account a larger realm of uncertainty. Since their information and communication are of lower quality, poor countries are simultaneously less able to anticipate their own spending needs and better able to prevent outsiders from learning what is going on. The former impels them to make large allowances for misjudgments; the latter, to prevent Finance from catching on too quickly. The combination of little money and large uncertainty makes departments in poor countries work harder — to use the most extensive strategic apparatus to preserve smaller amounts of money — than those in rich countries. Hence one sees greater use of strategies designed to increase income, more extreme versions of strategies used in rich countries, and more activity to accomplish less change in money variables.

How can we explain budgetary practices, especially those such as repetitive budgeting, that are common in poor countries but not in rich ones? One answer is that these practices have cultural roots. It was easy for American social scientists writing on poor countries in the 1950s and 1960s to attribute their difficulties to collective moral shortcomings. This is not so easy now that the United States is having its own troubles. The allegation is that people in poor countries adore bureaucracy, glory in delay, and love to frustrate one another. The persistence of repetitive budgeting across continents, races, and cultures, however, suggests that it is due rather to common problems faced by these countries. The basic cause of the phenomenon in low-income countries is extreme and extensive uncertainty which, when combined with severe scarcity of financial resources, narrows the time horizons of top officials to two or three months or less. The finance men responsible for the solvency of their country are held to a short time span because their environment keeps shifting on them. They have to renegotiate the budget throughout the year so as to move with the times.

In order to test our explanation it will be useful to look at organizations in rich countries that are poor financially but do not face uncertainty — even better to see what happens to these poor organizations when faced with an unaccustomed level of uncertainty. As we discussed in Chapter 6, American cities must deal with increasing demands for services within a context of constitutional limitations calling for a balanced budget. They act a little like poor countries in that they follow conservative estimating procedures in order to avoid running out of money. But for the most part their financial environment is certain, if bleak; they know how much they are spending and can estimate revenues with a high degree of accuracy. When, in the last years of the 1960s, however, expenditures rose rapidly because of inflation, and revenues decreased unexpectedly because of recession, predictability disappeared and uncertainty took its place. As uncertainty was joined to poverty, the characteristic budgetary behavior of poor countries began to appear in these American cities. The budget office was constantly trying to reprogram its funds; it went back on agreements with departments; it recaptured funds and held on to personnel vacancies; it made decisions only at the last moment; departments screamed that their lives were being disrupted and that they could not plan their work under these conditions.

A good place to find poverty joined with uncertainty in America is the Democratic National Committee. When last I looked, it was desperately seeking a way to repay a deficit from the 1968 presidential campaign and to mobilize resources for 1972. Its officials could not be sure how much money they would have on hand in the near future, nor what the demands on them for spending would be during that time. Consequently, there were innumerable complaints from people who did business with the national committee about delay in handling their requests. Admitting the truth of these complaints, the man in charge of the budget said that the delays were due to his reluctance to authorize expenditures: "You operate with that budget in front of you every hour of the God-damned day." Some requests get action more quickly than others, he added, because they have higher priorities.[9] Since both priorities and available funds shift rapidly, he delays in order to act on the most pressing need of the moment — just as a budgeter does in a poor country.

On the principle that analysis should begin at home, I shall provide a final example of the effects of adding uncertainty to poverty from the University of California at Berkeley. During the 1950s and most of the 1960s the university was reasonably well off. If certain unexpected costs materialized, they could be met within existing resources. Monies promised to schools and departments normally would arrive on schedule. But in the last few years financial stringency has hit the university. It no longer has a cushion of resources with which to absorb small elements of uncertainty from the environment. So the campus budget office must initially recapture funds that would ordinarily go to teaching units. But it cannot guarantee that these reduced allocations will remain with them. It sends out memoranda saying that reduced allocations made at the beginning of the year, and cut further a few months later, will have to be reduced again because certain unexpected costs have appeared on the horizon. Constant reprograming, pervasive delay, complaints about the arbitrary action of the budget office, have become everyday happenings. It will not be long, I suspect, before various elements of the university look for

[9] *The National Journal,* 3 (October 16, 1971), 2092.

special forms of funding in order to eliminate the current high level of financial uncertainty.

My hypothesis, then, does not apply only to poor countries. The behavior I have described, the syndrome of repetitive budgeting, should occur wherever severe financial constraints and a high degree of uncertainty coexist. Hemingway was wrong; Fitzgerald was right; the rich *are* different. But the poor are different, too, and that has been the burden of this chapter.

8
Political Structure and Budgeting: American States

What happens if the variables we have been using — wealth and certainty — are mixed in different proportions? After all, some governments may be richer than the poorest and poorer than the richest. American state governments are ideal for our purposes because some look like our model of the rich country (as in the U.S. federal government) and others are more like the poor-but-certain cities. At the same time, however, almost all states have certain governmental institutions in common — legislatures, an executive, and parties that differ in critical respects from those found at the municipal or federal level. Thus we can ask what difference it makes when, to the usual mixture of wealth and predictability, we add differences in political partisanship, formal powers, and expertise. Analyzing states lets us study a new variable — political structure.

The level of expertise in the three legislatures — Congress, state legislatures, city councils — varies. Does it influence the role which the institution plays or the manner in which it is being carried out? The chief executive's formal authority in budgetary matters is not the same in each. The president shares power with Congress; state governors have an item veto power, which allows them to annul certain legislative decisions; the manager or the mayor usually is the dominant figure in the municipal arena, confronted by a weak and unassuming council. How do these differences in formal powers affect the behavior of the chief executive himself, as well as the participants' reaction to him? Spending departments, likewise, operate under varying conditions of predictability. At the federal level they have much to gain or lose in the annual budgetary process. At the city level both the stakes and the probabilities of attaining them are much smaller. In the states the situation is indeterminate. In some states conditions are more like those of the federal government; in others they resemble the municipal scene. How does the amount at stake and the probability of loss or gain influence departmental behavior?

State budgets generally are much larger than those of cities, but smaller, of course, than that of the federal government. Like city governments, states cannot create money and are greatly limited in their borrowing capacity. They must fund spending by extracting resources from their residents and from the federal government. The state budgetary process resembles both federal and local budgeting, but, in toto, is not identical with either.

We will examine three basic questions:

1. The Financial Problem: What are the resource constraints?
2. The Strategic Problem: Who has the power and how do they use it to accomplish their purposes?
3. The Calculation Problem: How is budgeting made manageable?

THE FINANCIAL PROBLEM

The problem of resources at the federal level is less acute than at either the state or local level. Revenues are limited but so much larger than most agencies that budgeting involves resource allocation among competing programs and agencies. At the city level it is the most acute. Budgets must be balanced, revenues are inflexible, and expenditures grow rapidly. With severely limited resources, budgeting becomes a form of revenue behavior. The question is not so much what expenditures to undertake, but where to find the money to pay the incoming bills. The states are somewhere in the middle, operating under conditions that might push them either way. To understand budgetary problems in the states, we need to look at variations both in spending and in revenue constraints.

State expenditures share two general features with municipal expenditures: they grow mechanically even when the service level is kept unchanged, and most of the spending items are uncontrollable. The four largest items in the state budget — education, welfare, health, and highways — frequently (though not always) cost more each year since the clientele (students, welfare recipients, motorists, etc.) is increasing, and local governments are pressing to transfer more of their costs to state governments.[1] The cost of services (wages and prices) goes up but (seemingly) never down.

The ability of budgeters to control spending is greatly limited. Schick tells why. "In virtually every state, formulas set the level of state aid to school districts, welfare agencies, and many other functions. Coupled with these irreducible requirements are the fixed needs of existing programs and institutions."[2]

[1] For a trend analysis, see Stanley M. Wolfson, "Economic Characteristics and Trends in Municipal Finances," *The Municipal Year Book, 1973* (Washington, D.C.: International City Management Association, 1973), pp. 95–97.

[2] Allen Schick, "Control Patterns in State Budget Execution," *Public Administration Review,* 24 (June 1964), 104.

The executive's maneuverability, Anton tells us, is limited also by "the truly staggering complexity of the state's system of financial bookkeeping. Constitutional limitations, . . . incoherent divisions of financial accountability . . . and, worst of all, an intricate maze of general funds, special funds, revolving funds, loan funds, trust funds, federal funds, local funds . . ." [3] combine to confound the executive. Illinois, for example, has about 40 special funds in addition to the general purpose fund; Connecticut has 100; Wyoming, 168. With so many funds, how can one know what is going on, how much is being spent, or how much is coming in? Anton concludes that "The governor who hopes to fight for financial righteousness in these circumstances will surely be hard put to locate the battlefield, let alone lead his forces to victory." [4]

Earmarked taxes and federal grants contribute to this complexity and impose additional limitations on participants' discretion. Schick's conclusion is widely accepted. "The great dilemma confronting state budgeters [is that] so little of the budget is subject to effective expenditure controls. . . . Some budget officers have estimated that as much as ninety percent of the budget escapes careful examination." [5]

Revenues are critical since most states, like cities, operate under a constitutional requirement of balanced budgets. Having no monetary powers, and greatly limited indebtedness capability, state spending is revenue-constrained.

The state's taxing powers, however, are greater than those of cities. Though the federal constitution prohibits imposing taxes on interstate commerce or on international trade, states are free to levy any other tax which they deem necessary. Consequently, most states impose both an income and a sales tax in addition to a long line of excise and user taxes. (Twenty-six states have both sales and income taxes, twenty-two either sales or income tax, and only two states — Nebraska and New Hampshire — have neither sales nor income taxes.) [6] Unlike the property tax, both the income and the sales tax are highly elastic. They respond quickly to economic changes and, when the economy grows, their yield increases proportionally (depending, naturally, on the rates at which they are imposed). The probability that revenues may grow faster than expenditures is quite high. While cities struggle to meet their current spending, states may actually build surpluses.

A glance at aggregate national figures shows that since 1962 there has been a steady trend of increase in state surpluses (Table 8.1). A closer look

---

[3] Thomas J. Anton, "Roles and Symbols in the Determination of State Expenditures," in *Policy Analysis in Political Science,* ed. by Ira Sharkansky (Chicago: Markham, 1970), p. 213.

[4] Ibid., p. 214.

[5] Schick, "Control Patterns," p. 104. Schick cites: Tax Foundation Incorporated, *Controlling Federal Expenditures* (New York, 1964), and Tax Foundation Incorporated, *Earmarked State Funds* (New York, 1955).

[6] Thomas R. Dye, *Politics in States and Communities* (Englewood Cliffs, N.J.: Prentice-Hall, 1969), pp. 445–460.

Table 8.1. STATE REVENUES GREW FASTER THAN EXPENDITURES
IN THE 1960s
(in billions of dollars)

Fiscal Year	Revenue	Expenditure	Surplus
1970	$88.9	$85.1	$3.9
1969	77.6	74.2	3.4
1968	68.5	66.3	2.2
1967	61.1	58.8	2.3
1966	55.2	51.1	4.1
1965	48.8	45.6	3.2
1964	45.2	42.6	2.6
1963	41.0	39.6	1.4
1962	37.6	36.4	1.2
1961	34.6	34.7	−0.1[a]

Source: *The Book of the States, 1972–1973* (Lexington, Ky.: The Council of State Governments), p. 189. By permission.
[a] Deficit.

at individual states discloses a slightly different picture. Though most have surpluses, 15 (see Table 8.2) operate with deficits.

Nearly all the 15 states with deficits spend less than the national average on the 3 major state services — education, public welfare, and health.[7] Cur-

Table 8.2. MOST STATES HAVE SURPLUSES BUT SOME (28 PERCENT)
HAVE DEFICITS IN 1970
(in thousands of dollars, rounded)

State	Revenues	Expenditures	% Surplus
States with Surplus			
Alaska	1,212,000	354,000	70.70
Arizona	876,000	779,000	11.07
Arkansas	657,000	619,000	5.78
California	11,397,000	10,760,000	5.58
Colorado	956,000	885,000	7.48
Florida	2,226,000	2,116,000	11.50
Georgia	1,632,000	1,516,000	5.21
Illinois	4,348,000	4,069,000	6.41
Indiana	1,715,000	1,601,000	6.64
Iowa	1,714,000	1,714,000	0.00
Kansas	795,000	792,000	0.37
Louisiana	1,660,000	1,594,000	3.97
Maryland	1,670,000	1,541,000	7.72
Michigan	4,132,000	3,934,000	4.80

[7] For a more detailed analysis, see *The Book of the States, 1972–1973,* Vol. 19 (Lexington, Ky.: Council of State Governments, 1973).

Table 8.2. (continued)

State	Revenues	Expenditures	% Surplus
Minnesota	1,796,000	1,736,000	3.34
Mississippi	935,000	928,000	0.74
Montana	350,000	343,000	2.00
Nebraska	486,000	452,000	6.99
Nevada	288,000	267,000	7.29
New Hampshire	281,000	273,000	2.89
New Jersey	2,625,000	2,540,000	3.23
New Mexico	605,000	544,000	4.41
New York	10,351,000	9,894,000	10.08
North Carolina	1,945,000	1,830,000	5.91
North Dakota	289,000	281,000	2.70
Ohio	3,876,000	3,478,000	0.10
Oregon	1,035,000	1,019,000	1.54
South Carolina	926,000	892,000	3.67
South Dakota	254,000	240,000	5.50
Tennessee	1,273,000	1,271,000	0.15
Texas	3,649,000	3,345,000	8.33
Utah	553,000	528,000	0.45
Virginia	1,768,000	1,681,000	4.92
Wisconsin	2,133,000	2,019,000	5.34
Wyoming	228,000	214,000	6.14

States in Deficit			% Deficit
Alabama	1,351,000	1,370,000	1.40
Connecticut	1,237,000	1,348,000	8.97
Delaware	293,000	326,000	11.26
Hawaii	608,000	685,000	12.66
Idaho	315,000	317,000	0.63
Kentucky	1,264,000	1,291,000	2.13
Maine	420,000	433,000	3.09
Massachusetts	2,369,000	2,448,000	3.33
Missouri	1,480,000	1,503,000	1.55
Oklahoma	1,078,000	1,082,000	0.37
Pennsylvania	4,915,000	5,114,000	4.04
Rhode Island	439,000	445,000	1.36
Vermont	275,000	289,000	4.85
Washington	1,957,000	1,973,000	0.80
West Virginia	845,000	865,000	2.36

Source: The Book of the States, 1972–1973 (Lexington, Ky.: The Council of State Governments), pp. 194–195. Figures have been rounded. By permission.

rent programs consume all available revenues, and very little if anything is left for new programs or for the expansion of existing ones.

Although (with but few exceptions) state governments have the constitutional power to raise the resources they need, the mere existence of a power is no guarantee it will be used. Imposing new taxes or raising rates on existing ones is unpopular, the more so when the resulting increase in the tax burden is substantial. The legislature normally would oppose tax increases for this reason. If this happens, the governor may not be able to do much. The tale Malcolm Jewell tells could be repeated elsewhere:

> Governor Mennen Williams of Michigan had a greater instinct for political survival, but after twelve years of deadlock and financial crisis, he had not found the key to unlock a Republican legislature, and he left to study the politics of emerging nations in Africa, where opposition leaders rather than legislative programs are incarcerated.[8]

The relations between revenue and expenditure vary among the states, yet in the literature are treated as a constant. The assumption is that states are in a financial crisis similar to the one at the municipal level. In an article published in 1964 for example, Schick asserts that "tenuously balanced budgets now appear to be the norm in state governments. Gone (possibly forever) are the years . . . of bountiful surpluses and static tax rates." [9] Austin Ranney's assertion is regarded as common knowledge: "Most state governments . . . now face enormously increased demands for more and better schools, highways, welfare, recreational facilities, and so on — but most face them armed with very inadequate revenue sources." [10]

These conclusions serve as a basis for explaining the state budgetary process. Since expenditures grow but revenue does not keep pace, the governor's main concern must be with revenue, rather than with determining allocations. He is, therefore, pictured as engaged in a constant effort to curb the increase in spending and locate new revenue sources. This literature, while it may be relevant to the 15 deficit states, is inapplicable to the others with surpluses.

A far more serious limitation on our knowledge is not errors of commission but of omission. Studies about how budgetary decisions are made in states are scarce. Thomas Anton's *The Politics of State Expenditure in Illinois* is the only book-length study describing the participants, their goals, the environment in which they operate, the constraints and opportunities imposed on them, and the calculations and strategies they employ to carry out their tasks.

Another book that was published at the time this chapter was written is S. Kenneth Howard, *Changing State Budgeting*.[11] As the title suggests, the author attempted to deal with the states in general rather than with one or two

---

[8] Malcolm E. Jewell, "State Decision Making: The Governor Revisited," in *American Governmental Institutions,* ed. by Aaron Wildavsky and Nelson W. Polsby (Chicago: McNally, 1968), p. 545.

[9] Schick, "Control Patterns," p. 103.

[10] Austin Ranney, "Parties in State Politics," in *Politics in the American States: A Comparative Analysis,* ed. by Herbert Jacob and Kenneth W. Vines (Boston: Little, Brown, 1965), p. 91.

[11] S. Kenneth Howard, *Changing State Budgeting* (Council of State Governments, Lexington, Ky., 1973).

particular ones and to focus his analysis on changes which budgeting in the states is presumably undergoing. Essentially, the book does two things for the reader: first, it gives him a broad survey of the relevant general literature on budgeting, decision-making, systems approach, and PPBS. Second, it provides us with a survey of the literature on state budgeting. But it contains no new data. So the book is strong where the literature is strong and it is weak where the literature is weak. The rest of the literature can be divided into two parts. One deals with aggregative data in an effort to identify the determinants of state revenue and expenditures,[12] hence is unhelpful for explaining *how* decisions are made. The second is made up of a small number of studies about specific institutions such as legislatures, the governorship, the budget office, and spending agencies. Though limited in number and scope, we found these to be the most helpful.

To sum up, two types of budgetary syndromes emerge from this financial analysis. In one, revenues grow faster than expenditures, a surplus is accumulated, and budgeters need to be less concerned with cutting requests and finding money to fund current spending than with deciding whether or not to spend the extra monies — and if so, how and where. In the other, spending outstrips revenues and little is left for the budgeters' discretion. The budgetary process will revolve around revenue rather than expenditure. Budgeters will be concerned with curbing the rise in spending and with finding resources to fund current programs. This type, which resembles the municipal model, we have called *revenue budgeting*.

Having described the two types of budgetary process, we now move on to observe how they work in practice. We said that when spending outstrips income, revenue budgeting, in which the governor tries to curb increases in spending while devoting most of his energy to the quest for new sources of revenue, will result.

Thomas Flinn[13] has a detailed and insightful account of the budgetary decisions made by Governor Freeman of Minnesota in the late 1950s. Freeman was elected on the basis of a platform that promised an expansion in state programs, a promise which Freeman tried hard to keep but was unable to. Instead of dealing with expenditure decisions he found himself trying to expand revenues to meet the cost of the current budget. On entering office he quickly found that, "If [he] attempted merely to hold services at the same level, he would have to find new sources of revenue. . . . And if he wanted to expand state services . . . he would have to find a large amount of new tax money." [14] Since an increase in taxes was not considered politically feasible, the only course of action open to Freeman was to instruct his assistants to review

---

[12] An updated short review of this literature can be found in Ibid., p. 58 ff.
[13] Thomas Flinn, "Governor Freeman and the Minnesota Budget" (ICP Case Series, No. 60, University of Alabama: University of Alabama Press, 1961).
[14] Ibid., p. 6.

departmental requests and eliminate any item not essential to the continuation of existing programs.

While his assistants were busy paring fat from departmental requests, Freeman devoted his time and energy to locating new sources of revenue — tax increases that would be acceptable to the legislature and would not arouse much public opposition. Though after much juggling he succeeded in balancing the budget, he had to give up most of his promised expansions.

Anton's account of Governor Kerner of Illinois in the early sixties is almost the same story told in different words. When Kerner was elected there was a projected deficit of $12 million. Kerner's first task as governor was to balance the budget. No decisions on allocating resources could be made since there were no uncommitted resources. The problem Kerner faced was not on what to spend state money but where to find the sources to support whatever spending was currently under way. In Anton's words, "the principal concern of . . . the Governor was not so much the content of the budget as it was the problem of finding additional sources of revenue." [15] The Revenue Director describes how departmental requests were received: "I looked at them and told the Governor they were too high, that we couldn't raise that much money. So we began to cut things down." [16]

At the same time efforts were made to increase the state's income by intensifying tax collection, attracting more federal aid, and increasing tax rates. Kerner ended roughly where Freeman did. The budget was tenuously balanced, but no new major programs were considered. Budgeting revolved around revenue.

When income grows faster than spending and a surplus becomes available, the focus of attention moves from revenues to expenditures and from spending control — cutting departmental requests — to program expansion. Procedures normally used to cram a fattening budget into a slim-cut suit are replaced by others designed to enable budgeters to expand a skinny budget to fit a large man's clothes.

Studies of budgeting under conditions of surplus revenues are only now beginning to emerge. One of the first is John D. LaFaver's account of "Zero-Base Budgeting in New Mexico." [17] The state attempted, during 1971–1974 to institute a zero-base budget. The reform, designed to assist budgeters to eliminate duplication and outdated programs, came at a time when a surplus of $100 million, nearly 30 percent of the current general fund budget, was expected. The advocates of reform quickly learned that: "Since the state's fiscal outlook was optimistic there was little impetus to cut budgets or eliminate

---

[15] Thomas J. Anton, *The Politics of State Expenditure in Illinois* (Urbana: University of Illinois Press, 1966), p. 121.

[16] Cited in Ibid., p. 121.

[17] John D. LaFaver, "Zero-Base Budgeting in New Mexico," *State Government* XLVII:2 (Spring 1974).

marginal programs. Thus a budget system designed to locate duplication and thus reduce budgets was out of phase in a period of increasing revenue." [18]

Faced with the problem of surplus, reformers decided to abandon the zero-base requirement and to replace it with a "70 percent" base. The meaning of this was that agencies did not have to justify more than 30 percent of their last year's appropriation. But, this was still not enough, and in preparing the 1974 budget, agencies were asked to justify only their expansion items. Last year's appropriation became a rigidly defined base which was not subjected to the regular review process.

Even so there still remained slack to be taken up; hence "the decision range for most budgets would be between 110 and 120 percent of present appropriation." [19] Instead of having to protect what they already had, agencies were expected to commit themselves to higher expenditures. As LaFaver puts it, "Several years of accelerating increases in tax revenues have scarcely encouraged a critical analysis of current spending levels." [20]

To conclude, the question preoccupying governors and budget reviewers in the deficit states (as in the cities) is how much of the requests can be cut and where additional funds can be found to pay for unavoidable increases. The question confronting governors and budget reviewers in the surplus states is what should be done with the surplus; where can more money be spent? Now that we have portrayed the decisions that state budgeters have to make, we shall examine the strategies and calculations they employ to make them.

THE STRATEGIC PROBLEM

> A peek into the decision-making black box in most states . . . would probably reveal a system in which operating agency heads consistently request more funds, executive and/or legislative reviewers consistently reduce agency requests, governors consistently pursue balanced budgets at higher expenditure levels, and legislatures consistently approve higher appropriations while engaging in frequent disputes with the governor over revenues.[21]

The universal division of roles between spenders and savers is found at all three levels of government. Not surprisingly, departments in the states try to protect what they already have and increase their share in the pie. The budget office plays the watchdog, cutting and trimming agency requests so that the governor can make ends meet without having to increase taxes. In addition, it serves as a communication link between the governor and the departments, drawing attention to spending priorities and revenue constraints.

[18] Ibid., p. 109.
[19] Ibid., p. 111.
[20] Ibid., p. 112.
[21] Anton, "Roles and Symbols," pp. 216–217.

This is as far as the similarities go. State legislatures do not resemble city councils or Congress; and the governor's position differs from both the president's and the mayor's.

It is generally agreed that "The governor is the central political figure in American state politics." [22] He not only holds a highly visible and prestigious position, but also enjoys certain extraordinary powers. Most states (except Arkansas, Mississippi, South Carolina, and Texas)[23] have an executive budget, which "places the governor at the apex of state budgeting. Formally, it empowers the governor to review departmental estimates, to propose a plan of expenditures, and to control expenditures by executive agencies." [24] All governors (except in North Carolina) have veto power, and all but seven have an item-veto power for appropriation bills.[25] The item veto allows the governor to cut off or reduce a specific item without having to reject an entire appropriation bill. This is an immensely powerful tool, albeit a negative one, since it allows the governor to change the budget after appropriation according to his own liking. Not even the president can do this. The veto's high formal potency is buttressed by the fact that vetoes seldom are overridden. Malcolm Jewell tells us that "despite variations in the constitutional provisions for overriding vetoes and despite variations in party control of legislators, it is rare for a governor to have a veto overridden." [26] Spending agencies must secure the governor's consent to their requests. Without it, the probability of getting them through is very low. As a department head in Georgia says, "One of the first things I did (to win support for our budget) was to go talk to the Governor because I knew he plays the greatest part in getting it passed. He told me that he would see that we got it." [27] Convincing the legislature to appropriate more than the governor allowed the agency to ask for is not going to help since the item veto will be used to annul the decision. In an aggregate study on agency requests, Sharkansky has found that "the governor's support appears to be a critical ingredient in the success enjoyed by individual agencies in the Legislature." [28]

Though the governor may seem to be omniscient, most state constitutions

[22] Dye, *Politics in States and Communities,* p. 147.

[23] See Tables on "State Budgetary Practices" and "Elements of State Financial Organization," in *The Book of the States, 1972–1973,* pp. 162–170.

[24] Allen Schick, *Budget Innovation in the States* (Washington, D.C.: Brookings Institution, 1971), p. 177.

[25] See Table on "Legislative Procedure: Executive Veto," in *The Book of the States, 1972–1973,* pp. 72–73.

[26] Jewell, "State Decision Making," p. 549.

[27] Cited in Augustus B. Turnbull, III, *Politics in the Budgetary Process: The Case of Georgia* (unpublished Ph.D. dissertation, University of Georgia, Athens, Georgia, 1967), pp. 153–154.

[28] Ira Sharkansky, "Agency Requests, Gubernatorial Support and Budget Success in State Legislatures," *American Political Science Review,* 62 (December 1968), 1224. See also Arlene Theuer Shadoan, *Preparation, Review, and Execution of the State Operating Budget* (Lexington, Ky.: Bureau of Business Research, University of Kentucky, 1963), p. 46.

create extremely splintered structures of power. More often than not the governor has to share power with independently elected officials. Emmette Redford illuminates this aspect of the governor's position:

> The executive role of the governor can . . . be overemphasized. In about four-fifths of the states he shares power with other constitutionally elected officers: the secretary of state, the attorney general, and the treasurer, each of whom can be regarded as a present or potential competitor. Frequently, his power to appoint other major department and agency heads is limited or nonexistent and often his removal powers are subject to challenge. Especially in recent years, the creation of independent state agencies, boards, and commissions that have been equipped with their own fiscal and spending powers . . . has served to limit the governor's supervisory responsibilities.[29]

Limited tenure imposes additional restrictions on the governor's power.[30] A governor with only one term in office hardly has the time to get acquainted with the budget, to determine which way he would want to direct it, and to convince the administration and the legislature to implement his proposals. Since he is not expected to last, he can safely be ignored by legislature, spending agencies, and even by his own budget staff. He would have a hard time convincing the legislature to impose new taxes, or his agencies to limit the increase in spending. A governor with limited tenure, for instance, is not likely to initiate such an unpopular thing as a tax hike because he would not be around to reap the benefits. His term would have reached its end by the time the additional revenue would come in allowing for increases in spending. Unless there is a surplus, a governor with limited tenure will have few options open for action and would probably lack the incentive to undertake any.

In recent years there has been a strong trend toward removing most of the restrictions on tenure. At present only nine states have one four-year term, and one a two-year term. In the others the governor's tenure potential is equal to or better than the president's. If this trend continues, it would strengthen the governor's position vis-à-vis the legislature and the administration.

Consider now the governor's position. He is frequently elected on the basis of a platform promising expansion of state services and prevention of a

29 Emmette S. Redford, et al., *Politics and Government in the United States;* coordinating editor, Alan F. Westin (New York: Harcourt, Brace and World, 1965), p. 881. See also Albert L. Sturm, "Structural Factors in Management Analysis," in *Management Analysis for State Budget Offices,* ed. by James W. Martin (Lexington, Ky.: MASBO, Council of State Governments, 1969), pp. 7–16.

30 For an analysis of the governor's power and position bearing on this point, see, among others, Joseph A. Schlesinger, "The Politics of the Executive," in *Politics in the American States,* Jacob and Vines, eds. (Boston: Little, Brown, 1971) pp. 228–232. As of 1971 only seventeen have a four-year term with no restraint on reelection; sixteen are permitted to be reelected once; nine are limited to a single four-year term with no consecutive reelection; seven have two-year terms and can be reelected; and only one has a two-year term with a single reelection permitted. See *The Book of the States, 1972–1973,* p. 151.

tax increase. The two objectives, however, are clearly opposed to each other and cannot be pursued simultaneously. Depending on the particular conditions under which he operates and his own goals, the governor may lean either one way or the other.

The most critical variable is the financial situation. Since spending is highly uncontrollable, if it grows faster than revenues, governors, like city managers, would become budget balancers, and budgeting would become a form of revenue behavior. In Anton's words,

> the exigencies of their situation . . . force them to focus most of their attention on revenue, which typically must be increased just to keep pace with existing programs. . . . Governors may be regarded as "money providers" or as "budget balancers"; only infrequently can they be viewed as "decision makers" in the determination of state expenditures.[31]

When revenues grow faster than expenditures, the governor's constraints and opportunities are immediately different. He has more options to choose from. He may become an advocate of the status quo, supporting the cause of lower taxation, or he may join the ranks of those arguing for an expansion of state services.[32]

The governor's success depends on the course of action he chooses to pursue, on his formal powers, on the structure of his administration, and on the party composition in the legislature. The financial policy he chooses is the most important variable, since it determines the extent to which he would be able to make use of his formal powers and his relative position vis-à-vis legislature and administration.

Sharkansky has found that "Because of formal prerogatives, the governor appears to be in a more secure position when he reduces agency requests." [33] A conservative governor will find it easier to accomplish his goals because his veto powers give him the final say. He need not convince others to do what he wants; he has but to sit back and cut requests to the size he likes, whenever they do not conform with his spending goals. Since he can cut both before and after appropriation, he can cope effectively with both acquiescent agencies and a liberal legislature.

The success of a governor who wants to increase spending is less certain since it hinges on legislative approval. He cannot rely on his personal powers alone because they do not include the authority to appropriate. An unwilling legislature can, and most probably would, cut the governor's budget, leaving him without a leg to stand on.[34] The nature of the party system therefore is

---

[31] Anton, "Roles and Symbols," p. 215.
[32] See "Big Turnabout for the States — Now the Money is Rolling In," *U.S. News and World Report* (June 18, 1973), pp. 22–23.
[33] Sharkansky, "Agency Requests," p. 1231.
[34] Ibid.

critical in this situation. Where the governor's party controls the legislature and where there is a high level of party discipline, his chances for success would be high.

A splintered administrative structure, with many agencies headed by elected officials or directed by independent commissions, weakens the governor's position. Sharkansky has shown that

> In contrast, the presence of numerous separately elected executives appears to benefit agencies at the governor's expense. . . . In the states where there are many elected officials, agencies are more likely to get their acquisitive requests approved by the legislature, and the governor's recommendation is most likely to be altered in the legislature.[35]

Unless the governor elicits the cooperation of these officials, they will go over his head and make deals with the legislature. A carefully prepared budget, matching expenditures to available revenues, may thus easily dribble down the drain.

It is generally agreed that either the mayor or the city manager dominates actors in the urban budget scene; at the federal level power is shared between the executive and the legislature. But no similar statement can be made about state governments.[36] Where the governor has no restrictions on tenure, where there are but a few elected administrative officials in charge of spending agencies, and where the legislature is either of a city-council type or controlled by the governor's party, the governor can be as dominant as a mayor or manager.[37] These conditions seem to have obtained in Georgia in the late sixties. "Governor Saunders," Turnbull reports, "has completely dominated the show. . . . He hasn't lost a single spending program he wanted." [38] When these conditions do not hold, the legislature is more independent; the relations between participants then begin to resemble the federal model.

A third type unique to state governments is one in which allocation decisions are made by a legislative committee rather than by the executive. In South Carolina, for example, the budget is prepared by the state budget and control board. Among its members are the governor, the chairman of the senate finance committee, and the state treasurer. In this situation the governor plays a minor role and, according to Graham, "perhaps the state government in South Carolina could run just as well without a Governor." [39]

The balance of power and the division of roles shifts frequently. The

[35] Ibid.

[36] Ibid., pp. 1225–1226.

[37] Howard, *Changing State Budgeting,* pp. 268–279. For a similar conclusion, see Ira Sharkansky, *The Politics of Taxing and Spending* (Indianapolis: Bobbs-Merrill, 1969), p. 111.

[38] William O. Smith, *Atlanta Journal–Atlanta Constitution* (Feb. 6, 1966), p. 117. Quoted in Turnbull, *Politics in the Budgetary Process,* p. 259.

[39] Cole Blease Graham, Jr., *Budgetary Change in South Carolina, 1945–1970* (unpublished Ph.D. dissertation, University of South Carolina, 1971), p. 66.

weight moves from governor to legislature and back, depending on personality, and on political and financial conditions. A hard-nosed and ambitious governor may squeeze every last drop of power from his formal authority. A legislature united in its opposition to the governor's programs can successfully block any effort to increase spending or to increase taxation.

But beyond all else financial conditions determine who will be the central figure. A surplus increases the governor's importance because he wins the initiative. If, for example, he decides not to spend it, the legislature cannot force him. When the budget is tenuously balanced or when there is a deficit, the governor has an incentive to do nothing, because all options open to him are highly unpopular. A deficit means that he must balance the budget by either raising taxes or cutting spending, neither of which is likely to satisfy the public and the legislature.

Having referred so often to the legislature, we should now examine it more closely. Like the governor, state legislatures do not play a consistent role. Their behavior varies from a reflexlike approval of the governor's recommendations to advocacy of higher spending or guardianship. In a study of 592 agencies in 19 states, Sharkansky has found that "the legislature's final appropriation . . . varied from a cut of 8% below his [the governor's] recommendation to an increase of 19% above his recommendation." [40] To understand this inconsistent mode of behavior on the aggregative level, we must examine institutional characteristics and the position of state legislatures in relation to other participants in the budgetary process.

Though differences among state legislatures are substantial, they do share certain features.[41] Like city councils, most are part-time institutions and do not pay sufficiently high salaries to let their members engage only in their legislative work. Four states alone paid more than $15,000 a year in 1971 (California's $19,200 being the highest), six paid more than $10,000, twelve paid between $5,000 and $9,000, while twenty-seven paid less than $5,000, with the lowest pay being $5 per session day.[42] To understand how important this is, imagine the Speaker of the United States House of Representatives selling insurance policies to make a living. Absurd as it may seem, this is exactly what is forced on many state legislatures — including committee chairmen, speakers, and party leaders.

These men, almost none of whom can afford to work full time in their

[40] Sharkansky, "Agency Requests," p. 1224.
[41] Ibid.
[42] John C. Grumm, "The Effects of Legislative Structure on Legislative Performance," in State and Urban Politics, ed. by Richard I. Hofferbert and Ira Sharkansky (Boston: Little, Brown, 1971), pp. 308–309. See also Malcolm E. Jewell and Samuel C. Patterson, The Legislative Process in the United States (New York: Random House, 1966), pp. 251–253; and William J. Keefe, "The Functions and Powers of State Legislatures," in State Legislatures in American Politics, ed. by Alexander Heard (Englewood Cliffs, N.J.: Prentice-Hall, 1966), p. 59.

legislative job, with but few exceptions lack the staff aids required to let them develop an independent view on the numerous and complicated bills with which they are confronted daily. Their difficulties are well described by George A. Bell (Director of Research at the Council of State Governments):

> The legislative session may last only thirty, sixty, or ninety days, as it does in many states; few go beyond six months. In half of the states regular sessions are held only once every two years. Even during the session the legislator does not devote all his time to legislative tasks; he also operates his business or profession back home, and actually may be in the capital only three days a week. In the relatively small amount of time he has to give to legislative matters, the budget is only one of many hundreds of problems to which he must give attention.[43]

Turnbull reports that officials in Georgia confirm this view; "It is hard for the legislature to be here 40 days and then expect to control the budget for the remainder of the year. It is hard for them to get informed. . . . The members of the General Assembly don't have the time. They won't become expert budget officers in a 40-day session." [44]

Again in contrast to Congress, state legislatures, very much like city councils, suffer from low prestige and, thus, often from second-rate personnel. Sharkansky points out that "without a seniority system, state legislatures are unlikely to develop any financial expertise among their members. Where taxing and spending committees do not provide tenure and an opportunity for members to learn their jobs, they are likely to become highly dependent upon the recommendations of administrative agencies." [45]

Expertise is critical if the legislature is to do anything beyond rubber-stamping the governor's recommendations. Expertise comes through familiarity with the budget, with past decisions, with agency reputation, with costs of basic services, and so on. Without this knowledge, no one can make sense out of the budget proposal. The difference between members of the House Appropriations Committee and their colleagues at the state level is that the former spend years on the job. The promotion system forces them to become experts. Long service and competent staff help them to achieve this goal; state legislators have neither.

Time is an additional constraint on the legislature's maneuverability. A detailed budgetary review consumes a lot of time. Yet most state legislatures have only a few weeks in which to vote on the governor's budget. As Anton says:

> Constrained by constitution or by custom to dispose of major appropriations within a limited period of time, legislatures have little opportunity to do

---

[43] George A. Bell, "Executive-Legislative Relationships in Budgeting," in *Whatever Happened to State Budgeting,* ed. by Kenneth Howard and Gloria A. Grizzle (Lexington, Ky.: Council of State Governments, 1972), p. 143.

[44] Turnbull, *Politics in the Budgetary Process,* p. 287.

[45] Sharkansky, *The Politics of Taxing and Spending,* p. 91.

anything but approve the expenditures recommended by the governor. . . . Thus, whether in Kentucky, where the budget was introduced on Tuesday and passed by the following Friday, or in New York, where the legislature normally requires only two days to approve the budget, or in Illinois, where defeat for *any* appropriation bill is almost unheard of, legislative partici- pation in the determination of state expenditure is virtually non-existent.[46]

This explains why state legislatures sometimes behave like city councils, that is, adopting the governor's budget proposal as it stands.

Yet state legislatures often depart from this submissive mode of behavior. Why? Unlike city councilmen, state legislators are elected in partisan elections. They usually represent a narrow and specialized constituency. As Dye puts it, "State legislators clearly function to represent local interests in state politics." [47] Hence, in contrast to city councilmen, they not only have special interests to look after, but can also call on the support of their constituency.

Since most goods and services which states provide (education, highways, health, welfare, and recreation) are geographically specific, as is representation in the legislature, legislators are motivated to act either as advocates for spend- ing or as budget cutters, depending on the issue. Thus, "The General As- sembly," Turnbull observes, ". . . would prefer to reduce expenditures, and indeed threatens to do so. But its desire to cut expenditures is seldom as great as its desire to assuage the service demands of its constituents." [48] Sharkan- sky's findings support this contention. "Intense party competition and high voter turnout often work in favor of high expenditures. Under conditions of high turnout and competition, therefore, acquisitive agencies should be able to elicit the most support from the governor and the legislature." [49] Even so, we have to explain why the legislature sometimes acts as a spending advocate sup- porting agency requests against the governor, while at other times it assumes the guardianship role, paring down the governor's recommendations.

THE CALCULATION PROBLEM

Historically, state legislatures have tended to overappropriate rather than cut down the governor's proposal.[50] Indeed, in certain states this pattern be-

---

[46] Anton, "Roles and Symbols," pp. 215–216. Original studies to which Anton refers are: Douglas Kane, "Our Steamrollered Assembly," *The Courier-Journal Maga- zine,* February 20, 1966; Frederick C. Mosher, "The Executive Budget, Empire State Style," *Public Administration Review,* 12 (1952), 73–84; and Thomas J. Anton, *The Politics of State Expenditure in Illinois,* pp. 147–177.

[47] Dye, *Politics in States and Communities,* p. 145.

[48] Turnbull, *Politics in the Budgetary Process,* p. 301.

[49] Sharkansky, "Agency Requests," p. 1223.

[50] See Arthur E. Buck, *The Budget in Governments of Today* (New York: Mac- millan, 1934). Also see Schick, *Budget Innovation;* and Mosher, "The Executive Budget: Empire State Style."

came so prevalent that steps have been taken to limit the legislature's discretion. At present, in Maryland, New York, and West Virginia, the legislature may decrease but not increase recommended appropriations (except for its own and the judiciary's budget). In Nebraska, a two-thirds majority is needed to increase the governor's recommendations; a majority vote is required to reject or decrease them.[51]

In most states, however, overappropriation is permissible and frequently practiced.[52] Why? First, the governor (not the legislature) bears ultimate responsibility for balancing the budget. He is expected to apply the item veto when necessary to achieve this goal. Thus legislators can safely adopt each other's spending proposals (thereby satisfying their constituents) without having to share the responsibility for raising tax rates. Since they don't have to weigh the costs of increasing taxation vis-à-vis the benefits of expanding services, they are inclined to follow the spending path whenever they see the slightest benefit. According to Anton, in Illinois legislators, "unwilling to risk offense to legislative colleagues, aware of the need to carry on state activities, and generally uninformed with regard to either the nature of existing state activities or to alternative activities that might be necessary or desirable, . . . treated virtually all appropriations bills as "good things" and voted accordingly."[53] These spending incentives are even stronger when revenues exceed expenditures.[54] For legislators can then justify their decisions by arguing that "we have enough money."

The guardianship role is much more demanding. Since cuts are unpopular, they have to be backed by strong justifications. In order to withstand the pressure which agencies and their clienteles will exert, legislators must avoid random cuts. They cannot risk appearing arbitrary. To do the job well, they need to identify "fat," "padding," and "inefficiency." Selective cutting calls for a thorough familiarity with the budget. It is hard for any legislator, particularly a part-time one, to carry out these tasks without the help of a knowledgeable staff. Though there has been a growing awareness in recent years about the inadequacy of staff, and though some states have taken steps to provide more, most legislators still lack this professional assistance available to the members of Congress.[55]

Yet, even when the legislature is able to perform the guardianship role,

[51] *The Book of the States, 1972–1973,* p. 124.

[52] See, for example, Anton, *The Politics of State Expenditure in Illinois.*

[53] Ibid., p. 174.

[54] See, for example, D. Jay Doubleday, *Legislative Review of the Budget in California* (Berkeley: Institute of Governmental Studies, University of California, October 1967), p. 127.

[55] See the reports by Kenneth Bragg and Freeman Holmer, "Recent Developments in the Theory and Practice of State Budgeting," *Western Political Quarterly,* 14 (supplement) (1961).

it frequently chooses not to. California, for example, in addition to having one of the most prestigious legislatures among the states, also has a highly sophisticated staff system. Since 1941 the legislature has had at its command an Agency for Legislative Fiscal Analysis, under direction of a legislative auditor. The agency's analysts, who operate under the supervision and direction of a legislative commission, are instructed to prepare recommendations to the various committees of the legislature concerning revenues and expenditures — from a saving, rather than spending, point of view.[56] The analysts have been encouraged to take a stand on the issues which they examine and to formulate their recommendations in a "for" or "against" manner. They are expected to alert the legislature to any proposed new spending. They have to report any instance in which the administration failed to carry out the expressed intent of the legislature.

Still we find that in recent years the legislature has persistently appropriated larger budgets than the governor originally requested. In 1973, the budget passed by the legislature was $1.6 billion larger than that requested by the governor. This largesse evidently cannot be explained by arguing that the legislature cannot cut; it is more appropriate to say that it did not want to.

Though the capability of intervening in the budgetary process may vary among legislatures, the intervention itself as well as its nature will depend on the course of action which the governor chooses to pursue. A conservative governor, aiming to keep expense at the lowest possible level, may motivate the legislature to become the ardent protector and advocate for those who suffer from budgetary austerity. Overappropriation will result. A liberal governor aspiring to expand existing services and to introduce new programs may motivate the legislature to assume a guardianship role. Legislators would presumably perceive the danger of tax hikes and would try to prevent or at least minimize them.

The spending-saving roles are one of the constants of budgeting. No system can long persist unless both functions are performed. In both federal and local governments the same participants play the same roles most of the time. A similarly stable division of labor does not seem to exist in the states, where the governor and the legislature oscillate between guardianship and advocacy roles.

One thing is sure; spending departments will live up to their name. But how they advocate and how much they try to get will differ according to circumstances at the state level. Despite the similarity in goals which agencies at all three levels of government pursue, there are important differences in behavior.

The scope for decisions affecting its budget determines the department's

[56] Doubleday, *Legislative Review of the Budget in California*, p. 55.

behavior. Broadest at the federal level, the scope is most restricted in the cities, with states falling somewhere in between. In the federal government, relatively larger chunks of an agency's budget are subject to annual changes, and their absolute size makes even increments worth fighting over. Consequently, agencies are motivated to use a complicated array of calculations and strategies aimed at securing public support and favorable treatment from their department, the Office of Management and Budget, and the House and Senate appropriations committees.

At the city level, two factors make for a higher degree of certainty for agencies and consequently greatly simplify their budgetary strategies: (1) the nature of their expenditures is such that it hardly can be cut (70–80 percent of the budget goes to wages); (2) many services are financed by earmarked taxes and state grants and hence do not fall under the executive's control. Here the task which agencies face in protecting their budget is simple. They do not have to look for support and good will from numerous participants as federal agencies must. Knowing their requests are not the basis for decision, because there is not any money to allocate, they shoot for the moon and include everything they think they ideally ought to get, as though there were unlimited resources. If they wish to expand their budget, they must appeal to sources external to the city. Hence a common strategy for increasing the budget is to identify and adopt programs that the state or the federal government is interested in enough to pay for.

The scope for decision at the state level is almost as limited as in the cities. Mandatory expenditures, earmarked funds, and political structure (independently elected officials) all work to safeguard agencies' budgets. The main problem confronting state agencies is not how to protect their base from cuts, but how to expand their budget.

In those states where revenues fall short of current spending, the situation is similar to the municipal setting. Agencies would have to rely mostly on the federal government. In states where a surplus does exist, however, there is something to be gained from internal resources as well. Different conditions lead to different behavioral patterns. Because there is something to be gained, state agencies win nothing by advancing utopian requests; neither can they afford to stick to last year's budget. If they chose the former path, they would not be treated seriously and would probably be cut to the bone. If they chose the latter course, they would never get an extra penny.

Their efforts, therefore, will be aimed at winning the Governor's support. In most states (particularly those with weak legislatures) the legislature would be second in their list of priorities. There is less to be gained there. As Turnbull argues,

> The Congress of the United States customarily wreaks far more change in the federal budget than its counterpart, the General Assembly of Georgia, does to the state budget. . . . The Georgia agencies cannot indulge as freely

— or rather as successfully — in the customary federal practice of appealing to legislative champions of their programs.[57]

When requests are used as a basis for decision-making, they must be formulated so as to get the most favorable decisions. The first ground rule is, "Ask for more!" The second is, "But not too much! Be moderate and reasonable, and do not create the impression that your requests are reckless!" The third is, "Be persistent!" Sharkansky found that "agencies that request little or no increase over their current budget are generally treated well by the governor and the legislature, while those seeking large increases suffer the greatest reductions in their requests. Yet an acquisitive strategy appears to be a prerequisite for a substantial budget increase." [58]

Persistence is of special importance in the states compared to the other levels of government since the governor is usually inclined to eliminate new programs and obvious increases over last year's budget. Being forced to maintain a balanced budget, he must cut agency requests to hedge against the possibility of being left with empty pockets in the middle of the year. If he does not do it, the legislature will. The point is, however, that somewhere along that road the acquisitive agency may get an extra penny or two because the governor and the legislature might turn up a large enough surplus.

CONCLUSION

The most salient feature of state budgeting is its variability. The roles participants play vary under different financial conditions. The governor as a single individual has more power than anyone else in state government, but he emerges as the dominant figure only when legislature and agencies allow him to prevail through veto power.

The legislature's role depends largely on the course of action the governor chooses. A saving-oriented governor will induce the legislature to assume responsibility for spending advocacy. A spending legislature, however, has little chance for success since it has no weapon comparable to the governor's item veto. A spending governor, on the other hand, can more easily be controlled, particularly if he depends on tax increases to provide the additional revenues he needs. Since most state legislatures often are unable to perform guardianship functions, they are most powerful when the governor needs a tax increase, because they can refuse to authorize it, thereby throwing the ball of guardianship into the governor's court, and least powerful when a surplus is available, be-

---

[57] Turnbull, *Politics in the Budgetary Process,* p. 216.

[58] Sharkansky, "Agency Requests," p. 1231. For a similar conclusion reached in a case study of two state agencies, see Rufus P. Browning, "Innovative and Non-Innovative Decision Processes in Government Budgeting," in *Policy Analysis in Political Science,* Sharkansky, ed., pp. 304–334.

cause they cannot force him to spend it if he does not want to nor watchdog him if he does. Their only alternative in this latter situation is to bounce the governor's budget proposal back to him.

The most important variable determining the behavior of participants is the adequacy of revenues. Since state budgets must be balanced and since most expenses cannot be controlled, when revenues increase at a slower rate than spending, budgeting will become a form of revenue behavior. The governor will be engaged in a quest for monies to cover the increasing costs of state services. Spending agencies will have nothing to gain or lose internally; hence whatever strategies they may use will be directed toward sources outside the state government. The legislature, though advocating higher spending, will be engaged in constant disputes with the governor over revenues. When money comes in faster than it goes out, as often happens, more options become available. The governor stands to gain the most in this situation since he can use his formal powers effectively either to initiate or to prevent additional spending. The other participants, i.e., the spending agencies and the legislature, can and probably will advocate higher spending, but implementation depends on the governor's consent. Again, the conservative, saving-oriented governor will have the last word. Development of strategies becomes important for the spending agencies since there is something at stake in the budgetary process. Most of their effort will be directed toward the governor, for though only the legislature can appropriate monies, appropriation without gubernatorial support has little material value.

9
When a Budgetary Role
Is Missing: Deviant Cases

What if the division of roles between guardians and advocates, which lies at the heart of our observation of budgetary behavior, did not exist? Suppose a budgetary role is missing; maybe guardianship is out to lunch, or advocacy has gone fishing. Or perhaps both are at the dentist's. Then what? By observing the rare situations in which one (or both) of our roles is absent, we hope to learn more precisely what it means to have them there. Under what conditions do budgetary processes operate without the standard roles? What price do they pay? What benefits do they receive? In this chapter we shall describe and analyze four jurisdictions within the United States in which deviant behavior arises from the absence of these usual roles. These data should permit us to play variations on the major themes and see what happens when we ring changes on old favorites.

One of the constants of budgeting is the division of roles into spenders and savers, a result of the universal scarcity of resources. Claims and demands always outweigh the resources to satisfy them. Hence there are always people who want more than they have and those who show them they can't have as much as they would like. Officials in charge of carrying out the government's functions are oriented toward needs. They are always confronted with things that are not done but should be done. They fulfill their task best by advocating these needs. For this reason the government's purse needs guardians who would ensure that spending does not go beyond available resources and that all spending advocates get a share of what is available.

If this division of labor is so universal, how can we be sure the roles we describe really are determining budgetary outcomes? Could it not be that these roles are carried out perfunctorily as a matter of tradition, that they are not really essential, that they are merely a facade?

We learn to appreciate our health when we become ill. Remove one or more of the budgetary roles and you will see what difference they make. Finding such cases, however, is a difficult research task. No one knows where to start or in what direction to go. It is only by accident that a written account or even a reference can be found.

Three possibilities need to be considered: (1) no guardians, only spenders; (2) guardians but no spending advocacy (the guardians are making both spending and saving decisions); (3) neither role (there are no spending advocates and no one is guarding the public purse). In years of research I have come across only four such cases.[1] They are so different from the models of budgeting presented in this book that they may be labeled properly as deviant.

MISSING VARIABLE: GUARDIANSHIP

A principal task of budgetary guardians is to relate expenditure to income. By cutting and trimming spending requests, they ensure that there is always enough to pay incoming bills, and that taxes will not have to be raised constantly to provide necessary resources. The guardianship role is most pronounced in American cities due to the balanced budget requirement. Since cities are allowed to spend only as much as their tax revenues and external grants amount to, the guardianship role is more crucial to them than to others, such as the federal government, whose revenue constraints are less severe.

Americans generally assume that government agencies will be capable of assembling the resources necessary for their operations. The citizens of Haroldville, therefore, were quite surprised to read one morning that their city had sunk deep into debt and faced great difficulties in meeting immediate commitments. The city treasurer issued a report which warned the citizens, "In my opinion, it will be a herculean task just to meet payroll obligations." In the two years preceding this report, the city overspent current general fund revenue by $340,000 (total revenues in 1966–1967, $776,000) thereby accumulating a deficit of 39 percent.

How did such a thing come to pass and why did it take two years to become public? The crisis in Haroldville resulted from a temporary absence of budgetary guardians. Since no one tried to relate expenditures to revenues, and spending advocates were allowed to spend as much as they saw fit, expenses exceeded available revenues and a deficit was incurred.

In 1965 the council had appointed a new city manager, whom we shall

---

[1] The four cases are based on unpublished papers by graduate students in my course on budgeting and in a course given by my colleague, Robert Biller: (a) Richard W. Winnie, "The City of ——— Deficit" (December 1969); (b) Napier V. Smith, "Budgeting on the ———" (December 1964); (c) Robert S. Palmer, "An Administrative Board's Response to Statutory Control: A Review of the Budgetary Process in the ——— Water Conservation District" (December 1965); (d) T. M. Smith, "County Budgeting in a Rural Small Town Setting" (January 1965). Names of places and people are withheld.

call Tom. He was chosen primarily for his political skills, since he had virtually no previous experience in municipal administration. Tom himself said his reason for becoming city manager was promotional. He was hardly interested in administrative management. Rather, he wanted to accomplish certain community projects.

Thus from the very beginning he saw himself as a spending advocate rather than as guardian of the city's budget. Since he felt implementation of his pet programs to be more important than his more general administrative duties, the budget became an obligation rather than a powerful management tool. He looked on it as a spender, thinking of all those things that could or should be done, not as a saver viewing the scene in its entirety, and evidently never realizing that if one need was taken care of it was invariably at the expense of others, because there never is enough for everybody.

Normally a city manager would issue directives to the departments indicating how much they could ask for. More often than not he would stress the limitations of revenues and note that they would not be able to get much more than they did last year. When he received their requests he would review them with a critical eye, paring them down to meet revenue constraints. Tom did nothing of the sort. Instead, he said he had full confidence in his department heads and was sure they were not requesting anything they did not really need. He never told them how much they could ask for or hope to get, nor did he cut their requests once he received them. In his words, departments were cooperative in submitting "conservative budgets that required little cutting." (In contrast, the previous city manager had described those same department heads as habitually submitting exorbitant requests which required his closest scrutiny.)

Since departments were left to make their own spending decisions and were not subjected to a saving-oriented review, they reverted to a system of responding to the perceived needs of their clientele. Since everyone was concerned with his own professional needs, the well-being of the city organization as a whole was neglected. A program considered worthwhile by a certain department was immediately implemented; the question of sufficient money to carry it out never came up.

The city council, accustomed to having a guardian manager, assumed everything was fine and that outgo matched income. The councilmen were only part-time legislators without a salary out of which they could support themselves and their families and without any staff aids. They had little financial expertise and very limited knowledge about the city's budget. Like their colleagues around the country, they would have had trouble carrying out the guardianship tasks even if they wanted to. But nothing seemed to keep them from becoming spending advocates. Exposed to pressures from their constituents, they began to advocate implementation of certain programs, assuming that the manager (who did not have to concern himself with losing votes) would step in if necessary to shut off the financial faucet. Since he did not do so, they were content, naively trusting that money was available and happy to see their projects carried out. With few questions asked, the manager's budget proposal was adopted by the council; after that no one referred to it again. Spending commitments were fulfilled without verifying whether expected revenues materialized.

Even when the manager and the council woke up and saw that the city was sinking into debt, nothing was done to correct the situation. They assumed the political cost (of not responding to community demands) would be greater than the cost of a reaction against deficit spending (caused by expenses incurred in satisfying those very demands).

They worked out a number of strategies to facilitate this deficit spending. First, revenues were overestimated and expenditures underestimated, thereby creating the impression that slack was available (normally a reverse strategy is used to enable the manager to acquire slack). Second, promises to hold a bond election were made; but after the budget was approved those promises were forgotten. Third, monies were shifted from one fund to another in order to put out "local fires" and bolster the impression that all was well.

However, the chickens came home to roost in January 1967. The treasurer's second quarter report called to the city council's attention the critical nature of the city's financial condition, pointing out that between February 1, 1966, and January 31, 1967, general fund spending had exceeded revenue by $408,017.84! The report stated also that payrolls alone could not be met until sufficient cash became available.

Subsequent reports reinforced the reality of the financial crisis. A financial consultant was then hired, who revealed that:

1. City restricted funds such as the Water Fund, trust and agency accounts, and special revenue and miscellaneous accounts have been improperly used to pay General Fund obligations.
2. No effective system of budgetary control of expenditures exists. Expenditures that are over budget authorization are permitted without additional appropriations.
3. Expenditures for non-budgeted items are frequently made without proper authorization or consideration of the source of monies.
4. The City budget shows revenue and expenditure by source but lacks a summary of transfers or fund balances.
5. Use of current revenue for capital improvements has limited those resources available for municipal services. No long-range capital program nor capital budget exists.
6. Accounting records are inadequate to supply information necessary for administrative control of departments.

Apparently the treasurer's report was the first time the city council fully realized how much deficit spending had gone on in the preceding year and a half. Public reaction led to the resignation of the city manager. In order to allay rumors of impropriety, the council officially requested the district attorney to review city financial records and determine whether a grand jury investigation was warranted. The district attorney concluded that no impropriety had taken place, but in a private meeting he apparently threatened the mayor and city treasurer with charges of malfeasance if improvements were not made in the city's financial control.

So ends our story. With the appointment of a new manager, determined to play his role as it should be played, budgeting in Haroldville was brought back to normal. In Figure 9.1 we trace the relation between revenues and expenditures for a period of ten years. The years 1965–1967 during which Tom was manager are marked by a sharp increase in the city's deficit. As soon as Tom was replaced there was an immediate decrease in spending and movement toward a balanced budget.

MISSING VARIABLE: SPENDING ADVOCACY

Spending advocacy is also indispensable because priorities change; old problems disappear and new ones arise. To maintain viability those in charge of spending must constantly prepare and advance new programs to meet new needs. And advocacy serves another purpose: it simplifies the savers' task. Instead of going out and finding programs by themselves, they need only choose the best from among those proposed by the spenders. The competition and conflict in turn bring to light various aspects of policy proposals and help participants to make good decisions.

In the absence of advocacy the future might become a precise cast of the past; nothing can be gained or lost. Men lose motivation. Instead of trying to do better, they merely carry out their functions. Energy is wasted on trying to subsist within the system's constraints, instead of finding ways to break out. In this kind of static world, calculations and strategies are useless. There is no point in perfecting a spending program if you know for sure that it will be rejected.

In the absence of advocacy the savers will have a very hard job. They cannot make choices when there are no alternatives. When new problems surface, they will have to find their own solutions. Since policy alternatives will not be argued out through competition and conflict, it will be hard to separate the good from the bad. Not all of these outcomes are found in our next example, but many are.

The second example is a military installation, which performed what is known as "housekeeping" activity. Its primary function was to supply and maintain buildings, provide services and consumable materials to the tenant activities located in it, and to be responsible for the general operation and maintenance of the base itself. Each of the tenant activities had its own budget

Figure 9.1. ANNUAL GENERAL FUND EXPENDITURES AND REVENUES, 1959–1969 *(in thousands of dollars)*

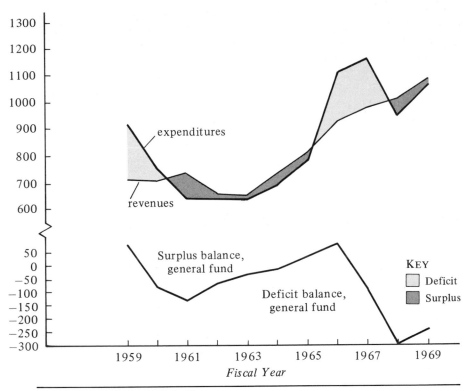

Source: *Annual Budget,* 1969–70

for individual expenses, funded by the parent bureau or activity under which the tenant activity operated. The installation's budget included only those funds necessary for operating and maintaining the base itself. Thus although the overall expenditure was $34.2 million in 1965, the actual budget of the base proper was only $4.3 million. The $30 million which the installation itself did not control went primarily for wages of military personnel attached to the various tenant activities and for operating several nonappropriated fund organizations in the base such as the commissary, the post exchange, and various clubs.

In an organization of this size, budget preparation is relatively simple. The various units within the station submitted requests to the controller, who reviewed the proposals, checked for justification and inconsistencies, and forwarded the budget to the base commander; he then sent it up the hierarchy for final approval. The process is as mundane as it could be except for one extraordinary procedure. The installation was instructed not to ask for funds exceeding its total budget for the preceding year. Since this was a military organization with a tight formal hierarchy, orders were carried out. If anyone thinks this goes without saying, a glance at the municipal scene would convince him that it does not. Spenders always try to increase budgets since their fate is closely related with their agency's spending. The fact that somebody tells them not to ask for more is not enough to keep them from doing so. Sometimes they would risk sustaining severe cuts in the short run to be able to increase their budget in the long run.

Budgeters in this installation, however, carried out their instructions because they had a strong incentive to do so. Their military careers depended on it. To achieve promotion they had to prove they were able to perform their tasks within the constraints imposed from above, and to behave as their superiors expected.

A spender in a governmental organization will win the praise and support of his clientele when he expands his agency's services; he will encounter severe criticism when he fails to do so. A spender in a military organization is more dependent on his superiors; hence, if they order him not to ask for more than he already has, he will obey.

What will he do when, at the same time his revenue is frozen, his costs keep rising? To keep the base running and to provide the services for which it was responsible, the budgeters had to find new ways for doing old things at a lower cost.

Two methods were used. The first was to eliminate all unnecessary functions and generally improve efficiency in the purely technical sense of the term. The second was to pull out from the budget every large item, such as purchase of new equipment, and include it in an addendum — a list of needs arranged along a priority scale and submitted with the regular budget to the approving authorities. When surplus monies become available, these authorities may use them to approve some of the needs listed in the addendum.

Responsibility for part of the station's budget thus was shifted to higher echelons in the military hierarchy. Those charged with representing the saving view now had to make spending decisions as well. The installation's commander did what he could with the available money and put everything else in the addendum. The addendum became a list of nearly everything the station needed, rather than a list of extraordinary expenses not related with routine operation, as originally intended.

Improvement of internal efficiency and elimination of fat became an end rather than a means. New programs to meet new needs, improvements which might cost more than existing procedures were not developed or initiated. Equipment which should have been replaced because it was no longer economical to repair was repaired, because money for purchases was not available. At the time of this study the base had reached the stage of deterioration in which, unless facilities were immediately replaced or totally overhauled at great cost, the service level would have to be lowered.

MISSING VARIABLE: BOTH SPENDING
AND SAVING ROLES

When only one role is missing, a budget system may be said to be out of balance; the one that is present dominates the process and outcomes flow accordingly. When both roles are absent or latent, we are dealing with a different world altogether. It is a world lacking conflict, hence lacking criteria by which to separate good from bad decisions. The absence of conflict may signify near universal agreement. Policies need not be well defined since no one has to be convinced to adopt them.

We will be looking at two different organizational structures operating in different environments. One is a water district; the other is a county. They have in common the absence of both vigorous spenders and rigorous savers.

The water district's enabling act (for reasons dating back to its inception in the early twenties) gives it the authority to raise the revenue required to cover its projects. The district is empowered also to incur bonded indebtedness, and no limit has been set on the amount of revenue to be raised by taxation or to cover interest and retirement of bonds voted by members.

The district's budgeters operate under extraordinary conditions. Rather than adapting expenditures to available revenues, they prepare a budget that would justify the maximum revenue they can raise. The effect of this opportunity on budgetary behavior is strengthened by the fact that the constraints imposed on revenues are extremely lax.

The district is relatively isolated from its environment. Though its total amount of tax revenues and bond monies may be significant from its budgeters' point of view, the individual taxpayer's contribution is too small to arouse his interest one way or another. Consequently few residents pay any attention to it. As long as water in adequate quantity and cleanliness reaches the taps at home or the pipelines in the fields, no one is likely to get involved in the district's politics.

The district's directors, usually appointed rather than elected for the simple reason that rarely is there more than one man interested in the job, are left to do pretty much what they want. It should come as no surprise if we say they want to maximize the district's revenues. The larger their revenue the more leverage they have and the more confident they can be in their ability to meet expenses. They have little motive for preventing increases in expenditure since, by so doing, they would lose revenue. For this reason they rarely get into conflict with spending administrative officials. The more the latter ask for, the more programs they advocate, the better the opportunity to increase the district's revenues. There is thus no more need for spending advocacy than for guardianship. Strategies and calculations are unnecessary because there is no competition and no conflict over resources. In order to get more one has only to ask.

Normally spending requests need very strong justification or they will almost certainly be cut. With so many needs competing over limited resources, spenders must convince guardians that the proposed programs are vital. In this water district spenders need not go to all this trouble. Since funds can be easily raised, there is no need to perfect program proposals.

Our second case in this section is a small rural county which we will call Sugarland. In Sugarland everyone knows everyone else and is familiar with what is going on. The point, of course, is that not much is going on. Things are rather stable. The county is not poor and is not particularly troubled by crime, pollution, overcrowded schools, noise, poor roads, or other such maladies normally associated with cities and around which some of the toughest budgetary battles are being fought.

The county's economy is not growing very fast, but neither is its population. Though resources are not expanding, neither are needs. The county government has enough money to carry out its operations and is not likely to encounter a shortage in the near future. The services provided by the county (sheriff, superintendent of schools, district court, agricultural department, hospital, and roads and bridge construction) are few, highly visible, and require relatively fixed spending (as long as there is no substantial population growth).

There is nothing extraordinary in all this that would have aroused anyone's interest except for the fact that budgeters in Sugarland do not behave as do their colleagues around the world. Let us begin with those in charge of spending. Usually men in these positions aspire to increase their budget. In order to achieve their purpose they use strategies such as padding. The spending officers in Sugarland rarely ask for more than they had last year. An annual increase of 1–2 percent to compensate for price hikes is the standard. Few ask for more than that, and when they do they have severe compunctions about doing so. Time and again they say they are satisfied with the way things are and have no interest in enlarging the domain of their activities.

Next comes the budget officer who, instead of paring down the departments' requests, approves them as is, with no questions asked. In the 12 years preceding this study he had not even once cut a request. When interviewed he said he rarely if ever discusses the budget with the spending officers and never issues directives to them. He explained this unusual mode of behavior by saying he knew his colleagues very well and was aware that their requests were as conservative as they could be. Since they never asked for something they did not really need, there was no reason to cut or even question their proposals. The county commissioners responded in much the same way. They too rubber-stamped spending requests. They made no policy decisions regarding the county's budget and relied completely on the department's initiatives.

When asked why no one seems to want to increase his budget, nearly every county official interviewed gave the same answer. "I try to keep the budget from going too high; after all, I'm a taxpayer too." In a county the size of Sugarland, people may have a clearer perception of the connection between expenditures and taxes. A director of a federal agency would have to stretch his imagination to visualize the possible connection between his efforts to increase his budget and his rising tax bill.

Since the county is small and its government operations are limited, and since officials know and trust one another and share the same values, budgetary strategies and calculations are unnecessary. Spending officials, content with what they have, know that if they need more they can get it just by asking. Though they do pad their requests slightly to create the slack necessary to hedge against uncertainty, they tend to return what is left of this surplus at the end of the year. Padding is not used as a strategy to expand the budgetary base.

The system has two major weaknesses: it can be abused by anyone who does not share the values on which it rests and, since there is no conflict and competition within departments and between departments, no one can say whether the system functions efficiently. Sugarland may be a "heaven of fools," as an old saying goes. Everybody trusts everybody else, but no one checks to make sure it is true. Hence, everyone believes that all is well, when it may or may not be.

A little story will illuminate both points. An annual increase of 1–2 percent is standard in the county. It was quite surprising, therefore, to find that in the year this study was made, the county's court budget was raised by 34 percent, a substantial increase by any standard. How did this happen in an environment where everybody seems to be so tax conscious and restrained?

The county clerk, a self-confident young man, recently appointed to the job, stated that he did not share the tax consciousness of his colleagues. Since he has to deal with a highly uncertain environment (it is extremely difficult to anticipate many of the court's expenses because no one knows how many and what kind of trials will be held), he normally inflates his budget request considerably to be able to meet unexpected expenses.

But this is not how he got the 34 percent increase. A few years before this study was made, there was a serious car accident, resulting in many complicated trials. The court requested and was granted a special fund to cover the unexpected and quite large expenses. No one questioned the request itself or its size, for everyone knew why it was made and believed the court clerk had asked for only as much as he needed.

When the trials ended, the clerk did not return the fund to the budget officer, as might have been expected. Instead, he "generously" chopped off one-third and kept the rest in his agency. Thus the new budget proposal which he submitted included a 34 percent increase over his previous year's appropriation. The request was approved along with the rest of the county's budget with no questions asked. At that time the clerk had not the vaguest idea of how the additional money would be spent, but forcefully indicated that he intended to spend it to the last dime. A new base has thereby been established for the court's budget and the clerk acquired slack which lets him cover his tracks by advancing, in the next few years, modest requests — Sugarland style.

Another example is the road and bridge fund. This is a "pork barrel" kind of item. The budgetary division of labor is indispensable here, perhaps more than it normally is. Roads and bridges provide tangible benefits to specific groups of people. A road leading from town to a remote ranch benefits only the rancher at everyone else's expense. Unless spending decisions are channeled through the spending-saving division of roles, an even distribution of resources might be difficult to secure.

In Sugarland, the road and bridge fund, by far the largest item in the county's budget, is the commissioners' exclusive responsibility. They decide where roads will be built, improved, and maintained; and they decide what equipment will be purchased. They are not required to request bids when buying new road machinery. Accusations have been made in budget hearings and elsewhere that the fund's monies have been used for political purposes, that the commissioners received kickbacks, and so on. Nevertheless, the commissioners have not once changed their road budget after a hearing. In six years, they pushed it up by about 25 percent.

Since the commissioners perform both spender and guardian roles, it is very hard for an outsider to find out what is going on in the fund, what is being done with the money, and why. The manager of a large taxpaying organization described the situation bluntly. "If you want to know the truth, the county commissioners' road and bridge account is nothing but a slush fund."

In such a system, it is also very difficult for outsiders to have an effect on the budgetary process. Since no county official needs to win a budgetary battle, nor is likely to lose one, no one needs to elicit the support of a clientele or listen to its criticisms. Representatives of some of the largest taxpaying organizations in the county, when interviewed, repeated the same story. They study the budget carefully, go to budget hearings, raise questions, and voice their criticism. Rarely, if ever, however, have they convinced the commissioners to cut or in any other way modify the budget. One of them expressed his feelings in a way that sums it all up. "We've gone to the budget hearings and beefed for years, but it hasn't done one goddamn bit of good."

Though on the surface things may seem a bit chaotic, they are not. In lieu of a formal division of labor, there are implicit shared norms of behavior. Participants share a common consciousness which induces them to keep their budget down. There is a general feeling of satisfaction with the way things are and few expressed an urge to expand their operations.

Since most spenders have internalized saving norms, guardians feel no need to question budget proposals, much less cut them. There is a self-reinforcing circle of mutual expectations. The spenders do not ask for more than they really need, because they are going to get exactly what they have asked for. Those in charge of guardianship do not cut spending requests because they believe the totals are not padded.

Since the organization is small in size, confronted with almost no severe problems, and relatively stable, this system of tacit understandings can function. It has advantages as well as disadvantages. It is economical and simple; it relieves budgeters from the need to go through the time- and energy-consuming process of defending and criticizing budget proposals. Since most of the activities are routinized and opportunities for policy decisions limited, it probably would have been tedious, if not useless, to try to describe them more accurately and provide justification for every step taken.

But the system is not without disadvantages. As the court clerk example shows, it is relatively easy to exploit. Since requests are never seriously questioned, anyone who wants to increase his budget may do so without being forced to compete with others over limited revenues. Budgeters are relieved from the need to justify every increase in their budget. Though in general they do not pad their requests, and though most of their annual increases result from higher costs, they can afford to waste money since they can always get as much as they need to provide the services for which they are responsible. Perhaps the most severe weakness is that the organization is isolated from its environment. Outsiders find it extremely difficult, if not impossible, to have an effect on budgetary decisions.

CONCLUSION

The four cases have shown that when a budgetary role is missing, "something" happens to the process and to its participants. All four are deviant in the sense that their modes or styles of budgeting do not resemble what is commonly found elsewhere. In the first two, the city of Haroldville and the military installation, one role is absent and the remaining role becomes dominant. In Haroldville, the absence of a vigorous guardian let the spenders dispense funds as they saw fit without paying much attention to the city's revenues. A financial crisis soon developed, since the city's resources were consumed and no money was left to provide for vital services. In the military installation, where spending advocacy was prohibited, unfortunate outcomes of a different kind resulted. Since the guardians dominated, cutting the budget became an end rather than a means. No new initiatives were made and the service level began to deteriorate.

In the last two examples, both roles are absent. Since there are no guardians or savers, there is little explicit conflict. The calculations and strategies which normally occupy most of the budgeter's time are of no use here and are not produced. Outcomes are less clear and dramatic than in the other instances. Though there is reason to believe that not all is well, both systems seem to operate smoothly and efficiently. In Sugarland this is so because the organization is small; its members know each other well and have internalized saving norms. Though budgetary roles are usually indispensable, under certain limited conditions (small size, abundant resources, mutual trust, shared values), the division of labor between spenders and savers may become unnecessary. Coordination need not imply a coordinator. The matching of expenditures to revenues can be achieved through informal arrangements.

III
Comparison

10

Strategies and Calculations

We have described budgeting in a composite of poor countries; in four rich ones; and in many American cities, states, and special jurisdictions. What do these processes have in common, how do they differ, and why? The purpose of this entire volume is to answer these large questions. Better answers may be available when efforts to reform as well as to maintain budgetary processes are considered. Here I want to begin the job of comparison.

A simple way to get at similarities and differences in behavior is to talk about strategies and calculations. How do budgeters go about getting what they want and how do they figure out what to do? Which strategies are found virtually everywhere, and which ones vary according to circumstances? What accounts for the frequency with which strategies are used? How do differences in budgetary environments — wealth, predictability, political institutions — affect the kind of strategy used and the rate of deployment? Similar questions can be posed about budgetary calculations. Why has there been convergence in modes of simplifying calculations in rich countries? Why are calculations in poor countries, which have less information at their disposal, more complex than in wealthy nations?

STRATEGIES

The thing that hath been, it is that which shall be; and that which is done
is that which shall be done; and there is no new thing under the sun.

Ecclesiastes 1:9

The words of Ecclesiastes represent the voice of experience. In like circumstances and conditions, men will behave in similar ways. The fundamental sameness of budgetary strategies around the world flows from the functional equivalence of budgetary processes. Everywhere there are those who want more than they can get, and others whose business it is to show them they can't have it. If nothing ever changed, so that the past precisely mirrored the future, there would be no point in trying to loosen the mortal grip of fate. Men could not hope to do better or fear that they would do worse; a quietistic fatalism would settle over the earth. But the prospect of advantage motivates men to adopt strategies designed to improve their position over what it might otherwise have been. Strategies connect the conflicting interests of spenders and savers with features of the environment they believe can be manipulated in their favor. On the assumption that men want to do better for themselves rather than worse, strategies are the behavior patterns that show how men believe it advantageous to act to achieve what they consider worthwhile. Uniformity in behavior, then, must stem from common positions they occupy and from the regularities in demands the environment imposes on them.

Some strategies originate from budgetary complexity. Central control organs, for instance, when faced with a sudden need to reduce spending, often resort to across-the-board cuts. They do this because the method is quick and because their knowledge is insufficient to make a considered judgment among the countless programs that would otherwise be candidates for selective treatment. Spreading misery around equally has its political costs, but so does playing favorites, as cutting collectively would no doubt be called. Spending departments, for their part, are fond of "the camel's nose," under which large programs are begun from seemingly small beginnings. They know that complexity of calculations turns attention toward increases. Since big programs are the most difficult to start, spenders are not above including new ones under the rubric of old ones, nor above beginning with sums too paltry to attract attention.

Other strategies are based on the division of roles in the budgetary process. Padding, for instance, is a means by which spending agencies show clienteles how they battle for their interests; it provides guardians with a starting figure from which to cut; and it preserves a margin of error on both sides. Padding is not something that just advocates do, but is part of their implication in a common system shared with guardians. Each actor gets a chance to look good and to be seen performing his role.

Strategic opportunities are created also by formal rules governing the budgetary process. Always on the lookout for easy places to reduce spending bids, guardians are likely to choose to cut a department down to what it actually spent in the previous year. The well-known habit of departments to increase their rate of spending toward the end of the fiscal year exists because they are not allowed to carry over funds. Having been fed this incentive to spend, there is little point in guardians remonstrating over rational adaptation to the end-of-year constraint — though, of course, the illogic of it all does not prevent the argument's being made.

Strategies are not merely ubiquitous, but contingent; they depend on time, place, and circumstance. Some strategies are used in certain environments but not in others. Strategies of dependence, for instance, such as those which revolve around the presence of aid donors and recipients, depend for existence on special conditions. Whatever else a budget strategist from the federal government of the United States might do, for example, he would not try to increase his supply of dollars by first getting a commitment from an international donor. In poor countries, however, precisely this strategy is followed, because taking in foreign exchange must have a high priority for finance ministries. They will often come up with the balance in local currency rather than lose the money they need to buy things from abroad. Even if a nation is rich, its subunits may be more or less poor, tempting them to make use of the opportunities a federal structure creates for those who wish to make much out of little. American cities may take on programs merely because federal funds are available; this may sound crass until one realizes that the monies are presumably being made available so that cities will have an incentive to respond to federal priorities. A delightful situation arises when many federal agencies, with different criteria, dispense funds to the same localities. Usually a growth-oriented agency tends to give funds to those best able to use them — a consideration that leads to putting money where there is quite a bit already. Another federal agency may be concerned with combating poverty or introducing considerations of equity into governmental dispersements. It will grant funds on the basis of need, possibly modified by some measure of tax effort. States, therefore, have an interest in appearing needy to one body and well-heeled to another, often doing both simultaneously by different interpretations of the same set of statistics.

The "claw-back" — refusing to dispense funds already approved in the budget — is found everywhere to a small extent, but in its most pronounced form in poor countries. Every nation sets up an apparatus for something like quarterly apportionments to even out the flow of funds. Poor countries, however, make it a normal, everyday practice to reconsider amounts allotted in the budget according to their latest financial and political developments. It is their multiple uncertainties, combined with poverty, that lead them to frequent changes of course. On occasion, financial exigencies may lead central control organs in rich countries to go back on their word, but this is rare, happening usually under circumstances in which there is a common recognition of desperate circumstances (such as the oil crisis of 1973–1974). When it looks as though reprograming of funds is becoming a way of life, participants seek an accommodation to smooth out the difficulties. When the 1967 devaluation under the Wilson Labour Government threatened a kind of perpetual chaos, for instance, the Treasury began to negotiate deals with the larger departments, who accepted less than they might have got in turn for more binding commitments into the future. The *service* vote is a protection against the claw-back in France. The efforts of the U.S. president to impound funds voted by Congress (which attracted notoriety precisely because the situation had never before come up in such aggravated and widespread form) threatened budgetary stability. If impounding were to become a daily exercise, so that passage of the budget by Congress had little predictive value, the effective budget would end up as reprograming by the executive.

The frequency with which strategies of all kinds are used, and the extremity of their departures from desired practices, vary directly with wealth and predictability. Strategies are least used and most moderate in units that are poor and certain. Everyone knows how much is available and usually it is not large enough to bother about since the chances for success are so small. Strategies are used most where uncertainty is the greatest. The poverty of poor countries aggravates their uncertainties. Unceasing strategic maneuver becomes the norm because spending agencies (rarely sure of what they have) find financial guardians always altering allocations to remain viable. Everyone shifts ground to keep up with the times. Since the formal budget is meaningless, the appropriation being more a hunting license than an actual kill, less attention is paid to it; thus there is an increased tendency for exaggerated estimates to be followed by severe and erratic reductions. The wealthy and less predictable, I presume, would show a lower level of strategizing, if only because their wealth created less need to take back what had once been promised; budgets may be late but, once enacted, more likely to be meaningful. The rich and the certain demonstrate modest amounts of strategic activity; there is a lot worth having, but ways and means of getting it are limited by strongly held expectations of desirable conduct. Penalties against asking for too much or making false claims are severe. It is easier to ferret out cheating and to invoke sanctions. Because there are fewer large fluctuations to take into account and because the budget hovers about a base, gross departures from known relationships become more obvious; because the budget is meaningful, failure to be included is a severe sanction. The least strategizing takes place in the poor-but-certain financial environments of American cities. There is little worth having and prospects for getting it aren't exactly brilliant. Since revenue drives expenditure, and spending is already close to constitutionally permissible limits, the margin of choice is very narrow. Also, the size factor for most cities means that getting a margin of allowable increases is usually pretty small potatoes.

Though, for budgetary purposes, they are more similar than different, the four nations that rank high in wealth and predictability are not at all alike in political structure. This provides an opportunity to see what difference political structure (within a reasonable range of types of democracy) makes for budgetary behavior. Surely the strategic moves are affected by how political institutions operate. Talking about strategies is another way of speaking of power. For in deciding how to go about increasing budgetary bases or defending them against cuts, spending departments necessarily have to make estimates concerning who has how much power over the subjects within their jurisdiction. To answer the question, "Where does one go to try for what there is to get?" is to say a lot about institutional power.

Everywhere people who want things out of government go to the great departments, which have the people and the expertise, and which are closest to the demands generating these expenditures and to the checkered experiences government has had in meeting them. Although these departments do not always get what they want, money rarely has to be forced upon them. Because they are expected to carry the burden of advocacy, programs they do not want are assumed to be unnecessary. Central control organs have enough trouble meeting all the demands made upon them without manufacturing others. Sufficient unto the day is the spending thereof! And, since the center is more interested in totals than in suballocations, departments regularly have the most say about where the money they do get will actually go. It is possible to get one's way by a frontal assault on the ministry in charge, but this strategy hardly ever comports with the doctrine of least effort.

Working with or through a department may prove fruitless, however, unless central control organs approve. They are always concerned about future financial implications of present decisions and always interested in actions that might create precedent for increased spending elsewhere. Masters of the totals, stewards of the tax rate, managers of the economy (always claiming to occupy the commanding heights with the broadest perspective), ministries of finance usually are the most prestigious administrative agencies, or close to it. Whether they attract the most talented personnel, or whether they are deemed talented merely by virtue of being there, ministry of finance people are likely to feel superior. And on occasion they act superior. It would be surprising if they spent years dealing with specific programs without having developed ideas of their own. Their long experience with spending departments creates not only the possibility of antagonism but also the opportunity for cooperation. They are likely to be well connected with other departments with whom they exchange favors. They are likely to have ministers who are more than usually prestigious and whose survival is more important to the government than is that of the ordinary run of cabinet member. So they are better able to act forcefully on the inside and resist pressures from the outside.

Conditions for the power of finance ministries may be better appreciated by contrasting those in Britain, France, and Japan with the relatively weaker central-control organ in the United States. In fact, there is no finance ministry in America. Taxation, economic management, and supply of money are held in some uneasy concatenation by the Treasury, the Council of Economic Advisers, and the Federal Reserve Board. The director of the Office of Management and Budget (OMB) cannot claim that spending must be held within a certain level with the same assurance he would show if his agency were the one really responsible for these determinations. Nor does the OMB have the final word. The fact that Congress can and does override its judgment weakens it considerably. The chances that finance ministries in the other countries will be overridden after the executive has made its decision are exceedingly slim. Finance people may anticipate the inevitable by graceful acquiescence in advance. They may be compelled to concede last-minute changes to party or prime minister or president. But, for the most part, they get their way within the executive and, after the budget leaves that level, they get their way entirely because legislatures do not alter it. The isolated instances of legislative action resulting in an expenditure change are exceptions that prove the rule by showing how extraordinarily skillful must be those who wish to penetrate the system from outside the executive. The single instance Guy Lord cites from France demanded the patience of Job, the cunning of David, and the wisdom of Solomon.

Now the similarities end and the differences in institutions begin. Once we leave the familiar landscape of advocates and guardians, we discover that each of our rich nations has distinctive budgetary institutions not duplicated in the others. Japan, to begin, has the only political party outside the legislature which takes a formal part in budgeting. The Liberal Democratic Party (LDP) participates in setting limits within which the budget is made, and its numerous substantive committees, on which its Diet members participate, are actively involved in the "revival negotiations" that divide up the last few percent. LDP influence may be found in the exceptional rise of rice subsidies for its rural constituencies and in the small public works projects strewn throughout the land wherever its supporters are congregated. Precisely because of its preeminent position as the governing party, however, there are limits on what the LDP can do. It cannot spend and spend because it is also responsible, broadly speaking, for the political consequences of tax rate increases. The LDP cannot reward only its friends, partly because it is so heterogeneous that many interests are included within it, and partly because it is responsible for maintaining the social harmony so important to the Japanese. Its most glaring weaknesses showed up several times when it tried actually to make a budget. This requires not merely general indications of benevolence, as in its "budget" today, but aggregation of preferences in all areas down to the last yen, bureau, and activity. In explaining this failure one should not overemphasize the party's lack of necessary expertise, because it could have obtained what it needed. The party failed in budget-making because its internal stability was threatened by endless disputes arising out of the need to make innumerable specific choices.

There is, of course, a sense in which parties in Britain and France also do make the budget. The party in power makes up the executive, which compiles and passes the budget. Japan is different because the *extra*-parliamentary party also participates in the budgetary process. No doubt party organizations outside Parliament in England and France also have occasional ideas, and party conferences are known to pass resolutions that later have an effect in setting priorities. But these occasions are few and far between, and there is no formal provision for the party as a party to be active in budgeting. Similarly, I suppose it is possible to find a plank in a party platform in America that would show some indirect influence on budgets. But the "convention" party exists for only a few days every four years, and is rivaled by the National Committee party and the Congressional party, each of which also has its separate preferences and its own internal incoherence. When parties lack discipline they cannot make or enforce a budget; when parties in Parliament are disciplined, as in England and France, they transfer their authority to a steering committee called the Cabinet.

Each of our wealthy nations has strong parties. It is not possible, looking at them in isolation, to compare the effects of partisanship per se. To do this we must look at differences between American cities that are or are not organized along party lines. There we discover that political parties energize otherwise weak legislatures. Partisanship enlarges the range of policy alternatives and enhances the potential for bargaining with the executive. Within the executive, elected officials, who have a partisan base, have the edge over appointed administrators.

That the American cabinet has atrophied is so well known as to require no further comment. But if the American one is a "has-been," the Japanese is a "never-was." Never — at least not since the Second World War — has the Japanese cabinet functioned as a body in making budgetary decisions. The Ministry of Finance (mostly) and the Liberal Democrats (partly) set the basic outlines. Further negotiations take place between individual ministers and Finance, or between ministries, their clientele groups, and the LDP. For the most part, the norm of balance is used to settle disputes before they reach Cabinet.

Before the days of the presidential regime, the French cabinet as a body had more to say about budgeting than it does now. Disputes that in Britain would be brought to Cabinet for settlement are, instead, handled in France through "arbitrage" at successive levels. Accurately perceiving that they were being left out, French ministers did try to participate in setting the global limits. They failed because the Ministry of Finance insisted on actively participating in the selection of items to be included within ceilings that the limits imposed; spenders thus discovered they were being subjected to an additional set of controls instead of winning new liberties.

The place of a nation's cabinet may stand in bolder relief if we ask where appeals are handled in these budgetary processes. Departments in Japan appeal to both the LDP and the Ministry of Finance in the "revival negotiations." Departments in France appeal seriatim to the Ministry of Finance, the prime minister, and the president. Ministers in Great Britain appeal to one another through the collective mechanism of the Cabinet. Now it is true that most arguments are settled at the civil service level in bilateral negotiations between departments and the Treasury. Differences that remain may be resolved in meetings with the Chief Secretary of the Treasury or the Chancellor of the Exchequer. The next step is to take the remainder to Cabinet committees and finally to Cabinet itself. Looking at this process from a strictly British point of view, observers may rightly wonder how much substance there is in collective decision-making when the Treasury is so powerful and the prime minister has a strong voice. Placed in comparative perspective, however, the British

Cabinet operates as a body that does make joint decisions. None of the other three nations comes close. For budgetary purposes, it turns out that the British Cabinet model applies only to Great Britain.

It appears to be true that the cabinet model, with or without a powerful cabinet, dooms a legislature to impotence. Or, it just might be that legislatures which actually do exercise power independent of the executive over a wide range of activities have become a rarity in the contemporary world. Among large- and medium-sized nations, only the United States Congress can claim that distinction. Members of the Japanese Diet act on the budget not as members of the legislature or even as adherents of the party in parliament, but by virtue of their association with the extra-parliamentary party. In any capacity, members of the House of Commons have little influence over spending; most of the bit they do have comes from belonging to the majority party. Deputies and senators in France may trade on their extra-parliamentary positions as civil servants or mayors to importune for favors before the executive budget is made up. The course of action required to convince the government to accede on one program or another is so involved that few try and almost none succeed. How, then, has the United States Congress been able to remain powerful; why also is its budgetary authority now under attack?

The usual answers remain important, but do not explain enough. Federalism, together with lack of party discipline, gives each congressman an independent base of support and prevents his subordination to an executive committee of legislative leaders. Yet there are places (the Philippines comes immediately to mind) where comparable conditions exist, but where the legislative power over appropriations has been nullified. These legislatures typically vote much larger appropriations each year than the national income will permit the government to spend, thus effectively transferring power over actual dispersements to the executive, who alone is willing to take on the burden of saying "No." Congress, under the leadership of its House Appropriations Committee, has preserved its power by maintaining the role of guardianship. By depending on the executive to play the advocate, Congress has asserted itself through selective cutting, which ties the executive to congressional figures. The controversy over impounding funds has come up just as Congress appeared to be acting more like an advocate and less like a guardian. When this is so, the executive can guard the Treasury and claim the final determination of increases on the grounds that it alone is responsible for placing revenue and expenditure in some sort of reasonable relationship.

Legislatures around the world suffer by being unwieldy in size and potentially incoherent; as a result they encounter delays in doing business. Congress mitigates these defects by arranging an internal division of labor and specialization, gluing the parts together by widespread acceptance of the norm of reciprocity (in which members regularly follow recommendations of their committees and subcommittees). By making manageable the problem of gaining knowledge and aggregating preferences, Congress can expedite its own activities and keep pace with events. The advantage the executive has is not that it is more intelligent or coordinated, but that it can more readily give the appearance of having both of these qualities. The president may spend only 20 hours a year on the entire budget and the chairman of the House Appropriations Committee may spend 2,000 hours, but the former may still appear more rational than the latter because he can announce a single set of figures, whereas the committee chairman must wait around for the actions of his colleagues. What appears to be happening in America is not so much that the president is usurping power, though this is not ruled out, but that congressmen have begun to lose faith in their own procedures and therefore make a less effective challenge when differences with the executive arise. Lack of legislative self-confidence is not the problem elsewhere because no one expects the legislature to need, have, or use power over spending.

Party politics either kill or cure legislatures. Partisanship kills under the Cabinet model with strong majority parties, because the party-dominated executive controls a legislature, which cannot oppose its own leaders. Coalition governments may provide more scope for legislative initiative but, unless the majority is so fragile that the votes of small parties are essential, party discipline will continue to prevail. Partisanship cures under the separation of powers because it gives an independently elected legislature an organizational base and and at least some programatic thrust. The party in the legislature becomes a counterpoise to the party in the executive. The importance of legislative ability to pay for full-time service, to gather expert staff support, and to gain knowledge through specialization, though most apparent in American cities and states, could be illustrated also in a negative sense in Britain, France, and Japan. Legislators there may criticize in their assemblies but if they want power, they must go elsewhere.

Britain is different because of its Cabinet, Japan for its Party, and the United States through its Congress. How does France differ? It has the only dual presidential and parliamentary regime. To understand what this combination means for the French, we must look at the situation from the standpoint of executive penetration of the budgetary process. The Japanese prime minister has few problems because he does not often try. Usually his initiatives are confined to foreign affairs. His job is to smooth troubled waters, not to make waves on domestic shores. To the extent he has leeway in choosing ministers, of course, he can indirectly affect major ministerial priorities, though his ministers themselves are limited by a strong civil service. British prime ministers do more. They help determine issues on which the Chancellor of the Exchequer will concede on spending bids, though prime ministers also are limited by the necessity to meet the chancellor's needs for financial management. Prime ministers would not ordinarily appoint a strong minister to a department whose spending was to be cut down, except perhaps in Defense, in which a man might still make a reputation from cuts rather than increases. The prime minister also can load Cabinet committees in his favor. Since his position requires that he not lose in Cabinet, however, he cannot afford to lead too often. Invading the prerogatives of ministerial colleagues, while possible on a limited basis, would create constant disharmony unless backed by a wider consensus within the Cabinet. The American president, precisely because he operates in a highly fragmented political system, provides the most concentrated center of power. His office produces streams of policy initiatives with financial implications. The very fragmentation that makes his initiatives so essential, however, also weakens his hold over them within both the bureaucracy and the legislature. The president can reach inside to the bureaucracy and outside to the legislature, but so can his competitors.

The French are in between. Executive penetration of the negotiations between spending ministries and central control organs is greater in France than in Japan or Great Britain, and less than in America. French ministers have their own cabinet, including people outside the civil service, and they cope with intradepartmental conflict more readily because the divisions are more autonomous and their differences require more arbitration than in Japan or Britain. Although there is less executive penetration of the bureaucracy in France than in America, the French are better able to close off government as a whole from outside pressures. The image evoked by Nathan Leites' splendid book on the French parliament, *The House Without Windows,* could stand as well or better for the French budgetary process.

What would the budgetary process look like where wealth and predictability resemble the levels obtaining in the federal government, but the structure of political institutions is markedly different? What form will it take where wealth is low, predictability is high — a situation pertaining in the cities — but where the executive is weak, or legislative partisanship is strong, or authority is fragmented among numerous elected officials? By looking at American state governments, the effect of political structure on budgetary processes can be more clearly observed.

The states vary greatly on all the dimensions affecting budgeting. Some are rich and getting richer as fast or faster than federal government. Others are as poor as most cities. Most have an executive budget, but in some the budget is prepared by a committee. The governor usually has the item veto power, which allows him to eliminate an item in a bill without vetoing it in its entirety.

State legislatures are part-time institutions with part-time resources and part-time abilities. Seldom does the legislature resemble Congress in specialization, expertise, and the time it devotes to budget review.

The existence of the item veto allows the legislature to engage in advocacy rather than guardianship, leaving the governor to assume responsibility for the painful and unpopular task of trimming the budget to fit expected revenues. A liberal governor trying to increase spending would motivate the legislature to assume its guardianship role. Unless the legislature is so opposed to his programs that it will be willing to throw the whole budget book back at him he should not expect to have much trouble. After all, few legislatures are equipped to perform the task.

The behavior of agencies depends on the financial situation. When revenues are not growing faster than expenditures, there is little hope of gaining anything internally. So, like their counterparts at the city level, state agencies look for external sources of money, choosing programs, clienteles, and strategies that are likely to win federal support. When the financial race pays a proper prize, and there is more money available than was spent last year, agencies scramble to get a share. They would, typically, focus their efforts on the governor, paying only minor attention to the legislature. The governor's consent is like money in the bank. If he objects, there is little reason to go to the legislature, for even if strong support can be mobilized there, it would only result in "overappropriations" that would be item vetoed.

By now it should be apparent that something is missing. Not a word (beyond departments and finance ministries) has been said about political institutions in poor countries. Why not? No one should conclude that strategies in poor countries are wholly independent of the structure of their political institutions. How agencies approach the executive is affected by whether the situation involves an army junta, leaders of a mass party, or representatives of economic interests. Basic modes of strategic interaction depend far more, however, on the extent of poverty and uncertainty than they do on how politics is organized. Strategies in poor nations differ far more from rich ones than from each other. Attention is devoted much less to what goes into the formal budget, much more to that series of reallocations during the year which actually convey the right to spend. The difference is not absolute, of course, but is one of degree. Reprograming goes on everywhere. But in poor countries redoing the budget is a (maybe *the*) way of life. It is not a method for occasionally modifying the budget, but actually is the normal way of allocating financial resources. Reprograming, not preprograming, is what they do most of the time.

The syndrome of repetitive budgeting, caused by widespread poverty and pervasive uncertainty, gives different directions to strategic behavior in poor countries. Repetitive budgeting increases the frequency with which strategies are used and leads to greater efforts to get around the regular processes of resource allocation. Unable to count on getting their hands on the money formally allocated in the budget, agencies seek earmarked funds and independent status to a greater extent than do their rich counterparts. Agencies in low-income countries have incentives to avoid rather than to use the governmental budgetary process. They seek (and often obtain) financing outside of the finance ministry. What does the existence of numerous independent budgetary entrepreneurs mean for the chief organs for resource allocation, the finance ministry and the political executive?

Under repetitive budgeting, the finance ministry is both stronger and weaker (though in different respects) than under incremental procedures preceding from a historical base. It is stronger in regard to the agencies within its jurisdiction because they must continually come to Finance for expenditure sanction. Its presence must loom large for agencies not only dependent for future favors but in constant danger of losing what they have. Finance is weaker in that it has a lower proportion of the nation's resources under its control — a proportion constantly in danger of dissipating. Its ability to sanction is greater than its ability to reward. Agencies may conform to Finance's dictates because they fear its wrath, but they are tempted also to engage in gross deceptions because they are so needy and uncertain. If Finance could guarantee funds into the future, agencies would have a positive incentive to go along. Inevitably the insecurity of both sides becomes mutually reinforcing; because neither can make good on their commitments, they see little advantage either in making or in keeping reasonable expenditure promises. Hence they pad and cut back by larger proportions, thus increasing the oscillations in the budgetary system.

The political executive, however constituted, is itself implicated in the syndrome of poverty and uncertainty that produces repetitive budgeting. Its instability is a major cause of uncertainty. The more rapidly ministers change, the larger the policy distance between the incumbent and his successor, the greater the reprograming efforts required to accommodate the new men, the less meaningful the formal budget. Everything is done on ad hoc basis. Not only increments, but also the budgetary base is subject to renegotiation. The demand for current information vastly increases while the supply declines correspondingly because the magnitude and scope of the contemplated changes are more difficult to assess. Political executives may promulgate many new laws and decrees but that is a far cry from finding resources and talents to implement those ideas. They may start but are unlikely to stay around long enough to finish.

If budgeting is our subject, and budgetary processes our main concern, then poor and uncertain countries operate in pretty much the same way regardless of political structure. The alliance of poverty and uncertainty is so strong as to diminish the importance of other relevant variables. That is why, however important these political structures may be for other purposes, I have not dwelt upon their variations from one country to another.

The differences that matter to us are those which produce variations in budgetary processes. Nowhere are they more apparent than in the calculations made in deciding how much to ask for or to appropriate.

CALCULATIONS

Ranking types of budgetary process according to the degree of complexity in the calculations used would show that they are the most simple for the poor and certain, most complicated for the poor and uncertain, with the rich and certain in between. American cities exemplify the extreme incrementalism produced by certainty and poverty. Their state constitutions mandate balanced budgets; revenues are difficult to increase; demands for services are close to the permissible limits on spending. City budget routines consist largely of adding on a little here and there when the revenue picture is good and cutting in similar proportions when it is bad. The larger they are, the more important such increments become, but usually they stay within a few percentage points of last year's base. Budgeters in cities need accurate accounting of the previous years' expenditures and estimates of next year's tax yields. So long as the past is a good guide to the future, that is, certainty holds, they should be able to make both calculations reasonably well. When one is talking mostly about adding or subtracting a few positions in a particular agency, the consequences are simultaneously easier to ascertain and less important to gauge just right.

Rich and certain nations generally budget by increments. The scope of their opportunities and their potential for difficulties are, however, greater than in American cities. Their ability to extract resources is considerable, limited only by available wealth and citizen protest. So is the ability to spend. Increments for rich countries are larger in absolute amount and in percentage than those in the cities. More important than the size of the increment, however, is the stability of the base from which it proceeds. Most agencies most of the time can count on getting something (plus or minus) like what they had before. Agreements entered into during the past few years will not often nor lightly be broken. Everyone can count on them. What can be taken for granted from year to year vastly exceeds what is open to dispute. That — the stability of the base — gives incrementalism its application. Nations that budget incrementally can concentrate on what they would do if they had a little less (or somewhat more) than in the previous year. Specific programs within a particular agency may experience greater volatility in a given year, but most programs and most agencies will carry on much as before. That is why central control organs and political executives can concentrate on a relatively few large items that involve significant departures from the past.

Rich but uncertain regimes face additional complexities. Their uncertainties lie in the political realm. These nations have skilled workers and good information but lack political cohesion. Budgets are still meaningful but often arrive late and must be renegotiated after ministerial shifts. Agencies, often working under old budgets long after the fiscal year has passed, are forced to begin over if the latest political shift produces a minister who wants change. The base is either too certain, failing to contemplate change because of governmental rigidity, or too uncertain, in that agreements made by one government are less likely to be kept by another. What can they do? Their best hedge against political uncertainty is to take as much of the past for granted as they can. Once they stumbled on a device such as the service vote in Fourth Republic France, which does exactly that, they latched on to it.

Most complex of all are the calculations of the poor and uncertain. Unlike conditions in American cities, poverty here extends far beyond lack of money. Unlike regimes such as the French Fourth Republic, uncertainties for the poor and uncertain extend beyond the political realm. Any one financial year is likely to be quite different from another in terms of revenue, expenditure, foreign aid, inflation, and even political leadership. Budgets lack predictive value, so they cannot stabilize expectations for so long a period as a year. It is hard to find out who has spent how much for what purpose; it is hard to estimate likely revenues; prediction is perilous. The poor and uncertain have more decisions to make involving proportionally larger amounts in shorter periods of time with less information at their disposal than do the rich. So they delay decisions, shorten the time span, and otherwise repeat their calculations throughout the year.

Nothing I have said should be interpreted to mean that the problems facing budgeters in rich countries are simple. They are not. Placed on some absolute scale, they would be considered incredibly complex, since they involve myriads of programs, each with a different technical component, political relationships, and uncertain effect on the others. Nowadays, moreover, governments spend proportionally more each decade than the one before, necessarily increasing the range and magnitude of the comparisons they must take into account. Instead of using increasingly complex *modes* of calculations, however, rich governments have made drastic moves to simplify their lives. Instead of moving away from incrementalism, they have gone toward it; instead of rejecting incrementalism as unworthy, they have embraced it.

THE INSTITUTIONALIZATION OF INCREMENTALISM

Incrementalism in budgeting has been attacked as mindless and irrational — mindless because most of the budget is not subject to scrutiny, irrational because most of the possible relevant comparisons are deliberately excluded. If, however, aids to calculation are, as I have argued, responses to the extraordinary complexity of governmental resource allocation, then the problem of calculation should have gotten worse in recent decades as government spending has increased manyfold. And indeed it has. With governments undertaking so many new programs and doing so much more under the rubric of old ones, we would expect greater rather than lesser emphasis on aids to calculation. More rather than less of the total budget would be taken for granted and a lesser rather than greater proportion of changes would be subject to serious scrutiny. This is just what has happened.

Incrementalism is becoming institutionalized in rich countries. Three out of the four for which information is available — Great Britain, France, and Japan — not only practice incrementalism but have built it into their formal machineries for making the annual budget. This is not incrementalism sub rosa, so to speak, as in the United States. (There it is adopted but not applauded, on the grounds that there must be something better but, at the moment, it's not clear just what.) Rather it is incrementalism with a vengeance, reinforced by procedures designed to compel incremental calculations. Since 1965 France has used the service vote in which all past spending is considered a continuing commitment. Parlement votes only on additions or, occasionally, subtractions from past totals. What is more important, the Ministry of Finances treats past commitments as if they were inviolable, with an inner life of their own. Since 1965 Great Britain has replaced the traditional estimates with five-year projections of the cost of existing policies. Called by the name of the official committee supervising it, the Public Expenditure Survey Committee (PESC), this new procedure is the mechanism through which funds are now allocated, in the form of annual white papers. PESC works. It has given the Treasury considerably greater control than it had heretofore exercised over the growth of public expenditure, a conclusion that will become apparent after we discuss PESC in Chapter 16. It is now much harder than it used to be to sneak in small items with large future spending implications. Containing the vices of its virtues, as most human mechanisms do, PESC also makes it correspondingly more difficult for old items to be taken out. And to make sure matters do not get out of hand, the Treasury has adopted two new devices — the relative price effect and the productive potential. Based on the questionable assumption that productivity in the public sector does not grow at the same rate as in the private sector, the relative price effect leads to a proportion of each year's budget being put away for safe keeping in case expenses go that much beyond expectations. Productive potential declares, by fiat, that productivity will not increase at more or less than 3 percent, thus establishing a small and constant margin for future increases. PESC works within a margin of a margin with a safety factor added on.

Incrementalism nowhere is better practised than in Japan. The Japanese can look incremental anyway you come at them, bottom-up, top-down, and seemingly sideways, too. For starters, the Ministry of Finance imposes a 125 percent ceiling over the past year. A quarter of the previous year's budget might seem large were it not for the fact that past spending goes unchallenged, and that every ministry is expected to get built-in increases amounting to a good half or more of that. In making up its critically important draft budget, therefore, Finance adds both "natural increases" (cost of living and mandatory items) and "seminatural increases" (those not required by law or price increases but which every sensible man knows will have to be made). Should the question arise of whether one ministry is to be preferred over others in obtaining increases, the norm of balance (*baransū*) is applied so that comparable programs and categories get essentially the same proportion of what there is to give. By the time Finance holds its own Important Items discussion, thinking is almost unnecessary in putting out its draft budget. Still, after all this, only a beginning has been made in performing the Japanese laminectomy on the yearly budget. Concerned lest there remain unadjusted grievances, the Ministry of Finance has put away a few percent of the total so that all those who feel they have lost out in the original process can participate in the "resurrection" (literally, to come back from the dead) negotiations. Within this rapidly diminishing margin, itself an increment of an increment, the Ministry of Finance allocates across-the-board proportions for salary and policy adjustment expenses, so that when top party officials and the Minister of Finance sit down for the final decisions, they are not overloaded with hard choices.

Apparently, central budget control organs in Britain, France, and Japan have largely given up, or retreated from, detailed scrutiny of budgetary proposals. They no longer appear anxious to use the budget as a means of imposing priorities on the rest of the government. What has happened? Why have they begun to abandon their ancient powers? What if anything have they got in return? Finance ministries have trimmed old expenditure powers so as better to preserve their authority over economic management. They have tried to limit conflict over the composition of individual expenditure items in order to enhance their general control over spending.

As spending has increased, the spenders have grown stronger. Flushed from past victories, feeding on desire for national grandeur or for social justice, righteous in their wrath against those who would deny citizens necessities of life, they have put their former controllers on the run. Threatened, for instance, by the Liberal Democratic Party in Japan and spending ministers in other countries — such as those who allegedly ganged up on the British Treasury's Chancellor of the Exchequer in the 1950s — central control organs have had to reconsider their function. At the same time also they have been deeply affected by the Keynesian revolution in economic thought. Except in the United States, where the Office of Management and Budget is not the same organization as the Treasury Department or the Council of Economic Advisers, the men whose job it is to control spending are part of a larger apparatus whose tasks include economic management. As politician and civil servant alike have grown assured and comfortable operating on seemingly simple Keynesian decision rules — spend when unemployment is high, cut back when it is low — they have identified their fortunes increasingly with their ability to affect the wider economic situation. Reducing the burden of calculation has meant not merely narrowing their job to considering increments to the budget, but also viewing spending as part of economic management, with the major emphasis and interest in total expenditures rather than specific programs. Ministers of finance and their civil-service advisers are not usually selected for their skill at cost-benefit analysis (which might be appropriate for choosing *among* spending projects), but for their ability to handle larger economic aggregates. And the politician's interest in holding down or manipulating the tax rate is served also by the same macroeconomic approach. Hence an implicit bargain has been struck. Ministries of finance have begun to loosen their hold over detailed financial scrutiny (made increasingly difficult anyway by the growing size of government) in return for control over the totals to aid economic management.

The shift from concern about composition of expenditures to interest in their total amount has alleviated some anxieties and created others. Less conflict crops up between spending ministries and their financial controllers over who has the expertise in a particular line of policy. But now central control organs begin to worry about whether they have gone too far, that is, whether anyone today is paying attention to public policy in the country except those with an ax to grind because they are the ones doing the work. Conflict has been reduced and authority maintained, but the rationality of spending is thrown into greater doubt than ever.

The strain between the polity and the economy, between maintaining consensus in the polity and rationality in the economy, goes to the essence of budgeting. If all that mattered was increasing income, no matter who received it, or maintaining harmony, no matter who suffered by it, resource allocation would be a lot easier. It is to this sort of conflict, then, that we must turn for a deeper insight into the dilemmas of budgeting.

11
Budgeting and Conflict

Each government has its own way of handling social problems. The calculations and strategies of its officials create a recognizable political style. Budgetary processes, inevitably part of that style, also contribute something of their own. That "something" is the subject of this chapter and the one following. My aim is to assess what budgeting has to do with handling conflict.

To make an acceptable budget for an entire year is a major achievement. For if the governmental participants and affected social interests are not reconciled to their lot, they will struggle against that allocation of resources not merely once a year but all the time, and thus undermine government stability. Indeed, the annual budget is one of the first reflectors of dissension about the role of government. Inability to agree on the budget shows that a common conception of government is lacking. But budgeting is not only a product of the political realities in which it is embedded; it to some degree also shapes these forces. Budgetary procedures can accent the animosities men bring to the bargaining table, or they can mitigate them. The way budgets are presented, the kinds of issues highlighted or cast into the shadows, the sequence in which decisions are made, the number and authority of the agencies involved, all may influence the amount and kind of conflict. Whether one feels that in a particular system there is too little or too much conflict, or even whether it is about the wrong things, one cannot escape knowing that the annual budget also is a mechanism for dealing with conflict.

To no one's surprise, this process is tightly linked to the political forces it tries to express. Budgeting is a subsystem of politicking, dominated by the political system. Strange, indeed, would be a system in which politics went one way and budgets the other; it would mean that actual resource allocation was being done elsewhere. Consider the circumstances under which national planning is merely window dressing while a nation's political forces make themselves felt through more binding mechanisms. Or, as in poor countries, see how budget documents lack predictive value because politicians do not express their real preferences until conditions evolve during the year. That politics dominates, however, does not mean that it is all-encompassing. Perfect congruence between political and budgetary systems is unnecessary. The budgetary subsystem may compensate for or reinforce defects of the larger political system. No one yet has addressed the interaction between political and budgetary systems. (Merely to say that budgeting *is* a political process, while better than maintaining the opposite, does not quite answer the question.) Let us start by considering, in this chapter, how budgeting reflects national modes of political problem-solving and, in the next, how it defuses or charges the existing mechanisms for shaping conflict.

CALCULATIONS AND CONFLICT

Calculations may be containers or sustainers of conflict.[1] If every year budgeters were required to redo the arguments on the desirability of each major expenditure — as called for in zero-base budgeting, and implied in program budgeting — they would stoke up the burners with old animosities to fan the flames of new conflagrations. Only poor countries come close to this state of affairs, not because they necessarily wish to do so, but because their uncertain financial position continually causes them to go back on old commitments in favor of new ones that are in turn replaced. Because past disputes are part of present conflicts, their budgets contain little of predictive value. If they feel they are working harder to accomplish less, that is only realistic. None of the rich countries do this. They accept past commitments as a given historical base, consigning themselves to a relatively narrow range of increases and, occasionally, decreases. The potential for conflict over these increments is limited because the scope for decision has been reduced.

Budgeting, as we know only too well, is serial, sequential, and specialized. It is not necessary, even if one could conceive of it, to solve each problem every year. Because budgeting recurs regularly, repeated attacks may be made on the same general problem. Participants know they will be able to make a series of efforts over the years, and can leave some things for the future. Nor need the agenda of problems within a single time period be dealt with all at once. Because budgeting is specialized, a number of participants (bureaus, departments, central control organs, executives, legislatures, parties, etc.) can take a crack at it. The magnitude and intensity of disagreement among participants is bound to be less than if the problems were treated all at once. By making choice more manageable, through what we can sum up as these aids to calculation, conflict is also reduced.

If it were necessary to deal with the effect of each issue on the others, or

---

[1] In writing this section I have benefited from contributions by Jonathan Bender and Richard Meisinger, students in my seminar on budgeting.

to trade off the substantive merits from one field of interest to another, participants would be constantly at loggerheads. One reason for the poor politics of program budgeting is that, if implemented, it would increase conflict by calling for simultaneous and clear-cut choice among major policy alternatives. Instead of bilateral bargaining in sequence, there would be the Hobbesian war of all against all. Classical budgeting is comparatively uncoordinated and relatively nonprogramatic. Attention, of course, is paid to totals. This total figure will emerge at the end of a long series of iterations by marginal reductions among a few programs, or even by smaller ones among all of them, rather than by deep and sudden cuts in a few. The major contrary examples are the reduction of British (after Suez) and French (after Algeria) military expenditures lasting a decade or more. Otherwise, disputes over accepted programs are treated as differences in monetary amounts. These differences, though important, are not likely to raise the same emotions as are challenges to fundamental merits, concerning which, in any event, conclusive information is likely to be scanty.

Why, despite the constant criticism to which they have been subjected, do budgeters persist in these aids to calculation? What would happen if they did not? The experience of both rich and poor countries is instructive.

Budgeting is bargaining. Participants usually have different policy preferences and often do not share factual premises about the likely effects of alternative courses of action — except in one respect. Among the rich there is certainty about money flows. It is known with relatively high reliability that revenues will be forthcoming as expected, and that expenditures in the budget will flow to officially designated spenders who will do their duty. Since there is disagreement over the values placed on policies, however, bargaining is necessary to resolve them. An essential criterion of successful budgeting, therefore, is that despite disagreement over policies, budgets are completed when they are supposed to be and are carried out as advertised.

Budgeting also is supposed to increase the knowledge devoted to public policy. If there is a mechanism for holding onto adequate solutions and sequentially proceeding to solve remaining problems, wise policy is more likely to result. Similarly, an agreement-producing process is more likely to work if past agreements can be retained, while the system works on an ever-decreasing set of unresolved issues. In both processes, two general types of error can turn up: extreme rigidity (retaining all past knowledge or locking oneself financially into the past) and extreme instability (rejecting all past solutions and past agreements). In budgetary systems, which are our concern, the first error amounts to leaving no financial flexibility to handle unexpected demands, whereas the second poses the problem of rebuilding from scratch a structure of agreements.

Base is to budgetary systems as habits are to organisms. A budgetary base is the routinized retention of old solutions. Clinging to last year's agreements (whether in the form of informal base norms in the U.S., or service votes in

France) is enormously economical of critical resources, particularly time and good interpersonal relations, which would be seriously impaired if all or most past agreements were reexamined yearly. In addition to having a "memory" of old agreements, budgetary systems must also have decision structures capable of generating new ones. The process of budgeting, which relates various levels to one another, performs this function.

The classical image of a hierarchy is a structure in which decisions move from top to bottom, each level providing the goal premises of the one beneath it. In the budgetary process, we observe not only hierarchies but "lowerarchies"; the flow is in both directions: aggregate figures are established at the top and passed down as constraints to lower levels, while conflicts are bubbled upwards. Ultimately, expenditure demands and spending limitations exert reciprocal influence on each other.

The two most important properties of the hierarchical aspect of budgeting are: first, the task of reaching agreement (on what is already a small subset of all possible budget decisions, since most were made last year) is partitioned into many small sub-tasks. Instead of confrontation with a very small number of widely diverging figures (as might happen if, say, the LDP in Japan actually managed to construct a genuine alternative budget so that the possible discrepancy with Finance might be large, and hard to resolve), the conflict breaks down into many small differences. Disparities between the bargainers are usually small enough to permit resolution of most decisions. But not all — and this is where the second feature is important. All four systems have mechanisms which act as coarse filters: agreements reached on lower levels usually hold for the rest of the system. The next level faces only decisions which were unresolved at the lower level (either because the spender refuses to accept a cutter's limit, or because both parties realize that the question is too controversial), and so on. In this way the system retains "successes" and resolves an everdwindling number of "failures." Potential overload is typically averted by those at lower levels who realize they must settle most disputes themselves. The higher official who does the cutting, moreover, usually sustains the "no" of his subordinate to keep an inordinate number of appeals from reaching his level.

Where is the real locus of decision-making — the "hierarchy" or the "lowerarchy?" Acceptance of the budgetary base pushes actual decision-making down to lower levels. Although a ministry's total budget is fixed, its funds for internal programs are allowed to vary; a minister may promote one program at the expense of another. Thus the more that successive levels of the administration lean on incrementalism, the lower down in the hierarchy will the real decisions among alternative expenditures take place. Only disagreements — the increment of the increment that differs from last year — are sent up.

Incrementalism may lead not only to uncertainty reduction, but also to a shift in the burden of uncertainty from one organization or level to another (i.e., reducing one level's uncertainty at the expense of another level). The focus on increments to the budget base reduces the uncertainty in the budget process for one or more participants. But if a higher level demands that a lower level rank the items within the increment of its increment, then that higher level is merely shifting part of the responsibility for final decision to the lower level.

The British do not usually try to do this, at least not in the short run. As evidenced by the Treasury's policy of "cutting by bargaining" rather than absolute "no's," the British budgeters' high degree of trust leads participants to share their problems rather than transfer them outright to another level. French budgeters, on the contrary, engage in more uncertainty-shifting strategies than the other three systems because the French budget process is more conflict-ridden. The budget division's strategy toward spending ministries is one of taking the offensive; at the start of the review, budget proposals are heavily criticized and many cuts are suggested. This strategy puts the spending ministry on the defensive and shifts back to it the burden of proof of program worth.

A typical agency strategy for shifting uncertainty to the budget division is to make cuts in important program areas; the cuts will have to be restored sometime during the year, and the budget division will be forced to find the resources to do so. But this behavior is risky. Uncertainty about actions taken at higher levels encourages bargaining at lower levels, for if there is disagreement in the "lowerarchy," there is no telling what the boys upstairs may do.

No one can say these mechanisms — for reducing conflict while allocating resources — have persisted for want of experience with others. For good or ill, budgetary processes can be shown to be adaptive mechanisms. The growing size and complexity of public expenditures have spawned efforts to limit the totals, increase the productivity of the rest, and enhance political control. From the late 1950s through the 1960s and continuing into the 1970s, our four rich countries have seen major budgetary changes. From the Public Expenditure Survey Committee, the Program and Analysis Review Committee, and the Central Policy Review Staff in Great Britain to the ceilings and revival negotiations of Japan, and from program budgeting in America to the service votes of France, the men of the 1930s and 1940s (not to speak of those in earlier historical epochs) would not easily recognize much of what now occurs, or how it happens. These modern devices all affect the nature and extent of conflict — who disagrees with whom how much over what — and most were explicitly recognized as increasing conflict in a desirable direction (for example the praise of American program budgeting for forcing trade-offs between comparable programs so as to cut down weaker ones) or deliberately reducing the scope of conflict (as Japanese ceilings, and the French service votes).

Many poor countries tried to adapt via program budgeting, but they could manage neither the calculations nor the strategies required; political support usually was nonexistent; even when it was forthcoming the necessary knowledge was lacking. Program budgeting, it turned out, was premised on achieving the very conditions — knowledge and power — initially required for its success. The real response of poor countries consisted precisely in those practices most condemned — adaptation to uncertainty by shifting from an annual budget to what was, in effect, continuous budgeting. They suffer today from inability to systematize these procedures to make the best of them.

For as long as poor nations pretend to make an annual budget that cannot be meaningful, calculations forced on them by the effort to maintain this fiction must increase conflict. Since the budget is a facade, but cannot be disregarded entirely, spending agencies and their associated interests are motivated to ask for more than they expect to get; finance ministries, lest they appear niggardly in public, are willing to give it to them — on paper. Accusations of bad faith are then added to the usual programmatic disagreements as Finance takes back what it only appeared to give and the spending interests feel let down. Every time the budget is renegotiated during the year there is additional possibility for disagreement. The more rapid the changes, the larger the departures from past spending patterns, the worse the conflict will get. The less confident each participant is in the formal budget, the less he is able to anticipate what others will do or to keep his own promises, the more necessary it becomes to compensate for these uncertainties by basing decisions on extreme calculations: the central control organs cut more to compensate for extreme padding and the spending interests accommodate deep cuts by deeper padding. Instead of decreasing conflict, calculations in poor countries actually widen the distance between opposing views.

Budgeters in poor countries would like to use incremental methods but they lack the stable base from which to proceed. Budgeters in rich countries could use different methods but they prefer to adopt an ever more incremental approach. Although these calculations, which limit conflict while budgeting, appear to lack an acceptable rationale, their very prevalence testifies eloquently that men in many countries come up with similar solutions to similar problems. Where they have not, it has been because of the turbulence of the financial environment, and not a preference for different methods. What is it about these aids to calculations, then, that appeals to all these voices of experience? How can we get a handle on what makes it work for them? If the essential mechanism at work is the reduction of problems into more manageable margins to be dealt with repeatedly at different times and by various authorities, let us ask whether some rich countries do more and others less of this sort of thing.

STYLES OF PROBLEM-SOLVING

The larger the number of relatively autonomous centers with a significant effect on the shape of the budget, the greater the potential division of labor, and hence the greater the opportunities for acting in sequence to reduce conflict. Merely listing the *levels* of budgetary decision (see Table 11.1) shows that the United States has by far the most, France a considerable number, and

Table 11.1. THREE WAYS OF COPING WITH CONFLICT

Levels of Budgetary Decision

United States (high)	France (middle)	Great Britain (low)	Japan (low)
Bureaus	Divisions	Departments	Ministries
Departments	Ministries	Treasury	Finance Ministry
OMB:	Finance Ministry	Cabinet	Party
President	Prime Minister		
House Appropriations	President		
Subcommittees			
House			
Senate Appropriations			
Committee			
Senate			
Senate Conference			
Committee			

Dominant Budgetary Norms

Legal arbitration	Legal	Interpersonal	Proportional
Interpersonal trust	arbitration	trust	balance
Proportional balance			

The Old School Tie

Low	High	Medium	High

Great Britain and Japan the fewest. Despite apparent similarities, these nations really have in common only institutionalization of the advocacy and guardian roles through spending departments and central control organs. Then differences begin to show up. American bureaus and French divisions are far more autonomous than their counterparts in Japan and Great Britain, where strong ministries are the rule. The cabinet as a collective entity is important only in Great Britain. There could be some disagreement over whether the president of the United States should be separated from the Office of Management and Budget, but I have separated them because he and his staff do serve as an important avenue of appeal, even though the OMB presumably is acting on his instructions in the first place. An even stronger argument can be made for separating the prime minister and president in France; there each can take initiative and each handles appeals. Japan is the one nation in which the party organization takes a direct hand in budgeting. The United States alone has a powerful legislature, including House and Senate, committees within them, and the Conference Committee, which reconciles their differences.

Before we can analyze the effect of differences in the number of decision levels on the budgetary processes in our four rich countries, we must know something about the relationship between those various levels within each country. By what norms — legal, interpersonal, proportional — do they regulate their relationships? How does the relative power of each level affect what they do to and with one another? What social bonds tie them together or pull them apart?

The norms we will discuss — trust, arbitration, and balance — are found to some degree in all four rich countries. Since formal rules can never cover all situations, there must be a degree of trust among participants in budgeting for anything to be settled; unless all disputes are resolved at the lowest levels (thus depriving higher authorities of their say), there must be ways to refer differences upward for arbitration; policy coherence and organizational stability require that like activities get similar treatment, and that departments not continually be subject to vast and sudden fluctuations of income.

What norms are most prevalent in which countries? We have little trouble here. Trust is the prevalent norm in Great Britain. Professionals that they are, high civil servants have relations mediated by common acceptance of dealing truthfully with one another. Participants do have different roles and organizational loyalties, and everyone accepts this; but they pass vital information to one another, and can rely on each other's commitments.

Trust, in France, is overshadowed by arbitration (*arbitrage*). Face-to-face relationships are played down.[2] Each organ pushes its own point of view, going to successively higher levels for arbitration and accepting the final results either through exhaustion or the lapse of time in the budgetary cycle.

Coordination — achieved in England by incessant "chats" and circulation of papers among top civil servants, and through courts of appeal in France — is accomplished by balance (*baransū*) in Japan. Though the Japanese do show trust and encourage appeals, they emphasize proportionality, that is, balanced consideration of ministries and of like activities in apportioning increases. Not only is the draft budget of the Ministry of Finance balanced, but "revival" negotiations also contain a significant element of proportionality. This is a system designed to guarantee that all gain something and no one loses entirely.

What about the United States? It has everything. Though Americans show trust among participants less than do the British, there is more than is found in France. Americans emphasize arbitration less than the French, but more than in Japan. Japan exceeds the United States in its devotion to balance, but American budgeting is not without some emphasis on fair shares. That America has something of everything is not without significance in understanding the nature of its budgetary process. For America lacks one thing all the other rich countries have — a strong bond of social cohesion among civil servants at the highest levels.

France and Japan are most extreme. All Japanese financial controllers come from Tokyo University (all but one from its law school). As in France,

2 See Michele Crozier, *The Bureaucratic Phenomenon* (Chicago: University of Chicago Press, 1964) for illustrations from other contexts in France.

they are recruited from the same upper middle-class backgrounds, go to the same few prestigious schools and, at appropriate ages, find their own kind strategically placed around the government. Britain is in a state of transition. The Oxford and Cambridge axis is still disproportionately represented in the higher civil service, but less so than in previous decades. The "old school tie," if one adds public schools like Eton and Harrow to "Ox-bridge," is being replaced by allegiance to the higher civil service. There is wide horizontal circulation between the Treasury, the departments, and the Cabinet Office. True, Treasury people are much more likely to head departments than are departmental people to come back and head the Treasury. Whether this trend represents Treasury imperialism or just the spirit of adventure, civil servants continue to work in many more different departments than they used to, and serve on many more top-level committees. Members of the prestige corps of the French civil service also move about a great deal, serving often in ministerial cabinets; but men from one department and division rarely serve in others. The same is true in Japan, where a lifetime of service is usually spent within a single ministry. The sense of proportion that British civil servants can get by learning how the world looks from a number of departmental perspectives is available in Japan only by widespread internalization of balance as a norm. France, Great Britain, and Japan, however, show little vertical mobility, from lower to higher levels of the civil service, and hardly any lateral mobility, that is, entry from the outside. Their civil service systems are relatively closed at the top and virtually impervious from the sides.

In all these respects the United States is different. No matter where you look there is mobility. But there is no longer, if there ever was — in the government as a whole, or in such elite departments as State and Treasury — a common social background. People at top levels of the civil service, or their immediate superiors in political positions, are unlikely to have known each other before they meet in Washington. Their relationships are shaped by need to interact with one another in various areas of policy. A good test of the open nature of the governmental machinery in the United States is provided by the flow between governments and interest groups. In Japan, France, and Britain it is customary for higher civil servants to take positions with interest groups, including those they have had some experience with in government. Rarely, if ever, do businessmen and trade unions come inside the government unless it be as part of a ruling party or coalition. In the United States the exchange is more even. Government personnel frequently join interest groups which, in turn, send their people to serve in government. It seems that the United States makes up for what it lacks by doing a whole lot of different things. The large number of levels of decision is part and parcel of its mode of handling conflict, just as the smaller number found elsewhere fit in with other nations' governmental ways of life.

France and the United States have the largest number of budgetary levels; but their underlying philosophies of government are almost diametrically opposed. The American style is diversionary; the United States confuses (and, it is hoped, diffuses) conflicts. The French throw up a fortress; France contains (and, it is hoped, controls) conflict. The one absorbs conflict into government, the other uses government to overwhelm it; one dissipates the force of conflict at every level, the other crushes it from above.

The highest reaches of French government stand as a bulwark against the flood crests that periodically threaten to engulf it. The government of the United States is like a network of small rivers in which, if a single one overflows, it does not add to the force of others as they carry away the sediment of conflict to different shores. The levels in the French budgetary process are like a succession of ever higher breakwaters, each holding back a certain amount of pressure until the flood recedes or the retaining walls collapse. The budgetary process in the United States is more like a series of sluice gates and diversionary canals gradually lowering the levels through successive reductions and, if that fails, deflecting the pressure into different channels. The retaining walls are smaller and weaker, but there are an awful lot of them, so that no single one is essential to the performance of the system. Crisscrossing and overlapping networks are characteristic features of the American budgetary process. The same issues undergo successive refinements within and throughout the executive and legislative branches. French budgeting, like French government, is unilinear; it goes up and down within the executive but not sideways to Parlement or crabwise within the executive. The French process is reinforced only between levels so, if the highest level collapses, the whole system may fall. The American process is redundant within each level as well; the system may confound itself, but it is less likely to fall apart.

France has, and needs, more levels of budgetary decision than Japan or Britain. It cannot count on a congruence between government and society and must, therefore, impose it. The president has to shore up the prime minister because otherwise the government is not strong enough. The many procedural constraints — service votes, global margins, limitations on debate in Parlement — force the budget process through to conclusion. Even a cursory knowledge of French politics suggests that the history of political fragmentation, instability, and consequential governmental uncertainty place a premium on formal mechanisms to ensure that the annual budget is made. The Gaullist reforms provide for a legal community because the social one is weak, in order to ensure that neither external social forces nor internal political ones will stalemate the budgetary process and immobilize the machinery of government. The French solution is to substitute a formal state apparatus for informal political community.

The British use fewer levels of budgetary decision because there has been less conflict for them to contain. They assume a closer congruence between government and society. Strong relationships of personal trust at higher levels of the civil service, reinforced by social bonds and common experience, reflect a fundamental social cohesion, at least at the upper levels of society. Budgeting concerns a handful of actors involved in face-to-face relationships. People know an enormous amount about one another, and about the policy preferences and organizational loyalties each brings to the budgetary game. Whether their knowledge of outside developments equals their superb grasp of inside events is more problematical. They assume congruence, but they can be mistaken. British networks are stable on the inside and closed to the outside.

The Japanese style is to avoid conflict; no matter how little there appears to be, they try to make it still less. The potential for conflict on the inside is reduced by common social ties and proportional norms among the few levels for decision. The ruling party, itself a heterogeneous coalition, is open to the outside. No major interests are neglected entirely; almost all can count on keeping what they have and getting a similar proportion of what is going.

Whatever the differences among them, however, the personal networks in all three countries are small enough for single actors to comprehend them. This comprehension cannot be had in the United States. Its absence helps to explain why budgeting in the United States is so difficult to understand.

The nexus between society and government in the United States, in its scale and complexity, is far beyond the cognitive capacities of any single actor, even if it were closed to the outside and stable on the inside, which it assuredly is not. In its size, the large number of elements involved, and the diffuseness of the power structure, the United States has less in common with any of the three countries than they have with each other. Holding these elements together is no mean task. The personalities involved are constantly changing in their identities and in their relationship to one another. That is why the United States uses, as we have observed, all the norms that prevail in the other rich countries. That is why both personal and legal relationships are necessary to link the vast array of components in the system if, indeed, there is to be a system that will produce a budget at all. In Japan and England people need to know each other to establish coordination at the top levels of the civil service, but in America they must be acquainted across policy lines to establish a minimum coherence necessary to get things done issue-by-issue. Trust in Japan and Britain helps participants carry out the public will that is assumed to preexist; confidence is essential in America so that participants can rely enough on each other to discover that will. Legal relationships, which in France make up for the lack of political community, in America provide more stable arenas in the midst of the prevailing flux.

The political arena in the United States may be likened to the operation of the marketplace in classical economics under the rules of free competition. The market mechanism sets optimal prices, vis-à-vis the preference schedules of the organized members of society, only to the extent that members are willing and able to articulate their real preferences. Various interest groups, including bureaucratic and political participants, act as watchdogs to support and struggle against each level of incremental decision according to their own preferences. Social preferences are better known because there are multiple points of access, few barriers to entry, and numerous levels of decision. Evoking preferences of the organized is all too easy. Implementing the resulting programs is exceptionally difficult because the same forces that assure multitudes of initiatives will also guarantee a diversity of responses.

France, Britain, and Japan are like monopolies whose franchise is subject to periodical renewal. Between elections, which is most of the time, they rely on consultation with major organized interests and their intuitions of public preferences. They can implement programs with astonishing rapidity and amazing completeness throughout the realm because governments are centralized and closed. The smaller number of preferences goes together with the fewer levels of decision. Execution is all too easy. But monopolies are correspondingly less able to gauge preferences and more prone to mistake the reaction to them. They can set prices all right, but these may be the wrong ones.

So far budgeting has been abstracted from both government and society. The stage has been set for marrying budgeting to conflict but the wedding has not yet taken place.

The extent to which budgetary processes affect conflict depends on how much conflict must be dealt with: what is the scope and intensity of conflict thrown up by the economic, social, and political systems to which budgetary processes are connected? Nations that are absolutely wealthier and growing relatively faster should generate fewer conflicts over spending than their poorer and declining neighbors. Though our measures are weak, few doubt that societies differ in their propensity to produce social conflict, some making more of their opportunities to disagree than others. The same can be said about political institutions and the elites who operate them. Politics may make strange bedfellows, but once in the same bed, some live together more happily or less miserably than others.

How does budgeting contribute to (or detract from) the ability to live together? Budgetary calculations narrow the distance between contending elements when they are rich, but widen the gap when they are poor. How does political structure affect the ways in which budgeting increases or decreases conflict? That question can be answered only in the rich countries. Poverty pulverizes processes; any poor country budgets more like another one than either budgets like any rich one. Tolstoy, in a famous passage, once suggested that happy families are all alike, whereas sad ones are each miserable in their own way. He would be quite wrong if he suggested that the budgets of the rich are all alike whereas the poor differed in the depths of their poverty. Quite the contrary. In the process of budgeting, poor nations have to resemble each other; only the rich can afford to be different. Let us begin, therefore, with the immediate antecedents of conflict over spending in our four rich countries.

12
Conflict and Budgeting

It would be nice to know how the demand for public expenditures measures up to a nation's ability to provide them, and how much conflict there is in each nation compared to the ability of governments to contain it. For if demands are small and resources are large by comparison, there need be less conflict over resource allocation. And if a society generates relatively little social conflict, then there is less need for governmental mechanisms to cope with it. Though it is easy to put these grand statements in a cavalier manner, it is very hard to analyze them convincingly. They encapsulate the ancient dilemmas of demand versus support and of legitimacy versus effectiveness. Involved are the relationships between citizen and government, and between opposing political forces. Thus we should not be surprised at our inability to progress very far, and we must be prepared to accept numerous compromises to go any distance at all. Now, prepared to use rough and ready measures, I will sketch in briefly the relative differences among France, Great Britain, Japan, and the United States along those dimensions which form the most critical parts of the environment for budgetary purposes.

WEALTH, TAXES, AND POLITICS IN RICH COUNTRIES

The absolute level or "stock" of wealth in a country is a simple indicator of those resources potentially available to the government.[1] Most citizens of a poor country can barely survive on a day-to-day basis, and little is left for the government. For rich countries, with potential wealth in the private sector,

[1] This section was co-authored with Aiden Vining, a student in the Graduate School of Public Policy, University of California, Berkeley.

Although technically per capita GNP is a measure of income (flow) rather than wealth (stock) the two measures are so close and the use of per capita figures so common we saw no reason to depart from custom.

Table 12.1. THE UNITED STATES IS STILL THE RICHEST

Gross National Product per head

United States	$4850
France	2920
Great Britain	2150
Japan	1910

Source: *OECD Economic Surveys: Japan 1972.*

what are the political costs and benefits of trying to transfer this wealth from the private to the public sector? A common way to describe this level of wealth is per capita Gross National Product (GNP). We can see from Table 12.1 that in terms of absolute wealth the United States still is the richest of our four rich countries by a considerable margin.

Absolute levels of wealth, however, do not give a complete picture of available resources. Equally important (or perhaps more so) is the rate of change over time in this wealth. Most macroeconomic planning now focuses on attempting to improve these economic growth rates. Economic growth in the four countries is dramatically different from existing levels of wealth. Japan (as seen in Table 12.2), with the lowest per capita product, has by far the highest rate of economic growth. The United States is over twice as rich as Japan but has a growth rate almost one quarter less. Britain is unhappily consistent — lowest in growth, second lowest in wealth — whereas France is more fortunate with both a healthy growth rate and a strong economic base (second to America) from which to proceed.

What then is the relative importance of these two indicators in budgetary terms? It depends on the relative tax effect. If the percentage increase in the budget is less than the percentage increase in GNP (leaving aside income distribution), we can expect the political consequences of the budget increase to be minimal. The reason is that since real wealth will have increased faster than spending, the government actually will be taking a smaller *share* of GNP than in the previous year. The net result will be a decrease in the relative tax burden. Wealth in the private sector of the economy, in addition, will have increased in

Table 12.2. JAPAN IS OUTDISTANCING THE OTHER COUNTRIES
IN ECONOMIC GROWTH

Average annual increase in GNP 1965–1970

Japan	12.1%
France	5.8
United States	3.3
Great Britain	2.1

Source: *OECD Economic Surveys: Japan 1972.*

absolute terms; real incomes will have gone up. Though the government still will be increasing its activity in real terms, the average citizen (unless tax shifts are designed to disadvantage him) should perceive that he is better off than in the previous year. This type of budgetary growth might best be described as "perceptually painless" — the government is doing more without any apparent cost to people beyond what they are used to paying.

We can contrast this type of painless budgetary increase with an increase that is greater than the growth of GNP. As such, it necessarily relies for finance on existing levels of wealth. Borrowing may do for a time, and a degree of inflation may be acceptable, but eventually the rate of taxation has to be increased to cover extra spending. This is unlikely to be politically popular. An increase in GNP, on the other hand, automatically generates additional revenues, even without a higher tax rate. Where economic growth has been high, the tax burden remains approximately the same; where growth has been low (see Table 12.3) taxes have risen. Central governments in Japan and France have not had to dip into existing levels of wealth to finance their increasing expenditures; Britain and America have. With rapid economic growth it is possible to expand the budget without taking more citizen income than in the past.

The tax burden in Japan dropped from 16.5 percent of GNP to 15.6 percent. One might assume that government spending actually fell; this is not so. In fact, during the sixties, central government spending climbed every year on the average by a factor of 116 percent over the previous year,[2] but sizeable budget expansion was more than offset by the average GNP growth of 12.1 percent. With a per capita GNP of $462 at the beginning of the decade in Japan, very little budget expansion could have been achieved by trying to increase taxation levels on existing wealth.

Because its economic growth was considerable, France experienced only a

Table 12.3. RAPID GROWTH HOLDS TAX RATES DOWN; SLOW GROWTH INCREASES THEM

	Tax rates 1954–1955	Tax rates 1968–1969	Growth rate 1965–1970	Percentage change in taxation 1955–1969
Japan	16.5%	15.6%	12.1%	−0.9
France	21.8	22.5	5.8	+0.7
United States	21.9	25.2	3.3	+3.3
Great Britain	25.5	30.1	2.1	+4.6

Source: *OECD Economic Surveys: Japan 1972.*

2 John Creighton Campbell, "Japanese Balanced Budgeting" (prepared for the Research Conference on Japanese Organization and Decision-Making, Maui, Hawaii, January 5–10, 1973), p. 39.

slight tax increase, hardly noticeable given the increasing real wealth in the private sector. Therefore, in Japan (and substantively in France) Wagner's Law — which postulates a rising share of GNP being appropriated by the government — does not even come up.[3] The United States increased its tax burden by 3.3 percent in spite of steady growth rates. It financed increased government spending out of both the growth in wealth and the already existing levels of wealth. At the beginning of the sixties, the U.S. had sufficiently high levels of wealth to make such a course of action possible and not too painful; the American citizen, with a $2000 higher per capita GNP than his French counterpart, obviously was the better target.

Great Britain presents a gloomy picture — a slow growth rate and a relatively low per capita GNP. Any major increases in the expenditure budget must be financed almost exclusively by increasing taxation levels, a difficult job in view of the relatively low per capita wealth. The tax burden as a share of GNP rose from 25.5 percent in 1955 to 30.1 percent in 1969. Britain therefore is in the worst position of all four countries; without the high growth rates of Japan and France, and high levels of existing wealth in the United States.

The method of taxation also may affect the associated political consequences. The tax structure, as Table 12.4 shows, varies considerably from country to country. What is important for our purposes is that some taxes are more "visible" than others to taxpayers. In general, individual income tax,

Table 12.4. THE COMPOSITION OF TAXES VARIES IN ALL FOUR COUNTRIES
(*percentages for all levels of government in 1961*)

	United States	Great Britain	France	Japan
Individual income	32.2%	35.5%	15.8%	20.3%
Corporate income	16.3	4.0	6.0	26.8
Death, gift, net wealth	1.8	3.2	0.7	0.5
Property	13.2	9.5	1.0	5.7
Excise, sales, customs	21.4	34.6	44.8	33.1
Social Security contributions	14.1	13.4	26.2	12.4
Other	1.0	—	5.5	1.2
Total taxes	100.0	100.9	100.0	100.0

Source: Richard Abel Musgrave, *Fiscal Systems,* Studies in Comparative Economics, 10 (New Haven: Yale University Press, 1969); and *Excise Tax Compendium,* U.S. Congress, House Committee on Ways and Means, 88th Congress; Part I; June 15, 1964.

[3] See Richard Abel Musgrave, *Fiscal Systems,* Studies in Comparative Economics, 10 (New Haven: Yale University Press, 1969).

death, gift and net wealth taxes, property taxes, and social security contributions from employees tend to be felt more directly by the individual taxpayer than are corporate, income, excise, sales, and customs taxes, and social security contributions from private employers. If we rearrange Table 12.4 to reflect this separation, we get (in Table 12.5) a better picture of countries with more visible tax structures.

Japan and France derive revenue largely from tax sources that are less apparent to the individual taxpayer and voter. The United States and Great Britain collect most of their taxes from more visible sources. Those countries which have the highest absolute tax levels and which have increased the tax burden (Table 12.3) have tax structures (Table 12.5) that make these increases highly visible to the general public. By putting together wealth (both absolute and relative in consideration of growth rates) and tax efforts (in both total and type) we should be able to arrive at a more precise notion of the political burdens each nation must face in its spending process.

Figure 12.1 shows the four nations according to their relative economic growth and the level of wealth. The wealth axis is used within the context of rich countries; by absolute standards all are wealthy. The ideal position is represented by *, the least desirable position by o. Three of the four countries are in a relatively sound position on at least one of the axes. In addition, a good position on the growth axis suggests that the country also will have a good position on the other axis — high wealth. Thus it is estimated that in the next five years Japan will pass Britain in per capita wealth. We would expect the British government to have the greatest difficulty in raising the government share of the budget, given low growth and relatively low wealth. We would expect also for the United States to have some trouble, since financing by "dipping into" the level of wealth is politically more difficult than financing by growth. The situation in these two countries is exacerbated by the fact that they have high levels of taxation and a readily visible tax structure.

It may be worth noting that Japan and France, which are in a favorable position, have been dominated for the past two decades by one party (Liberal Democrats and Gaullists, respectively). Perhaps a party that cannot increase government services without increasing tax levels can expect to lose power.

Table 12.5. THE U.S. AND GREAT BRITAIN HAVE MORE VISIBLE TYPES OF TAXES THAN FRANCE AND JAPAN

	Visible	Invisible
France	24.4%	75.6%
Japan	32.9	67.1
United States	53.8	46.2
Great Britain	55.8	44.2

Note: Data are given in percentages.

Figure 12.1. THE WEALTH-GROWTH AXIS

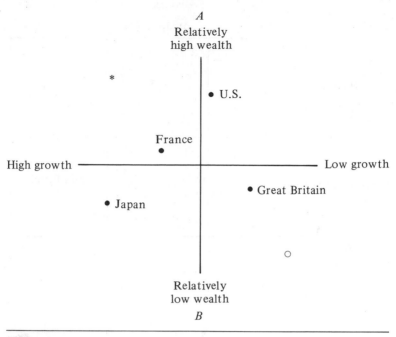

*Ideal position   ○Worst position

The demand for services depends heavily on what they cost. Where the price was comparatively high — as in the United States and Great Britain — the offending parties (the Democrats and the Labour Party) were voted out of office. For present purposes, the immediate objections and qualifications to this simple-minded hypothesis, the variables left out, and doubts about the direction of causality are not of immediate interest. It has been enough to provide rough measures relating wealth and taxes to political problems of expenditures.

How rich are these countries in their ability to support public spending? Our concern is to rank the four nations in relation to one another, not in any absolute terms. It is hard to say, for budgetary reasons, whether per capita GNP is the best measure, or whether the rate of growth determines the allowable margins. So I have taken both measures and, failing any better rationale, given them equal weight to get the wealth-growth index (see Figure 12.2). Along the sides I put relative wealth per capita, with the United States highest, France next, and Great Britain and Japan lower. Along the top, I have relative rate of growth per capita, with Japan definitely the highest, France way down but still high, the United States in a lower range, and Britain, again, on the lowest level. Arbitrarily assigning each a rating — 3 for high, 2 for medium, and 1 for low — the U.S.A. has a score of 5; France, 4.5 (because its growth has been significantly higher than America's), Japan, 4; and Great Britain, 3 on

Figure 12.2. THE WEALTH-GROWTH INDEX

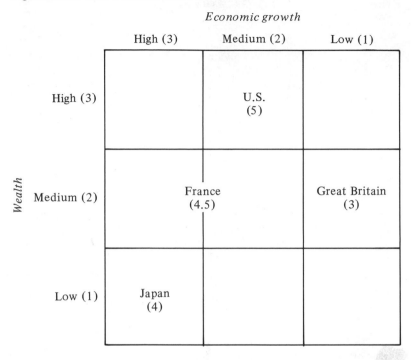

Economic growth

	High (3)	Medium (2)	Low (1)
High (3)		U.S. (5)	
Medium (2)		France (4.5)	Great Britain (3)
Low (1)	Japan (4)		

Wealth

the wealth-growth index.[4] Following a similar procedure, it seems useful to construct an index (Figure 12.3) to highlight political problems in extracting tax resources from the population. On the left (classified as previously indicated) is the visibility of taxes. The United States and Great Britain score high; France and Japan come in low. On the top is increase or decrease within each country in the total rate of taxation. Japan is lowest because it has actually reduced its demands on citizen income; France is treated similarly because of its minimal increase; the United States, with substantial increases, is in the middle; Great Britain is clearly the highest. Using the usual arbitrary weights we get the visibility-of-tax-increase index. It seems intuitively right that a growing burden of more visible taxes should lead to greater political problems than reduction or maintenance of taxes less directly experienced.

[4] It could be argued that ordinal scales are inappropriate. However, as the growth data has a much greater range (Japan is growing six times as fast as the United Kingdom) than the wealth data (the United States is only about twice as wealthy as Japan) use of cardinal measures (that is, the original figures) would, in fact, weight growth more heavily than wealth. Let us take an example. Imagine two countries with per capita GNP of $5,000 and $1,000 respectively and annual growth rates of 2% and 10% respectively. If we simply multiplied these values (i.e., $5,000 × 2% and $1,000 × 10%) each would receive the same score — 10,000. This would be an oversimplification. It will still, in fact, take the less wealthy country many years to get to the position of the richer. Our procedure is an attempt to standardize for this phenomenon.

Figure 12.3. THE VISIBILITY OF TAX INCREASE INDEX

Increase in tax rates (1955–1969)

	High (3)	Medium (2)	Low (1)
High (3)	Great Britain (6)	U.S. (5)	
Medium (2)			France (3)
Low (1)			Japan (2)

Visibility of taxes (vertical axis label)

The purpose of this exercise is to construct a ratio — the wealth-growth index over the visibility-of-tax-increase index — relating a nation's wealth to the demands made on it for taxation. Let us call it the support-on-spending (SOS) ratio (see Figure 12.4). A high SOS ratio, as in Japan and France, suggests that available resources far exceed the calls made on it; a low one, half of unity, as in Great Britain, implies that demand far exceeds the wherewithal to support it. The ratio for the United States is at unity, suggesting that America is just about making it.

The support-on-spending ratio is meant to provide a calculus for the budgetary problems facing rich countries. The higher the ratio in a given time period the easier the problem. The SOS ratio, then, should help determine certain structural features of the budgetary processes, specifically the degree to which they are incremental and proportional. My hypothesis is that the higher the SOS ratio the less incremental and the more proportional are the budgetary processes in each country. The rationale is straightforward: the more funds available at a lower political cost the greater the increments over the past years; the more there is to spread around the more equally is this largesse likely to be shared.

It could be argued to the contrary that if institutionalizing incrementalism has a practical effect, the processes of nations involved should reveal the telltale signs. Percentage increases and decreases in departmental budgets should

Figure 12.4. THE SUPPORT-ON-SPENDING RATIO

	The wealth-growth index			The visibility of tax increase index
Great Britain	3	3/6	(0.50)	6
United States	5	5/5	(1.00)	5
France	4.5	4.5/3	(1.66)	3
Japan	4	4/2	(2.00)	2

vary with the incremental features of the process; Japan, Britain, and France then should be more incremental than the U.S.A. And so they would be, if only the formal process mattered. But we have seen that wealth has a pervasive influence on budgeting. At the extremes, where nations are further apart relatively and absolutely, budgeting by increments must take on different meanings. The richest can afford to treat everyone well; the poorest must make hard, hard choices to avoid stagnation. For them, more for one department necessarily means less for another. That is why the higher a nation is on the SOS ratio (which sets wealth and growth against the pain of resource-extraction) the less it should show evidence of incrementalism. Only when nations have roughly equivalent scores would we expect specific features of their budgetary processes, such as a format for incrementalism, to become fully effective.

We must recognize that the budgetary processes in all four nations are likely to be more rather than less incremental because they belong in the wealthy-and-predictable category where calculations take on the form of increase-decrease analysis from an existing base, whether or not these tendencies are reinforced with such formal devices as PESC or the service vote. According to our hypotheses, however, the relative ranking of our small sample of rich countries should conform to the order of their SOS ratios.

Now for the computations. To get at incremental size, we look at changes in an agency's budget from the previous year. The smaller the change in the budget, the more we would describe budgetary outputs as incremental. Table 12.6 combines these percentage changes in all four countries for all agencies over a period approximately covering the 1960s.

In Britain, departmental budgets change by quite small percentages in absolute terms. In over half of all agencies the change from the year before was less than 5 percent. The United States exhibits somewhat less incrementalism, but still two-thirds of agency appropriations are within 10 percent of the base. France and Japan, on the other hand, are much less incremental. Japanese agencies vary from the previous year's budget by 10 percent or more almost three-quarters of the time, and French almost three-fifths.

However, incrementalism obviously is an incomplete measure of agency

Table 12.6. BRITAIN AND U.S. ARE THE MOST INCREMENTAL: PERCENTAGE CHANGE BY AGENCY FROM PREVIOUS YEAR'S BUDGET

	Period	0–5%ᵃ	5.1–10%	10.1–15%	15.1–20%	Over 20%	Degree of incremen-talism
Great Britain	1960–1970	52.1	17.7	14.6	4.2	11.5	Highest
United States	1959–1968	36.7	30.4	10.1	7.0	15.8	
France	1960–1969	21.7	20.8	17.9	7.9	21.7	
Japan	1961–1970	8.4	16.9	29.2	8.5	27.0	Lowest

Sources: For Japan, unpublished Ministry of Finance tables were provided by John Campbell. *The Budget of the United States,* 1958–1963, and The Budget in Brief, 1964–1968. For Britain, *Annual Abstract of Statistics,* #107 (London: Her Majesty's Stationery Office, 1970). For France, *Annuaire Statistique de la France,* 1960–1969 (Paris: Institut National de la Statistique et des Etudes Economiques).

ᵃ Categories are + or −; thus 0–5% change from previous year is actually a 10% range, i.e., from 95% to 105%.

budgetary activity. If an agency budget remains the same while the total budget is growing, that agency is losing ground to rival departments. There is thus a conflict between incrementalism and maintaining a fair share (or equal proportion) whenever the total budget is increasing. We need to measure proportionality another way, that is, to see how an agency budget keeps pace with general budget growth. Table 12.7 provides such a measure.[5] It takes the percentage change of an agency from its previous year's budget (say, 115%) and compares it with the change in the total budget (say, 120%). Thus, in this case the agency budget "deviated" 5% from the total budget change (120%−115%). If the total budget change is 110%, but the agency changes by 125% of the previous year, we have a 15% deviation. We would have the same result if the agency change was 95% (i.e., a decrease) while the total budget change was 110%.

Japan in this table exhibits a high degree of proportionality. Fully three-quarters of agencies deviate from overall budget growth by less than 10 percent. France shows a similar pattern. In fact, we can see that Table 12.7 is roughly the reverse of Table 12.6. Since there has been some growth of the total budget in all four countries, this inverse relationship is not surprising. If many agencies are displaying highly incremental behavior (and therefore show small changes in Table 12.6) while the total budget is growing, then these same agencies must also be falling behind in achieving their "fair share" (and therefore produce large changes on Table 12.7). When there is budget growth, there is tension between incrementalism and balance.

[5] This index of proportionality, or "shares of growth," was suggested by John Creighton Campbell.

Table 12.7. JAPAN AND FRANCE ARE THE MOST PROPORTIONAL:
AGENCY GROWTH/TOTAL COMPARED TO BUDGET GROWTH

	Period	0–5%[a]	5–10%	10–15%	15–20%	Over 20%
Japan	1961–1970	57.1	19.2	13.6	5.0	5.6
France	1960–1969	49.5	25.7	12.4	0.0	12.4
United States	1959–1968	37.4	29.7	14.2	9.0	9.7
Great Britain	1960–1970	18.8	34.4	13.5	13.5	19.8

Sources: For Japan, unpublished Ministry of Finance tables were provided by John Campbell. *The Budget of the United States*, 1958–1963, and The Budget in Brief, 1964–1968. For Britain, *Annual Abstract of Statistics*, #107 (London: Her Majesty's Stationery Office, 1970). For France, *Annuaire Statistique de la France*, 1960–1969 (Paris: Institut National de la Statistique et des Etudes Economiques).

[a] Categories are + or −; thus 0–5% change from previous year is actually a 10% range, i.e., from 95% to 105%.

The hypothesis expressed again in Table 12.8 appears to be confirmed: incrementalism varies inversely, and proportionality directly, with the SOS ratio. Each of the four nations appears in the predicted order and approximately in the right magnitude. Comparing the two extremes — Britain and Japan — tells the story. Britain's extremely low SOS ratio means that most agencies must have correspondingly low increments. For Britain to show a high degree of proportionality, however, would mean that virtually all agencies (and the programs within them) would have to be kept within the same low bounds. This is unlikely, if only because mandatory items (agricultural price supports, unemployment benefits, etc.), which are beyond anyone's control in the short run, are likely to vary considerably from the norm. Efforts to raise the SOS ratio, so to speak, by improving the productivity of the economy, or to adjust to a low status by redistributing governmental services, would also cause disproportional increases or decreases in the budgets of selected agencies.

The magnitude of the predicted differences, though within tolerable limits, requires additional discussion. Japan has a ratio four times larger than Britain's but its budgetary process (see Table 12.8) is almost six times more proportional. Japan is also somewhat more proportional than the SOS ratios would

Table 12.8. THE HIGHER THE SOS RATIO THE LESS THE INCREMENTALISM
AND THE MORE THE PROPORTIONALITY OF AGENCY EXPENDITURES

	SOS ratio	Incrementalism	Proportionality
Japan	2.00	lowest	highest
France	1.66	lower	higher
United States	1.00	higher	lower
Great Britain	0.50	highest	lowest

suggest, compared to France and the United States. Perhaps a variable has been omitted, most probably the norm of balance, which is important in guiding elite behavior. A good or better explanation than saying the hypothesis has been misspecified is one which relies on measurement error. The whole operation is admittedly crude.

No one, least of all the author, wants to lend a spurious air of specificity to these indices and the ratios made up from them. Though each dimension that makes up the indices is related to real-world numbers and observations, the distances between rankings are, at best, approximate; giving them equal value is defensible, if at all, only if we are interested, as we are, in gross comparisons. These difficulties increase when we enter into the even more judgmental area of citizen feelings about governments and their relationships to their countrymen.

SOCIETY, POLITICS, AND CONFLICT

To understand the part played by budgetary processes in ordering conflict we need some notion of how much conflict each society is likely to produce, and how well its governmental apparatus is able to keep it under control. These are tall orders, and existing knowledge is far from reaching them. Nevertheless, in keeping with the spirit of the enterprise, I can try, at least, not to falsify what is known in making estimates of the comparative rankings.

My initial interest lies in establishing a potential for social conflict within each nation. At the simplest level — it is hard to rise above that — conflict is conceived to be a product of social diversity and of the political intensity with which these differences are expressed. The more homogeneous a people (along racial, religious, class, and regional boundaries) and the less they polarize themselves along the cleavages that do divide them, the less conflict there is likely to be. The United States is by far the most diverse nation along all these categories, divided as it is by race, religion, and geography, followed by France, where some religious differences still persist, and then by Japan and Great Britain, who share with the others the usual class divisions. I am at my most judgmental when I say that the British make the least of their divisions, with the United States and Japan doing pretty well on occasion, and France near the brink of turmoil on occasion. None of these nations has escaped occasional explosive civic turmoil. Thus the United States and France, for somewhat different reasons, score highest on the diversity-intensity index (Figure 12.5), with Japan below, and Great Britain showing the least combination of diversity and the disposition to make something of it.

The ability of governments to contain conflict depends not only on how much they have to handle, but on how strong they are. This strength, in turn, depends on how disposed citizens are to defer to governmental judgment and how much agreement there is on governmental form. A regime constantly un-

Figure 12.5. POTENTIAL FOR CONFLICT: THE DIVERSITY-INTENSITY INDEX

Diversity of population

	High (3)	Medium (2)	Low (1)
High (3)			
Medium (2)	U.S. (5)	France (4)	Japan (3)
Low (1)			Great Britain (2)

Intensity of differences within population

der attack — because its citizens either disagree with a range of specific policies or (worse still) continually question the form of government — is likely to create as much, or more, conflict than it can resolve. How shall we discern citizen consensus on the form of government? The simplest measure appears to be the existence of parties with substantial followings who challenge the form of government or even democratic procedures themselves. Bearing this criterion in mind, we find Great Britain and the United States high in consensus. There are no competitors of any size to the prevailing constitutional arrangements. Japan and France, on the other hand, are low on political consensus because there are sizeable parties opposed to the prevailing form of government.

Turning to citizen deference to government, it is necessary to recognize that no people agree with everything a government does, or fail on occasion to protest. The question is whether government *normally* operates with greater or lesser pressure from its citizens. My ranking is only a matter of judgment reached by reading books and newspapers about what happens in these countries. By all accounts, citizens in Great Britain show considerable deference to government. This does *not* necessarily mean that they like their governments better or agree more with its decisions, but only that they are not disposed to challenge them. Whether citizens love their government or merely feel powerless to alter its policies, they defer. France, Japan, and the United States receive a middle ranking because most governmental decisions are accepted without much difficulty, but there is a continuous pattern of resistance to at least some of them. [These rankings are based on experience of the last decade; had I been thinking about the late 1940s and 1950s, the United States might have ranked higher and France lower on deference to government. Had I considered only 1974, Japan, and especially Britain (in view of its disruptive coal strike) would have come in lower.] Combining the rankings, for want of a better way to proceed, we find (Figure 12.6) that France and Japan show the lowest consensus-deference index, and Great Britain the highest, with America slightly lower.

What I am aiming at is some comparative relationship between the propensity of nations to produce conflict and the ability of their governments to contain it. Hence I have combined the diversity-intensity and consensus-deference indices to produce the containment-of-conflict ratio (COC). When containment is placed on top and conflict below, it appears (Table 12.9) that Great Britain can contain a great deal more conflict than it produces, Japan and the United States are just about even, and France is in a deficit position.

The purpose of this exercise is to let us compare the relative financial positions of these nations with their political situation. The support-on-spending ratio presents one side of the story and the containment-of-conflict ratio the

Figure 12.6. POTENTIAL FOR CONTAINING CONFLICT: THE CONSENSUS-DEFERENCE INDEX

Citizen consensus on form of government

	High (3)	Medium (2)	Low (1)
High (3)	Great Britain (6)		
Medium (2)	U.S. (5)		France Japan (3)
Low (1)			

Citizen deference to government

Table 12.9. THE CONTAINMENT-OF-CONFLICT RATIO

Great Britain	6/2	3.00
Japan	3/3	1.00
United States	5/5	1.00
France	3/4	0.75

other. The remaining task (Figure 12.7) is to juxtapose the financial and polit-ical rankings to get an approximate notion of the budgetary problems facing these nations. Remembering that our concern is with rough relative rankings the COC ratio appears on the left and the SOS ratio on the bottom with coun-tries ranged on both from very high to very low. Those to the left of the dotted diagonal have political but lack economic strength, whereas those on the right are in the reverse position.

Britain is able to compensate for low support on spending through the ex-ceptional ability of its government to contain conflict. Its situation is symmetri-cal but precarious; should dissatisfaction with the inability of government to meet demands spill over into the broader political system, or should deference or consensus decline in any significant way, the nation would be exposed to far

Figure 12.7. THE CONTEXT FOR BUDGETARY CONFLICT

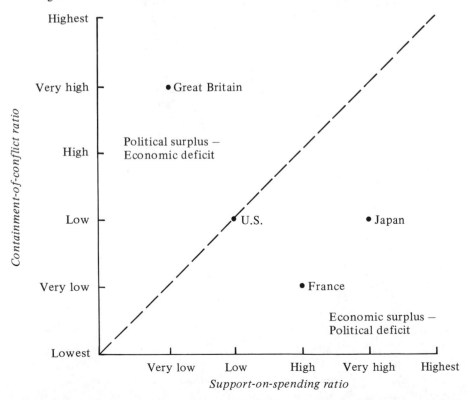

greater turbulence than it has been accustomed to in the past. Japan, where support for expenditures exceeds the tax demands on the population, needs no help from its political apparatus, and gets more than it needs. Its balance on containing conflict might, however, become fragile if support for spending falls due to a decline in its rate of growth. France needs a little assistance in containing conflict, and gets a lot from a tax structure that is more than acceptable. Economic trouble would find little political solace. The United States appears remarkably evenly balanced between demand for expenditures and capacity to supply them, and between production and absorption of conflict. Its delicately wrought balance remains a mystery to supporters and detractors alike. Whether it is true that God takes care of fools, drunkards, and Americans, could be debated. By relating budgeting to politics, I shall try to show that there is a reasonable rationale to the American equilibrium, just as there is to the distinctive styles of confronting conflict in France, Britain, and Japan.

BUDGETING AND POLITICS

In Chapter 11 I tried to evoke four national styles of governmental budget-making; in this chapter I have tried to account for their propensity to generate and resolve conflict apart from budgetary processes; still to be explained is how budgeting interacts with politics to affect conflict. The budgetary process in Japan is more explicitly geared to reducing conflict than is the rest of its political system. The huge Japanese "surplus" on the support-of-spending (SOS) ratio and its balance on the containment-of-conflict (COC) suggest that it is not absolutely necessary to bring almost everyone along at the same level, to conduct revival negotiations, or even to distribute funds according to a proportional norm. No doubt the historical circumstance of a seemingly permanent and heterogeneous majority party requires due allowance for widespread dispersal of small public works to settle, as they say, the intraparty situation. Japan's extraordinarily high rate of economic growth might, as well, suggest little reason for cutting back but is insufficient to require that ministries be advanced in roughly the same proportions. Some programs, and the ministries in which they are found, could have been pushed ahead more vigorously and others less. Yet, except for rice subsidies in Agriculture, this did not take place. Perhaps the Japanese know themselves better than outsiders do. Perhaps their social and political accord is more fragile than appears on the surface. The Japanese would rather not be half-safe.

Britain definitely needs help in overcoming the large deficit in its SOS ratio and for that purpose can use the even larger surplus in its COC ratio. It can try to improve its position by resisting demands for expenditure and following policies to increase its economic growth. Ministries may be treated differentially, each receiving markedly different shares of whatever increases are going with some actually subject to sharp declines. This requires strong central control. And so we see; greater authority has been given to (or seized by) the Treasury. Its power to set totals has been enhanced by its monopoly of macro-economic forecasting, which means that arguments over allowable totals are always arguments over the Treasury's figure. The Treasury has created a double margin of error through the relative price effect and productive potential. Although PESC does nothing to guarantee that public spending will be more rational (in the sense of leading to the highest economic growth), it does help the Treasury ensure that the expenditures that are supposed to grow will be the ones that do in fact increase. Now the Treasury is caught between the control advantages of the Public Expenditure Survey and the new experiments in providing policy analyses for Cabinet which, if successful, would lead to still greater deviations within the total by providing a rationale for substantially increasing some programs and severely cutting others. Whatever happens with these new developments, however, the main tendency is clear: in trying to cope with the problems created by its deficit on the SOS ratio, the British expenditure process enhances government centralization.

So far the United States maintains its equilibrium. Its SOS and COC ratios are at unity. The parts of its political system, which might appear to fly off in all directions at once, are, in fact, components of a larger system in which the elements keep each other in check. But only just. The budgetary process helps sustain this equilibrium in quintessential American style by moving subsystems in opposite directions. The president, acting through the OMB, provides a centralizing element not found elsewhere; the budget is the president's greatest opportunity to impose his own sense of direction on governmental activities. The congressional process, on the other hand, fragments decisions through the various House appropriations subcommittees heaped on top of the regular substantive (or legislative) committees. As a whole, therefore, the budgetary subsystem is even more fragmented than the political system. The result is a larger number of smaller conflicts than there would be if the president controlled appropriations or if there were a single set of committees to deal with them in Congress.

The French boast a large surplus on support for spending but a small deficit on containing conflict. Yet French problem-solving shows a style, not of ameliorating or deflecting conflict at its source, but of bolstering governmental authority. And the French budgetary process does just that — no more and no less. No one is asked to feel better or deny his cause; everyone gets several opportunities at arbitration before time runs out and the government imposes its will. Here, too, the cultural element — product of centuries of central control — shows its strength. For France is overreacting to the opportunities of the 1970s through the institutional collective memory of less happy days. France may now better be able to afford the "luxury" of a Fourth or Fifth Republic, but it still remembers the bad old days. French political elites are taking no chances. Perhaps they know something we don't.

What do budgetary processes do? Rich and certain nations build on their strengths. Budgeting intensifies the main strengths and diversities in each nation's style of government. Developments in the budgetary process further centralize Britain, fragment the United States, harmonize Japan, and bulwark France. For poor and uncertain countries budgeting accentuates their weaknesses. Poverty and uncertainty exacerbate one another. Spenders and savers make life worse for each other, one by holding back what was allegedly allotted, the other by taking special funds away from the central treasury. The poor budget more but like it less.

The budgetary subsystem overidentifies, as it were, with its political system. Budgetary processes push other political processes in the same direction they were going, only harder. There we have the importance of budgeting as a political process — it is more royal than the King, more religious than the Pope. How likely is it, then, that budgets would become regicides by espousing the heresies of reform?

IV
Reform

13
Planning, Budgeting, and Reform

Wombs of war have ever been pregnant with seeds of peace. Wartime experience leads to peacetime innovation. The adoption of program budgeting (a short term for Planning, Programming, and Budgeting Systems, or PPBS) in the 1960s had its recent origins in the need for planning during the Second World War and the following era of reconstruction. Systems analysis gained its vogue through the new men, with their new techniques, who worked on military operations during the war and on weapons systems afterwards.[1] To make systems out of weapons required specifications of programs to which a variety of alternatives might contribute. Thus all the elements of PPBS were in place — planning, programing, systems. As the initials suggest, planning came first, for World War II also unleashed forces that led to independence for former colonies and creation of a multitude of new nations.

PLANNING

It is not surprising that planning should offer itself as an attractive solution to the problems facing leaders of poor nations.[2] The twentieth century, more than any earlier historic period, emphasizes the potentialities of planning. Man contrasts with other creatures of the planet less because of his superior technological prowess than because of the ability to shape his own fate. Other forms of life have shown themselves capable of myriad adaptations to their varied, changing, and complex environments; but man aspires to control his

---

[1] Aaron Wildavsky, "Practical Consequences of the Theoretical Study of Defense Policy," *Public Administration Review,* 25 (March 1965), 90–103.
[2] This section has been adapted from Naomi Caiden and Aaron Wildavsky, *Planning and Budgeting in Poor Countries* (New York: Wiley, 1974), copyright © 1974 by John Wiley and Sons; and Aaron Wildavsky, "If Planning is Everything, Maybe It's Nothing," *Policy Sciences,* 4 (June 1973), 127–153.

future: hence planning, whose powerful appeal depends on its promise to harness destiny.

In the poor countries, particularly those struggling toward political independence, the tasks were all too obvious — an urgent need to improve living standards, to restore to the people that rightful inheritance up to now misappropriated by their colonial masters, to establish economic independence and social justice. Such aims could not be fulfilled by a policy of drift; the need was for deliberate action — a positive thrust to make up for the negative years, and imposition of present sacrifices for the sake of future generations. It was essential that society find a confident new direction toward national goals. The intuitive answer was to plan. To the question implicitly posed to their leaders by the liberated masses: "What will you *do*?," the response after, as before, independence was almost automatic: "We have a plan. . . ."

In espousing planning, the new elites of poor countries, of course, had more to go on than intuition. A variety of circumstances pointed toward its acceptance as a generalized concept and its adoption in a particular form — comprehensive economic planning. First there was the force of example. A series of five-year plans in the Soviet Union dating from 1929 had shown the possibilities of national economic planning as a means of mobilizing national effort. As the last vestiges of laissez-faire theory disappeared under the force of the depression of the 1930s and the World War of the early 1940s, government initiative, now called Keynesian economics, became respectable in leading Western nations. The idea that government might control fluctuations in the economy became increasingly palatable. Following the war, national planning, modified to fit the mixed economy, was designed to rebuild Western Europe. Postwar European planning emerged from its early rough-and-ready phase to become a recognized discipline, accepted (or at least tolerated) in the top echelons of government service. Influential technocrats, who tried to elevate national policy-making for economic growth to a more rational level, got much of the credit for economic recovery. The mixed economy, it appeared, was no obstacle to national planning.

Rich countries found themselves with rapidly growing expenditures and increasing state intervention in society. Their ability to mobilize financial resources outstripped their capacity to spend wisely. "Welfare" and "warfare" states called for rapid rates of economic growth, so they could do more and feel it less. Finance ministries responded by concentrating on growth. The traditional function of budgeting — expenditure control — became an adjunct of economic management. Spending departments traded away a say over totals for larger leeway over allocations within these amounts. Hence the parallel rise of economic planning and incremental budgeting. Hence the split between macro- and microeconomics — further centralization of money flows, tax revenues, fiscal policy; enhanced decentralization of expenditure decisions. The amount of public works might be controlled from the center, but the contents of programs and projects were determined at the periphery of national government. This incongruity slowly created strain. If economic rationality was good for the big picture, for macroeconomic management, why was it also not good for whatever else ailed the country, that is, for social policy through microexpenditure analysis? The bastions of budgeting were under seige.

Budgeting on the Defensive

During the 1960s, concern with improving financial practices centered on the relationship between budgeting and planning. Defects in budgeting were viewed as the exact obverse of virtues of planning. Budgeting would have to improve by taking on the features of planning.

The reports of United Nations Budgeting and Planning Workshops testify to complaints against budgeting authorities in all parts of the world. Ministries of finance have a bad reputation in many countries; they have been castigated for rigidity, arbitrary behavior, overcentralization, and delay. To detractors their conservatism seems a total lack of flexibility. All that red tape jeopardizes projects in progress; their lack of vision, an inability to go beyond purely monetary considerations, aborts others. The budgets Finance concocted, even where they related to reality (and did not simply appear after the event), provided little information as to the efficacy of expenditures. Finance, said its critics, was still preoccupied with housekeeping — or, at best, managing — in an age which needed a much more sophisticated approach in keeping with the state as promoter of economic development.

It would seem planning was far superior to budgeting in technique. Whereas budgeters could stretch their imaginations only as far as the current year (thereby arbitrarily chopping up long-term project funding into annual appropriations), planners could think years ahead. Planning could apply a systematic analysis to claims and projects. Planning could introduce the rationality of an overall vista in place of those haphazard results of the political bargaining which characterized budgeting.

Budgeting, by assimilating some of the attributes of planning, may take on some of its aura. Program budgeting has been one adventure in this direction. Budgeting can adopt multi-year budget outlooks, providing long-term instead of one-year estimates. Budgeters also can use the tools of planning: cost-benefit analysis, structuring programs around their contribution to entire sectors of activity, and so on; they can learn to quantify progress on projects in terms of broad economic, as opposed to narrow financial, criteria. Note the emphasis: proper coordination between plans and budgets, with planning in the lead, would assure rational resource allocation.

To understand contemporary budget reform, therefore, one first must try to comprehend national planning. Planning is the attempt to determine the consequences of actions; the more consequences we determine, the more we have succeeded in planning. To use somewhat different language, planning is the ability to control the future by current acts. Instead of waiting to discover his fate in the future, rational man plans in the present to make it in his own image. Virtually everyone would agree that planning requires: (1) a specification of future objectives and (2) a series of related actions over time designed to achieve them. We can now try to discover in general terms what is entailed by national planning.

Planning as Cause

Beginning with the implementing actions, we can say that the first requisite of national planning is causal knowledge: the existence of theory, with at least some evidence to support it, specifying causal relationships. If X and Y are done, then Z will result. If the consequences of contemplated actions cannot be appraised accurately, specified objectives will be achieved only by accident. Causal knowledge is even more essential in long-range planning because the consequences of each action become the basis for succeeding steps. Each error in prediction is magnified because of its effect on future decisions.

It will help if we specify what kinds of causal knowledge planning requires: a knowledge of the relationships in each of dozens of areas of policy from fisheries to foreign exchange. These relationships may be further subdivided: (1) interaction among elements of the policy itself, (2) incentives for the people involved to carry out the policy, or mechanisms for ensuring compliance, (3) sufficient resources at the time required. In agriculture, for example, knowledge of the elements of the policy itself — technology of production, mechanisms of distribution, availability of markets — must be complete if the policy is to work. If farmers will not plant the crops called for or if the prices do not bring them sufficient remuneration, they will sabotage the policy, either overtly or through passive resistance. If there is insufficient money for seeds or fertilizer or if the farmer lacks the education or the motivation to employ the necessary techniques, the policy will fail.

Even if good theory exists somewhere in the world, people in a particular society must be able to apply it in the specific context of their own country. Yet knowledge of how to apply theory is often as weak as the theory itself. Social circumstances may make a mockery of general principles. There may be few men who can put existing theory to practical purposes. Where causal theory is absent or imperfect, where applications are poor or nonexistent, where personnel to carry out policies is lacking or poorly trained, the preconditions of planning (and hence of PPBS) cannot be met.

Scarce as causal theory is within specific areas of policy, it is superabundant compared to the lack of knowledge of interaction effects. Energy policy, for example, cannot be pursued apart from transportation, industrial, and agricultural policy. The major consequences of each set of decisions for other areas of policy must be known; if they are not, some objectives will be won at the expense of others or none at all will be achieved. Yet there are no useful models of economies as a whole; either they contain so few variables as to be too general, or so many that one cannot understand what goes on inside them, let alone in the world to which they are supposed to refer.

Causal knowledge is necessary also for relating policies of the nation over time to changes in the international economy. Low-income countries are especially vulnerable to fluctuations in the price of imports and exports and in the willingness of previous donor nations to supply aid. But rich nations may also be set back if critical commodities, like oil, rise rapidly. Should the plan require a certain amount of foreign currency, it can easily disintegrate if commodity prices drop, imports rise, and foreign aid disappears. Yet there are no good predictive models of international prices or of willingness to supply aid.

National planning provides a hard test of causal knowledge. Men, resources, and institutions must be mobilized and related to one another at successive stages in time in order to obtain predicted results that lead to the achievement of objectives. Planning demands causal knowledge and the ability to wield that knowledge effectively in society. Power and planning are different ways of looking at the same events.

Planning as Power

Power is the probability of changing the behavior of others against opposition.[3] Where disagreement over social goals or policies exists, as it must, there can be no planning without the ability to make other people act differently than they otherwise might. There would be no need to plan if people were going to do spontaneously what the plan insisted they do authoritatively. Planning assumes power.

Planning requires the power to maintain the preeminence of the future in the present. The nation's rulers must be able to commit existing resources to accomplishing future objectives. If new rulers make drastic changes in objectives, the original plan is finished. The continuity of the regime, of course, is one of the more problematical features of the poor country. Its unity may crumble, its devotion to original objectives may be undermined from within, and its ability to command the nation's resources may be dissipated through disagreement. The same is true for rich countries subject to periodic political instability. Either rulers must stay in power long enough to accomplish their original purposes or their successors must have the same commitments.

If planning is to be more than an academic exercise, it must actually

---

[3] See Andrew McFarland, *Power and Leadership in Pluralistic Systems* (Stanford, Calif.: Stanford Univ. Press, 1969); Herbert Simon, *Models of Man* (New York: Wiley, 1957); John Harsanyi, "Measurement of Social Power, Opportunity Costs, and the Theory of Two-Person Bargaining Games," *Behavioral Science*, 7 (January 1962), 67–80; Robert Dahl, "Power," *International Encyclopedia of the Social Sciences* (New York: Macmillan and Free Press, 1968), Vol. 12, pp. 405–415; James March, "The Power of Power," in *Varieties of Political Theory*, ed. by David Easton (Englewood Cliffs, N.J.: Prentice-Hall, 1966), pp. 39–70.

guide the making of governmental decisions. Governmental actions (and the private activities they try to influence) must in large measure conform to the plan if it is to have practical effect. To plan, therefore, is to govern.

Implementation depends on planners' ability to ensure that the public sector moves consistently toward plan objectives; governmental resources must be directed toward this end, and not diverted away from plan purposes. If the plan is to be meaningful, then it must be reflected in the budget. If the plan goes one way and the budget another, the plan is ignored. That is why planners strive to influence budget allocations.

But they have failed. Why? Because planners need knowledge and power and they cannot get either.

Planning versus Finance

Planners claimed a comprehensive rationality that would allow them to determine where a nation should go and how it should get there for years ahead — in regard to both economic policy and resource allocation, among sectors and within major projects. Finance ministries met the challenge by bolstering their capability in economic management and by mobilizing those in political power to ignore the plans whenever they thought necessary (which was quite often). Whether it was because planners in Japan did not anticipate so much economic growth, or whether those in England predicted so little, or whether planners in France missed on inflation, or because none could get into the budget, nowhere were planners' targets met or even roughly approximated. What is important for present purposes, however, is not the fate of the plan but rather the nature of the conflict between Finance and Planning about spending.

Planners are spenders. Their raison d'être is economic growth. Typically they underestimate spending and overestimate revenues to leave room for investments they believe are necessary for accomplishing the goals they wish to achieve. Planners are natural allies for large spending departments whose projects planners believe desirable for securing economic growth. For the same reasons, planners are natural enemies of financial controllers who want to limit expenditure. An all-too-brief recapitulation of experience in Great Britain and Japan must suffice for illustrative purposes.

The Department of Economic Affairs (DEA) in Britain, and the National Economic Development Councils which preceded it, postulated high rates of economic growth. Although there was no theoretical rationale for doing so, spending departments and their allies found it convenient to assume they could grow with the rate of increase in gross national product. Consequently, when economic growth fell below announced figures, the Treasury found expenditures rising far more rapidly than incomes, with subsequent balance-of-payments and inflationary difficulties. Nor did the Treasury want just a lower publicized rate of growth; rather, it wanted no public rate of growth at all because it knew politicians would not let themselves be accused of selling the country short; hence the figure would inevitably be higher than experience justified. So it fought the DEA and eventually secured its abolition.

The Japanese Bureau of the Budget was not at all happy with the publication of planned expenditures years into the future, for it knew that spending ministries would use the figures as a floor from which to lobby for additional increments. The Budget Bureau insisted on treating the plan figures as maximums from which they were free to cut according to the conditions of the times as they interpreted them. Since the planners lacked power over spending, and since they vastly miscalculated the rate of economic growth in each plan, they found few willing to listen to their stories.

If planning could not control budgeting, budgeting might yet become a form of planning. By expanding budgeting to include planning, the same goals could be achieved from a different direction. The idea is marvelous; if planners suffer a power deficit, they balance their books by becoming budgeters, who have a power surplus. Budgeters are powerful but ignorant; planners are knowledgeable but powerless; what could be more desirable, thought the proponents of PPBS, than combining the virtues of both classes by making budgeters into planners. Instead of dealing with budgetary inputs (such as personnel and maintenance) for purposes of narrow control, the budget would be organized around categories emphasizing outputs, so as to improve choice. By providing quantitative indicators of inputs and outputs, ranking programs according to merit in achieving objectives, and extending these considerations further into the future, resource allocation would be done in a more rational way.

Was this hubris or justice? That depends on whether the requisites of planning — power and knowledge — can be transferred to budgeting. Power requires fitting into the particular political style (its structure and norms) of each country. If the American style is to diffuse conflict and the French is to put up a bulwark against it, for instance, budgeting by programs might not work equally well in both nations. Knowledge calls for causal theory relating alternatives to consequences for all areas covered by the budget, which is to say, for all of government. (To do less would mean only that some program analysis existed amid regular budget categories, a circumstance true long before PPBS, thus taking away its justified claim to novelty.) But societies differ in the ability to support causal theories. Japan and Indonesia, with their vast disparities in wealth and personnel, can hardly plan or budget in the same way. Reform must be based on understanding the context in which it is expected to operate.

To make good on its implied promise — if the changes proposed are made, then the desirable consequences predicted (and not the terrible ones feared) will actually occur — reform must connect to its environment. As soon as one hears about those damnable obstacles to change, that monotonous litany of the critical conditions that prevent progress, one is about to be put on, for these are usually the characteristic conditions of environments in which change must occur. Removing obstacles that the reform is designed to overcome should not be a precondition to its success. If reform will work only when it is not needed — if these products of reform must be present before it has a chance — why bother?

To avoid the "obstacle" syndrome it is helpful to delineate the distinguishing features of budgetary environments with which reformers must cope. Theory about budgetary processes works well for this purpose. It moves from environmental conditions to specific attributes of governmental units that engage in resource allocation. It relates practices (such as repetitive budgeting) to larger causes that produce them (such as poverty and uncertainty).

For convenience, I shall summarize the first twelve chapters by means of figures which trace the hypothesized causal connections for each type of budgetary process. Presumably reform must proceed by altering these connections so that results will be different than they were before. The requisites of reform at which we have been aiming, therefore, are nothing more or less than a reversal of the constituent elements of our theory — Can poverty be overcome? Can uncertainty be mitigated? Can institutions be altered or norms reversed? With these questions I shall continue the search for the requirements of reform.

BUDGETING

Let us turn to the theory recapitulated in Figure 13.1, Five Types of Budgetary Processes. The limiting conditions (endless wealth and bottomless poverty), which make budgeting unnecessary or futile, are indicated on the left. There can be no budgeting without resources to allocate or scarcities to require allocation.

Because the combination of low wealth and low predictability leads to repetitive budgeting, with its intensive strategic byplay, no matter what the political structure or economic rate of growth, it will be convenient to begin with the bottom portion of the figure. The lessons for would-be reformers are immediately evident: political change alone, whether revolutionary or reformist, does not affect the main features of the budgetary process so long as these nations remain poor and uncertain. Powerless planners may become powerful budgeters only to discover that they have taken on those very features of the environment they were committed to change. Strategies of reform must either get at wealth — perhaps by exploiting the possession of vital commodities — or at predictability, so that the budget can be relied on to do what it says for the period it covers. Because getting rich overnight is still the exception rather than the rule, however, attention should be devoted to relieving uncertainty. The worst imaginable approach (alas, the very one adopted) would be to foist budgetary devices derived from governments operating in wealthy and predictable environments on countries with precisely the opposite characteristics.

Figure 13.1. Five Types of Budgetary Processes

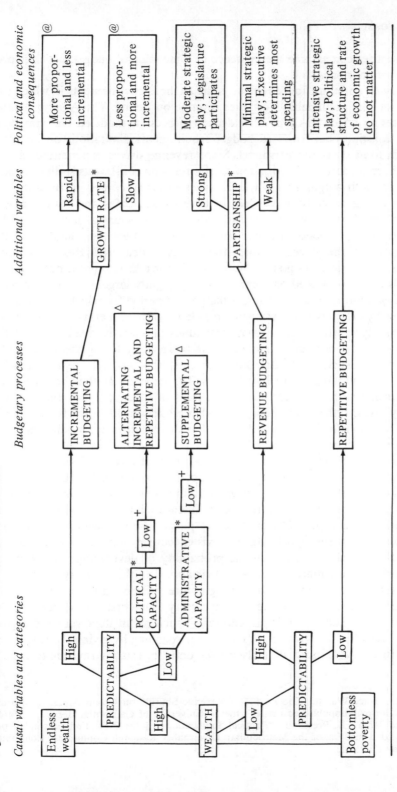

Causal variables and categories   *Budgetary processes*   *Additional variables*   *Political and economic consequences*

*The text shows that the variable requires consideration only in this position.
+The text shows that only the "low" category of this variable requires consideration.
@Additional processes and developments are shown in Figures 13.2 and 13.3.
△No contemporary examples of these processes were found.

Rich countries can assume the existence of a meaningful budget, which is precisely what poor ones lack.

Moving up in the flow chart, we come to those environments in which low wealth but high predictability produce revenue budgeting. The American cities and states on which this type of budgetary process is modeled are characterized by constitutional balanced budget requirements, limitations on taxation, and high fixed costs for personnel. Since revenue drives expenditure, as we know, the main thrust of reform must lie in relaxing constraints so that income keeps pace with outgo. This is where revenue sharing comes in. By using the superior taxing capacity of the federal government, cities and states are enabled to spend more. What happens under revenue sharing, however, is determined by the amounts, the time period for which they are granted, and the tax structure in the places to which the money is delivered. Relatively small amounts mean that cities go to a lot of trouble for a little money, because new demands are now focused on them, with only slightly larger resources to meet them. Even more serious, perhaps, is the limited period for which the money is guaranteed, for cities become overcommitted by hiring permanent personnel that add to their fixed costs. Fearing that funds may not be available after the initial five-year period, cities and states are more likely to use them for single-shot ventures, such as capital improvements, that do not require massive amounts of continuing future expenditures. Tax structure matters because cities overburdened with relatively inelastic sources of revenue (such as sales and property taxes, rather than income taxes) are likely to use such funds for tax relief. The result in all three instances is that sharing does not modify the basic characteristics of revenue budgeting.[4]

Under these conditions, and in view of the relatively small size of municipal budgets, there is likely to be little change from one year to the next; an increment of a small base is likely to be a small increment. What part, then, does politics play? Nonpartisanship reduces political mobilization and gives power to appointed executives. The existence of parties, by increasing political mobilization, strengthens legislatures vis-à-vis executives and increases the use of strategies. Partisanship increases the probability of developing a program of some sort to differentiate the sides in their appeal to the citizenry. Opposition also increases the likelihood that the legislature will obtain the minimum staff resources for developing the expertise necessary to understand the budget. The presence of specific institutional features — such as an item veto for a governor — can alter the strategic situation over spending by giving the legislature an incentive to vote more, thus placing the onus for relating revenue to expen-

[4] See Bruce Wallin, "The Impact of Revenue Sharing on Urban Areas: California and New Jersey," unpublished master's thesis, University of California, Berkeley, March 1973; and Jeffrey L. Pressman, "Political Implications of the New Federalism," paper prepared for a meeting of the Metropolitan Governance Research Committee, Columbus, Ohio, May 17, 1974.

diture on the governor. The political complexion of the executive also matters; if it takes on the spending advocacy role, for instance, the legislature is more likely to assert itself through taking a cutting stance, especially if the majority is of a different party. Where revenue budgeting prevails, therefore, reform requires a contextual analysis. Rather than trying to install new budgetary devices, reformers might begin with revenue. Next might come party structure and the provision of support for legislators. Altering the form of the budget, just by itself, would come last, as a palliative to alleviate surface symptoms. Yet the traditional approach to budgetary reform has (almost) always been administrative.

Here it may be helpful to look at the experience of Third and Fourth Republic France — a nation rich in financial resources and predictable in administration but uncertain in regard to political continuity — from the vantage point of budgetary reform. The French knew, within reasonable limits, how much they were spending and how much they could expect to raise in revenue. Their problem was their famous political instability, which led to rapid changes of government, often resulting in inability to agree on the budget. Proponents of budget reform could opt either for drastic political surgery or for mitigating the worst evils of the existing situation. They did both. They first put a Band-Aid on the budgetary process by stipulating that last year's budget would automatically become this year's budget unless it were changed. Agencies could count on getting what they had the previous year. Then the replacement of these other regimes by the Gaullist Fifth Republic created, at least for a time, the stability that had heretofore been lacking, so that France became like other wealthy and predictable nations.

I know of no contemporary examples of wealthy nations whose unpredictability comes from administrative incapacity rather than from political instability. Here we would be talking about an administrative infrastructure that was weak in itself or that could not keep pace with rapid and unpredictable changes in society. Another brief excursion into the past, however, will serve up an example good enough for present purposes. The Confederate States of America, whose creation led to the American Civil War, was a government that sprang full-blown, like Minerva from the head of Jove, without past experience on which to base future expectations.[5] Much has been said about the undesirability of having this year's budget resemble last year's. But consequences flowing from government without a budgetary base should give pause to anyone. Unable to anticipate its income, dependent on a single commodity (cotton), the Confederate Treasury behaved very much like the finance ministries in poor countries. But the spending departments behaved even worse. They tried to behave normally by asking for twice as much as they thought they

[5] See Carl V. Patton, "Budgeting under Crisis: The Budgetary Process of the Confederate States of America," paper submitted to Aaron Wildavsky's seminar on Budgets as Political Instruments, 1974.

needed, but they could have used four times as much because they had no way of anticipating actual expenses and inflation rapidly eroded what they did get. This administrative incapacity led to supplemental budgeting; agencies waited until they were running out of money before they put in a new request. Then, at scattered intervals, they would run out again and repeat the procedure. Although the causes of this extraordinary situation have only recently been studied,[6] the havoc created by supplemental budgeting is well known to students of the Confederacy. What they needed most, the Treasury and agencies alike, was what they could never get — a budgetary base to provide a stable set of expectations so that they would know what they were doing and others could rely on them.

Incremental budgetary processes, which stem from a combination of wealth and predictability, are specified at the top of Figure 13.1. If a rapid growth rate is added to their stock of wealth, nations that fit the typology are likely to be less incremental and more proportional in their budgetary output. Fast growth facilitates proportional increases because there is enough to go around. Governments with slower rates of growth are likely to be more incremental and less proportional because they are obliged to make harder choices among competing agencies and programs; only a few programs go way up or down while most stay pretty much the same. Thus ability to hold down spending and reallocate resources may be more important in countries experiencing faster rather than slower growth rates. Such countries would be well advised to avoid policies that lead to long-term commitments to spend large amounts, for if the growth rate should slow, the resources to maintain prior expenditure would also decline. Reform should be related to growth rates but rarely is because, so long as there is enough to go around, little competition exists.

All rich and certain nations have solved the problem of making a meaningful annual budget. Their problem is whether the expenditures that will flow predictably from the budget document are the right ones. Are they economically productive? Are they socially worthwhile? Do they help keep society together or pull it further apart? The recent emphasis in budgeting has been on economic rationality. Reform has less to say about social desirability because the distribution of income, psychic as well as economic, is usually outside the scope of the analyses. It has least to say about political rationality, that is, about the contribution of budgeting to maintaining the right to rule. Because this book is about budgetary processes in governments, *my focus is on conflict and accommodation* as well as on gross national product.

The political context for spending must be approached from two directions — the ability of government to contain social conflict, and to gain support for public spending. I ranked four rich nations on the containment-of-conflict ratio by placing the consensus-defference index over the diversity-intensity in-

6 Ibid.

dex (see Chapter 12, Figures 12.5 and 12.6, and Table 12.9, pp. 244, 245, 246). I obtained the support-on-spending ratio by placing the wealth-growth index over the visibility-of-tax-increase index (see Chapter 12, Figures 12.2–12.4, pp. 238–240). Juxtaposing the two ratios in Figure 13.2, we obtain the context for budgetary process in each of our four countries. Britain is in a symmetrical but precarious position; it is very high on ability to contain conflict, but very low on ability to support public spending. Should its political strength decline, its economic situation would pose great difficulties. For Britain, reform has to begin outside the expenditure process by increasing the interaction between government and society so as to improve the economy; internal budget reform must be concerned with both restraining expenditure and increasing its productivity. With the economy placing such strain on the polity, Britain must hesitate to buy policies that might create conflict it could otherwise afford. France lies almost, but not quite, in the opposite position. It is very low on ability to contain conflict, rather high on ability to support public spending. The French concern must be with their political system, and hence

Figure 13.2. THE BUDGETARY PROBLEM: CONTAINMENT OF CONFLICT (POLITY) VERSUS SUPPORT OF SPENDING (ECONOMY)

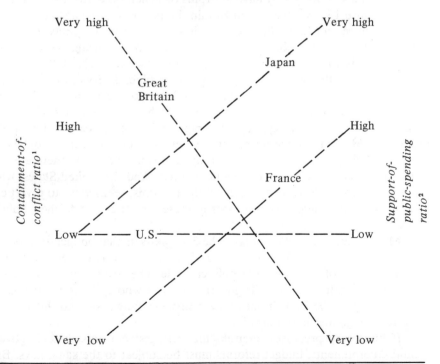

[1] This ratio is determined by dividing the Consensus-Deference index by the Diversity-Intensity index.
[2] This ratio is determined by dividing the Wealth-Growth index by the Visibility-of-Tax-Increase index.

with the contribution their budgetary process makes to resolving conflict. The position of the United States is symmetrical and balanced. Its abilities to contain conflict and to support spending are about even both within each ratio and between them. Unless one is contemplating a radical restructuring of the federal government, budgetary reform in the United States must be concerned with maintaining this balance by relating expenditures to revenue, executive to legislature, and substantive to appropriations committees. The Japanese ability to support public spending is very high but capacity for containing conflict is just at par. Perhaps their exceptional economic growth has masked political difficulties. If their growth rate begins seriously to decline, how budgeting is conducted will become an index of social cohesion. The Japanese will want to ensure that economic decline does not take place at the expense of political viability. All this, of course, is pure supposition. It remains to be seen how the budgetary processes in these countries actually have adapted to their differing contexts.

I have conceptualized the context in which budgetary problems arise as a relationship between containment of conflict and support of spending. Containment may be conceived as the political dimension and support as the economic dimension. Any country may have a surplus or deficit on these two dimensions. Thus in Figure 13.3 we see that in Britain the polity is stronger than the economy, in France and Japan the economy is stronger than the polity, and in the United States they are about equal. The next step, following the analysis in Chapter 11, is to ask how the budgetary processes in each of the four rich countries deal with their particular budgetary problems. Style, the reader may recall, is a combination of the number of levels of decision and the norms regulating conduct among elites. Britain — with few levels of decision, and trust as a norm — has a style of resolving conflict at the center. Japan, with proportionality as the main norm and few levels of decision, has avoidance of conflict as its style. France — where arbitration is the norm and there are more levels of decision — chooses to contain conflict. And the United States, which has many levels of decision and uses all three norms, seeks ways to divert conflict. What do the budgetary processes in these countries add to their political styles?

My answer, as the title of Figure 13.3 suggests, is that budgetary processes do more of whatever was done before. They carry to a further extreme the main tendencies of their country's political style. The British budgetary process is even more centralized than its government as a whole, the American is further fragmented, the French put up ever stronger bulwarks, and the Japanese strive for still greater harmonization.

If budgetary processes intensify the strongest currents in their governmental environments, budget reforms must be subject to the same laws. Budgeting cannot be the Archimedean lever of the political system; it cannot square the circle. *Budgetary processes may modify but they cannot substantially alter political processes.* Budgeting remains, as I have repeatedly urged, a subsystem

Figure 13.3. BUDGETARY PROCESSES INTENSIFY THE POLITICAL STYLE OF EACH GOVERNMENT

Country	Context of budgeting		Political style (number of levels plus norms of conduct equals style)	Result
United States	Economy balances polity	+	Trust Many + Proportionality = Diversion Arbitration	→ Further fragmentation
France	Economy stronger than polity	+	Medium + Arbitration = Containment	→ Stronger bulwarks
Japan	Economy stronger than polity	+	Few + Proportionality = Avoidance	→ More harmonization
Great Britain	Polity stronger than economy	+	Few + Trust = Absorption	→ Greater centralization

within a larger political system. The political system dominates the budgetary subsystem, not the other way around. It follows that those who desire drastic changes in budgetary processes must, lest their desires prove defective, first alter the larger political system to which budgeting primarily responds. A budgetary reform in the United States that attempts to upset its political balance at one point must compensate at another; otherwise, constituent elements in the political system will overwhelm it. Presumably President Nixon discovered this when his "reform" — incessant impounding of funds after they had been appropriated, something akin to an item veto — was successfully challenged by Congress. Reforms in Britain that promise further centralization as well as economic effectiveness (such as Program Analysis and Review) will do better than a proposal that sacrifices one for the other. Changes that propose to make elite relationships in Japan less harmonious through repeated adversary encounters over budgets must first restructure the party system to allow and sustain these conflicts. And any process that will increase the level of conflict in France would obviously have a hard time justifying itself.

The "ABCs" of power relations in budgeting were covered in Chapter 10. Support of most if not all major power wielders is essential for budgetary reform. Lateral attacks (as with the Central Policy Review Staff in Britain) rather than frontal assault on the Treasury (as in the old Department of Economic Affairs) are likely to be more successful. Reforms that bypass the Cabinet, such as the committee of nonspending ministers in Britain, or that try to give cabinets collective control, such as the abortive effort to establish global margins in France, are likely to fail because they run counter to the political style of their respective countries.

Just because the question is obvious — In whose interest is the proposed reform? — does not mean that it should not be asked and answered. A serious proposal for reform can never be merely a technical device to increase the efficiency of government operations but must always affect who gets what the government has to give, and who will be in charge of whatever is ultimately done. Because interests in society and government are affected by changes in budgeting, compiling lists of potential losers and gainers constitutes only reasonable forethought. Figuring out how to overcome expected resistance is not an extraneous but rather an intrinsic part of reform. Good ideas that nobody wants make bad analysis. Divorcing reform from its requisites is a recipe for ruin.

Budgetary calculations affect reform in two significant ways: Can the operations specified in the reform actually be carried out; What will they do to the level of conflict? There is not much point in struggling for power over budgets only to find that one's preferred reform demands unavailable knowledge or leads to unanticipated and undesirable consequences. Because calculations are connected to conflicts, the ways in which actors go about figuring out things cannot be a matter of indifference. Analyzing the base rather than the increment evidently affects the scope as well as the outcome of conflict. Governments in political deficit will seek economic surplus, not further borrowings on their ability to contain conflict. Suppose, however, that the two goals — economic growth and political consensus — do not complement but oppose one another. How much growth at the expense of how much consensus? Actually, the dilemma is older and broader than that. For contradiction as well as complementarity of goals has been the existential state of budgeting for as long as recorded history.

HISTORY

In the most ancient times, in Babylonia and Assyria, ancient China, Egypt under the Pharaohs — think back to Joseph the Provider — there was no accepted medium of exchange. Taxes were collected and resources were allocated in kind. That explains the vast storehouses necessary for the Pharaoh's provisions and his wealth. Keeping all the king's resources at the center meant that there would be pilferage of his revenues on the way there and spillage when sent back to discharge local payments. Leaving a significant part in the hinterlands may have simplified disbursements but at the risk of political suicide when local satraps commandeered the king's due and then rose up to challenge the central authority. Then, as now, budgeters had to take their chances in a world that rarely let them have it all their own way.

Until relatively recently in the history of mankind, there was no distinction between public and private. The accounts sculpted on temple walls by Athenian treasurers to report their stewardship were the rare exception; the rule was the commingling of state funds with those of the men who wielded power. At various times in the ancient world, as under the late Roman emperor Septimus Severus, there were attempts to distinguish between the monarch's private patrimonial resources and those of the state. Such attempts rarely lasted long. For the greater the resources a king could command, the greater his power. Because control over resources meant control of the state, kings enhanced their authority by personal surveillance of the Treasury when it was possible and by appointing men they hoped were trustworthy as their financial agents when it was not.

But without norms and procedures that differentiated public and private resources and the technical capacity to record the distinction, state agents, like the king, had strong motivation to enlarge their own holdings. Ancient and medieval kings often employed punitive sanctions to set the example that might, they hoped, induce their officials to respect the king's fiscal rights. Just as the Egyptian Pharaoh Harmhab I threatened dishonest treasurers with amputation of their noses and banishment to the outer reaches of the Arabian desert,[7] medieval French kings executed and punished numerous treasurers be-

---

[7] James Breasted, *A History of Egypt from the Earliest Times to the Persian Conquest* (New York: Scribners, 1916) p. 406; Eberhard Otto, *Aegypten, Der Weg des Pharaonenreiches,* 3rd ed. (Stuttgart: W. Kohlhammer [Urban]), 1958, p. 171.

cause of role confusion — their failure to distinguish between their private
pockets and the state purse.[8]

The problem of establishing and maintaining a distinction between public
and private was compounded for states that lacked the organizational ability
to administer their own finances. At various times and places in the past, governments used market administrative methods as substitutes or supplements to
state bureaucracies. These governments sold the right to collect specific taxes
to private agents called tax farmers. In the transactions between governments
and the men who farmed taxes or bought offices for a fee, reciprocity governed the terms of exchange. States leased out tax franchises and sold offices
to achieve fiscal certainty. In addition to the payment of tax farming contract
fees in advance of collection, states could borrow from tax farmers when revenues were short. During the turbulent last century of the Roman Republic, as
in Byzantium, England under the Stuarts, or France in the *ancien régime,* governments tried to stabilize cash flow by obtaining advances from tax farmers.
But they rarely succeeded, for payment in advance held the penalty of smaller
receipts. The motive to buy offices or to engage in the risky business of tax
farming was the potentiality for large personal gain. Those who held public
office as private property could exploit their investments to obtain the maximum yield. In the process by which venal officeholders manipulated state finances, the fiscal system's productivity was sharply reduced. The state often
lost out as market administrators siphoned off from a quarter to half the potential revenue yield.[9]

To eliminate market administration and replace it by a state bureaucracy
selected by merit was but one focus of earlier reforms. The reforms we are
concerned with today, then, are only the latest in a series that goes back for at
least a thousand years. For most of mankind's history, governments could not
budget for the conception of annual allocation of a comprehensive accounting
of state resources did not exist.

Suited to conditions when accessibility was limited by primitive modes
of transport and poor communications, the allocation procedures of ancient,
medieval and early modern governments were highly fragmented. From the
taxes collected in outlying territories, the local collectors — state officials, men
who held office as property, tax farmers, or the military — were authorized
to make local payments. Even in the cases where central governments demanded an accounting of provincial revenues and expenditures, there was no
way to ensure their collectors' honesty, or the comprehensiveness of their ac-

[8] Rene Stourm, *The Budget* (New York: Appleton and Co.) 1917, pp. 536–541;
J. P. Bosher, "Chambres de Justice in the French Monarchy," in J. P. Bosher, ed., *French
Government and Society, 1500–1850, Essays in Memory of Alfred Cobban* (London:
Athelone Press, 1973), pp. 20–40.

[9] Julian Dent, *Crisis in Finance, Crown, Financiers and Society in Seventeenth Century France* (Newton Abbot: Davis and Charles, 1973), pp. 35–40.

counts. Thus in the late Roman Republic, Cicero railed against Verres, corrupt governor of Sicily, for the brevity of his accounts:

> . . . Let us see how he gave in his accounts; now he . . . will . . . reveal his character. "I received," says he, "2,235,417 sesterces; I spent, for pay to the soldiers, for corn, for the legates, 5,417 sesterces." Is this giving in accounts? . . . What does this mean? What impudence it is! What audacity! . . . [10]

Seven hundred years later, during the Puritan revolution in England, London merchants, suspicious of the management of revenues by parliamentary committees, voiced a similar concern when they complained that the committees

> . . . have arranged the receipts and revenues . . . so disorderly and ineffectually that the Kingdom cannot but be unsatisfied concerning the due employment thereof and doubt that much of the publick money hath been employed to private ends and remains obscured in the hands of such as were intrusted the collection of those assessments. . . .[11]

Large state expenses paid out by central governments in past ages were allocated by earmarking, a technique that worked well for governments with limited expenditures. During periods of rapid expansion, however, the earmarking technique became inflexible and unwieldy as the variety of taxes and the objects of expenditure became far too numerous either to comprehend or control. Under the usual conditions in which government finance was conducted in past ages, then, merely to obtain a surplus to buffer emergencies was often the kings' sole fiscal goal.

By the early eighteenth century, many of the conceptual elements on which comprehensive budgeting is based had already emerged. Annual accounting of state revenues and expenditures gradually became customary, first in the northern Italian communes in the early renaissance, later in England, when, following the Restoration, Parliament sought to limit the executive's arbitrary power by rationing his funds. Long before formal estimation techniques had been invented, governments drew up accounts at the year's end or sometime afterward to provide a basis for determining what funds would be needed in the following year. It does not matter that the accounts were incomplete and the arithmetic faulty. Compared to the haphazard revenue procurement of earlier eras, this rough procedure reflected the emergence of a key concept of budgeting — that of the expenditure base.[12] Control of expenditures by means of reliable accounts kept in arabic numerals and according to

---

[10] A. H. M. Jones, *A History of Rome Through the Fifth Century*, Vol. 1, *The Republic* (New York: Walker & Company, 1968), p. 101.

[11] W. R. Scott, *The Constitution and Finance of English, Scottish and Irish Joint-Stock Companies to 1720*, Vol. 1 (Cambridge: University Press, 1912), p. 235.

[12] O. A. Ranum, *Richelieu and the Councillors of Louis XIII* (Oxford: Clarendon Press, 1963), pp. 125–126.

double-entry technique was known and widely used in business by the seventeenth century, though most governments were yet to adopt the method. Experimental attempts to regularize the funding and amortization of government debt were tried briefly in the early eighteenth century, then abandoned long before the time needed for organizational learning had elapsed. But, gradually, public perception of the losses that resulted from corruption associated with venality of office, public servants' mismanagement of multiple earmarked funds, and archaic administrative methods, led to pressures for change.

If a benchmark is needed, formal budgeting began with the reforms of William Pitt the younger, Chancellor of the English Exchequer in the late eighteenth century. Pitt's reforms combined the multiplicity of special funds into a single consolidated fund from which nearly all expenditures were made, authorized account-keeping according to double-entry technique, and introduced control over funding and amortization of the state debt. But it was a long time after that before all state revenues were collected in the same way and allocated all together to ensure budgetary comprehensiveness. Regular annual budgets that incorporate all the state's revenues have appeared only in the last century.

For all of this time, continuing to this very day, the control purpose of budgeting has dominated. In earlier reforms, control had been achieved by piecemeal accretion of procedures. New methods were superimposed on the old; these existed in parallel for a time and eventually the old were abandoned. With dual focus, early reforms — like the Roman emperor Diocletian's of 301 A.D. — aimed at increasing tax receipts through comprehensive assessment of a newly specified base.[13] However, most early reforms in financial administration focused on the revenue side, aiming at increasing tax yields by asserting forceful control from the center. To this end, diverse governments on repeated occasions tried to strengthen the center's influence over the outlands by creating new offices that duplicated the functions of old ones. Thus, from the periodic centralizing edicts of Chinese emperors, to Henry VIII who emasculated the medieval English Exchequer by establishing parallel revenue courts that duplicated its function, to Sully, Mazarin and Richelieu in the French *ancien régime* who imposed layer upon official layer in a vain effort to check the abuses of a vast and amorphous provincial bureaucracy, to Frederick William I, the Great Elector of eighteenth-century Brandenberg Prussia, who actually accomplished that task by means of a personal cadre of financial espionage agents, we see a series of incremental efforts to change existing procedures.

Hesitant to offend supporters who held offices, successive governments preserved old rules and procedures when the real substance of financial ad-

---

[13] Mikhail Rostovtseff, *The Social and Economic History of the Roman Empire* (Oxford: Clarendon Press, 1926), pp. 466–467.

ministration had been transferred elsewhere. The changes in organization and method that occurred in the late eighteenth and early nineteenth century English Exchequer illustrate the process of administrative evolution by gradualism. As the holders of antiquated sinecures died or retired, their offices were abolished. A new breed of salaried professionals slowly replaced them.[14] Sometimes — China and France provide good examples — displaced elements managed repeatedly to regain influence and control, which led to cycle on cycle of attempted reform. But rarely — only in times of extreme crisis — have governments tried to develop new procedures from scratch. There have always been drives for economy — from the sumptuary laws of ancient kingdoms to those of Japan in the eighteenth century that regulated the amounts of gold or silver thread that could be woven into garments worn by noblemen,[15] to the limitations on travel expenses incurred on government business today. But it is only since the late eighteenth century that the administrative technology that would make orderly allocation possible was adopted by governments. The basis of present reforms promoting efficiency — achieving a given objective at least cost, or getting the most of a given objective out of a stated sum of money — is really a twentieth-century phenomenon.

Eventually, ideas of technical efficiency became an accepted part of budgetary practice. This movement is known in America as performance budgeting and elsewhere as value for money or by some other designation. The idea is to take repetitive activities, determine their lowest costs, and try to enforce these notions by means of activity or performance budgets. The planning orientation that program budgeting brought with it, emphasizing the productivity of expenditures over time, added another budgetary innovation.

PROGRAM BUDGETING

PPBS emerged from at least three distinct but closely related strains of development. These strains — economic development planning, the administrative reforms of the early decades of this century, and management of national economies to control cyclical fluctuations — all rest on a legacy of the Enlightenment, the optimistic confidence in the power of intelligence to order man's environment and improve human welfare. In the processes by which

[14] Sir Edward Bridges, *Treasury Control* (Oxford: Clarendon Press, 1957), pp. 108–109.

[15] Augustus Boekh, *The Public Economy of the Athenians* (London: John Murray, 1828), Vol. II, pp. 378–9, 381; Albert E. Trever, *History of Ancient Civilization,* Vol. II, *The Roman World* (New York: Harcourt Brace, 1939), pp. 141, 268; George Sansome, *A History of Japan, 1615–1867* (Stanford: Stanford University Press, 1963), pp. 160–161; M. Miyamoto, Y. Sakudo, and Y. Yasuba, "Economic Development in Preindustrial Japan, 1859–1914," *The Journal of Economic History,* Vol. XXV, No. 4 (December 1965), p. 42.

development, efficient government, and economic stability would be achieved, the contemporary paradigm of science provided a model. When implemented successfully the new methods would permit the planner, policy-maker, and administrator to achieve the same objective control of government, economy, and society as could, theoretically, be attained in a laboratory. So, too, the administrative reforms of the early years of this century aimed at purifying government by taking politics and personality out of it. Advocates of the new economics, coming later in time, were far less naive; nonetheless a strong strain of technocracy has been associated with proposals for economic stabilization. PPBS, by merging the long-term perspective of planning with the systematic analytic methods of economics in the name of administrative reform is thus but the latest of a long chain of proposals to introduce a greater rationality into the processes of government.

As Allen Schick put it in his discerning study of American experience, "The Road to PPB: The Stages of Budget Reform,"

> In the initial stage, the primary emphasis was on central control of spending and the budget was utilized to guard against administration abuses. The detailed classification of objects of expenditure was the main control mechanism. The second stage was management-oriented. It was concerned with the efficient performance of work and prescribed activities. The performance budget, officially introduced by the Hoover Commission, was the major contribution of the management orientation. The third stage is reflected in the planning orientation of the new PPB system. It had roots in Keynesian economics and the new technology of systems analysis.[16]

Any budgetary process, Schick insists, must be able to handle budgetary control, budgetary efficiency or management, and budgetary planning. The reforms of the future, such is their heavy burden, have to do all that was done by the reforms of the past as they attempt to float in on the waves of the future.

This time the future arrived first in the United States. The fact that planning, programming, and budgeting systems were first spawned there may be the result of this country's special cultural interest in the productivity of work — the many variations of Taylorism that employed time and motion studies first developed in America. A huge defense budget, coupled with government's permeability by outside forces, are situational factors that favored the development of PPBS. Together these factors fostered an interest in analysis of defense programs and led to the emergence of a cadre of defense intellectuals outside the government who applied systems analysis to military problems. Yet it may appear surprising that a budgetary reform with an avowed planning orientation should develop in the one country without even the pretense of formal economic planning. Ideological objections to national planning have resulted in

---

[16] Allen Schick, "The Road to PPB: The Stages of Budget Reform," *Public Administration Review*, 26 (December 1966), pp. 243–258.

vague euphemisms for planning, like the various commissions on national goals, that attempt to salvage the substance without giving offense by the form. Had PPBS been successful, it would necessarily have become America's version of planning, the curse evidently taken off the word by surrounding it with echoes of efficiency — programming, budgeting, and systems.

On August 25, 1965, President Johnson announced that he was asking all federal agency heads to introduce "a very new and revolutionary system" of program budgeting which would produce the "most effective and the least costly" way to accomplish national goals.[17] Program budgeting has no standard definition. The general idea is to make budgetary decisions by focusing on end products and on gross categories of output such as governmental objectives, instead of on such discrete inputs as personnel, equipment, or maintenance. Like cost-benefit analysis, to which it owes a great deal, program budgeting lays stress on estimating the total financial cost of reaching goals. Cost effectiveness (also called cost-utility analysis) is used in order to select among "alternative approaches to the achievement of a benefit already determined to be worth achieving." [18] When priorities among objectives are set up, budgeting by programs is supposed to determine how much should be spent on one program versus another. Programs should be seen as interrelated wholes, to determine the best expenditure mix in the annual budget for producing the largest future benefits.

Although there were a few historical precursors,[19] program budgeting really came to life via the federal government. With amazing rapidity, it then spread in the 1960s to many American cities and states, governments abroad, and international agencies. The literature has become so vast that full-scale bibliographies have blossomed — with, no doubt, a bibliography of bibliographies now in the offing. Clearly, from the standpoint of effort and publicity, PPBS is the major budgetary phenomenon (perhaps *cause célèbre* would be more accurate) of our time. Hence it needs and deserves attention. But where to begin?

In my experience, discussions of PPBS suffer from being too abstract. Musing about whether important values suffer from quantification, or whether budgeting by outputs is superior to budgeting by inputs, makes it very hard to see real people, on the job, grappling with the intricacies of program budgeting. So, drawing on my own research, I will present and then analyze two case

[17] Lyndon B. Johnson, "Transcript of the President's News Conference on Foreign and Domestic Matters, Thursday, August 26, 1965," quoted in *Program Budgeting: Program Analysis and the Federal Budget,* ed. by David Novick (Cambridge: Harvard Univ. Press, 1965), p. v.

[18] Alan Dean quoted by George A. Steiner, "Problems in Implementing Program Budgeting," in Ibid., p. 311.

[19] See Allen Schick, *Budget Innovation in the States* (Washington, D.C.: The Brookings Institution, 1971), and David Novick, *Origin and History of Program Budgeting* (Santa Monica, California: RAND Corporation, October 1966).

histories: one, in Chapter 14, the zero-base budget, an experiment to see if a PPBS-type mechanism would work; and the other, in Chapter 15, a later attempt to implement the real thing.

Efforts to sponsor change, with their attendant struggles, often bring into bold relief the stakes participants have in the status quo. It is one thing to talk about budgeting as a political process and quite another to watch this politics at work. When we see real actors consciously attempting to manipulate program budget categories to gain advantage, the connection between form and fortune becomes more vivid. If the categories in which budgets are calculated delineate agency programs, they also establish organizational boundaries, so we will not be surprised that program definition invokes the territorial imperative. The critical question is not only what a budget category contains, but who it is for. Willingness to supply information depends on a coincidence of interests between supplier and consumer. Being able to observe the variance in the truth content of the categories, depending on who is emerging as the client, breathes life into what otherwise might appear as merely technical discussions.

Both episodes have their locus in the United States Department of Agriculture. The risk, for the reader, is that he will learn far more than he may want to know about this department. The opportunity, I hope, is to ask why the "after" differed so little from the "before." Unlike the man in Charles Atlas advertisements, this 99-pound weakling did not become a strong hero. I want to find out why, after agencies tried this wonderful new method, the crowd in the budget department — unlike the friends of our man in the classic advertisment — did not break into loud cheers when the novice flexed his new muscles.

That PPBS has yet to win those cheers will become only too apparent as we survey experience in other parts of the world. Why has it failed so often, despite variation in personnel, locations, and circumstances?

Perhaps the problems were only political. Maybe PPBS ran up against vested interests. Threatened by what program budgeting would uncover about failure to reach goals, or, merely wedded to old ways of doing things, defenders of the status quo possibly just refused to let PPBS work. Or maybe it had hidden political defects that it was proper for wise and good men to resist. In order to explore these potential political explanations in Chapter 16, we must place program budgeting in the context of the economic doctrine from which it was derived by investigating "the political economy of efficiency": how much of PPBS is devotion to efficiency and how much politics clothed in the rhetoric of economic rationality?

Categories are strategies. To define an exhaustive set of budgetary categories is to say what government should do. The measure is the program. Men do what they are measured by. So it is not surprising that the politics of advice is fought out over seemingly exotic categories and apparently esoteric measures of what constitutes merit. Speaking about cost-benefit analysis may seem almost antiseptic; altering or maintaining the distribution of income generates passion; yet the first is based on (and affects) the last. Analysis affects outcomes. Indeed, system analysis is supposed to tell you what your problem is as well as what you might do about it. The systems analyst tells you where to get off as well as how to get there. It is a dangerous occupation.

But suppose PPBS had internal deficiencies as well as external enemies. Suppose that on its own merits it could not work because society did not know how to perform the necessary calculations. If PPBS had defects in principle, if its internal rationale was defective, as I argue in Chapter 18, then it would not (because it could not) work anywhere. To argue a contrary point one would need to show that somewhere — anywhere — program budgeting succeeds in its own terms. As the worldwide survey in Chapter 17 shows, I am still waiting for the first example. Yet there is one successful budgetary reform in Great Britain which, though different from PPBS, had major consequences for the way resources are allocated. The nineteenth chapter is an attempt to understand why this reform worked and PPBS did not. The last and twentieth chapter represents my effort to practice what I preach by proposing reforms that are based on an understanding of how different budgetary processes work.

14

Some Butterflies Were Caught, No Elephants Stopped: The Zero-Base Budget, a Precursor of PPBS

Before budgeting by programs was unleashed on the Federal Government of the United States as a whole, an extreme variant actually was tried out for a year in the Department of Agriculture. Largely ignored at the time, this experiment reveals significant clues as to the difficulty of putting together and practicing this kind of system. Like the deliberately exaggerated displays in medical museums — which present views of pathology several times larger than life — the zero-base budget magnifies everyday experience to show aspects of behavior which might otherwise escape attention. Tracking down the origins of the zero-base idea should help us better understand those dissatisfactions with traditional budget processes which led reformers to think up new ways to do business.

A CONTROVERSY

Whatever else they may be, budgets obviously are political documents. They engage the intense concern of administrators, politicians, leaders of interest groups, and citizens interested in the "who gets what and how much" of governmental allocations. Participants in budgeting drastically simplify their task by concentrating on the relatively small portion of the budget that is politically feasible to change. A previous year's budget, the largest part of which is composed of continuing programs and prior commitments, is usually taken as a base needing little new justification. Attention normally is focused on a small number of increases and decreases which signal significant departures from the established historical base of the agency concerned. Parts of the total budget are given to various administrative agencies, appropriations subcommittees, presidential staff, and other interested parties for special attention. Fragmentation is increased because all budgetary items are not evaluated together, but are dealt with in sequence by the various participants, so that only a small number of items need be considered by any individual at any one time. There is heavy reliance on feedback from interested parties, if a decision turns out to have adverse consequences for others. The existing budgetary process, therefore, may be described as incremental, fragmented, and sequential.

Much of the literature on budgeting in the United States has been devoted to criticizing the present process.[1] Such aids to calculation as the incremental method have been called arbitrary and inefficient. Fragmented and sequential budgetary operations have been severely attacked for leading to lack of coordination and neglect of important values. Failure to consider the budget as a whole, each item competing for funds with the others, has been characterized as irrational. Although many statements could be cited to show how long and how consistently these views have been held, only a few illustrations seem necessary here. Writing in 1924, E. Hilton Young asserted:

> It must be a temptation to one drawing up an estimate to save himself trouble by taking last year's estimate for granted, adding something to any item for which an increased expenditure is foreseen. Nothing could be easier, or more wasteful and extravagant. It is in that way obsolete expenditure is enabled to make its appearance year after year long after reason for it has ceased to be.[2]

Benton Biser beat this drum again in 1941: "Appropriations generally are built upon the basis of the preceding year's expenditure, plus or minus any known items of increase or decrease, without considering whether or not the past year's experience is the result of efficient and economical administration."[3] Arthur Smithies was even more positive: "In general final expenditure decisions should not be made until *all* claims on the budget can be considered"[4] (italics supplied).

These norms still operate. According to Maurice Stans, budget director

---

[1] See, for example, W. F. Willoughby, *The Problem of a National Budget* (New York: D. Appleton, 1918); A. E. Buck, *Public Budgeting* (New York: Harper, 1929); Commission on the Organization of the Executive Branch of the Government (1947–1949), *Budgeting and Accounting* (Washington, D.C.: U.S. Government Printing Office, 1949); Jesse Burkhead, *Government Budgeting* (New York: Wiley, 1956); Arthur Smithies, *The Budgetary Process in the United States* (New York: McGraw-Hill, 1955); and Edward A. Kolodziej, "Congressional Responsibility for the Common Defense: The Money Problem," *The Western Political Quarterly,* 16 (March 1963), 149–160.
[2] Quoted with evident approval by A. E. Buck in *The Budget in Governments of Today* (New York: Macmillan, 1934), p. 172.
[3] "Some Shortcomings of Present Budgetary Practice," *Toward Better Budgeting* (Detroit: Governmental Research Association, 1941), p. 6.
[4] Smithies, *The Budgetary Process in the United States,* p. 16.

under President Eisenhower, "*Every item* in a budget ought to be on trial for its life *each year* and matched against *all* the other claimants to our resources" [5] (italics supplied). Such critics would prefer a budgetary process in which coordination would become the explicit concern of a central hierarchy, which would consider a wide range of alternative expenditures and investigate rather fully their probability of occurrence and the consequences of each. No item would automatically be included; each would be considered anew every year in the light of its relative priority. Instead of a historical base, there would be no base at all; therefore, this comprehensive budget is labeled "zero-base."

Although it is evidently possible to talk about comprehensive, zero-base budgeting, the question arises as to whether it is possible to do it.[6] This question cannot be shunted aside as unimportant, when one considers the constraints imposed by limited time and comprehension; the lack of theory to predict consequences or means to calculate them fully; the widespread political consensus on many ongoing programs, and the statutory necessity of proceeding with others; and inability to resolve the perennial question of the comparability of different preferences held with varying degrees of intensity. A direct test of the comprehensive approach was not possible before because (to the best of our knowledge) no major attempt was ever made to try a zero-base budget. The effort of the Department of Agriculture to work with a zero-base budget in 1962 provides, therefore, a unique opportunity for a direct test. The analysis of a "deviant case" (when compared with the usual mode of budgeting) has special advantages in highlighting features of the budgetary process that might otherwise escape notice.[7]

---

[5] U.S. Senate, Committee on Government Operations, Subcommittee on National Policy Machinery, *Organizing for National Security; The Budget and the Policy Process,* 87th Congress, 1st Session, 1961, Part 8, p. 1107.

[6] David Braybrooke and Charles E. Lindblom, *A Strategy of Decision; Policy Evaluation as a Social Process* (New York: The Free Press of Glencoe, 1963); also Lindblom's "Decision-Making in Taxation and Expenditure," in *Public Finances: Needs, Sources, Utilization; A Conference of the Universities — National Bureau Committee for Economic Research,* National Bureau of Economic Research Special Conference Series, 12 (Princeton: Princeton Univ. Press, 1961), pp. 295–336.

[7] See Patricia L. Kendall and Katherine M. Wolf, "The Two Purposes of Deviant Case Analyses," in *The Language of Social Research,* ed. by P. F. Lazarsfeld and Morris Rosenberg (Glencoe, Ill.: The Free Press, 1955), pp. 167–170. For excellent examples of the insight to be derived from an unusual case, see Herbert A. Simon, "Birth of an Organization: The Economic Cooperation Administration," *Public Administration Review,* 13 (1953), pp. 227–236, and Seymour Lipset, et al., *Union Democracy: The Internal Politics of the International Typographical Union* (Glencoe, Ill.: The Free Press, 1956).

The study is based on an extended series of interviews, during the summer of 1963, with budget officers, directors or assistant directors, and staff people in nearly every agency in the Department of Agriculture, as well as with department-level officials. We tried to interview every person at a high level who was intimately involved in the zero-base budget experiment, and succeeded in talking with at least one person in all but two small agencies. Our 57 interviews constitute an overwhelmingly large sample of the important men available for discussion. All those interviewed were encouraged to comment on a draft of this paper and to amplify their remarks. Twelve reinterviews were under-

PROCEDURES

The experiment in zero-base budgeting goes back to three circumstances: (1) The general climate of opinion favored comprehensive budgeting. (2) A letter from Director of the Budget, David Bell, to the Secretary of Agriculture, Orville Freeman, suggested that a more comprehensive approach to budgeting was in order. Dated August 16, 1961, the crucial sentence reads: "I think we should in a real sense reconsider the basic funding for each program — 'justify from zero' in the budgetary phase." (3) Freeman had developed a strong interest in budgetary problems as governor of Minnesota.[8]

When the decision was made, staff members in that department's Office of Budget and Finance quickly surveyed the literature and discovered that although much had been written criticizing traditional methods of budgeting and advocating a comprehensive approach, there was little to be found about zero-base budgeting. After the staff had consulted with leading department officials in order to get a clearer idea of the objectives, they began preparations.

In April 1962, the Department Office of Budget and Finance sent out "Instructions for 1964 Agency Estimates," which called for radical changes.

> A new concept has been adopted for the 1964 agency estimates; namely, that of zero-base budgeting. This means that all programs will be reviewed from the ground up and not merely in terms of changes proposed for the budget year. . . . The *total* work program of each agency must be subjected to an intensive review and evaluation. . . . Consideration must be given to the basic need for the work contemplated, the level at which the work should be carried out, the benefits to be received, and the costs to be incurred. . . .
>
> The fact that certain activities have been carried out for a number of years will not, per se, adequately justify their continuation. Nor will the fact that programs are prescribed by statutory law necessarily be a controlling consideration. Program goals based on statutes enacted to meet problems or needs that are today of lesser priority must be reevaluated in terms of present conditions.
>
> It is implicit in the zero-based budget approach that the need for programs and their recommended magnitude in the fiscal year 1964 be clearly and specifically demonstrated. . . . The justifications should be prepared on the assumption that *all* [italics supplied] information needed for making budget decisions should be included.[9]

---

taken in order to check on disputed points. Quotations represent a transcription of notes taken during interviews or, when indicated, comments in letters written in response to the first draft.

[8] Thomas Flinn, *Governor Freeman and the Minnesota Budget,* Inter-University Case Program, No. 60 (Birmingham, Ala.: Univ. of Alabama Press, 1961).

[9] It should be understood clearly that this approach was being tried only at the Department of Agriculture and not in the Budget Bureau or Congress. As the "Instruc-

Instructions for preparing a zero-base budget called for three major types of calculation: (1) justification of the need for agency activities and programs without reference to congressional mandate or past practice; (2) justification of the requested level of expenditure based on the needs; (3) justification of the costs of needed programs from the ground up. How did agency officials react? How did they go about putting together the huge amount of necessary information?

Application of Zero-Base Concept

All agencies had serious difficulty in conceptualizing circumstances in which there were no legislative mandates, no past commitments, no consideration of items to be included because of demands by other participants in the budgetary process, no programs for which support could not conceivably be expected; in a word, no history or learning based on that history. The words of one official, "Justifying the whole program is silly; it just equals rehashing the original legislation" were echoed by many others. So the agencies either assumed or quickly decided that their programs *were* needed. Many programs were justified at least in part by references to the language of their enabling legislation, despite the statement in the instructions that this would not be an overriding consideration. Besides pointing to statutory requirements, agencies gave priority to showing how their program met objectives of the Kennedy-Freeman program: increasing recreation facilities, aiding low-income groups, and generally advancing rural development. This is, of course, what the agencies normally would have done in justifying their budgets, except that they added more detail and greater documentation. Furthermore, time was precious and in short supply. "We didn't have time to analyze much" was a typical comment, reflecting the tendency for effort to be channeled into the large and pressing task of compiling supporting data.

One budget officer estimated that any "real examination" of the need for the programs carried out by his agency "would take at least a year." As a result, he explained, continuation of major programs was not reexamined.

Calculations involved in determining the precise figures were described by one agency head in terms generally applicable throughout the department: "In the matter of preparing budget estimates, the dollar emphases (priorities) are intended to represent a program which represents what the secretary and Congress want to give emphasis to at that time. The dollar figures represent a

---

tions" pointed out, "Since it is anticipated that the Department Estimates for 1964 will be submitted to the Budget Bureau in accordance with existing ... instructions, the justifications ... will be primarily in terms of changes from 1963." Thus a list of "Increases and Decreases, 1964, Compared with Latest Estimate, 1963," was also requested of each agency.

compromise among the guidelines given by the need for the service (what the public has asked for), the wishes of the president and secretary, and the indications given by Congress at 'Hill' hearings ('Hold the line on this program next year!')." Other officials mentioned certain limiting factors — availability of trained personnel, or physical resources — which set upper limits to what they could do. Clearly agency people lightened their burdens by actively seeking guidelines or constraints — what Congress would approve, what the statutes required, what could be done with available personnel and resources.

Agency people were far more concerned with the level of their programs than with whether there was a need for them at all. One stated, "We told our program people, 'These are the areas Congress has authorized us to participate in. Which need to be implemented in your state, and at what level?' "; and even here, "Mostly this was a justification of what we had." Program officials reported, apparently without realizing the totally contradictory implications for the theory behind the zero-base budget, that in preparing estimates, "We had to start from the previous year, then determine what increases we wanted for 1964." "Each staff officer reviewed his office. We all decided we needed what we had. Then we decided whether to ask for increases." Business as usual.

Since the zero-base budget was designed specifically to avoid this incremental procedure, we challenged respondents to explain and defend their approach. Some were not even aware at first that they were still following an incremental procedure. At times they became agitated: "You've got to start from where you are!" They made two main points to support this proposition. First, since they were best informed about their present status, they could make some reasonable estimate of the effect of more or less money for particular programs. But they had no idea what drastic changes — such as eliminating their programs, or cutting them in half, or doubling them — would mean: "Increases or decreases are about all we can swallow." At department budget hearings such comments were reinforced; we saw agency representatives typically confronted with the same kinds of increase-decrease statements as in previous years: "How many people do you have now? What did you spend for that last year? What do you propose to do with the extra funds?"

The second argument was that the whole procedure was unreal. Why so much trouble for a procedure which nobody with experience could see leading to significant results? Everybody knew certain programs were mandatory, others could not be modified, and still others had to be supported at approximately their current level, unless the president and the Secretary of Agriculture were prepared to make many more enemies than appeared to be so: "We knock our heads against the wall and then we know it will all turn out the same." All this "waste of time and effort" when they might have been working on programs about which they could really do something.

Yet the instructions for the zero-base budget did contain some guidance: "One of the department's objectives will be to reduce overall net expenditures for the Department of Agriculture in 1964 and subsequent years below presently estimated levels for 1962 and 1963." If agencies were expected to make a fundamental analysis of the needs for their programs, regardless of budget constraints, such an admonition would seem superfluous.[10]

"My first reaction was to jump out the window," an agency budget officer revealed. As agencies began work to justify the cost elements in their estimates, however, initial difficulties were forgotten in the frantic attempt to meet requirements set down for the zero-base budget. Those agencies whose activities or experience lent themselves easily to workload analysis reacted differently from those whose activities made this procedure impossible or inappropriate. An agency with a well-developed and widely accepted mode of workload measures could meet the requirement that expenditures be justified from "the ground up" by attaching an explanation to tables of workload statistics, supporting the expenditures. As one budget officer put it, "Workload data is great for us. We're pioneers in this area. We'd been developing this data for years." A high-ranking official was explicit in stating that in his agency, "the zero-base approach made no difference, because to meet rapidly changing conditions, we're always preparing our budget zero-base style. Economic assumptions lead to size of expected program (required by statute), which leads to cost on basis of previous staffing and material needs. We don't know what the estimate will be until it pops out of the calculating machine." They might account for their costs per unit of work but that hardly provided justification for the level of effort or rationale for the program itself as the spirit of zero-base budgeting would have required.

For agencies that did not or could not use workload data, calculating the expected level of expenditures in zero-base style was much more difficult, and officials tended to react much more negatively. "I don't know of any budget officer who liked zero-base budgeting," was a typical comment. "Workload data is inappropriate for us," they explained. "It's not like building a bridge or something — you don't have 'units,' you have subject matter, and it is very

[10] An official at the department level writes that this "sentence . . . appears to . . . contain an erroneous conclusion. As the author of the sentence referred to, I can clearly recall that at the time we very explicitly rejected the proposition that zero-base budgeting as such had to take place without regard to overall limitations on financial resources. I felt then, and still feel, that the 'ceiling' technique and zero-base budget development and justification are logically compatible. As the article points out, the zero-base budget approach that was used involved not only the question of whether or not work should be done but also the amount of work proposed and the price tags. Each of these aspects is logically a variable but can be adjusted within a program or between programs in the light of overall available resources. The reason the sentence was included in the instructions (and in a sense it was superfluous) was merely to make it very explicit to the agencies that we were not making the assumption that the budget decision-making system would suddenly tolerate all 'justifiable' expenditures merely by virtue of a change in the technique of presenting the budget, and that the secretary in fact had an overall objective that he wished to attain with respect to the department as a whole. The sentence, of course, was not intended to mean, and did not mean, that the objective applied to each individual program and activity separately."

difficult to know how many technical people are needed." Unable to talk in terms of so many applications processed, operations performed, or similar measures, agencies with no workload statistics had to find another rationale. Some tried to explain the problem and to justify proposed levels of expenditure by projecting into the future the rate of growth of the previous few years. A few agencies tried to develop new ways of dividing activities, although they did not think this realistic, and expected no benefits from what they called "arbitrary categories." Developing supporting data meant breaking down costs differently and engaging in many hurried calculations without any feeling that something positive would result. As a result, these agencies were overburdened with work in which they had little confidence, although they did manage to submit estimates as much as ten or more times longer than previous ones. Six weeks after the instructions for the zero-base budget had been sent out, twenty-five sets of binders representing agency estimates, most taking up three feet of shelf space, appeared in the Office of Budget and Finance. "It nearly created a surplus storage problem," one official remarked pointedly.

Comprehensiveness of Zero-Base Approach

"Theoretically," a department official said, "a zero-base budget is a way of evaluating needs and priorities more systematically and comprehensively than usual." How did officials at the department level [11] analyze the voluminous material presented? Did they try to evaluate the relative merits of every item or program compared to every other? What procedures were actually used in making agency allowances?

The main problem was lack of time. "We knew we were getting into something horrendous," said one respondent, "and it was obvious in advance that it would be impossible for all of us to analyze the material at all stages. The range of decision — the number of decisions to be made — increased almost infinitely. Although individual steps of the process at the department level were the same as always, this made such a quantitative difference as to amount to a qualitative one." Another official observed, "The stuff the agencies submitted was very complete, obviously too bulky for the secretary himself to wade through." Direct confirmation came from an authoritative source who said that the Agriculture Secretary "didn't read a great deal of material; he only has time for summary material." But he did spend more time than before on the budget. Of the eight members of the Budget Committee of the department — the undersecretary (chairman), six assistant secretaries, and the Director of Budget and Finance — it is doubtful that more than one or two actually had time to read all the material submitted. That the zero-base budget came up

---

[11] The Secretary of Agriculture and his staff, the six assistant secretaries and their staff assistants, and the Director of Budget and Finance and his staff.

during the Billie Sol Estes episode and at a time when the appropriations bill was seriously behind schedule in Congress may have added to the time problem. The consensus, expressed by a high department official, was "There was too much material in the zero-base budget for us to digest and use. I haven't read it all." What, then, did they do with the material they could read and digest?

The crucial question centers on the degree to which comparisons were made as to the relative desirability of programs spanning several different agencies. Nothing approaching a comparison of every program with every other (or of most programs with each other) was made. On the contrary, most comparisons made by department officials concerned programs and activities within individual agencies. An official explained, "Questions at department hearings were in the same categories as usual — Why this program? Why this level? What would alternatives cost? — but in more detail. In analysis, we didn't consider why 65 rather than 64 or 66 man-years for project X, but why 3 times as much for project X as project Y." Only for a few closely related programs in different agencies, where this already had been the practice, were comparisons made across agency lines. In fact, most of the analysis, as in previous years, dealt with justifying an individual program at a particular level of expenditure. "Unavoidably," a department official revealed, "we ended up talking about how much more, about increases. Budget people seem to talk about a budget request of $5 million when actually that's just the increase."

When we faced him with these findings one department official declared that:

> The ideal of a zero-base budget is actually impossible: It would require investigating why each research lab is where it is (which is tough to trace), giving an objective measure of how much can be justified for research in a given area, etc. If you have the type of program where you can identify units of work, budgeting on zero-base is relatively simple. But in a case like the Department of Agriculture, that often doesn't work. Our activities are so varied as to make quantitative comparisons between programs impossible. I don't agree that just because we put emphasis on increases, no one pays attention to the rest of it. We are always evaluating some programs in a basic sense and always trying to make improvements in management. If we do [place emphasis on increases] it's because that's the way appropriations committees like to operate.

This official and others appear to be saying (1) that they do not know how to make the calculations required for a zero-base budget; and (2) that a comprehensive approach is not necessary, because they do, from time to time, investigate various programs intensively, within the limitations of their time and knowledge. It is clear that those who like the zero-base budget will have to show how it can be done if they wish to see it put into practice.

THE STAFF

Those who were analyzing the budget at the department level tried hard to avoid increase-decrease analysis. "Naturally," a staff man explained, "we were interested in the fact that a program would be a new investment; that fact might raise or lower [its] priority. But increases and decreases as such were for the Bureau of the Budget [and later for submission to Congress]; they weren't even included in the detailed justifications." This procedure raises a question of some interest: If, as we have seen, top officials showed greatest interest in increases and decreases for the purpose of making recommendations on the budget, what purpose was served by providing them with other kinds of data and analysis?

When we asked department people about this, they began to alter the rationale originally offered for the zero-base budget. Two major lines of thought developed. The first professed to see in the zero-base budget a combination of psychological reassurance and strategic utility: "There has been a great hue and cry about the size of the agriculture budget. The purpose of it [the zero-base budget] is to reassure, if we can, the secretary, the Director of the Budget, the members of the appropriations committees, that money is not being wasted and that it is being used to carry out only the most important projects in work that furthers the national interest." Although related to the first in its emphasis upon the psychological aspect, the second post hoc rationale leans on the benefits to be derived from any radical change in habits of work and thought. "We were interested," proponents of this view asserted, "in the zero-base budget as a therapeutic device for agency and budget people. It's easy to get into the habit of doing things the same way. Starting out with the idea that nothing is sacred is therapeutic in itself. Any device that will encourage people to give a deeper and broader consideration of operations will lead to better understanding of what is going on and of areas where improvements might be made." Notice that the focus has shifted from external phenomena, like comprehensive calculation from the ground up — from analyzing programs comparatively — to internal psychological states, like breaking up people's habitual patterns of thinking and reassuring leaders. To what extent did "better understanding" lead to improvements? Consider the consequences of the zero-base budget for budgetary decisions within the department. What difference did it make in the kinds of decision made?

INTENDED OBJECTIVES

The major purpose of the zero-base budget was to examine all programs at the same time and from the ground up to ferret out programs continuing through inertia that did not warrant being continued at all or, minimally, at the present level of expenditure. Money released by spotlighting these "obsolete" programs might lead either to a decrease in the overall size of the funds requested by the Department of Agriculture or to more rapid expansion of the highest priority programs than was possible under the traditional incremental approach to budgeting. In brief, for the first time, detailed information about all programs would be available for departmental review in one place at one time. As a result, relative priorities of total amounts for all programs could be considered and not merely amounts of increase and decrease for some programs.

We therefore asked each person interviewed to tell us whether any decision made by him or by others could in any way be attibuted to the zero-base budget. Did the agency or department officials recommend different programs, different amounts for programs, or distribute funds among programs differently as a result of the zero-base approach? Overwhelmingly, the answer was no.

Most statements were variants of "I don't think it made a damn bit of difference," or, "I don't think anyone would honestly tell you that they changed their budget." Agency personnel continually reiterated their doubts that the department was adequately staffed to digest such vast amounts of material. Asked for evidence, respondents usually replied that, "The figures we put in have never been referred to as far as I know," or, "It [the zero-base budget data] was sent across the street [where the department offices are located] and we never heard of it again." A few respondents hedged: "I don't know that I personally learned anything new or different, but . . . I suspect it did make some difference, but I'd hate to have to prove it." A couple of times an exceedingly small change was reported though not without qualification. Although there was "no difference in the overall amounts requested or received from the department, analysis did lead to the transfer of $20,000 among programs. This analysis was, however, planned before the zero-base budget. . . ." An excess expenditure for files in one agency was also mentioned. In one instance a department official did say, "I am confident that decisions were made which would not have been made or even considered in the absence of a zero-base budget." But even he could give only one specific change — a reduction of $100,000 in an obsolete research program. The paucity of changes attributed to the zero-base budget is evident in the fact that this example was brought up repeatedly. (Many officials said they had heard of a change somewhere, but it always turned out to be this same one.) Another department official insisted that the zero-base budget procedure was not useful in "ferreting out all the sorts of dark and sinister things that shouldn't be done, which would turn up quickly anyhow." Our general conclusion can be stated in the words of a person in a position to get a general view: "Some butterflies were caught, no elephants stopped."

There are a number of explanations for the scarcity of changes. First, as one agency official put it, "Budgeting is continuous." Individual programs are constantly being evaluated. When authorizations run out, new studies usually are undertaken and new justifications prepared. A change of party in the White House or the appearance of a new agency head often results in the reevaluation of some programs. Interest in Congress or the Bureau of the Budget (as it was then called), demands by clientele groups, and changes in the economy or in technology may lead to intensive analysis of specific programs. These take place in addition to periodic reviews scheduled within the agency in order to adjust to changing circumstances. Second, some of the Agriculture Department's programs have always been budgeted more or less in zero-base fashion because their operations lend themselves to quantification of the level of operations. These include the price support programs of the Commodity Credit Corporation, which make up the largest single item in the budget. For such programs, justifying a $600,000 program and justifying a $100,000 increase in a $500,000 program amount to much the same thing. Therefore requests coming from those agencies — certainly a major determinant of what departmental officials will approve — were much like those of previous years. Third, administrators are responsible for seeing that resources are expended for the programs they believe have the highest priorities. The head of one of the larger agencies pointed out that when he goes to Congress with a request for an increase in his agency's budget, he must always be ready to admit that the increase will finance work of lower priority than is already being done; otherwise he will be criticized because he has not already transferred funds to the higher-priority activities! Nearly all agencies have many more programs than they can undertake or expand with the funds they have or are likely to get; they are not likely, therefore, to allow an obsolete program to continue to drain resources from programs they deem more worthwhile.[12] Even those interested in expanding their organizations can seek expansion of those programs they believe most worthwhile.

The main reason that budgets turned out pretty much the same, however, is that the process by which they are calculated and justified is only one — and by no means the most important — determinant of program size, distribution, and content. Budget officials, particularly at the departmental level, continually qualified their remarks by saying that, after all, "The zero-base budget didn't affect the basic economic and political facts of life." There are mandatory programs such as price supports for which expenditures must be made and which cannot be easily altered. The level of programs may depend a great deal on the state of the national economy (for service programs), on the existing state of knowledge and the availability of trained personnel (for research programs), and not on how programs are analyzed or written up. As many officials remarked, "Decisions are made on criteria other than the justification of the

---

[12] See the statement to this effect by the late William A. Jump, a noted budget officer in the Department of Agriculture, quoted in Aaron Wildavsky, *The Politics of the Budgetary Process,* 2nd ed. (Boston: Little, Brown, 1974), pp. 23–24.

program itself. Frequently the figures are based on judgment factors of what the environment will permit taken in total." Whether political support exists for a program depends on party alignments in Congress and the executive branch; preferences of the president, director of the budget, members of appropriations committees and other officials; and the activities of clientele groups. Budget people know full well, for example, that the most compelling justification may have little influence against a powerful budget-cutting drive. Such factors do not figure in the zero-base approach; therefore in a budgetary system which necessarily stresses "what will go," [13] a zero-base approach will not necessarily make much difference.

Despite widespread agreement that the zero-base budget did not significantly affect outcomes, nearly half of those interviewed commented quite favorably on the experience after it was over. Was this merely a show of bureaucratic loyalty or were there other reasons for the favorable attitude? This unexpected finding led us to ask further questions.

UNANTICIPATED CONSEQUENCES

Activities may have unanticipated, even unperceived, outcomes.[14] Preparing a zero-base budget resulted in a number of unexpected consequences which were probably more important (and certainly more interesting) than those anticipated.

One difficulty faced by reflective people engaged in budgeting is that they hold implicit beliefs about desirable methods of calculations — comprehensive and simultaneous evaluation of means and ends being considered as synonymous with rationality — while they practice quite different — incremental and sequential — methods. For the large minority who expressed positive feelings about zero-base budgeting, the experience appears to have satisfied a longing to believe that they were in fact proceeding according to canons of rational calculation. When asked why they liked zero-base budgeting, they would answer by describing the method and pronouncing it good: "Considering everything from the ground up at the same time is, well, good, the right way

[13] Ibid., "Deciding How Much to Ask For," pp. 21–31. Despite our stress on the political aspects of budgeting, more than one official wrote: "Greater emphasis perhaps could also have been placed on the importance of the political imperative on the budgetary process. At the point that budgeting begins, i.e., gathering of base information, there is often only meager guidance on economic and other assumptions on which to base estimates which are compatible with sound practices. This guidance consists of admonitions to be economy minded — guidance which may become meaningless if interest in program emphasis suddenly increases."

[14] See Robert K. Merton, "Manifest and Latent Functions," in *Social Theory and Social Structure* (Glencoe, Ill.: The Free Press, 1957), pp. 19–84. We have avoided use of Merton's "manifest and latent functions" because functional analysis has inappropriate implications.

to do it, and not just letting things grow, like Topsy." "The major benefit may well have been the much more intensive, thoroughgoing review, from the bottom up." So, if the zero-base budget did not lead to changes, did people at least learn more?

Here there was a sharp split in the responses of most of those who approved the zero-base budget. Some claimed that they learned nothing new; they had known about all their operations before. How, then, was the zero-base budget helpful? Agency personnel answered that the department people must have benefited; department-level personnel answered that agency personnel had benefited! "The zero-based budget," said an agency man, was "enlightening to department officials who reviewed it. To us it was just an exercise." "We knew what was going on," department officials would say. "It was helpful in the agencies. I can't prove this, but I have no doubt that things turned up in the agencies that were never passed on." A variant of this argument came from one agency head: "I don't know that I personally learned anything new or different. But some of my staff who prepared material for me produced clearer presentations than in other years." For these officials, the zero-base budget was good because it benefited other people.

The rest of those administrators who were favorably disposed toward zero-based budgeting did feel that they themselves had learned something new. Without exception these were people who had been in their positions less than three years and had not yet discovered how useful perusal of budgetary material could be in adding to their store of information. "I think everyone came out of this process with a great deal more information than they'd ever had before," a new appointee declared. "I went through all of the material, spent more time on budgeting than before [the previous two years], learned more about the scope of operations." Like others in his position, he knew what programs were being undertaken, but had not realized the full extent of the operations until he read the budgetary data.

If this were so, why did not these officials use their new knowledge to alter their preferences or otherwise make somewhat different decisions? An important clue was furnished by one of these "learners" who remarked, "Some of these things I wouldn't have needed to know." Indeed, further questioning revealed that much of what was learned was simply not appropriate to the kinds of choices available to these men or, at least, was not perceived by them as being relevant in the context in which they operated.

Those who disliked the zero-base budget complained that they had done a lot of extra work for nothing in the way of changes. But those who liked the zero-base budget were far from unhappy and seemed to find positive advantage in this circumstance. One official explained, the zero-base budget was good because "it tended to confirm what you had a notion of otherwise." It felt good "to satisfy yourself that you're doing a conscientious job," said another official, "instead of following the inevitable least resistance, less deep analysis, of the increases and decreases approach." The happy coincidence of finding out that one had done budgets right all along was a morale booster. Before they had come to the department they had heard complaints that many of its programs were wasteful and unnecessary. Now that it had been demonstrated in detail just what the Department of Agriculture was doing and why, they were more certain of the necessity of programs for which they were responsible.[15] The strength of this feeling may go a long way toward explaining their favorable reaction to the zero-base budget and all its extra work — even — indeed, *especially* when few changes were made as a result of it.

The zero-base budget experiment had focused attention on the budgetary process itself. For the first time in many years, a Secretary of Agriculture had attended department budget hearings and had made it known that he considered budgeting of primary importance. As a result, many officials informed us, "There was a higher interest in budgeting than ever before." Much more time was spent on budgeting: "I worked ninety hours a week and still didn't have nearly enough time." "A tremendous number of man-hours were involved. I spent at least twice as much time on budgeting this year, lots of Saturdays and evenings." Budget people discovered that their function was rated more highly as program people became more involved in budgeting and were "forced . . . to sit down and justify their programs." And, as program personnel worked on budget justifications, they liked the feeling of being more involved in their activities regardless of any desire for change. They might well have learned as much (or more) in other years had they spent as much time and energy on budgeting. The zero-base approach had value here not so much because it was necessarily a better way of planning a budget, but because it was a *different* one which prompted them to focus their attention on budgeting.

A large part of the felt benefits of engaging in zero-base budgeting may stem, therefore, from the well-known Hawthorne effect[16] in which the content

---

[15] The reassurance function of the zero-base budget is clear from two quotations. A newcomer said: "Coming into a big department like this you need landmarks on which to justify your own opinions of the budget. This is difficult when the budget this year is based on last year which is based on the year before. You sometimes had the feeling that they were building it like a sort of poor skyscraper, piling on more and more steel, without knowing where the building was headed. [After the zero-base budget] you had the feeling that you understood the programs better . . . and had more confidence in the value of the services being performed."

An old-timer in the department confirmed this view and gave it a special twist in terms of the functions performed for the agencies. "When new administrators come in, they see things they didn't know the Department of Agriculture was doing. They figure this is just the top of the iceberg and get worried. If you take the whole iceberg out of the water and drop it on their desks, and they're too overwhelmed to look at it, they don't have an excuse to nag you any more. This is the major benefit from the agency point of view: to the extent that their superiors looked at the stuff they were reassured; to the extent they didn't, they no longer have an excuse to nag them [the agencies]."

[16] Elton Mayo, *The Social Problems of an Industrial Civilization* (Cambridge: Graduate School of Business Administration, Harvard University, 1945); Fritz Roethlisberger, *Management and Morale* (Cambridge: Harvard Univ. Press, 1941).

of the experiment is less important than the fact that the sense of importance of those engaged in the experiment is enhanced. Greater interest and attention is devoted to the activity in question and the people who engage in it. Consequently, they feel that, perhaps, their problems are in some sense better understood, regardless of whether this understanding is objectively real or leads to specific consequences for the pattern of decisions. Thus agency people felt good at being able to educate their departmental superiors. Top departmental officials believed that the zero-base approach helped agency people see their work in perspective. Through being compelled to justify the existence of their agency's programs, they would see how it fit into the total operations carried out by the Department of Agriculture. This line of reasoning may help explain why many officials were certain that the zero-base approach had helped people at other levels in the hierarchy, even if they were unable to suggest any way in which it had helped them.

Political Use of Budget

This analysis would not be complete without noting that the zero-base method of budgeting — whose advocates present it as a means of focusing on costs and benefits rather than on political maneuvering — was used also for strategic purposes, thereby enhancing its appeal to certain officials who felt that the zero-base procedure was useful in dealing with outsiders. "We've examined these requests from the ground up," they would say in justifying their requests as "solid" and not subject to cuts. By stating that the desirability of changes had been made clear from the zero-base analysis, several officials were able to call attention to changes they had wanted in previous years. In this way one agency won approval for building funds denied the year before. In general, the zero-base experiment helped those who had previously decided they did want to review a program by giving them an excellent reason for not delaying review. Resistance to providing essential information was overcome to some extent because top agency officials "were armed with weapons which forced . . . the disgorging of the information they needed to get. . . . This is often like pulling teeth." And, having proposed the change they had in mind, responsible officials could manipulate the belief that the zero-base approach was more rational to make their colleagues more amenable to the change.

Attitude toward Annual Zero-Base Budget

No one suggested that the zero-base approach be followed every year. Among those who felt that the experiment should be repeated, the most common suggestions were: "not every year but periodically," "at intervals, every few years," or "every five years or so." Since new officials would benefit most, such officials reasoned, a zero-base budget would be useful only with changes in administration. Another view was that budgets changed little from year to year, so that an annual zero-base budget would result in "duplicating the same pages." The authors were cautioned to "remember that the budgetary process is not the only decision-making process for setting policy. Parts of operations are considered through other channels all the time." The general conclusion was that the zero-base method might serve every five years "for a reference document," or "to find out where you are now," or so "we'll have a more recent base." It is apparent that even those who found some use for the zero-base approach began to assimilate it to the more familiar incremental method. They would use it from time to time, to "take inventory" as one put it, and then take their bearings for the immediate future from that date. Whatever these comments suggest about failure to understand the essence of zero-base budgeting, they are eloquent testimony to the effect of experience. Comprehensive budgeting vastly overestimates man's limited ability to calculate, and grossly underestimates the importance of political and technological constraints. The required calculations could not be made and would not have led to substantial changes. As a result, a great deal of effort went into zero-base budgeting with few specific changes attributable to this costly method.[17]

ZERO-BASE BUDGETING IN TWO STATES

Of late we began to hear rumors about successes scored in the implementation of zero-base budgets. We have good reason to doubt that they are

---

[17] If one makes the conservative estimate that at least 1000 administrators above the level of clerk-typist and messenger were involved in bringing together parts of the zero-base budget throughout the Department of Agriculture and its many field offices, and that they spent an average of 30 hours a week for 6 weeks preparing the data, above and beyond their usual budgetary work, then at least 180,000 man-hours may be charged directly to this activity. With the generous estimate that $200,000 worth of changes (without going into their desirability) can be attributed to the zero-base budget, it appears that the government achieved a return of something more than a dollar per hour (leaving out the cost of facilities, paper, clerical help, and depreciation of human talent). Nor do we know what these officials missed in terms of opportunities foregone during the time they worked on the zero-base budget. The point is not that the reader should place too much credence in these estimates (respondents differ as to whether we are too high or too low) but that under any reasonable estimate, the return to the government would be very small. Had anything like the same amount of effort been devoted to studies of filing, the flow of paper, or similar operations, much greater returns might have been achieved. Since half of these men were not usually involved in budgeting, however, there might well have been important intangible benefits that we have not taken into account.

One respondent went further and wrote, "The author might find it advisable or worth while to really set about analyzing the present cost of budget preparation and justification throughout its entire process. While this is an important activity, there is little written evidence as [to] the resources going into the preparation and justification of agency budgets within the department, the Bureau of the Budget, and the Congress of the United States. A careful analysis might reveal that possible shorter steps or involvement by fewer people would be in order."

founded. To convince ourselves, if not our readers, we decided to look into the matter.

Peter A. Pyhrr, a management consultant, claimed that, ". . . as experience in Texas Instruments, Inc. and the state of Georgia has indicated, this kind of budgeting (zero-base) need not add heavily to the burdens of budget making. In fact . . . it can actually reduce the burdens of budget making while significantly improving management decision-making and allocation of resources." [18] Unfortunately we know little about Texas Instruments, but we do know something about Georgia and New Mexico, two states which did attempt to institute zero-base budgets in recent years.

Did zero-base budgeting in fact reduce the burdens of budgeting? Mr. Pyhrr's own account suggests the opposite. "In the state of Georgia, with 10,-000 decision packages and 65 agency workings, the volume was too great for the Governor to review all packages." [19] A far more important question, however, is whether zero-base budgeting did or did not change the way in which budgetary decisions were traditionally made. Pyhrr claims that it did and offers the following description.

> . . . the Governor concentrated on the summary analyses and reviews provided by his financial staff in the budget bureau. He had a review with each agency, and concentrated his time on reviewing policy questions, major increases and decreases in existing programs, new programs and capital expenditures, and a few specific packages . . . where there appeared to be problems.[20]

If the reader suspects that he may have seen this description elsewhere he is perfectly correct. This is the way in which most governors make budgetary decisions. If Pyhrr has changed the governor's decision rules, then his description should differ from that furnished by Turnbull who describes the Georgia budgetary process in the late sixties.

> The Budget Bureau prepares a "Summary of Agency Requests for Increase in State Funds" which outlines the major increases requested by each department. . . . It serves as the major guide to consideration of the budget by the Governor. . . . The Governor [Saunders] favored supporting established programs at a level that would allow progress. New programs of less than immediate need were quickly eliminated. . . .[21]

We leave it to the reader to decide if there is such a difference. Had we switched the descriptions, no one would have been able to say which was which (pre-

[18] Peter A. Pyhrr, *Zero-Base Budgeting: A Practical Management Tool for Evaluating Expenses* (New York: John Wiley & Sons, 1973).
[19] Ibid., p. 97.
[20] Ibid.
[21] Augustus B. Turnbull, III., *Politics in the Budgetary Process: The Case of Georgia* (unpublished Ph.D. dissertation, University of Georgia, Athens, Georgia, 1967), pp. 236–243.

versus post–zero-base). Another reviewer, Donald Axelrod, reached a similar conclusion.

> By his own (Pyhrr's) account the Georgia experiment was hardly a success story. . . . With some exceptions the quality of decision packages and analysis ranged from poor to mediocre. There were no major cutbacks in on-going programs to finance high-priority programs. Few discernible benefits in cost reduction or management improvement flowed from the process. . . . The large volume of decision packages swamped large agencies as well as the budget bureau.[22]

Things were not very different in New Mexico. John D. LaFaver describes lessons learned after a few years of attempts to implement zero-base budgeting. "It simply was not reasonable to expect an agency to routinely furnish information that might result in a lower appropriation."[23] "The Legislative Finance Committee realized that the abolishment of an agency, no matter what its performance record might be, is usually impossible."[24] "A budget addressed to justifying an agency's existence does not examine the critical issue facing a finance committee — that of how much should be allocated."[25] Despite these difficulties, LaFaver tells us that the Finance Committee decided to retain zero-base, albeit in a modified form. We were ready to take notice when we suddenly read about the "modification." "The major modification was the abandonment of the level of effort below the present base. Thus, a rigidly defined base was the first level of effort and expansion items only were ranked in priority order."[26] If zero-base budgeting means preparing a budget as if it was done for the first time, paying no attention to the past, then New Mexico (like Georgia) does not have an operative zero-base procedure.

Had much more time been available, it might have been possible for the advocates of zero-base budgeting to develop workload measures for more programs. With more time and experience, the initial confusion might also have been overcome; but the basic problems of the zero-base budget still would not have been solved. It would still not be politically feasible; nor would anyone be able to make the necessary calculations. In order to compare activities on a department-wide basis under a zero-base budget, top officials would have had to develop categories cutting across agency programs, together with methods of relating their costs and benefits. Present methods of calculations are not equal to this task, as the subsequent experience with program budgeting was to reveal ever more conclusively.

---

[22] Donald Axelrod, "Post Burkhead: The State of the Art or Science of Budgeting." *Public Administration Review* 33:6 (November/December, 1973), p. 582.
[23] John D. LaFaver, "Zero-Base Budgeting in New Mexico," *State Government* XLVII:2 (Spring, 1974), p. 109.
[24] Ibid.
[25] Ibid.
[26] Ibid., p. 110.

15

Whose Place in the Sun? PPBS in the Department of Agriculture

Following President Johnson's August 1965 announcement of PPBS, the new revolutionary budgeting system for federal agencies, Orville Freeman introduced it on October 27, 1965, in the Secretary of Agriculture's Memorandum No. 1589, saying that PPBS would (1) define program objectives in specific terms capable of being analyzed; (2) specify time horizons for accomplishing objectives; (3) measure program effectiveness — "indicators" would tell how well things were going; (4) develop and compare alternative ways of attaining the objectives. Groupings of activities would cut across agency lines in order to provide a program structure that would facilitate meaningful analysis. Thus bureaus would be asking the following questions: "What do we do?" (program); "Why do we do it?" (objective); and "How are we doing?" (output in relation to objectives — i.e., results).

To underscore the significance he attributed to PPBS, Secretary Freeman underlined his special commitment: *"I will personally participate in the evaluation and approval of the Department's Program and Financial Plan."* Within the Office of the Secretary, a staff working for the undersecretary would put together special studies to help the Program and Budget Review Committee in its task of coordinating the review of Department policy. A special assistant appointed to the undersecretary would work with selected bureaus (including the Forest Service and Soil Conservation Service) to develop approximate program categories. Bureau staffs, reporting directly to bureau heads, were to begin full-time work on these categories within the next three months.

Let us see how the implementation of this plan affected the Department of Agriculture, particularly the Forest Service — my second case history.

From Chapter 5, "Program Budgeting: A Macroanalysis," from *The Budgeting and Evaluation of Federal Recreation Programs: Or Money Doesn't Grow on Trees,* by Jeanne Nienaber and Aaron Wildavsky, © 1973 by Basic Books, Inc., Publishers, N.Y.

CREATING THE ORIGINAL PROGRAM
CATEGORIES

In response to the question "What do we do?" the bureaus submitted their lists of proposed categories. The department responded by suggesting the following 14 program categories.

1. Adequate Supply of Farm and Forest Products (includes conservation and development of land, water, and forest resources; research designed to enhance our future capacity to produce farm and forest products; storage operations for adequate reserve stocks; etc.)

2. Protect and Enhance Income Position of Commercial Farm Families (includes price support programs, programs designed to withhold excess productive capacity, and supporting research)

3. Improving Efficiency of Marketing System (includes marketing research, market news, Commodity Exchange Authority, etc.)

4. Improve Quality and Variety of Farm and Forestry Products (includes research to develop new products and new uses, and improve quality; product grading activities; etc.)

5. Improve Food Diets and Nutrition (includes food distribution programs, nutrition research, etc.)

6. Protect Human Health (includes meat and poultry inspection, pesticide regulation and research, pollution control, etc.)

7. Enhance Personal Development of Rural People (includes Job Corps; extension education and development activity, including work with youth and low-income families; research on human development problems; etc.)

8. Rural Community Improvement (includes water and sewer systems loans; telephone and electricity; R, C & D: Rural Renewal; RCDS)

9. Provide Adequate Housing in Rural Areas (housing loans and grants, and related research)

10. Recreation and Natural Beauty (Forest Service recreation, wildlife, and natural beauty programs; hunting, fishing, other recreation; etc.)

11. World Trade Expansion (includes food fairs and other market development activities; Title IV of P.L. 480; international negotiations; supporting research)

12. Foreign Food and Development Assistance (food and technical assistance programs and supporting research, etc.)

13. Nonmission Oriented Basic Research (residual category for research activities unable to allocate to above objectives)

14. General Administration and Program Support

Program Category 1, Adequate Supply of Farm and Forest Products, which covered most of the Forest Service budget, was broken down so that planned accomplishments might be expressed in quantitative, but not necessarily financial, terms. The measures below represented direct (or primary) outputs of department programs. Yet these outputs were expressed in units that presented problems in analyzing possible trade-offs where all or part of one program might be substituted for another. The trade-off between miles of terraces and acres of irrigation, for example, calls for a common unit for weighing, which does not exist.

Measures for Category 1: Adequate Supply of Farm and Forest Products

1. Water resources development conservation, which would concern itself with additional acre feet of water storage by output units, reducing volume or weight of sediment per unit of streamflow, decreasing in depth to the permanent water table, seeking to improve BOD (Biological Oxygen Demand) rating, and increasing cubic feet per second of streamflow and the additional acres irrigated.

2. Land resources development and conservation would be expressed in acres limed, drained, fertilized, etc.; acres terraced, cleared; miles of windbreak; acres protected from flood hazard by levees, etc.; acres converted to pasture, fallow use, timber or other non-crop use; acres of reduced erosion; and animal unit months of forage provided for livestock.

3. Credit insurance output units would include acres, volume or weight of specified crops and number of firms insured by size class of firm; acres, volume or weight of specific crops and number of firms receiving capital improvement loans by size class of firm and type of improvement; and acres by type of farm and number of firms receiving emergency loans by size class of firm.

4. Wood production output units would be board feet of sawtimber and veneer harvested on National Forests; cubic feet of bulk timber products harvested on National Forests; additional board feet of growth of sawtimber and veneer on National Forests; additional cubic feet of growth of bulk timber products on National Forests; and additional board feet or cubic feet of growth on private woodlands.

5. Maintaining standby sources of supply output units measuring additions to storage capacity by volume units and commodity, volume units of commodities stored, and number of firms by size class and commodity class participating in storage program.

6. Research and education.

7. A separate category might be necessary to handle mineral claims and certain special uses in National Forests.

In the Forest Service budget, the following items, together with proposed amount of funding, fell within the definition of Program Category 1: forest protection and utilization ($222 million), forest roads and trails ($87.6 million), acquisition of lands for national forests ($1 million), cooperative range improvements ($700,000), access roads ($1 million), assistance to states for tree planting ($1 million), timber-development organization loans and technical assistance ($1 million), and permanent appropriations, primarily to states ($60 million).

The Forest Service also was supposed to conduct some of its activities under Program Category 4, Improve Quality and Variety of Farm and Forestry Products. One subelement of this category would be developing and improving new uses, products, and by-products of forest materials which could be measured in output units according to their number, weight, or volume. Developing and improving product quality also would be a concern, to be measured by increases in volume or weight of commodity output in desired grades or by the number of grading systems improved or newly developed. Finally, maintenance and guarantee of product quality would be judged in output units either of volume or weight of commodities inspected, or by increases in weight or volume of a commodity marketed on a grade basis. The Forest Service "crosswalk" (conversion) to its regular appropriations structure would be in terms of the "Forest products utilization research" line item of $5.9 million, though it was possible that the line item for marketing research might also come within this program category.

Wildlife Production, which could be included in Program Category 10, Recreation and Natural Beauty, would be placed in output terms according to the number of hunter or fisherman days or in terms of visitor days. Visitor days also would be the chosen unit for the Outdoor Recreation Opportunities subcategory. Natural Beauty, a most difficult subcategory to which to assign output units, would be measured in terms of acres, areas, or miles of improved scenic environment by the units of floral products, ornamental shrubs, trees, and grass seed produced, or in terms of technical assistance and research provided to the private sector. If none of these seems closely related to natural beauty and its measurement, it is not surprising. The Forest Service line items proposed to be cross-walked into this program category were "Recreation — Public Use" ($28 million), "Wildlife Habitat Management" ($4 million), "Forest Recreation Research" ($500,000), and "Wildlife Habitat Research" ($700,000).

Here then was the original program category setup proposed by the Department of Agriculture, with special attention given to those categories into which Forest Service budget line items would be expected to fit. Thereafter a memorandum from the Planning, Evaluating, and Programming (PEP) Staff Director called for meetings with each of the affected agencies in the Department to review the program elements assigned to them. This is the Director's depiction of the categories involving resource agencies:

CATEGORY 1: *Adequate Supply of Farm and Forest Products.* Includes action, research information, education, and other supporting programs whose outputs directly and primarily enhance capability to provide adequate supplies of farm and forest products at reasonable prices or shift production to higher priority agricultural uses. These programs are designed to affect actual current production, capacity for future production, or the maintenance of standby supplies or productive resources for emergency needs. One major group of programs is concerned with the growing and harvesting of forest products on both federal and nonfederal lands. Another group aims at conservation measures to enhance or safeguard the capacity of land for production of farm products, or to shift land to higher priority agricultural uses both now and in the future. A third group includes programs oriented toward storing minimum reserve stocks of agricultural commodities or protecting agricultural industries and associated resources for emergency need.

CATEGORY 4: *Improve Quality and Variety of Farm and Forest Products.* Includes principally research programs with outputs that primarily enhance the development of higher quality and greater variety of farm and forest products. Incentive programs to achieve these ends would be included here. One group of programs would be designed to develop new food products from farm products and to improve the quality and variety of existing food products. A second group of programs would be designed to produce new industrial products from farm and forest products and to improve the quality and variety of presently produced industrial products made from agricultural products.

CATEGORY 10: *Outdoor Recreation and Natural Beauty.* Includes action, research, information, education, and other supporting programs to enhance the supply of outdoor recreation and natural beauty through conservation measures and development of facilities and services.

Outdoor recreation includes hunting, fishing, camping, picnicking, hiking, swimming, and similar opportunities on federal and nonfederal lands.

Natural beauty programs are aimed primarily at upgrading the aesthetic appearance of U.S. natural resources and related public and private improvements. Examples are research to develop more attractive flora for urban and rural use, vegetation management to maintain aesthetic roadside, shoreline, and landscape zones, and development of sites for viewing scenic vistas.

A PLACE IN THE SUN, A CATEGORY OF ONE'S OWN

How would leaders in administrative agencies be expected to look at this (or any) classification of their activities? One problem in institutionalizing evaluation is that even the first step, defining objectives, may be viewed as a hostile act by the agencies affected. This proved to be true of the 14 categories introduced in the Department of Agriculture.

When considering its place in a new budgetary arrangement, each bureau naturally asks whether its own activities will receive good treatment under the general categories and whatever measures are proposed for giving them value. Each bureau wants its activities included in as many categories as possible, so that it may justify them as contributing to the enhancement of as many valued goals as possible. If necessary, bureaus will request that new categories be created to reflect their special contribution to the public interest. To be left out of a category, or to fail to have a beloved activity included, might signify the loss of organizational jurisdiction, leading to aggrandizement of one's competitors.

The Forest Service claimed that conservation should not be submerged in the first category, Adequate Supply of Farm and Forest Products; instead, it proposed that resource conservation should be set up as a separate output category. The National Forest System activities of the Forest Service, together with its own conservation action and research functions and those of bureaus within the Agriculture Department, were said to affect 75 percent of the nation's land and water surfaces. Conservation of water, soil, and scarce minerals, the Forest Service argued, would therefore come under a Natural Resources Conservation category. Not only would this classification point up the leading role which the Department of Agriculture plays in this area, but it would afford an opportunity to consider conservation allocation at the highest level. Conservation outputs, though difficult to evaluate, are certainly no more unquantifiable than natural beauty, but when placed alongside the "hard" production activities of Category 1, conservation outputs become "soft" in comparison. The whole concept of stewardship of national forests, so dear to the Forest Service, would be lost when considered in the Category 1 setting of timber production.

In another attempt to protect its interests, the Forest Service claimed that Category 2, Protect and Enhance Income Position of Commercial Farm Families, should include the income effects of forestry along with those arising from farming operations. Similarly in Category 8, Rural Community Improvement, it argued that emphasis should be broadened to include urban improvements from watershed management, which benefited many cities through protection of their municipal water supplies. These attempts were in keeping with the unwritten rule of planning a crosswalk, namely, claim to be a piece of the action whenever it is possible, especially on a coming issue such as urban problems.

In order to show that the reaction of the Forest Service is not unique, it is useful to consider the response of a similarly situated bureau. Following meetings called by the Department Director of PPBS with various agency staffs to review program elements under the proposed fourteen category headings, a top administrator of the Soil Conservation Service took issue with the proposed categories, calling them unacceptable to his service. His major objection was that the categories did not reflect any integration with or appreciation of the program structure and categories of agencies beyond the Department of Agriculture. "For example, the proposed categories tend to obscure the important work the department performs in the 'Conservation and Development of Natural Resources' category." As many departments and agencies could well be integrated and coordinated through the National Water Resources Council, he felt that top level staff should recognize this relationship. Equally unfortunate, this official wrote, would be the burial of the Conservation and Development of Natural Resources item within one of the existing tentative categories, such as Rural Community Improvement or Adequate Supply of Farm and Forest Products.

This SCS official evidently felt that the proposed categories in the Department of Agriculture, with their lack of emphasis on resource conservation, would give the Department of Interior an advantage in the decades-old struggle to determine which one had primary responsibility for natural resources. So he wrote to the department director on December 15, 1965:

> We think these categories fail to project in the present program structure that the department is concerned with nearly all the private lands of this country and some 186,000,000 acres of public lands. No other department has a greater role in the conservation and development of our land, water, and related natural resources, yet the present program categories fail to recognize this. The Soil Conservation Service feels sure this recognition will not be neglected by the Department of the Interior and others.
>
> Yesterday the Central Planning Staff implied that there would be great difficulty in measuring the outputs from a program category called "Conservation and Development of Natural Resources" or "Conservation and Development of Water and Related Land Resources. . . ." We contend that this reasoning has little merit because in the total program structure these activities will occur at some level and it will be necessary to design input-output measures. It will make no difference whether the benefits are short term or long term. Each program aggregate will need to reflect its portion of the output contribution to some larger aggregate.

He then suggested a "Conservation and Development of Natural Resources" program category which would include planning, research, education, technical and financial assistance, and the installation of appropriate measures directly affecting the use and development of water and land resources to meet demands now and into the foreseeable future. Included in this comprehensive group of programs would be the preparation of river basin and watershed plans. Individuals, groups, state and local governments, and other federal agencies, he insisted, must be drawn into the picture. As major objectives under such a category, he suggested including watershed protection, flood prevention, erosion control, sediment reduction (as well as pollution and chemicals abatement), reduction of the adverse effects of droughts and water excesses, fish and wildlife development, reserving scarce reservoir sites for future municipal usage, and contributing to the beauty of the countryside.

This administrator was making a plea on behalf of program categories to preserve (and even enlarge) rather than decimate the clientele of the Soil

Conservation Service. The great strength of the SCS has been the members of the soil conservation districts that are found throughout the country. By suggesting that the SCS was not part of the nationwide conservation movements, the proposed program categories robbed it of connection with a value important to many Americans. Not only was conservation an important value politically, but the organizational implications of the categories caused concern that SCS might be afforded a lower place than it then had in national funding priorities. Although some people may have thought that they were talking about program categories that would improve analysis, this administrator of the Soil Conservation Service believed that they were talking about policy questions affecting the health and prosperity of his agency.

THE RELUCTANT CLIENT

Alternate proposals from agencies were not the only source of direction for the Department of Agriculture; the Bureau of the Budget suggested reduction to seven or eight categories as a means of sharpening the focus on internal conflicts among the different programs. The BOB suggested, for example, that Categories 1 and 2 (Supply of Products and Farm Income) could be viewed as the same activity, first as a supply problem in an aggregate sense and then as an individual farm-income problem. A benefit in the supply category might be a cost when looked at as affecting the individual farmer's income. To gain the benefits of a better fresh vegetable and meat supply through better management, the BOB observed, might inflict a cost on the farmer insofar as his income might become lower as a result of the more efficient market.

According to the Department of Agriculture, the greater the number of categories, the less the chances of overlap, i.e., the more likely it was that an existing program would be viewed from various quarters as belonging in one (and only one) place on the list. Hence, the greater the number of categories, the fewer the conflicts created. Rather than confront a set of differing goals, it would be easier for the department to create separate categories for them. For the Budget Bureau, however, that juxtaposition of different aims was the precise reason for the existence of PPBS. If the Department of Agriculture did not want to arrange its program structure into a smaller number of categories which forced critical choices to be made among programs, then the Budget Bureau had to shoulder this responsibility.

Consider for a moment the effect of this type of thinking on PPBS. If program budgeting were to be a departmental tool, for better or worse, it had to be a product of departmental thinking and needs. If the Department of Agriculture thought fourteen categories were needed, should it not have fourteen? Of course, if the BOB were designing the program structure for its own purposes, then possibly seven or eight would be a better solution. The basic question was: "For whom was the system created?" If the departmental contact with BOB occurred only at the end, then the Budget Bureau would handle nothing more than the "B" of the PPB sequence. It would have no contact with departmental planning or programing but only with budgeting.

The fact was that even in 1965 when Secretary Freeman introduced PPBS into the Department of Agriculture, the Bureau of the Budget was already transforming itself from a producer of guidance for the new system into its single largest consumer. Once the BOB had gained access to the planning and programing as well as to the budgeting level, the PPB system seemed to exist entirely for its convenience. It was not yet clear, however, whether the Bureau of the Budget was prepared to make PPBS serve its purpose.

Two years later, in order to determine whether it was being well served, the BOB staff prepared "A Year of Transition — PPB in the Department of Agriculture," an examination of the PPB process in 1967. It was a tough-minded and hard-hitting report. The staff found that inertia, lack of credibility, and continuing disagreements over what constituted appropriate outputs had left decision-makers disaffected with PPBS. The staff asked basic questions: How realistic was it to expect line officials to make decisions on a five-year time frame? Was such long-range planning depriving officials and budgeters of the necessary short-term view so vital to ongoing budget decisions? To what degree did PPB structures preclude alternative program structures which might also provide evaluational insights?

Outputs were appraised by the Budget Bureau as having absorbed an unusually high proportion of the energies of those involved. The sheer bulk of the PFPs and PMs (program and financial plans and program memoranda) was felt to have deprived departmental staffs of time that might better have been given to "thoughtful analysis." Nevertheless, the report stated, the secretary and his Budget Policy Review Committee might benefit from the new categories, although their final decisions regarding the 1968 budget did not seem to reflect any significant changes, departing little from the last year's submission. Regarding strengths and weaknesses of the PMs the report continued:

> With several exceptions — Timber Production, and Housing Programs — all of the PMs suffer from the deficiency of poorly stated objectives which are not explicit. In at least one department program — Crop Insurance — it is difficult to find any statement of objective whatsoever. Members of the Program Evaluation Staff have suggested that the department analysts ought to stand off with a cold critical eye and question whether the Department of Agriculture ought to be administering certain programs — commodity programs, crop insurance, etc. — at all.

The memorandum posed the following questions to the director:

> Which decision-maker is the PM designed to serve: BOB, secretary, bureau head? Can one PM serve them all?

Should the PM provide a means for presenting a set of programs to show input, output, etc., or should it instead consist of selected analyses which concentrate on a major question or issue and be aimed at a specific decision? If the latter, how does it differ from a "special study?" If the former, would not the major proposals in the PM necessarily be backed up by special studies?

Do we really need a PFP, and if so, what form should it take to provide the information BOB will need for director's review purposes? The submission last year contained information that we did not need on the one hand, and did not go into enough detail on a bureau-by-bureau basis on the other hand to permit the division to structure its director's review material in terms of the department's program categories.

In closing remarks, the staff noted that a member of the BOB Program Evaluation Staff had volunteered to take several of the proposed department studies and prepare analytical papers which would set forth alternative study proposals. It was hoped that this work would be ready for the meeting of the director with the Department of Agriculture's secretariat.

This BOB official's critique of the existing program structure concluded that "in producing their program memoranda and financial plans, they [the Department of Agriculture] have really failed to relate particular programs to each other and to the achievement of general goals"; that is, the department had failed "to state its larger objectives in a meaningful way." An interesting argument was then made for determining categories on the basis of the conditions that justify governmental intervention, such as monopoly, income transfer, and externalities. However, though these suggestions made a good deal of conceptual sense, they would, if their implications were followed, result in drastic changes in the activities of the Department of Agriculture. The author of the paper felt that program budgeting would not be useful either to the department or to the Bureau of the Budget unless such major changes were made.

Recalling their doubts over these alternatives, members of the BOB staff informed us that their staff critic had certainly set forth one way of representing a useful basis for arraying the goals of government. They doubted whether this was the best system for relating outputs and costs to objectives, or whether it asked the right questions, for they doubted that a "best" or "right" one existed. They questioned the usefulness of asking why the Department of Agriculture existed. The controversial memo, according to staff critics, did not recognize the necessity of confining recommendations to small changes in programs that might conceivably be implemented.

Even if these had been the right questions, however, the staff concluded that it was not then the time to initiate more changes, for the past year (1967) had been the first for the department under its newly negotiated program structure within its own agencies. To ask it to renegotiate its internal PPBS division would be unfair. In fact, many of the shortcomings of the 1968 submission were blamed on this prolonged negotiation process between the department staff and the agencies. The chief reason why the 1968 submission had little utility, the staff decided, was because of its analytical flaws. Hereafter, the BOB staff agreed that the push must be toward better analytical studies and toward their integration into the decision-making process.

The value of the controversial BPB memorandum lies not only in its thought-provoking economic argument, but in what its reception teaches us about why a powerful and consistent set of categories is unlikely to be adopted. The intellectual demands are formidable and, even if remotely met, would face the most severe political objections. The cost of modifying the new system, in terms of bargains renegotiated, procedures altered, concepts abandoned, and tempers frayed, would seem prohibitive. The short-run advantages of securing modest improvements in the near future would always seem preferable to vague long-term benefits from the proposed new set of categories. If the Bureau of the Budget were not interested in a set of consistent categories designed to rationalize choice in the Department of Agriculture, then no one was.

The years between 1965, when President Johnson initiated PPBS in the federal government, and 1968, when the new administration took over, showed that the Bureau of the Budget was not prepared to sponsor the new way. No director of the Budget was able to use the information the system conveyed in order to make difficult choices — or indeed, choices of any kind whatsoever. Day-to-day events drove out long-term policy considerations. The director found it more convenient to make his hard choices in terms of the old line-item categories. Although the program-evaluation staff understood the spirit of the new order, many other members of the BOB staff did not. And little effort was devoted to converting them. Yet it was these lowly examiners who would have to impose the idea of analysis on recalcitrant bureaus and departments. When it came to a crunch, the Budget Bureau found it more convenient to ask departments what they wanted than to insist on what it wanted. (For the most part, of course, the Budget Bureau did not know what it wanted, other than good analysis, and it could not tell the agencies how to do that.) With the Bureau of the Budget unwilling to assume the mantle of leadership, either the departments would run the show or it would not be run at all.

The Department of Agriculture soon learned some basic political lessons involving the choice of program categories. Because the categories involved policy preferences, they had to be negotiated with each and every bureau. Initially, it seemed that the larger the number of categories, the easier the task of negotiation because the extent of conflict was minimized. Only later did the department learn that it was possible to move in the opposite direction with even greater effect. For if the number of categories was reduced to a basic minimum — say, three or four — they would become so large, include so heterogeneous a collection of elements, that they would not commit anyone to anything. It was only possible to get agreement on a set of categories either so numerous that they precluded comparison or so few as to lack specificity. Once that lesson had been learned — once the political nature of the categories had become manifest through experience — the department set about using its program categories to build support for its policies.

STRUCTURE AND SUBSTANCE

It should be clear by now that program categories are not simply "out there" waiting to be found. They must be invented by man. The form of the budget is no minor technicality but instead an important shaper of policy, for it helps determine what kinds of program comparison are made and therefore what kinds of decisions are reached. If this were not true, there would be no reason to consider program budgeting at all, because it preeminently involves a change of budgetary form. No one should be surprised, therefore, when agencies object to program categories that do not put them in the best possible light or that fail to provide measures for values they deem important. It is only a matter of time before everyone concerned begins to understand the strategic nature of program categories.[1]

A quick look at the categories established in 1968 in the Department of Agriculture reveals essentially strategic functions. It is with more than a small sense of excitement that one reads about "Communities of Tomorrow," "Dimensions for Living," "Resources in Action," "Growing Nations — New Markets," "Income and Abundance," and "Science in the Service of Man." Only a Scrooge could turn down expenditures requested under these glorious rubrics (although "General Support" might be easier to resist).

The first thing to note about these program categories is that no one conceivably could use them to make decisions. How would one know whether to prefer Communities of Tomorrow to Dimensions for Living or Income and Abundance to Growing Nations? If they sound good, they have more than fulfilled their purpose.

Perhaps, then, it is not the program categories but the subcategories that can be acted upon for purposes of decision? Not so. How could one decide in the abstract to do something about the subcategory Farm Income or Agriculture Marketing and Distribution System, both found under Income and Abundance? One might have ideas about the subcategory Resource Protection and Environmental Improvement, but it would not tell one whether to prefer the snow-survey program element to the land-acquisition program element, which are both covered under this subcategory. Nearly everyone engaged in program

---

[1] According to Interior Department officials, the following discussion can apply equally to that department.

budgeting would agree that, to the extent actual decisions are made in program terms, they result almost entirely from consideration of program elements. One just might base decisions on analysis of program elements such as national Forest Timber Production, or Food and Nutrition Research, or the Food Stamp Program.

Let us look, then, and see if program elements (circa 1969) in the Department of Agriculture met PPBS requirements. The basic idea is that individual programs should be compared with one another to see which ones contribute most to common objectives. The idea of comparison is central to program budgeting because its proponents claim that traditional line-item methods lead to duplication and obfuscation of activities which ostensibly serve common purposes. In the Department of Agriculture most existing programs are contained within single bureaus, whereas proper analysis would require comparison among programs covered in several bureaus. Over two-thirds (119) of the department's program elements are included in one and only one bureau, and most of the remaining forty-six are concerned largely with relatively small research activities. Hence it is true to say that the bulk of analytic activity involves no comparison across bureaus (and therefore programs); that which does is relatively unimportant. In the Income and Abundance category forty-three out of fifty-three elements are in one agency, and eight of the ten others involve research. Turning to the category that interests us most because it contains resource activities, "Communities of Tomorrow," we find thirty-seven out of fifty-four program elements contained within a single bureau. Of the seventeen remaining elements, twelve involve research. This leaves five potentially interesting programs that cover more than one agency. The first is a bit of a disappointment because the Outreach Program is small and involves a good deal of traditional extension activity. "Timber Disease and Pest Control" is a minor regulatory program. The three programs that appear interesting — Flood Prevention, Water Protection and Management, and Resource Conservation and Development — all involve the same two bureaus, the Soil Conservation Service and the Farmers' Home Administration. All three are small, and all concern incentives for regulating resource activity. From the look of things, then, one would conclude that program budgeting as practiced in the Department of Agriculture is either equivalent to attempting analysis of individual programs within single agencies, or is misleading if it suggests that the activities of the department as a whole somehow are being compared, contrasted, integrated, interconnected, coordinated, interfaced, or what have you.

Taking a more modest view of program budgeting, we would regard it as a success if it even encouraged sustained use of analysis within bureaus. Our investigation shows, however, that the primary interest of bureaus in program categories and elements lay in protecting their jurisdictions. They saw categories not for analysis but for dividing territories. To them program structure was not a way to cooperate with others to produce better policy but a treaty with foreign powers.

HAS PROGRAM BUDGETING LED
TO CHANGE?

At the beginning of this study we said that evaluative activities would be inefficient, costing more than they were worth, unless they led to change. So, has program budgeting made for any changes in decisions within departments? Some people say "yes" and others say "no." Because of the complex nature of power relationships, the fact that many decisions are not made so much as accreted, and that other events in the world such as racial conflict have had an immeasurable effect, no one can say for sure. The previously discussed analysis by the Budget Bureau's staff suggests that few, if any, important changes had come about. But perhaps officials directly concerned could cite some decisions that were profoundly affected by the program budgeting procedure.

We are really asking if anything is new in the way individual programs are analyzed. In order to bring even some small amount of objectivity to the question, we looked into the way agency budgets are presented to congressional appropriations committees. The idea is that any fundamental changes in agency programs or in criteria for decision must ultimately end up in agency justifications. We have, therefore, adopted the procedure of looking at policies related to land and recreation, and asking what kinds of justifications and measures have been used over the years to support them. Since a book might be written on this subject, we decided to take just three points in time and to accept only the most blatant trends as worthy of notice.

We shall deal with only two aspects of the outdoor recreation[2] budget process: (1) the different types and numbers of justifications[3] used by the various advocating agencies before the House of Representatives for their programs, and (2) the types and numbers of quantitative measure used by the various agencies in defending their programs. The period investigated spans

[2] It would be edifying to present a common definition for outdoor recreation, but none exists. One such definition describes outdoor recreation as a system of scarce or depletable resources, the allocation and distribution of which can be analyzed by using economic models. This definition could be used for all natural resources. In another kind of definition, recreation is considered a service system. A recent (1969) National Academy of Sciences Report on "A Program for Outdoor Recreation Research" views recreation as a "social institution whose purpose is to enhance human life by offering satisfaction and by enriching human capital." Since such a definition can cover sex as well as a chain of ice cream parlors, however, we find it a bit too broad. We will do the best we can.

[3] The limited definition of justification, as used in this investigation, is any reason mentioned by an advocating agency for money to be spent on a certain project or service, and, more particularly, why an increased appropriation is needed for recreational activity. The following plea from a director of the National Park Service is a good example: "On Shasta Lake there was a terrible accident where two little girls were killed by a speedboat. We did not have enough personnel to patrol that lake. There have been other instances like that, and protection of this property has to be taken care of adequately. That is why we need more personnel."

twenty-two years, from Fiscal Year 1948 to F1969, and concentrates on three particular years: 1949, 1958, and 1969. The source of information was the record of hearings before the Subcommittee of the Committee on Appropriations of the House of Representatives. The executive branch agencies covered were the National Park Service, Forest Service, Bureau of Land Management, Bureau of Outdoor Recreation, and the Bureau of Sports Fisheries and Wildlife.

The frequency with which justifications were used by resource agencies, Table 15.1 shows, declined somewhat in 1958 and rose sharply in 1969. Justifications such as the importance of the social, spiritual, and educational values of outdoor recreation to the entire population, particularly to urban youth, are relatively new. This type of justification, which follows recent trends in social thought, appeared only once in 1958 but ten times in 1969. The contention that outdoor recreational activities alleviate social problems in the cities (crime, riots, etc.) is even newer and appears at high frequency (nine times) in the 1969 record; it is the agencies' counterattack to all competing requests for additional money to solve city problems.

Table 15.2 shows a continuous increase in the frequency with which quantified measures are used in each fiscal year. The increase between 1958 and 1969 is much larger than that between 1949 and 1958. The type of measures,

Table 15.1. SHARP INCREASE IN FREQUENCY OF DIFFERENT JUSTIFICATIONS FOR RECREATION ACTIVITIES OVER THE PAST DECADE

Type of Justification	Occurrences per Fiscal Year			
	1949	1958	1969	Total
Expanded responsibility	3	1	4	8
Increased users pressure	6	5	7	18
Facilities and personnel inadequacy	10	3	6	19
Cost increase	1	2	2	5
Other agencies need help	2	1	2	5
Private inholdings menace	1	1	1	3
Uncontrolled disasters	1	1	4	6
Economic value	2	2	5	9
Planning, analysis, coordination	2	3	7	12
Resources, conservation, and protection	2	2	6	10
Social, spiritual, educational values	. . .	1	10	11
Alleviation of city problems	. . .	. . .	9	9
Total number of occurrences	30	22	63	115

Source: Compiled by Ehud Levy-Pascal.

Table 15.2. MEASURES CHANGE VERY LITTLE BUT THEIR
FREQUENCY INCREASES CONTINUOUSLY

Type of Measure	Per Fiscal Year			Total all Years
	1949	1958	1969	
Standard expenditure comparison[a]	10	14	28	52
Development and planning[b]	4	5	10	19
Service output statistics[c]	2	6	10	18
Other units of measurements[d]	3	4	10	17
Visitors statistics[e]	1	4	12	17
Additional areas data[f]	1	2	7	10
Individual areas expenditure[g]	2	2	3	7
Crime statistics[h]	2	2	1	5
Disaster damage cost[i]	1	1	2	4
Obligations comparison[j]	3	2	1	6
New area studies[k]	1	1	8	10
National recreation economics data[l]	. . .	1	4	5
Total	30	44	96	170

Source: Compiled by Ehud Levy-Pascal.

[a] Traditional line-item categories such as salaries, travel, materials, etc., and major activities with their detailed breakdown: construction, administration, maintenance, protection, etc. presented in a table form comparing the basis or the previous year appropriation with the amount asked for the present year and showing the difference between the two.

[b] Data pertaining to development of specific new areas and larger overall plans for the future. Such data include cost of access roads, utilities, construction, maintenance, protection, and planning itself.

[c] Service output statistics pertains to accomplishments such as new areas developed, family units, campsites, miles of road and trails, buildings, etc.

[d] 1949 — dollars, visitors, miles of roads and trails; 1958 — same as above plus family unit; 1969 — same as above plus visitor days, camper days, square foot of buildings, parks area, visits per acre, visits per road and trail mile, visits per campsite, visits per $1,000 of maintenance and rehabilitation funds, visits per $1,000 invested in buildings and utilities, number of beaches, campsites, and picnic tables.

[e] Visitors statistics show the number of visitors per year and indicate the increase from previous years and future estimates. Many times it is followed by the sum of revenues collected.

[f] Every year additional recreation areas were given to the agencies and their number and requirements are delineated. A continuous growth in frequency is indicated (three-and-a-half-fold for 1969).

[g] Tables breaking down the various expenditures for each area are brought up every year and comparisons are made between the present and previous years.

[h] Statistics about the amount, type, and disposal of crimes committed in the parks, forests and recreation areas.

[i] Some kind of disaster or emergency occurs about every year and statistics are shown about its frequency (such as number of forest fires) and the cost of the damage.

[j] Data are shown for every year in table form about the different recreation area acquisition and construction contractual obligations and their financial status.

[k] More new areas are added each year than the agencies can develop. Stud-

however, remained practically the same; the only new category observed is "National Recreation Economics Data."

The great jump in the frequency of units of measurement in 1969 demonstrates an increase in the quantity of analyses, but not a change in the types of analysis. No use of the Planning, Programing, and Budgeting System was observed in the record, although many expenditure breakdowns by program (as compared with classification by activity) were evident in 1969. Elements of analysis still lacking include definitions of benefits or effectiveness, quantitative goals, specifications of problems, investigations of alternatives, and, therefore, broad range trade-off analysis between one program and another.

So far as we can determine from congressional hearings, the emphasis placed on quantification in program budgeting is amply warranted; the kind of justification and measure used remained relatively constant, but they appeared with much greater frequency. Essentially, the same justifications were used twice as often (and the same measures three times as often) in 1969 as some twenty years earlier. The quantity of argument has evidently increased at a much faster rate than its quality (if quality is associated with new measures or justifications).[4]

Those changes we do find cannot be attributed to program budgeting. The contribution of recreation to national income had appeared by 1958, before program budgeting, and undoubtedly stemmed from continued efforts in the analytic community to measure the possible benefits of recreation. The focus on urban areas and spiritual benefits of recreation, of course, is precisely the type of adaptation to emerging values we would expect from the political administrators who ran the traditional budget. The program budget was supposed to contribute new analytical perspectives; but that it did not do. Congress increasingly demanded greater detail in budget hearings and it got just that — more of the same.

Congress never used PPBS and, indeed, rejected it. The chairman of the House Appropriations Subcommittee of the Department of the Interior, for example, refused to examine PPBS documents and even threatened to abolish the department's Office of Program Analysis by cutting off its funds. It was

---

[4] Because congressional hearings vary in their focus, concentration on a particular year may give a distorted impression. We could not study every year from the late 1940s through the 1960s but we were able to look at another study. Jay Starling observed trends in justifications and measures for 1948, 1957, and 1968 in the hearings from the Forest Service, Park Service, and Bureau of Land Management. Starling's work also shows that the increase in the frequency with which measures and justifications were used far exceeds changes in type.

---

ies are made to decide which to develop, and accurate estimates must be made of development costs.

[1] Its aim is to show the importance of the recreation activity in the nation's economy and its part of the gross national product and revenue. It includes the contribution of recreation to gross national product, taxation, and the transportation and hotel industries.

frequently perceived as a tool of the Budget Bureau, and was, for that reason, distrusted.

The Bureau of the Budget response to the Department of Agriculture's efforts brings into sharp focus the unresolved question: Which clientele is PPBS supposed to serve — bureaus, departments, or the Bureau of the Budget? A department which sensed that *it* was the client took steps to make the program categories politically attractive. Prudence suggested that we take a look at actual changes in policy rather than surface movement in budgetary definitions, terms, and classifications. A survey of changes in justifications, and in the measures used to support them, in recreation and land policies, suggests that change in policy has been more apparent than real. PPBS apparently leads to the greater use of the same old quantifiable measures to support the same old justifications.

Two case histories do not add up to a conclusive argument. But they are suggestive; they do constitute a source of hypotheses. No one who studies what they have to teach will be surprised to discover that other efforts to implement PPBS reveal both the presence of political opposition and the absence of societal knowledge to support the enterprise.

16

Should the Economic Tail Wag the Political Dog? Political Foundations of Program Budgeting

What would politics be like if it were organized according to the principles of PPBS? What political assumptions lie beneath its seemingly neutral search for efficiency?

THE POLITICAL ECONOMY OF EFFICIENCY

Once upon a time the meaning of economic efficiency was reasonably clear. An objective met up with a technician. Efficiency consisted in meeting the objective at the lowest cost or in getting the maximum amount of the objective for a specified amount of resources. Let us call this "pure efficiency."

The desirability of trying to achieve certain objectives may depend on the cost of achieving them. If so, the analyst (he has graduated from being a mere technician) alters the objective to suit available resources. Let us call this "mixed efficiency." Both pure and mixed efficiency are limited in the sense that they take for granted the existing structure of the political system and work within its boundaries.

Yet the economizer, he who values efficiency most dearly, may discover that the most efficient means for accomplishing his ends cannot be secured without changing the decision-making machinery. He not only alters means and ends (resources and objectives) simultaneously but makes them dependent on changes in political relationships. Although he claims no special interest in or expertise concerning the decision apparatus outside of the marketplace, the economizer pursues efficiency to the heart of the political system. Let us call this "total efficiency." In this vocabulary, then, concepts of efficiency may be pure or mixed, limited or total.

A major purpose of this chapter is to take several popular modes of achieving efficiency — cost-benefit analysis, systems analysis, and program budgeting — and show how much more is involved than mere economizing. Even at the most modest level of cost-benefit analysis, I will try to show that it becomes difficult to maintain pure notions of efficiency. At a higher level, systems analysis is based on a mixed notion of efficiency. And program budgeting at the highest levels leaves pure efficiency far behind its thrust into the structure of the political system. Program budgeting, it turns out, is a form of systems analysis, that is, political systems analysis. By placing program budgeting in the context of the other techniques for decision-making out of which it has grown, and on which it is dependent for its analytical utility, I hope to come up with a fuller statement of what is involved in PPBS.

COST-BENEFIT ANALYSIS

... One can view cost-benefit analysis as anything from an infallible means of reaching the new Utopia to a waste of resources in attempting to measure the immeasurable.[1]

The purpose of cost-benefit analysis is to achieve an efficient allocation of resources produced by the governmental system in its interaction with the private economy. The nature of efficiency depends on the governmental objective, usually postulated to be an increase in national income. In a crude sense, this means that the costs to whomever may incur them should be less than the benefits to whomever may receive them. The time streams of consumption won and lost by a project are its benefits and costs.

The aim of cost-benefit analysis is to maximize "the present value of all

---

[1] A. R. Prest and R. Turvey, "Cost-Benefit Analysis: A Survey," *The Economic Journal,* 75 (December 1965), 683–735. I am much indebted to this valuable and discerning survey. I have also relied on:

Otto Eckstein, "A Survey of the Theory of Public Expenditure Criteria," in *Public Finances: Needs, Sources, and Utilization; A Conference of the Universities — National Bureau Committee for Economic Research,* National Bureau of Economic Research Special Conference Series 12 (Princeton: Princeton Univ. Press, 1961), 439–504.

Irving K. Fox and Orris C. Herfindahl, "Attainment of Efficiency in Satisfying Demands for Water Resources," *American Economic Review,* 54 (May 1964), 198–206.

Charles J. Hitch, *On the Choice of Objectives in Systems Studies* (Santa Monica, The RAND Corporation, 1960).

John V. Krutilla, "Is Public Intervention in Water Resources Development Conducive to Economic Efficiency," *Natural Resources Journal* (January 1966), 60–75.

John V. Krutilla and Otto Eckstein, *Multiple Purpose River Development,* Studies in Applied Economic Analysis (Baltimore: Johns Hopkins Press, 1958).

Roland N. McKean, *Efficiency in Government Through Systems Analysis with Emphasis on Water Resources Development* (New York: Wiley, 1958).

benefits less that of all costs, subject to specified restraints." [2] A long view is taken, in that costs are estimated not only for the immediate future but also for the life of the project. A wide view is taken, in that indirect consequences for others — variously called externalities, side effects, spillovers, and repercussion effects — are considered. Ideally, all costs and benefits are evaluated. Projects whose benefits are greater than costs may then be approved, or the cost-benefit ratios may, with allowance for relative size, be used to rank projects in order of desirability.

Underlying Economic and Political Assumptions

A straightforward description of cost-benefit analysis cannot do justice to the powerful assumptions that underlie it or to the many conditions limiting its usefulness. These assumptions involve value judgments which are not always recognized and, even when recognized, are not easily handled in practice. The limiting conditions arise partly out of severe computational difficulties in estimating costs, and especially benefits. Here I can only indicate some major problems.

Cost benefit analysis is based on superiority of the marketplace,[3] under competitive conditions and full employment, as the measure of value in society. Any imperfection in the market works against the validity of the results. Unless the same degree of monopoly were found throughout the economy, for example, a governmental body which enjoys monopolistic control of prices or outputs would not necessarily make the same investment decisions as under free competition.

The economic model on which cost-benefit analysis depends for its validity is based on a political theory. The idea is that in a free society the economy is to serve the individual's consistent preferences as revealed and rationally pursued in the marketplace. The individualist theory may assume as valid the current distribution of income. Preferences are valued in the marketplace where votes are based on disposable income. Governmental action to achieve efficiency, therefore, inevitably carries with it consequences for the distribution of income. Projects of different size, location, and composition will transfer income in different amounts to different people. Although economists might estimate the redistributive consequences of various projects, they cannot, on efficiency grounds, specify one or another as preferable. How is this serious problem to be handled?

2 Prest and Turvey, "Cost-Benefit Analysis," p. 686.
3 In many important areas of policy such as national defense it is not possible to value the product directly in the marketplace. Since benefits cannot be valued in the same way as costs, it is necessary to resort to a somewhat different type of analysis. Instead of cost-benefit analysis, therefore, the work is usually called cost-effectiveness or cost-utility analysis.

Cost-benefit analysis is a way of trying to promote economic welfare. But whose welfare? No one knows how to deal with interpersonal comparisons of utility. It cannot be assumed that one can measure the desirability of rent supplements versus a highway on a single utility scale. There is no scientific way to compare losses and gains among different people or to say that the marginal loss of a dollar to one man is somehow equal to the gain of a dollar by another.

The literature on welfare economics is notably unable to specify an objective welfare function.[4] Ideally, actions would benefit everyone and harm no one. As an approximation, the welfare economist views as optimal an action that leaves some people better off and none worse off. If this Pareto criterion were applied in political life, it would result in a situation like that of the Polish Diet in which anyone who was damaged could veto legislation. To provide a way out of this impasse, Hicks and Kaldor proposed approval of decisions if the total gain in welfare is such that the winners could compensate the losers. But formal machinery for compensation does not ordinarily exist and most modern economists are highly critical of the major political mechanism for attempting to compensate, namely, logrolling by trading votes in Congress on public works projects.[5] It is a very imperfect mechanism for assuring that losers in one situation become winners in another.

Public works projects have a multitude of objectives and consequences in addition to redistributing income. Projects may generate economic growth, alleviate poverty among some people, provide aesthetic enjoyment and opportunities for recreation, improve public health, reduce the risks of natural disaster, alter travel patterns, affect church attendance, change educational opportunities, and more. No single welfare criterion can encompass these diverse objectives. How many should be considered? Which can be quantified? The further one pursues this analysis, the more impassable the thicket.

Limitations in the Utility of Cost-Benefit Analysis

One possible conclusion is that right now certain types of cost-benefit analysis are not meaningful. In reviewing the literature on the calculus of costs

[4] Abram Burk-Bergson, "A Reformation of Certain Aspects of Welfare Economics," *Quarterly Journal of Economics,* 51 (February 1938), 310–384; N. Kaldor, "Welfare Propositions and Interpersonal Comparisons of Utility," *Economic Journal,* 49 (September 1939), 549–552; J. R. Hicks, "The Valuation of Social Income," *Economica,* 7 (May 1940), 105–124; I. M. D. Little, *A Critique of Welfare Economics* (Oxford: Clarendon Press, 1950); W. J. Baumol, *Welfare Economics and the Theory of the State* (Cambridge: Harvard Univ. Press, 1952); T. Scitovsky, "A Note on Welfare Propositions in Economics," *Review of Economic Studies,* 9 (1941), 77–78; J. E. Meade, *The Theory of International Economic Policy,* Vol. II: *Trade and Welfare* (New York: Oxford Univ. Press, 1955).

[5] For a different view, see James M. Buchanan and Gordon Tullock, *The Calculus of Consent, Logical Foundations of Constitutional Democracy* (Ann Arbor: Univ. of Michigan Press, 1962).

and benefits in research and development, for example, Prest and Turvey comment on "the uncertainty and unreliability of cost estimates . . . and . . . the extraordinarily complex nature of the benefits. . . ." [6]

If the analysis is to be useful at all, calculations must be simplified.[7] The multiple ramifications of interesting activities can be taken into account only at the cost of introducing fantastic complexities. Prest and Turvey remark of one such attempt, that "This system . . . requires knowledge of all the demand and supply equations in the economy, so is scarcely capable of application by road engineers." [8]

Whether or not a proposed project is desirable depends on the rate of interest that is chosen to discount its streams of costs and benefits over time. An interest rate measures the preferences people have for present versus future costs and benefits. Thus, as Otto Eckstein has observed, ". . . the choice of interest rates must remain a value judgment." [9]

If the efficiency of a project is insensitive to interest costs, then these costs can vary widely without mattering much. But Fox and Herfindahl discovered that if Corps of Engineer projects raised their interest (or discount) rate from 2⅝ to 4, 6, or 8 percent, then 9, 64, and 80 percent of their projects, respectively, would have had a benefit-cost ratio of less than unity.[10] This single value choice among many has such large consequences that it alone may be decisive.

The Mixed Results of Cost-Benefit Analysis

Cost-benefit analysis is shot through with political and social value choices, and surrounded by uncertainties and difficulties of computation. Whether the many noneconomic assumptions and consequences actually result in basically changing the nature of a project remains moot. Clearly, we have come a long way from pure efficiency, to verge on mixed efficiency.

Its dependence on a prior political framework does not mean that cost-benefit analysis is a useless or trivial exercise. Decisions must be based on something. Quantifiable economic costs and benefits may not be everything, but a decision-maker would not wish to ignore them entirely. The great advantage of cost-benefit analysis, pursued with integrity, is that some implicit judgments are made explicit and subject to analysis. But not yet judgments about politics. Leaving out explicit consideration of political factors is a serious deficiency.

[6] Prest and Turvey, "Cost-Benefit Analysis," p. 727.
[7] David Braybrooke and Charles Lindblom, *A Strategy of Decision; Policy Evaluation as a Social Process* (New York: The Free Press of Glencoe, 1963).
[8] Prest and Turvey, "Cost-Benefit Analysis," p. 714.
[9] Eckstein, "A Survey of the Theory of Public Expenditure Criteria," p. 460.
[10] Fox and Herfindahl, "Attainment of Efficiency in Satisfying Demands for Water Resources," p. 202.

Whenever agencies and their associated interests find out that they cannot do what they want, they may twist prevailing criteria out of shape: Two projects may be joined so that both qualify though one, standing alone, would not. Costs and benefits may be manipulated, or the categories may be so extended that almost any project qualifies. On the other hand, cost-benefit analysis has some political uses which might be stressed more than they have been. The technique gives the responsible official a good reason for turning down projects, with a public interest explanation the Congressman can use with his constituents and the interest group leader with his members.

Cost-benefit analysis can certainly tell decision-makers something about what they will be giving up if they follow alternative policies. The use of two analyses, one based on regional and the other on national factors, might result in an appraisal of the economic costs of federalism. The burden of calculation may be reduced by following cost-benefit analysis for many projects and introducing other values (federalism, party strength, distribution of income to selected groups, etc.) for only a few. To expect, however, that the method itself (which indulges some and deprives others) would not be subject to manipulation in the political process is to say that we shall be governed by formula and not by men.

Because the cost-benefit formula does not always jibe with political realities — that is, it omits political costs and benefits — we can expect it to be twisted out of shape from time to time. Yet cost-benefit analysis still may be important in getting rid of the worst projects. Avoiding the worst where one can't get the best is no small accomplishment.

SYSTEMS ANALYSIS

The good systems analyst is a "chochem," a Yiddish word meaning "wise man," with overtones of "wise guy." His forte is creativity. Although he sometimes relates means to ends and fits ends to match means, he ordinarily eschews such pat processes, preferring instead to relate elements imaginatively into new systems that create their own means and ends. He plays new objectives continuously against cost elements until a creative synthesis has been achieved. He looks down on those who say that they take objectives as given, knowing full well that the apparent solidity of the objective will dissipate during analysis and that most people usually do not know what they want because they do not know what they can get.

Since no one knows how to teach creativity, daring, and nerve, it is not surprising that no one can define what systems analysis is or how it should be practiced. E. S. Quade, who compiled the RAND Corporation lectures on systems analysis, says it "is still largely a form of art" in which it is not possible to lay down "fixed rules which need only be followed with exactness." [11] He examined systems studies to determine ideas and principles common to the good ones, but discovered that "no universally accepted set of ideas existed. It was even difficult to decide which studies should be called "good." [12]

Systems analysis is derived from operations research, which came into use during the Second World War when some scientists discovered that they could use simple quantitative analysis to get the most out of existing military equipment. A reasonably clear objective was given, and ways to cut the cost of achieving it could be developed, using essentially statistical models. Operations research today is largely identified with specific techniques: linear programing; Monte Carlo (randomizing) methods; gaming and game theory. Although there is no hard and fast division between operations research and systems analysis, a rough separation may perhaps be made. In systems analysis there is more judgment and intuition and less reliance on quantitative methods than in operations research. The less that is known about objectives, the more they conflict, the larger the number of elements to be considered, the more uncertain the environment, the more likely it is that the work will be called a systems analysis.

Systems analysis builds models that abstract from reality but tries to represent the crucial relationships. The systems analyst first decides what questions are relevant to his inquiry, selects certain quantifiable factors, cuts down the list of factors to be dealt with by aggregation and by eliminating the (it is hoped) less important ones, and then gives them quantitative relationships with one another within the system he has chosen for analysis. But crucial variables may not be quantifiable. If they can be reduced to numbers, there may be no mathematical function to express the desired relationship. More important, there may be no single criterion for judging results among conflicting objectives. Most important, the original objectives he has been given, if any, or the ones he has postulated, may not make sense.

It cannot be emphasized too strongly that a (if not the) distinguishing characteristic of systems analysis is that the objectives are either not known or are subject to change. Systems analysis, Quade tells us, "is associated with that class of problems where the difficulties lie in deciding what ought to be done — not simply how to do it — and honors go to people who . . . find out what the problem is." [13] Charles Hitch, the former Comptroller of the Defense Department, insists that:

> . . . learning about objectives is one of the chief objects of this kind of analysis. We must learn to look at objectives as critically and as professionally

[11] E. S. Quade, ed., *Analysis for Military Decisions* (Amsterdam: North Holland Pub., 1970), p. 153.
[12] Ibid., p. 149.
[13] Ibid., p. 7.

as we look at our models and our other inputs. We may, of course, begin with tentative objectives, but we must expect to modify or replace them as we learn about the systems we are studying — and related systems. The feedback on objectives may in some cases be the most important result of our study. We have never undertaken a major system study at RAND in which we are able to define satisfactory objectives at the beginning of the study.[14]

Systems analysts recognize many good reasons for their difficulties in defining problems or objectives. Quade reaches the core: "Objectives are not, in fact, agreed upon. The choice, while ostensibly between alternatives, is really between objectives or ends and non-analytic methods must be used for a final reconciliation of views." [15] It may be comforting to believe that objectives come to the analyst from on high and can be taken as given, but this easy assumption is all wrong. "For all sorts of good reasons that are not about to change," says Hitch, "official statements of national objectives (or company objectives) tend to be nonexistent or so vague and literary as to be non-operational." [16]

What is worth doing depends on whether it can be done at all, how well, and at what cost. Hence, objectives really cannot be taken as given; they must be made up by the analyst. "In fact," Wohlstetter declares, "we are always in the process of choosing and modifying both means and ends." [17]

Future systems analysts are explicitly warned not to let clients determine objectives. A suggestive analogy is drawn with the doctor who would not ignore a patient's "description of his symptoms, but . . . cannot allow the patient's self diagnosis to override his own professional judgment." [18] Quade argues that since systems analysis has often resulted in changing the original objectives of the policy-maker, it would be "self-defeating to accept without inquiry" his "view of what the problem is." [19]

I have stressed this point that the systems analyst is advised to insist on his own formulation of the problem, because it shows so clearly that we are dealing with a mixed concept of efficiency.

Adjusting objectives to resources in the present or near future is difficult enough without considering the tremendous uncertainty of future states of affairs. Systems analysis is characterized by the aids to calculation it uses, not to conquer, but to circumvent and mitigate some of the pervasive effects of uncertainty. Before a seemingly important factor may be omitted, for example, a sensitivity analysis may be run to determine whether its variation significantly

---

[14] Hitch, *On the Choice of Objectives*, p. 19.
[15] Quade, *Analysis for Military Decisions*, p. 176.
[16] Hitch, *On the Choice of Objectives*, pp. 4–5.
[17] Albert Wohlstetter, "Analysis and Design of Conflict Systems," in *Analysis for Military Decisions*, ed., Quade, p. 122.
[18] Quade, "Methods and Proceedings," in Ibid., p. 157.
[19] Ibid., pp. 156–157.

affects the outcome. If there is no good basis for calculating the value of the factor, arbitrary values may be assigned to test for extreme possibilities. Contingency analysis is used to determine how the relative ranking of alternatives holds up under major changes in the environment, say, a vast increase in the demand for energy, or alterations in the criteria for judging the alternatives — such as a requirement that a system continue to work well if coal must be used instead of oil. Contingency analysis places a premium on versatility as the analyst seeks a system that will hold up well under various eventualities even though it might not be quite as good for any single contingency as an alternative system. Adversary procedures may be used to combat uncertainty. Bending over backward to think up advantages for low-ranking systems and handicaps for high-ranking systems is called *a fortiori* analysis. Changing crucial assumptions in order to make the leading alternatives even, so that one can judge whether the assumptions are overly optimistic or pessimistic, is called break-even analysis.[20] Since all these methods add greatly to the burden of calculation, they must be used with some discretion.

In the famous study of the location of military bases, conducted by Albert Wohlstetter and his associates at the RAND Corporation (widely acknowledged as a classic example of systems analysis), Wohlstetter writes, "The base study . . . proceeded by a method of successive approximations."[21] Many aspects of a problem must be simply put aside. Only a few variables can be considered simultaneously. "Otherwise," Roland McKean tells us, "the models would become impossibly cumbersome, and . . . the number of calculations to consider would mount in the thousands."[22] Formulas that include everything may appear more satisfactory but those that cannot be reduced "to a single expression are likely to convey no meaning at all. . . ."[23] Summing up their experience, Hitch and McKean assert that ". . . analyses must be piecemeal, since it is impossible for a single analysis to cover all problems of choice simultaneously in a large organization."[24]

Although admitting that much bad work is carried on and that inordinate love of numbers and machines often gets in the way of creative work,[25] practi-

---

[20] Herman Kahn and Irwin Mann, *Techniques of Systems Analysis* (Santa Monica: The RAND Corporation, 1957), believe that *"More than any single thing,* the skilled use of a fortiori and break-even analyses separates the professionals from the amateurs." They think that convincing others that you have a good solution is as important as really having one.

[21] Wohlstetter, "Analysis and Design of Conflict Systems," in *Analysis for Military Decisions,* ed., Quade, p. 725.

[22] R. N. McKean, "Criteria," in Ibid., p. 83.

[23] Quade, "Pitfalls in Systems Analysis," in Ibid., p. 310.

[24] Charles J. Hitch and Roland N. McKean, *The Economics of Defense in the Nuclear Age* (Cambridge: Harvard Univ. Press, 1963), p. 161.

[25] See Hitch on "Mechanitis — putting . . . machines to work as a substitute for hard thinking." Charles Hitch, "Economics and Military Operations Research," in

tioners of systems analysis believe in their art. "All of them point out how the use of analysis can provide some of the knowledge needed, how it may sometimes serve as a substitute for experience, and, most importantly, how it can work to sharpen intuition." [26] The claim is that systems analysis can be perfected: mere intuition or unaided judgment can never be improved.

Yet there is also wide agreement that systems analysts "do philosophy," [27] that they are advocates of particular policy alternatives. What Schelling calls "the pure role of expert advisor" is not available for the analyst who "must usually formulate the questions themselves for his clients." [28] Beyond that, Wohlstetter argues that systems analysts can perform the function of integrating various values. New systems can sometimes be found that meet diverse objectives.[29] The politician who gets what he wants by inventing policies that also satisfy others, or the leader of a coalition who searches out areas of maximum agreement, performs a kind of informal systems analysis.

All these men, however, work within the existing political structure. Although cost-benefit analysis may contain within it implicit changes in existing governmental policies, it poses no direct challenge to the general decision-making machinery of the political system. Program budgeting is a form of systems analysis that attempts to break out of these confines.

PROGRAM BUDGETING

Not everyone would go along with the most far-reaching implications of program budgeting, but the RAND Corporation version, presumably appropriated from the Defense Department, definitely does include "institutional reorganization to bring relevant administrative functions under the jurisdiction of the authority making the final program decisions." In any event, there would be "information reporting systems and shifts in the power structure to the extent necessary to secure compliance with program decisions by the agencies responsible for their execution." [30] Sometimes it appears that comprehensiveness — simultaneous and complete examination of all programs and all alternatives to programs every year — is being advocated. Actually, comprehensiveness has

"Economics and Operations Research: A Symposium. II," *Review of Economics and Statistics,* 40 (August 1958), 199–209.

[26] *Analysis for Military Decisions,* ed., Quade, p. 12.

[27] Ibid., p. 5.

[28] T. C. Schelling, "Comment," in "Economics and Operations Research: A Symposium. V," *Review of Economics and Statistics,* 40 (August 1958), 222.

[29] Wohlstetter, "Analysis and Design of Conflict Systems," in *Analysis for Military Decisions,* ed., Quade, p. 122.

[30] Roland N. McKean and Melvin Anshen, "Limitations, Risks and Problems," in *Program Budgeting: Program Analysis and the Federal Budget,* ed. by David Novick (Cambridge: Harvard Univ. Press, 1967), pp. 286–287.

been dropped (though not without regret) because "it may be too costly in time, effort, uncertainty, and confusion." [31]

Programs are not made in heaven, nor do they exist naturally in the world; they must be imposed on it by men. No one can teach people to create programs. There are as many ways to conceive of programs as there are of organizing activity,[32] as the comments of the following writers eloquently testify:

> It is by no means obvious . . . whether a good program structure should be based on components of specific end objectives (e.g., the accomplishment of certain land reclamation targets), on the principle of cost separation (identifying as a program any activity the costs of which can be readily segregated), on the separation of means and ends (Is education a means or an end in a situation such as skill-retraining courses for workers displaced by automation?), or on some artificially designed pattern that draws from all these and other classification criteria.[33]

> Just what categories constitute the most useful programs and program elements is far from obvious. . . . If one puts all educational activities into a broad package of educational programs, he cannot simultaneously include school lunch programs or physical education activities in a Health Program, or include defense educational activities (such as the military academies) in the Defense Program. . . . In short, precisely how to achieve a rational and useful structure for a program budget is not yet evident.[34]

> A first question one might ask is whether, given their nature, health activities merit a separate, independent status in a program budget. The question arises because these activities often are constituents of, or inputs into, other activities whose purpose or goal orientation is the dominating one.[35] Outlays by the Department of Defense for hospital care, for example, though they assist in maintaining the health of one segment of the population, are undertaken on behalf of national defense, and the latter is their justification.[36]

The space program illustrates difficulties with the program concept. On first glance space projects seem ideally suited for program budgeting because they look like physical systems designed to accomplish different missions. Ac-

---

[31] Arthur Smithies, "Conceptual Framework for the Program Budget," in Ibid., p. 45.

[32] A look at the classic work by Luther Gulick and Lyndall Urwick, et al., *Papers on the Science of Administration* (New York: Columbia Univ. Press, 1937), reveals considerable similarity between their suggested bases of organization and ways of conceptualizing programs.

[33] Melvin Anshen, "The Federal Budget as an Instrument for Management and Analysis," in *Program Budgeting,* ed., Novick, pp. 19–20.

[34] Melvin Anshen, "The Program Budget in Operation," in Ibid., p. 356.

[35] For a related example in Transportation, see Smithies, "Conceptual Framework for the Program Budget," in Ibid., p. 41.

[36] Marvin Frankel, "Federal Health Expenditures in a Program Budget," in Ibid., pp. 219–220.

tually, there is a remarkable degree of interdependence between different missions and objectives — pride, scientific research, space exploration, military uses, etc. — so that it is difficult to divide costs on a proper basis. Consider the problem of a rocket developed for one mission and useful for others. To apportion costs to each new mission is purely arbitrary. To allocate the cost to the first mission and regard the rocket as a free good for all subsequent missions is ludicrous. The only remotely reasonable alternative — making a separate program out of the rocket itself — does violence to the concept of programs as end products. The difficulty is compounded because facilities that have multiple uses (such as boosters and tracking networks) tend to be very expensive compared to the items that are specific to a particular mission.[37] Simple concepts of programs evaporate on inspection.

Political realities lie behind the failure to devise principles for defining programs. As Melvin Anshen puts it, "The central issue is, of course, nothing less than the definition of the ultimate objectives of the federal government as they are realized through operational decisions." The arrangement of the programs inevitably affects the specific actions taken to implement them. "Set in this framework," Anshen continues, "the designation of a schedule of programs may be described as building a bridge between a matter of political philosophy (what is government for?) and . . . assigning scarce resources among alternative governmental objectives." [38]

Because program budgeting is a form of systems analysis (and uses a form of cost-benefit analysis), the conditions that hinder or facilitate its use have largely been covered in the previous sections. The simpler the problem, the fewer the interdependencies, the greater the ability to measure the consequences of alternatives on a common scale, the more costs and benefits that are valued in the market place, the better the chances of making effective use of programs. Let us take transportation to illustrate some of the conditions in a specific situation.

Investments in transportation are highly interdependent (planes versus cars versus trains versus barges, etc.) as well as connected with decisions regarding the regional location of industry and the movements of population. In view of the powerful effects of transportation investment on regional employment, income, and competition with other modes of transport, it becomes necessary to take these factors into account. The partial equilibrium model of efficiency in the narrow sense becomes inappropriate and a general equilibrium model of the economy must be used. The combination of aggregative models at the economy-wide level with inter-region and inter-industry models that this approach requires is staggering. It is precisely the limited and partial character

---

[37] See the excellent chapter by Milton A. Margolis and Stephen M. Barro, "The Space Program," in Ibid., pp. 120–145.

[38] Anshen, "The Federal Budget as an Instrument for Management and Analysis," in Ibid., p. 18.

of cost-effectiveness analyses, which take so much for granted and eliminate so many variables, that makes them easy to work with for empirical purposes. Furthermore, designing a large-scale transportation system involves so close a mixture of political and economic considerations that it is not possible to disentangle them. The Interstate Highway Program, for example, involved complex bargaining among federal, state, and local governments and reconciliation of many conflicting interests. Developing certain "backward" regions, facilitating the movement of defense supplies, redistributing income, creating countervailing power against certain monopolies — not to mention the political needs of public officials — were all involved. Although cost-utility exercises might help with small segments of the problem, J. R. Meyer concludes that, "Given the complexity of the political and economic decisions involved, and the emphasis on designing a geographically consistent system, it probably would be difficult to improve on the congressional process as a means of developing such a program in an orderly and systematic way." [39]

About one condition for effective use — reorganization of the federal government to centralize authority for wide-ranging programs — proponents of PPBS are markedly ambivalent. The problem is that responsibility for programs is scattered throughout the whole federal establishment as well as decentralized to state and local authorities. In the field of health, for example, expenditures are distributed among at least twelve agencies and six departments outside of Health, Education, and Welfare. A far greater number of organizations are concerned with American activities abroad, with natural resources, and with education. These multiple jurisdictions and overlapping responsibilities violate the concept of comprehensive and consistent programs. It "causes one to doubt," Marvin Frankel writes, "whether there can exist in the administrative echelons the kind of overall perspective that would seem indispensable if federal health resources are to be rationally allocated." [40] To G. A. Steiner it is evident that "The present 'chest of drawers' type of organization cannot for long be compatible with program budgeting." [41]

The inevitable resistance to wholesale reorganization would be so great that, if it were deemed essential, it might well doom the enterprise; hence, the hope is expressed that translation grids or crossover networks could be used to convert program budget decisions back into the usual budget categories in the usual agencies. Recognizing that a conversion scheme is technically feasible, Anshen knows that there are "deeply frustrating" issues to be resolved. "The heart of the problem is the fact that the program budget in operation should not be a mere statistical game. Great strategic importance will attach to

---

[39] John R. Meyer, "Transportation in the Program Budget," in Ibid., p. 170. This paragraph is based on my interpretation of his work.

[40] Frankel, "Federal Health Expenditures in Program Budgeting," in Ibid., p. 237.

[41] George A. Steiner, "Problems in Implementing Program Budgeting," in Ibid., p. 348.

both the definition of program structure and the establishment of specific program objectives (including magnitude, timing, and cost)." [42] The implications of program budgeting, however, go far beyond specific policies.

It will be useful to distinguish between policy politics (which policy will be adopted?), partisan politics (which political party will win office?), and system politics (how will decision structures be set up?). Program budgeting is manifestly concerned with policy politics, and not much with partisan politics, although it could have important consequences for issues that divide the nation's parties. I contend that *the thrust of program budgeting makes it an integral part of system politics.*

Program budgeting contains an extreme centralizing bias. Power is to be centralized in the presidency (through the Budget Bureau) at the national level, in superdepartments rather than bureaus within the executive branch, and in the federal government as a whole instead of state or local governments. Note how W. Z. Hirsch assumes this to be desirable when he writes: "These methods of analysis can guide federal officials in the responsibility of bringing local education decisions into closer harmony with national objectives." [43] G. A. Steiner observes that comprehensiveness may be affected by unrestricted federal grants-in-aid to the states because "such a plan would remove a substantial part of federal expenditures from a program budgeting system of the federal government." [44] Should state and local officials be reluctant to use the new tools, Anshen suggests "that the federal government may employ familiar incentives to accelerate this progress." [45] Hirsch concludes that "It appears doubtful that a natural resources program budget would have much impact without a good deal of centralization." [46]

Under PPBS there would have to be strong executives inside great federal organizations designed to encompass the widest ramifications of basic objectives. Cutting across the subunits of the organization, as in the Department of Defense, the program budget could be put together only by the top executive. A more useful tool for increasing his power to control decisions vis-à-vis his subordinates would be hard to find. [47]

In any event, it is hard to justify on scientific grounds the idea that all decisions ought to be made by the most central person in the most centralized body capable of seizing them.

The virtues of the program budget are said to be its usefulness in relating ends to means in a more comprehensive fashion, the emphasis it puts upon the

42 Anshen, "The Program Budget in Operation," in Ibid., p. 359.
43 Werner Z. Hirsch, "Education in the Program Budget," in Ibid., p. 206.
44 Steiner, "Problems in Implementing Program Budgeting," in Ibid., p. 347.
45 Anshen, "The Program Budget in Operation," in Ibid., p. 365.
46 Werner Z. Hirsch, "Program Budget for Natural Resources Activities," in Ibid., p. 280.
47 See Aaron Wildavsky, *The Politics of the Budgetary Process* (Boston: Little, Brown, 1974), p. 140.

policy implications of budgeting, and the ease with which it permits consideration of the budget as a whole while each program competes with every other for funds. Interestingly enough, the distinguishing characteristics of the program procedure are precisely the reverse of traditional practices. Federal budgeting today is incremental rather than comprehensive, is calculated in bits and pieces rather than as a whole, and veils policy implications rather than emphasizing them. It is evident that program budgeting is supposed to lead to different (it is hoped, more rational) decisions. But it is not immediately clear that PPBS is also likely to affect the type and level of conflict over annual resource allocation through the budget.

The incremental, fragmented, nonprogrammatic, and sequential procedures of the present budgetary process help to win agreement and reduce the burden of calculation. It is much easier to agree on adding or subtracting a few thousand or a million than to agree on whether a program is good in the abstract. It is much easier to agree on a small addition or decrease than to compare the worth of one program with that of all others. An incremental approach reduces conflict by reducing the area open to dispute. In much the same way the burden of calculation is eased because no one has to do the whole job. Calculations are made sequentially, in small segments, by subcommittees, and are accepted by the Congress as a whole. If each subcommittee challenged the results of the others, conflict would be greatly exacerbated. If each congressman rejected the decisions of the subcommittees most of the time there would be (assuming that time was available for making the necessary calculations) continual disagreement over most items instead of only a few as at present. Finally, agreement is much more likely when disputed items can be treated as differences in dollars instead of basic differences in policy. Calculating budgets in monetary increments facilitates bargaining and logrolling. It becomes possible to swap an increase here for a decrease there or for an increase elsewhere without always having to consider the ultimate desirability of programs blatantly in competition.[48]

Procedures that deemphasize overt conflicts among competing programs also encourage secret deliberations, nonpartisanship, and the recruitment of personnel who ordinarily feel comfortable in sidestepping policy decisions. Prospects for agreement within the House Appropriations Committee are enhanced by closed hearings and markup sessions, and by a tradition against publicity. Were deliberations to take place in public — "open covenants openly arrived at" — committee members might find themselves accused of "selling out" as they made concessions. Willingness to compromise, to be flexible, is a quality sought in choosing members to serve on appropriations committees.

---

[48] See William H. Brown and Charles E. Gilbert, *Planning Municipal Investment: A Case Study of Philadelphia* (Philadelphia: Univ. of Pennsylvania Press, 1961), for an excellent discussion of the desire of elected officials to remain free to shift their commitments.

If party ties focused attention on policy differences between the two political persuasions, agreement could be disrupted. Instead, party differences are submerged during committee deliberations. Thus the usual process of taking something from a program here, adding to a program there, swapping this for that, can go on at the committee stage without having to take the kind of "yes" or "no" party positions that may be required at the voting stage on the floor.

Consider by contrast some likely consequences of program budgeting. The practice of focusing attention on programs means that policy implications can hardly be avoided. Gains and the losses for the interests involved become far more evident to all concerned.[49] Conflict is heightened by the stress on policy differences and increased still further by a built-in tendency to an all-or-nothing, "yes" or "no" response to the policy in dispute. The very concept of program packages suggests that the policy in dispute is indivisible, that the appropriate response is to be for or against rather than bargaining for a little more or a little less. Logrolling and bargaining are hindered because it is much easier to trade increments conceived in monetary terms than it is to give in on basic policy differences. Conflict would become much more prevalent as the specialist whose verdict was usually accepted in his limited sphere gave way to the generalist whose decisions were fought over by all his fellow legislators — who could claim as much or (considering the staggering burden of calculation) as little competence as he.

Let me be clear. I am not saying that the traditional method of budgeting is good because it tends to reduce the amount of conflict; many of us may want more rather than less conflict in specific areas. What I am saying is that mitigation of conflict is a widely shared value in our society; we must realize that program budgeting is likely to affect that value. Program budgeting may affect not only economic benefits but also political costs.

POLITICAL RATIONALITY

Political rationality is the fundamental kind of reason, because it deals with the preservation and improvement of decision structures, and decision structures are the source of all decisions. Unless a decision structure exists, no reasoning and no decisions are possible. . . . There can be no conflict between political rationality and . . . technical, legal, social, or economic rationality, because the solution of political problems makes possible an

---

[49] See Stanley T. Gabis, *Mental Health and Financial Management: Some Dilemmas of Program Budgeting,* Public Administration Program Department of Political Science Research Report No. 3 (East Lansing: Michigan State University, 1960), p. 46. Gabis writes that "under program budgeting the increase or decrease in the power and influence of each program would be spelled out in detail. It would be surprising if each addition or subtraction were not accompanied by a complicated process of maneuver and counter-maneuver among the affected program heads."

attack on any other problem, while a serious political deficiency can prevent or undo all other problem solving. . . .[50]

Non-political decisions are reached by considering a problem in its own terms, and by evaluating proposals according to how well they solve the problem. The best available proposal should be accepted regardless of who makes it or who opposes it, and a faulty proposal should be rejected or improved no matter who makes it. Compromise is always irrational; the rational procedure is to determine which proposal is the best, and to accept it. In a political decision, on the other hand, action never is based on the merits of a proposal but always on who makes it and who opposes it. Action should be designed to avoid complete identification with any proposal and any point of view, no matter how good or how popular it might be. The best available proposal should never be accepted just because it is best; it should be deferred, objected to, discussed, until major opposition disappears. Compromise is always a rational procedure, even when the compromise is between a good and a bad proposal.[51]

In the literature discussed above there appears several times the proposition that "the program budget is a neutral tool. It has no politics." [52] In truth, the program budget is suffused with policy politics, makes up part of partisan politics, and tends toward system politics. How could men make so foolish a statement? Perhaps they identify program budgeting with something good and beautiful, and politics with another thing bad and ugly. McKean and Anshen speak of politics in terms of "pressure and expedient adjustments," "haphazard acts . . . unresponsive to a planned analysis of the needs of efficient decision design." From the political structure they expect only "resistance and opposition, corresponding to the familiar human disposition to protect established seats of power and procedures made honorable by the mere facts of existence and custom." [53] In other places we hear of "vested interests," "wasteful duplication," "special interest groups," and the "Parkinson syndrome." [54]

Not so long ago less sophisticated advocates of reform ignored the political realm. Now they denigrate it. And, since there must be a structure for decision, it is smuggled in as a mere adjunct of achieving efficiency. Who is to blame if the economic tail wags the political dog? It seems unfair to blame the evangelical economizer for spreading the gospel of efficiency. If economic efficiency turns out to be the one true religion, maybe it is because its prophets could so easily prevail.

It is hard to find men who take up the cause of political rationality, who

[50] Paul Diesing, *Reason in Society: Five Types of Decisions and Their Social Conditions* (Urbana: Univ. of Illinois Press, 1962), pp. 231–232. Reprinted by permission of the author.

[51] Ibid., pp. 203–204. By permission.

[52] Anshen, "The Program Budget in Operation," p. 370.

[53] McKean and Anshen, "Limitations, Risks, and Problems," pp. 289–290.

[54] Ibid., p. 359.

plead the case for political man, and whose chief concerns are the laws that grease the political machinery. One is driven to a philosopher like Paul Diesing to find the case for the political:

> . . . the political problem is always basic and prior to the others. . . . This means that any suggested course of action must be evaluated first by its effects on the political structure. A course of action which corrects economic or social deficiencies but increases political difficulties must be rejected, while an action which contributes to political improvement is desirable even if it is not entirely sound from an economic or social standpoint.[55]

Hardly a single political scientist would claim half as much. Political scientists' desire to invent decision structures to facilitate the achievement of economic efficiency does not suggest a full appreciation of their proper role.

A major task of the political system is to specify goals or objectives. "Goals" may well be the product of interaction among key participants rather than some *deus ex machina* or (to use Bentley's term) some "spook" which posits values in advance of our knowledge of them. What we call goals or objectives may, in large part, be operationally determined by policies we can agree upon. The mixtures of values found in complex policies may have to be taken in packages, so that policies may determine goals at least as much as general objectives determine policies. In a political situation, then, the need for support assumes central importance. Not simply the economic, but the *political* costs and benefits turn out to be crucial.

Let us see if spelling out what is meant by political costs can bring better understanding of the range of requirements for political rationality.[56] A political leader incurs exchange costs when he needs the support of other people to get a policy adopted. He has to pay for this assistance by using up resources in the form of favors (patronage, logrolling) or coercive moves (threats or acts to veto or remove from office). By supporting a policy and influencing others to do the same, a politician antagonizes some people and may suffer their retaliation. Mounting hostility costs may turn into reelection costs which can decrease his chances (or those of his friends) of being elected or reelected to office. Election costs, in turn, may become policy costs if he cannot command the necessary formal powers to accomplish the desired policy objectives.

In the manner of Neustadt, we may also talk about reputation costs, i.e., not only loss of popularity with segments of the electorate, but also loss of esteem and effectiveness with other participants in the political system, and loss of ability to secure policies other than the one immediately under consideration. Those who continually urge a president to go all out — that is, use all his resources on a wide range of issues — rarely stop to consider that the price

---

[55] Diesing, *Reason in Society*, p. 228. By permission.
[56] I am indebted to John Harsanyi for suggestions about political rationality.

of success in one area of policy may be defeat in another. If he loses popularity with the electorate, as did President Truman, Congress may destroy almost the whole of his domestic program. If he cracks down on the steel industry, as did President Kennedy, he may find himself constrained to lean over backward in the future to avoid unremitting hostility from the business community. If he attacks the information media, as did President Nixon, he can surely expect to suffer when his guard is down.

A major consequence of incurring exchange and hostility costs may be undesirable power redistribution effects. The process of getting a policy adopted or implemented may so increase the power of various individuals, organizations, and social groups that later it will be used against the political leader. The power of some participants may be so weakened that the political leader is unable to enjoy their protection.

The legitimacy of the political system may be threatened by costs that involve the weakening of customary political restraints. Politicians who try to suppress opposition, or who practice election frauds, may find similar tactics being used against them. The choice of a highly controversial policy may raise the costs of civic discord. Although the people involved may not hate the political leader, the fact that they hate each other may lead to consequences contrary to his desires.

The literature of economics usually treats organizations and institutions as if they were costless entities. The standard procedure is to consider rival alternatives (in consideration of price policy or other criteria), calculate the differences in cost and achievement among them, and show that one is more or less efficient than another. This typical way of thinking is sometimes misspecified. If the costs of pursuing a policy are strictly economic and can be calculated directly in the marketplace, the procedure should work well. But if the costs include making one or another organization change its policies or procedures, then these costs must also be taken into account. Perhaps legal, psychological, or other impediments make the required changes either impossible or difficult. Or the changes may require great effort and result in incurring a variety of other costs. In considering a range of alternatives, one is measuring not only efficiency but also the cost of change.[57]

Studies based on efficiency criteria are much needed and increasingly useful. My quarrel is not with them as such. I have been concerned that a single value, however important, could triumph over other values without explicit consideration being given these others. I would feel much better if political rationality were being pursued with the same vigor and capability as is economic efficiency. I would then have fewer qualms about extending efficiency studies into the decision-making apparatus.

[57] See Aaron Wildavsky, "The Self-Evaluating Organization," *Public Administration Review,* 32 (September/October 1972), 509–520.

I have not wanted to accuse economizers of doing what comes naturally. Rather, I have tried to emphasize that economic rationality, however laudible in its own sphere, ought not to swallow up political rationality — but may do so, if political rationality continues to lack trained and adept defenders.

I should have added a critical qualification to the last sentence. Economic rationality, as embedded in PPBS, might have bad consequences, if it works as intended, indeed, *if it can work at all*.

17

Potemkin Villages:
Around the World with PPBS

British, French, and Japanese governments have had unsatisfactory flirtations ("experiences" would be too strong a word) with program budgeting. From the outset central budget agencies were ambivalent — divided functionally between traditional types, and program budgeters who themselves were unsure of how far they could or should go. In Japan, for example, program budgeting had to fit in with pervasive norms mandating equity among participants. If program budgeting could be shown somehow to be more scientific, so that its results were both more desirable and more acceptable, everyone would feel that justice had been done. But the sponsors of PPBS had the usual trouble figuring out what to do, and the usual difficulty in getting anyone who was disadvantaged to agree that what they did was good. The program structures were confusing, the analysis was not convincing, and the losers (who in Japan would have had to agree) would not assume the required position. So PPBS was aborted before it fairly got started.

Information on the French *Rationalisation des Choix Budgétaires* (RCB) is sparse, but conversations with a few people who are in a position to know suggest that it is still an ephemeral part of French budgeting. RCB exists but is not yet taken seriously. No one has suggested that RCB has actually affected important budgetary decisions. Nor is it entirely clear whether its future emphasis will be upon discrete policies, taken one at a time, as in Britain, or on program structures, *à l'américain*.

The evolution of Great Britain's thought and practice is most instructive. When all the publicity surrounding program budgeting reached Britain, the Public Expenditure Group in the Treasury was well served by its customary caution. Observers, sent to America, came back enticed but wary of the innumerable pitfalls they faced. They proceeded pragmatically in two directions: they encouraged a few departments with interested personnel to try out the creation of program structures and categories, and they gave part of the time of one of their bright young men to work with local government officials in actually introducing program budgeting at that level. Let them struggle. Thus when neither group was able to advance because they could not figure out how to make the system work, the Treasury had no substantial investment to abandon.

Yet the Treasury could not sit still. Its own concern about the adequacy of program review was exceeded by that of the Conservative Party and its associated businessmen who wanted to give the prime minister and Cabinet more adequate tools for making expenditure decisions. Instead of rushing into program budgeting across the board, however, the Treasury persuaded businessmen to join with them in creating a mechanism for Program Analysis and Review (PAR) aimed at encouraging departments to analyze a few major programs each year with the knowledge that they would be subject to Cabinet review. PAR, still in its infancy, has hardly had time to make an impact. But it exists. Its viability may depend in part on whether another new apparatus, the Central Policy Review Staff (CPRS), which the Conservative businessmen designed to aid the prime minister and Cabinet in reviewing policy and adhering to party programs, will also be able to maintain itself in the heretofore closed world of top level British political administration. Thus the Treasury now faces competition not from planners with grandiose general schemes, but from analysts who are interested precisely in having an effect on the choice among major alternatives in the annual allocation of resources.

A QUICK TOUR OF PROGRAM BUDGETING AMONG THE RICH

Experience with program budgeting in rich countries outside the United States is hard to come by. Yet these brief encounters are all we have — encounters not without their own instructive charm. Most comments are by civil servants whose caution is exemplary:[1] "At the time of reporting," according to one such writer, "there had been no decision by the Australian federal government on the application of programme budgeting . . ." [2] In New Zealand, "Introduction of programme budgeting is at an early stage . . ." [3] All we know

---

[1] These accounts appear in a book prepared by David Novick, the leading American proponent of program budgeting. They may fairly be taken as representative of the best that can now be said. See David Novick, ed., *Current Practice in Program Budgeting (PPBS): Analysis and Case Studies Covering Government and Business* (New York: Crane, Russak, 1973).

[2] David Novick, ed., *Current Practice in Program Budgeting (PPBS): Analysis and Case Studies Covering Government and Business* (New York: Crane, Russak, 1973), p. 57.

[3] Ibid., p. 138.

from Belgium is that "At the present time, studies of PPBS are being pursued. . . ." [4]

Things are apparently further advanced in France where "The development of [Rationalisation des Choix Budgetaires] has now reached the point of leaving the experimental stage. . . . Difficult problems will have to be solved in the near future." [5]

Men with experience in trying to apply PPBS are careful: ". . . although the Japanese people in general might be impatient to see results, the people involved in instituting this new management tool must realize that it will be a long and very difficult avenue to travel before satisfactory results are realized." [6] The Irish are pretty much the same: "Assuming that the results of the pioneer efforts in the selected departments are such as to confirm the feasibility of making the system generally operational, it would be unrealistic not to anticipate a difficulty. . . ." [7]

Are there anywhere results to show? Our Canadian authority says ". . . it is not possible, at least for this writer, to cite a clearly documented instance where a decision to undertake program *A* rather than program *B* or *C* was arrived at on the basis of analysis . . ." [8] How about the Mother Country? "Much of the discussion surrounding the introduction of programme budgeting into local government is concerned with the question of defining a programme structure for an authority. . . . No matter how formal the programme structure being adopted, there are few signs as yet of any attempts to replace the traditional financial budget with a new budget structure based on programme heads. . . ." [9] In Austria, "It would therefore be premature to expect public authorities to put program budgeting into practice less than a year following the circulation of information about it." [10]

Here, as elsewhere, there are fragmentary reports of budding developments. The blooms, however, are found at the stage of intention and preparation. Thus, "The newly founded Ministry of Science and Research *intends* to apply it in planning its legislative and expenditure program, and . . . the Ministry of Finance *is preparing* a ten-year investment program for the central government sector [italics supplied]." [11]

The federal government of the United States, first to introduce program budgeting, was also the first to abandon it. The Office of Management and Budget experienced extreme difficulties in negotiating the pathways between

4 Ibid., p. 67.
5 Ibid., p. 117.
6 Ibid., p. 128.
7 Ibid., p. 123.
8 Ibid., p. 77.
9 Ibid., p. 108.
10 Ibid., p. 63.
11 Ibid.

knowledge and power. The OMB was neither able to produce information from program categories appropriate to the level of the user nor to impose such preferences as it did have on the recalcitrant and unwilling. Spending agencies played along because they thought PPBS was for the OMB, whose favorable opinion was useful to them. When they discovered that the OMB was as much in the dark about what to do as they were, and that program budgeting was supposed to be for them, the spenders used program structures as the latest in the long series of devices for self-advertisement in the struggle for funds. After PPBS was disestablished in a circular commenting on the reduction of unnecessary paperwork in the federal government, it was a good two years before the OMB finally began to receive inquiries from people who noticed something was missing. What happened?

PPBS in the U.S.

No doubt the most extensive experience with program budgeting has taken place in the country of its origin. There, in the United States, the cycle of early enthusiasm, wide diffusion, and later disillusion, has been played out to its fullest extent. And the end is not yet in sight. For as old jurisdictions drop the burden, new ones pick it up. They drop program budgeting because they literally cannot hang on to it. Their central dilemma — to be unable to get a handle on what *seems* to embody rationality — is our subject.

We know already what PPBS is supposed to have done for us; the question yet to be answered is, what did it actually accomplish when efforts were made to implement it? Did it change the traditional budgetary process as advertised? If not, what (if any) other effect did it have?

Right now we do not wish to argue either for or against PPBS; we want to survey the experience with implementation.[12] We have here what lawyers call evidence; fortunately we have plenty of it, for PPBS was introduced throughout the federal government, tried by numerous cities and counties, and adopted by at least half the states. Unfortunately, the literature on PPBS is a vast ocean in which the literature on implementation is a hardly noticeable drop. Still, much can be learned from the few good accounts of what actually occurred in the process of trying to put PPBS across.

Three categories emerge: implementation in name only, PPBS established but never really used as a decision-making tool; PPBS operative but without noticeable effect; PPBS having made a difference but we do not yet know how much or what kind. The criterion for this classification is the degree of success in replacing the traditional decision rules with PPBS methods — i.e., identification of programs, specifications of their inputs and outputs, comparative anal-

---

[12] This section was written with the collaboration of Brian Tannenbaum.

ysis of costs and benefits, extension to future years — and, once the apparatus is in place, the extent of implementation.

PPBS IN NAME ONLY. In its days of glory, many considered PPBS to be the philosopher's stone of budgeting. The pressure to put it into practice was strong, both formally (as in President Johnson's executive order), and informally (because budgeters were told that for the first time, they would really know they were acting rationally). Often, however, implementation never got past the stage of "I will." Some administrators did not know where to begin and what to do. Others lacked sufficient resources to embark on any kind of reform. Hence, PPB was implemented in form but not in substance. Titles of budgetary forms were changed to include the term PPBS; instructions were sent out to all budget officials indicating that a PPB system had been installed and that everyone should submit requests in programmatic form, backed by analytic studies. But, if the format of the budget document was new, its content was not. Schick found that this pattern of underlying behavior belying surface appearances applied to most state governments:

> The most important fact to note about PPB is that it is approaching operational status in only a few states. Most states have gone no further than the preliminaries — training courses and program structures — and have not taken adequate steps to build PPB into the decisional structure. Only a few have made the critical investment in commitment, resources, and boldness to give PPB a fair chance against the prevailing budget traditions.[13]

Many cities display a similar state of affairs. Let us take three examples — New York City; Oakland, California; and Washington, D.C. In New York Mayor Lindsay called for budget reform on taking office in 1965, and a PPB system was advanced under the direction of Frederick O'R. Hayes. "He [Hayes] briefly tried but then deemphasized the more formal aspects of PPBS such as restructuring the budget format. He settled on an analysis-oriented strategy." [14] In fact, Hayes "deemphasized" the basic nature of PPB to the point of nonexistence. New York's budgeting system could not be considered a PPB system, for it was not on a program basis. Budgeters continued to use a line-item format: "The examiners still have the basic responsibility of putting line budget together. They handle the line schedule. But their primary function is budget administration." [15] Nothing was really changed in New York City. A heavier analysis orientation has been introduced; but, after all, analysis was part of budgeting long before PPBS was born.

---

[13] Allen Schick, *Budget Innovation in the States* (Washington, D.C.: The Brookings Institution, 1971), p. 103.

[14] Frederick O'R. Hayes, "Creative Budgeting in New York City: An Interview with Former Budget Director Frederick O'R. Hayes," *Journal of Urban Analysis,* 1 (1973), 120.

[15] Ibid., p. 124.

In Oakland, California, the Board of Education tried to implement a PPB system for the fall of 1973. In 1971, a program budget was produced for the 1971–1972 fiscal year. This was not the actual budget for that year, but was commissioned to give the Oakland School Board an idea of what program budgeting was all about. The actual budget, on the basis of which allocations were made, was much shorter and done on the line-item format. The sample program budget was no more than a detailed line-item budget, a voluminous 595-page report which, despite its imposing length, contained no programatic material. It merely broke the line-item budget down, school by school, into functional categories such as administration, instruction, supplies, etc. This information is available in the traditional budget, but is just not included in the final budget statement. As such, then, there is no real difference between the two.[16]

Washington, D.C.'s budget for the 1971 fiscal year was advanced as a program budget of two parts. The first was a standard line-item accounting of reviews and expenditures; the second was a breakdown of the budget by activities. This second part did not correlate expenditures with proposed objectives. Indeed, objectives were very poorly stated. If the "program element" of Police Street Patrol — "To prevent and detect crime" — tells us very little, for example, the program description tells us even less:

> Activities of the Patrol Division, Traffic Division, and Special Operations Division of the *Metropolitan Police Department* are directed to crime prevention and control. Both regular and special assignments of police manpower to patrol duties are used in the effort to curb criminal activities.
> The FY 1971 budget recommends the authorization and funding of 5,100 police officers. The bulk of this manpower will be assigned to street duty. The increased police manpower in the District of Columbia should deter the commission of crime, especially street crime, as more officers are recruited, trained and assigned to patrol duty.[17]

Since it does little more than restate objectives, the program is described inadequately.

What is more, there appears to be no program structure. Street patrol comes under the aegis of the Patrol, Traffic, and Special Operations Divisions. The structure is not built on the lines of the street patrol program; rather, street patrol is worked into the various divisions of the police department. One strongly suspects that decisions of city council members would be based on the line-item portion of the budget, for the program budget part tells one very little about programs, does not budget in any detail, and does not correlate spending with objectives any more than traditional budgets do.

16 Jesse J. McCorry, "School Budgeting in Oakland" (mimeographed).
17 Washington, D.C., *The Fiscal Year 1971 Program Budget for the City of Washington, D.C.* (1971), p. 45.

New York State began PPBS in 1964. In 1970 it was discarded and succeeded by Program Analysis and Review. From 1965 to 1967, New York's PPB system emphasized planning but included little budgetary work. The primary purpose of the system was to develop government planning with particular stress on long-range plans. PPBS was to develop five-year program plans, although twenty-year projections of needs were desired. This approach "made impossible demands on the data and decisional resources of the participating agencies." [18] And, not surprisingly, budgeters found the system to be burdensome. In 1967, officials in New York decided to revamp their PPB system, since their initial approach had accomplished so little. They downgraded the planning aspect of PPBS and pressed for program structure, analysis and budgetary work. The emphasis was on budgeting with some program reporting as a secondary characteristic. However, the second approach to PPBS did not improve matters. Schick makes it clear the "PPB never made it in New York. . . . Second-generation PPB was little more than a reporting system, as distant from program and financial decision-making as its predecessor had been." [19] Any budgeting changes were minor, and traditional budgeting remained intact.

In 1970 Program Analysis and Review (PAR) was introduced to replace PPBS. The idea of PAR was to subject a few matters to analysis; in effect, it turned out to be the traditional budget cake with an icing of extra analysis. Whatever else PAR is, it is not a system of annual or longer-term budgeting by program categories.[20] Since PPBS was not strongly anchored, the moment the wind changed it quietly drifted away.[21]

Before PPBS was officially established at the federal level, there were two major efforts to implement PPBS-type mechanisms. One, the zero-base budget in the Department of Agriculture (see Chapter 11), tried having budgetary decisions made from the ground up, as it were, by reconsidering the desirability of each and every expenditure as if it were new. The chief result? Mountains of paperwork. The experiment failed both because no one could figure out how to make the comparisons, and because no one was willing and able to make the necessary drastic reallocations.[22]

The second major effort took place in the Department of State; it was called Comprehensive Country Programing Systems (CCPS). Frederick Mosher and John Harr, in *Programming Systems and Foreign Affairs Leader-*

---

[18] Schick, *Budget Innovation in the States,* p. 123.
[19] Ibid., p. 125.
[20] New York State, Division of the Budget, *Guidelines for Program Analysis and Review* (1970).
[21] Schick, *Budget Innovation in the States,* pp. 1–3.
[22] Aaron Wildavsky and Arthur Hammond, "Comprehensive versus Incremental Budgeting in the Department of Agriculture," *Administrative Science Quarterly* 10:3 (December, 1965), pp. 321–346.

ship — An Attempted Innovation,[23] note that CCPS was not enthusiastically received or supported by the department's hierarchy, including Secretary Rusk. They also report that CCPS met with "hostility or apathy" from embassies in those foreign nations where the system was supposed to be implemented.[24]

The State Department did succeed in developing comprehensive programs for a select group of countries, but was unable to put them to work. A chief reason, according to Mosher and Harr, was agency independence. If an agency working overseas but not part of the State Department refused to accept a recommendation made on the basis of the program, no one except the president could force it to. "The State Department desk officer was negotiating from a position of weakness and his counterpart in the other agency from a position of strength, and both knew it. Because of this situation, there was reluctance to raise issues at all. . . ." [25]

No one in the programing group wanted to develop a PPBS system for the State Department alone. They could not do much because "Not much of what the State Department did was 'programable.' " [26] State either worked at a "high level" of negotiating, reporting, and advising on policy or at a "low level" of providing administrative support around the world to other agencies. PPBS met strong opposition from most line officials because, they believed, "It is virtually impossible [in many or most or all] foreign affairs activities to measure outputs in terms of national objectives. . . ." and that "A systems approach . . . simply adds another layer to the existing excess of reports and paperwork." [27]

The Nixon administration brought a new wave of reform into the foreign affairs arena. When Henry Kissinger became the president's counsel on foreign affairs, initiative went from the State Department to the White House. The department thus had more serious business than PPBS to face — climbing back on the horse. "As of October 1969, the new administration had made no significant announcement about PPBS." [28]

As it did everywhere else, PPBS in the State Department died quietly. Did it leave a residue behind? Mosher and Harr were reluctant to take on this tricky question. They did say, however, that the experiences with CCPS and PPBS are not likely to encourage additional efforts to rationalize foreign policymaking. In their words, "There remains a need for marrying quantitative analysis with judgment based upon qualitative considerations, but it does not ap-

---

[23] Frederick Mosher and John Harr, *Programming Systems and Foreign Affairs Leadership: An Attempted Innovation* (New York: Oxford Univ. Press, 1970), pp. 68–69.

[24] Ibid., p. 61.

[25] Ibid., p. 103.

[26] Ibid., pp. 117–118.

[27] Ibid., pp. 205–206.

[28] Ibid., p. 200.

pear that a romance between the two was materially encouraged by the events described in this story." [29]

PPB ESTABLISHED IN FORM BUT WITHOUT AFFECTING DECISION-MAKING IN FACT.

> Evaluation, analysis, and program budget categories are all useful tools, but the moment of truth is the decision. The real point of PPBS is to establish a process for bringing the relevant tools to bear at the right moment so that decisions are made in the light of maximum information about present and future consequences of alternative courses of action.[30]

Most efforts to implement PPBS never left the ground. Most often, PPBS was initiated by the executive branch as an experiment, and preliminary implementation was started. The first steps amounted to hiring program budgeting staffs of various sizes, who would produce papers and studies dealing with reorganization of the bureaucracy on program lines, and to their efforts to reorient people toward the goal of budget definition and program analysis. Beyond this, very little took place; PPBS never replaced traditional budgeting in decision-making.

Many practitioners would still agree with the student who concluded that, "In fact, the materials produced under the auspices of PABS [California PPBS] were not used in budget-making, and their quality generally was unsatisfactory." [31] Multi-year projections have been discarded. Though a few people fiddle with program structures, our interviews reveal that their music is neither heard nor appreciated by others. The line-item budget is still what the Department of Finance itself uses to make its decisions.

The experience of the State-Local Finances Project of the George Washington University is also instructive. Its staff, charged with a technical assistance mission, worked with a group of state and local governments for several years to install PPBS. This demonstration effort was called the 5-5-5 project because the group of governments included five states, five counties, and five cities. When the staff discussed what they had learned from those efforts they found that these fifteen governmental units lacked some important requisites for a successful system. There was no significant study capability and, more important, no strong chief-executive support. The program structure was not used "significantly," operational outputs were not defined, and only three govern-

[29] Ibid., p. 238.

[30] Alice M. Rivlin, "The Planning, Programming, and Budgeting System in the Department of Health, Education, and Welfare: Some Lessons in Expertise," in *Public Expenditures and Policy Analysis,* ed. by Robert H. Haveman and Julius Margolis (Chicago: Markham Press, 1970), p. 513.

[31] Don Loarie, "Budgeting in the California Department of Public Health" (submitted to Wildavsky's seminar on "Budgets as Political Instruments," University of California, Berkeley, 1969).

ments actually completed a study or a program analysis.[32] As the project staff said, "Governments wishing to implement PPB should expect to invest considerable time and effort before significantly useful products can be achieved." [33]

Implementation in the federal government began in 1965 following President Johnson's directive that all federal agencies adopt the new method. The Bureau of the Budget relied heavily on the model developed in Defense, without adapting it to the conditions under which civilian departments operate. Instructions were extremely general and vague, and the agencies were never requested to replace their traditional budget with a PPB system. Throughout PPB's lifetime, the Budget Bureau continued to issue separate instructions for program budgeting and for the traditional budget.

Most agencies tried to do what they were told, but since the instructions were so general, nearly every agency ended up with its own interpretation. But what nearly all agencies had in common was the inability to make PPBS work. The PPBS staffs just couldn't "penetrate the vital routines of putting together and justifying a budget." [34] They managed only to submit a number of analytical studies to the decision-makers.

Marvin and Rouse conducted 400 interviews in a large number of agencies with discouraging results. "Detailed PPB processes have been developed in . . . a . . . group of agencies; for example, Interior. With the exception of the work in an occasional bureau, the materials produced through these processes have not been used extensively by decision-makers. . . ." [35] In another group of agencies, "well-developed analytic activities have contributed to decision-making and did so long before the advent of PPB. . . . The result is that PPB's contribution in restructuring the decision-making process in these agencies has been marginal." [36] Jack W. Carlson, in another study, looked at 26 agencies and discovered, similarly, that though program structures have been developed, "the formal structure has been only partially successful." [37] Benefits derived from their preparation were mainly educational.[38]

And the first shall be last. Since 1961, Defense has been held up as the prime example of what PPB can do and how well it can succeed. According to

---

[32] Selma J. Mushkin, et al., *Implementing PPB in State, City, and County: A Report on the 5-5-5 Project* (Washington, D.C.: State-Local Finances Project, George Washington University, 1969), pp. 12–26.

[33] Ibid., p. 23.

[34] Allen Schick, "A Death in the Bureaucracy: The Demise of Federal PPB," *Public Administration Review,* 33 (March/April 1973), 147.

[35] Keith E. Marvin and Andrew M. Rouse, "The Status of PPB in Federal Agencies: A Comparative Perspective," in *Public Expenditures and Policy Analysis,* eds. Haveman and Margolis, p. 448.

[36] Ibid.

[37] Jack W. Carlson, "The Status and Next Steps for Planning, Programming, and Budgeting," in Ibid., p. 374.

[38] Ibid., p. 375.

G. W. Shipp, however, ". . . aside from the statements by DOD officials there is little evidence that the use of program elements has revolutionized budgeting." Indeed, *"the DOD still relies on the most part on incrementalism."* [39] (Italics mine.)

PPBS did not have the anticipated effect on budgetary decisions in DOD to any significant degree. Rather, it was yearly appropriations which limited the programs. John P. Crecine, in an intensive study of the subject, concluded that, "In spite of the many differences in necessary procedures under PPBS, the methods of arriving at dollar figures for the line items in the appropriations request, consistent with the fiscal constraints on the total . . . are not dissimilar from those utilized during the Truman-Eisenhower administrations." [40] Department tactics and strategies of the budget process remain the same as before PPBS. The appropriations request submitted to the president and to Congress is a traditional line-item statement. Budget reviewers in DOD, when forecasting cuts that are going to be made, base their budget decisions on those of the past. "Basically . . . *experience with the decision system* [the 'base' in our terms] *is the prime ingredient in the budget review exercise."* [41] (Author's emphasis.)

PPB's application to DOD's final budget is insignificant; but, within the department, could it be thought to have had an effect? This does not appear to have been so, for two reasons: first, "PPB decisions are always made to conform to appropriations decisions made during the October-December budget crunch," and second, "The current PPB system does not do what any foreseeable budget decision system has to do if it is to be the primary determinate of DOD resource allocation; it has to adapt to external, fiscal constraints." [42] PPBS, apparently, is not only a "has been" in Defense but may well be a "never was."

WHERE PPBS MAY HAVE HAD SIGNIFICANT EFFECT, BUT WE DO NOT KNOW FOR SURE. Three states — Hawaii, Pennsylvania, and Wisconsin — still hope to make PPBS work. For them the Scottish verdict — unproven — is still the appropriate one.

"Certainly," Schick concludes, "in design and on paper, Pennsylvania's PPB system is a more comprehensive and bolder departure than has been tried elsewhere in the United States. But it is one thing to design and install, and

---

[39] G. W. Shipp, "Program Budgeting in the Defense Department: A Small Change" (paper submitted to Wildavsky's seminar on "Budgets as Political Instruments," University of California, Berkeley, 1966), p. 240.

[40] John P. Crecine, *Defense Budgeting: Constraints and Organizational Adaptation,* Discussion Paper No. 6 (University of Michigan: Institute of Policy Studies, 1971), p. 38.

[41] Ibid., p. 49.

[42] Ibid., pp. 54–55.

quite another to use, a new system." [43] Hawaii, in Schick's opinion second only to Pennsylvania in developing a comprehensive system, is significant in that it is the only state in which the legislature was the prime moving force behind PPB. No current information is available on what has happened under the recent law placing elements of PPBS into the budgetary process. According to officials,

> ... Wisconsin already has two major accomplishments: a program budget that is genuinely and closely related to the accounting and appropriations processes, and possibly the most informative budget documents of any state. In each succeeding biennium the scope and amount of program information in the budget has been expanded. ... Yet the goals that Wisconsin has set for the future are more difficult than those it has already achieved. The state has established the informational groundwork for planning, analysis, and evaluation; it remains to be seen whether the information will be put to these purposes.[44]

After this chapter was finished we wrote to practitioners in a number of states in order to find whether they had something new to report. We asked them to tell us if, in their opinion, PPBS replaced traditional budgeting in their state. None of the responses we received suggested to us that PPBS was alive and kicking. The general tone of the letters was, "We are trying; a comprehensive review of the status of PPB is scheduled; as of now we cannot list any changes in budgetary decisions resulting from PPB." Typical of the responses was one from a close official observer: "From my own personal standpoint, I would not honestly state that as an overall concept PPBS has been implemented in the state."

If these practitioners had had real success with PPBS they would have hailed it with trumpets and fanfare. We were told that efforts in implementing PPBS are still being made in these states and that we will be kept posted with any advances made. We will believe it when we see it; as of today, we haven't seen it.

In states where program budgeting is still alive, PPBS staffs often claim advances in the area of policy analysis and support it with claims of a few successful analytical studies. The point, of course, is that had implementation really succeeded, there would have been so many analytical studies that displaying one or two would have been a tremendous understatement. The few analytical studies which PPBS officials hold out as proof for advancement are praised because they are unique, or as Schick says, like a "museum piece ... exuberantly displayed for outsiders, but a 'hands off' practice bars their use in actual decisions." [45] Still, where there is life. . . .

---

[43] Schick, *Budget Innovation in the States*, p. 153.
[44] Ibid., pp. 137–138.
[45] Ibid., p. 104.

Conclusion: The World Still Goes Its Own Way

Observers of the budgeting process agree that PPB has had limited influence on the major resource allocation decisions in domestic agencies of the federal government.[46]

Except for one or two states, PPB has not penetrated the decision-making arenas of state governments.[47]

We have not been able to find one successful example of PPBS at work. Even where implementation was seriously carried out, and a large investment made, the primary goal — changing budgetary procedures and decisions — has never been achieved. PPBS was abolished in the federal government and discarded by most cities and states. Disillusionment with its ability to deliver was universal.

There still are a few places where PPB holds on. Given time and continuous care, they tell us, PPBS *will* work. Why dispute the claim? Time will show whether or not it is valid. Meanwhile, progress has been limited, even in these supposed examples of success. Programs are not yet fully and adequately defined. Inputs and outputs have not been identified or measured. Decisions on allocation of resources are still being made on the basis of traditional rules and procedures. No legislature that we know of, with the possible exception of Hawaii's, has changed its review and appropriations procedures to adapt to the new system. Any achievements are, as yet, indirect ones. More data are available, though it is doubtful whether this can be considered an improvement since it is not at all clear that more data lead to better decisions. In the absence of a theory relating inputs to outputs, abundant data on both will not enlighten anyone. Though the number of analysts has increased, it is hard to separate the effect of PPBS from the generally increased interest in evaluating programs. Budgeters receive increased formal training; but usually this amounts to a limited exposure to ideas involved in PPBS such as cost-benefit analysis. Whether or not they can use these concepts after the usual short course is doubtful.

One hears often that although PPBS did not stand up to its promises, and disappeared from the scene much sooner than its advocates may have desired, the budgeting world will never be the same again. PPB's greatest success, its advocates argue, has been in changing the budgetary atmosphere. It focused wider attention on the need for improving analysis and developing more rational decision rules. This might very well be true; it would be ironic, how-

[46] Edwin Harper and Fred A. Kramer, "Implementation and the Use of PPB in Sixteen Federal Agencies," *Public Administration Review,* 29 (November/December 1969), p. 632.

[47] Schick, *Budget Innovation in the States,* p. 86.

ever, if a system based on economic analysis, which failed, could yet convince budgeters of the need to improve their analytic capabilities!

PROGRAM BUDGETING IN POOR COUNTRIES

Despite all this evidence that program budgeting does not work in the United States, it has nonetheless been exported, and its worldwide attractiveness is easy to understand.[48] Besides being the newest fashion for every nation that wishes to be considered advanced, program budgeting promises also to center the budgetary process around the productivity of expenditures, a tempting prospect for poor countries. But PPBS experience has been the same story abroad; no country, rich or poor, knows how to do it. Although the words — planning, programing, systems — trip easily off the tongue, no corresponding operations flow from them. No one understands how to put together program structures that relate objectives to one another, because no one has operative theories that reliably relate available resources to desired objectives over the broad range of public policies. Consequently, many different things go under the name of program budgeting. On occasion it simply means naming as a program whatever a bureau is doing. Or it may mean modeling a new system of accounts so as to discover the cost of particular activities that might interest decision-makers. Elsewhere it means trying to learn how much is being spent on individual projects. Rarely does program budgeting in practice come to mean relating financial resources to achieving objectives.

Remember that program budgeting calls for a high degree of conceptual ability, a new accounting or information system, and a political leadership ready and willing to use it. No one should be surprised, then, to find that it runs into serious trouble in poor countries. A full study of program budgeting in low-income countries would fill another book. The reader may, however, get an idea of the problems encountered from comments of some officials in a few of the countries we visited.

Lack of information is the most obvious problem. In order to evaluate programs — an essential part of program budgeting — one must be able to measure progress in some uniform way. If, as in an example cited by a Chilean informant, the goal of a program is to lower the birthrate, success or failure cannot be measured by counting pregnancies, because "it would be impossible to locate such figures." Information ultimately may be available, but probably too late to be of any use. For example, after the month of liquidation (when accounts are closed), a Peruvian official explained, "we know how much has been spent in each area. But of course, that it too late to be helpful in preparing the budget for the next year."

---

[48] The material here is taken from Naomi Caiden and Aaron Wildavsky, *Planning and Budgeting in Poor Countries* (New York: Wiley, 1973).

Program budgeting involves not only a need to measure the resources used but also a sensible way of relating them to goals. Often such unit-cost measurement is out of the question in countries where conditions and standards differ widely. Apart from the difficulty of applying standardized measures, programs themselves may be hard to identify. Program budgeting depends on qualified personnel with a clear understanding of its aims and methods. Such people often don't exist in low-income countries. We were told that in Argentina "the most difficult problem at the beginning was to determine what were the most appropriate programs. Looking at all the ministries you found a multitude of agencies and a multitude of ostensible programs. But there was no integration between the two." Even at the level of ongoing activities, identification may be difficult because of differences in nomenclature. A Peruvian official declared with some exasperation, "Everyone who works in the national bureaucracy has a different language. Plowing is called one thing in one region, and another thing in another. Activities have been given names and descriptions according to the points of view of different participants. It is, of course, impossible to set goals based on activities if everyone speaks a different language." Faced with time-consuming problems of program identification and classification, it is sometimes easier not to bother. In Chile, we were told that "different ministries simply divided their traditional budget into four or five parts, and called these programs. The program budget is program in name only, not by structure."

Not only is the talent necessary for program budgeting often in short supply, but conversations with a number of people involved reveal that the people in charge may be so valuable they are taken away to perform other activities. A report prepared for a leading foundation includes comments that inadvertently show this up. The writer notes that "two officers who were originally members of this unit have left, one to join the X Foundation and another the Y Institute." Again, he states that, even as the cabinet secretariat was exhorting departments to do performance budgeting, the man who had prepared the major proposal "left the finance ministry and joined the X Foundation." The circulation of elites makes reform difficult. Program budgeting needs commitment as well as expertise.

Ministers have been less interested in the intrinsic merits of the new budgeting system than in its ability to pry loose greater appropriations. "They cannot conceptualize programs," an experienced participant said, "but only greater and greater resources." The program budget, it turned out, was less a way of determining what was best than it was a mechanism for selling an approved program to others. "What is supposed to be a technical process to determine agencies' needs soon boils down to bureaucratic politics." When political considerations caused program analysis to be abandoned in favor of intervention by top officials, operators of the program budget were disillusioned. Chile decided to halt transportation projects in favor of social welfare projects over the short term, for political reasons. "You might say," a wise Chilean remarked, "that economic development is postponed in favor of political development."

Programing is not only a way of deciding what to do; it is also getting and spending funds. Departmental participants in program budgeting soon see its strategic aspects. Consider the question of how many programs there should be: the more programs, the less flexibility in spending because national laws often prohibit transfers among programs. Unless programs have easily quantified goals, so that relating resources to them is simple, departments are better off with fewer, more general ones. If one aspect does not proceed as scheduled, they can then shift funds within the program category.

Similarly, legislatures may find that program budgeting cuts across their previous practices. Legislators in the Philippines continue to insist that they receive a line-item budget in addition to the program budget, lest the latter inhibit the usual "pork barrel" public works projects.

Honesto Mendoza (a Filipino whose name perhaps displays a certain bias) finds that "the most depressing reason for the present superficial adoption of performance budgeting in the government is the complete reversal of the position of Congress with respect to performance budgeting. It is incomprehensible why the very body that compelled the government to adopt performance budgeting would demand . . . line-item for appropriations. . . ." The answer is that each member of Congress can be sure his district is getting what has been agreed on only with a line-item budget to spell it out. This is useful also for bargaining purposes because he can trade refusal to vote for one such item in return for receiving another.

Program budgeting may be looked at more positively — valued not for what it is but for the opportunity any new system gives for making changes. A Peruvian organization, for instance, found itself with thirty different categories of salaries. An enormous amount of time was spent haggling over petty details concerning individual transfers. This organization used the program budget to trim the number of categories. The Peruvian official in charge admitted that "we might conceivably have reduced the number of categories to six even without the program budget. But you must realize that a lot of people profited unfairly from the confusion of the old system. When we introduced the brand-new program budget, it was a lot easier to skim away antiquated practices on the assumption that it didn't fit into the new system."

Introducing program budgeting has not been easy, and there have been many false starts and disappointments. Often program budgeting seemed to be introduced as a whim of the moment. At the first snag, it was abandoned or left in a state of suspended animation to await the next campaign for efficiency and progress. At a later date newly arrived personnel might again introduce program budgeting, but without building on the ruins of the old effort. The word from Argentina was that "in the central administration there has been a general discrediting of the program budget because it was never promoted in a vigorous or continual way, but reintroduced on several occasions without carrying it to completion." In Chile we were told, "there has not been any sustained, strongly taken decision to implement this system here, so the concept has been only superficially absorbed." Our Peruvian reporter says that "the program budget hasn't worked very well here, primarily because most people don't have any idea of what it is about." The one initiated in 1962 "was only a law, a series of sentences. No effort was made to teach the people how to use it."

Program budgeting also can lead to consequences directly contrary to those intended. A Peruvian agency found that PPBS meant increasing the number of financial categories (or *partidas*) from 25 to 300. These programs turned out to be much more expensive to run because each one insisted on having its own administration. "Each of the 300 programs arranged for its own transportation supplies, which meant a considerable duplication of transport." That agency then reduced its 300 categories of independent programs to 12 areal zones. But because each zone had a multitude of individual programs, the "tremendous task of cost control and cost determination," we were told, would not be completed for a very long time, especially because "we have good people, but they lack the technical capacity to fulfill this type of a budget."

Could we find no examples of reasonable success? A controversial example came from the health service in Chile whose participants were divided on whether a real program budget existed or, if it did, whether it was effective. Those who thought it extremely successful spoke of several conditions unlikely to be repeated elsewhere. To begin with, there was strong hierarchical control. "Each service unit is not an independent little factory, but is closely tied to the national organization. When an order is given here, it is executed in every one of the locales in the same manner." Moreover, "implementation of the program budget has the consistent support of executives in the agency. This political support comes from a stable directorate. It was not a situation in which top personnel changed continuously and didn't want to work even halfheartedly to get the system adopted." According to our informants the organization has excellent personnel and a high level of information. A great deal of time was spent explaining to the local people that they would get information useful to themselves, and in expanding their confidence in those who were implementing the system. So far as we can tell, the program budget consisted of the cost of various services. These were not related to any idea of how effective they were in meeting program objectives, but gave managers a notion of how much they were spending. The tendency for program budgeting to end up as performance budgeting (where efforts are made to improve the efficiency with which repetitive activities are performed) shows once again.

Successful initiation of any reform, especially one as complex as program budgeting, will depend largely on the attitudes of those who have to make the new system work. Unless the reform changes their objectives, their primary learning will be directed toward gaining the same ends from the new system as they did from the old. Strategies will be adapted (but not abandoned) and new ones devised to make the new system work according to the needs of participants. Where this happens, the net results may be little different from before. The aims of participants, in program budgeting, remain unchanged: departments want maximum resources, and the ministry of finance wishes controlled spending.

But program budgeting suffers from one disability that does not affect most reforms — one can churn out paper endlessly but no one really is able to do the necessary operations. It is frustrating to watch experts from the Philippines and America recommend practices to Ceylon and Nepal that have never worked in their own countries. When one asks the most sophisticated officials in these poor countries how program budgeting might help them they immediately disavow its central features. In their circumstances they never imagined quantifying the relative contribution of different policies to the nation's general objectives. Ceylon has trouble getting accounts of public corporations speeded up to being only three years late, and funds in Nepal often aren't released until a year or more after they have been approved. No, leading officials in these countries would be satisfied with much less. "Today," a minister of finance told us, "I get a single sheet from a department saying they have a project, it cost so much last year, and they want 20 percent more for the next year. If only I could get them to give me three pages explaining the merits of the projects, breaking down the costs in major parts, saying how much progress has been made and is expected, I would consider myself a fortunate man." So far as I know, program budgeting has yet to bring fortune to anyone, in this or any other respect.

18
Why PPBS Fails

Why does PPBS fail? There can be no single answer. The problem is that PPBS fails for so many different reasons that it is difficult to sort them out. As Herman van Gunsteren observes in the best analysis of the subject that has appeared to date,

What would PPB have to accomplish to prove itself successful as a system? Probably things like providing better decisions, generating new and/or better arguments and alternatives, providing information at the time and level where they are needed. As far as we have evidence, PPB scores negatively on those criteria. So PPB seems to have failed. But one may ask whether the criteria for evaluation are not too ambiguous. This may be so, but need not concern us here, because most believers in PPB take different routes to avoid being convinced by negative "evidence." In the first place they point out that we have insufficient causal knowledge to attribute a negative score on the success scale to PPB. The quality and outcomes of the decision-making process are not determined by PPB alone. Secondly, they say that PPB has not really been tried properly, so that speaking of success and failure does not make sense. It is too early to evaluate. Let us examine this second argument somewhat more closely.

In quite a few cases PPB is operational only in name. Budgeters often do not understand PPB, budgetary decisions are taken without paying attention to analytical studies, program structures are virtually ignored, etc. In those cases PPB cannot be evaluated, because it has not been properly tried. There are other situations where PPB is more than nominally operational, but where other conditions, necessary to give PPB a decent try, are not fulfilled. Lack of funds, incomplete information systems, lukewarm or hostile top leadership, inter- and intra-organizational hostilities and rivalries, etc. may all disturb or spoil the PPB experiment. When presented this way, the argument sounds convincing. It is really too early for evaluation, because PPB has not really been tried. . . . How can they maintain that PPB has not been tried, while admitting that many people are trying hard to make PPB a success?

Theoretically the "decent try" argument cannot be refuted. In practice, however, we have tried decently, given our limited powers of invention and the kind of world in which we have to operate. Since the "decent try" defenders of PPB maintain that there is nothing wrong with PPB, or at least that this has not been shown, what must be wrong in their eyes is the world in which we have to live and try and govern and make budgets. When a proposal does not work as intended, one has always a choice. One can say that something is wrong with the proposal, or that something is wrong with the world. Saying that something is wrong with the world is not a priori foolish. It may be relatively easy to make the world fit for our proposal. But in the case of PPB this is not so. It seems impossible, or very difficult and costly, to make the world fit for PPB. (In some situations it may be right or justifiable to maintain that something is wrong with the world, even when we cannot make the world fit for our proposal — e.g., love, peace, dignity. But this is not the case with PPB.) The world changes, we can influence this change, we can imagine worlds, there is not one "real" world out there . . . etc.: All this makes rejection of the present world (as it is seen by some people) always at least a defensible option. There is always a choice between the world and our proposal. Empirical evidence cannot logically decide this dilemma.[1]

My own view is that PPBS fails because it cannot meet a necessary condition for its success — the human knowledge required for performing the operations it stipulates. Although it may fail for many other reasons, such as lack of political support or trained personnel, it always fails for lack of knowledge, when and if it is allowed to get that far.

Let us begin by reviewing the knowledge deficit (or the cognitive lack) that PPBS showed when it first appeared in full flesh, and where it was practiced most intensively, in the United States federal government. Then I shall try to show that the cognitive explanation accounts for the data on worldwide failure of program budgeting as well.

WHY DEFENSE WAS A BAD MODEL

A quick way of seeing what went wrong with PPBS is to examine the conditions under which this approach was used in the Defense Department, from which it was exported throughout the federal government.[2] The immediate origins of PPBS are to be found in The RAND Corporation,[3] where, after the Second World War, a talented group of analysts devoted years of effort to un-

[1] Herman R. van Gunsteren in E. Shlifer, ed., *Proceedings: XX International Meeting The Institute of Management Services,* vol. 2 (Jerusalem: Academic Press), p. 683. By permission.
[2] This section comes from Aaron Wildavsky, "Rescuing Policy Analysis from PPBS," *Public Administration Review* XXIX:2 (March/April, 1969), pp. 189–202.
[3] See David Novick, *Origin and History of Program Budgeting* (Santa Monica, Calif.: RAND Corp., October 1966).

derstanding problems of defense policy. It took five years to come up with the first useful ideas. Thus the first requisite of program budgeting in Defense was a small group of talented people who had spent years developing insights into the special problems of defense strategy and logistics. The second requisite was a common terminology, an ad hoc collection of analytical approaches, and the beginnings of theoretical statements to guide policy analysis. When Secretary of Defense Robert McNamara came into office, he did not have to search for men of talent nor did he have to wait for a body of knowledge to be created. These requisites already existed in some degree. What was further necessary was his ability to understand and to use analytical studies. Thus the third requisite of program budgeting is top leadership that understands policy analysis and is determined to get it and use it.

The fourth requisite was the existence of planning and planners. Planning was well accepted at the various levels of the Defense Department with the variety of joint service plans, long-range requirement plans, logistical plans, and more. Military and civilians believed in planning, in coping with uncertainty, and in specifying some consequences of policy decisions. The problem as the originators of PPBS saw it was to introduce cost considerations into planning; they wanted to stop blue-sky planning and to integrate planning and budgeting. They wanted to use the program budget to bridge the gap between military planners, who cared about requirements but not about resources, and budget people, who were narrowly concerned with financial costs but not necessarily with effective policies.

That part of defense policy dealing with choices among alternative weapons systems was ideally suited for policy analysis. Since the cost of intercontinental missiles or other weapons systems ran into the billions of dollars, it was easy to justify spending millions on analysis. The potential effectiveness of weapons like intercontinental missiles could be contemplated so long as one was willing to accept large margins of error. It is not unusual for analysts to assume extreme cases of damage and vulnerability in a context in which the desire for reducing risk is very great. Hence a goal like assuring sufficient destructive power so that no enemy strike could prevent devastation of one's country may be fuzzy without being unusable. If one accepts a procedure of imagining that possible enemies were to throw three times as much megatonage as intelligence estimates suggest they have, he need not be overly troubled by doubts about the underlying theory. If one is willing to pay the cost of compensating against the worst, lack of knowledge will not matter so much. The point is not that this is an undesirable analytic procedure — quite the contrary — but that extreme cases were allowed to determine the outcomes.

Inertia

The introduction of new procedures that result in new policies is not easy. Inertia is always a problem. Members of the organization and its clientele groups have vested interests in the policies of the past. Efforts at persuasion must be huge and persistent. But there are conditions that facilitate change. One of these is a rising level of appropriations. If change means that things must be taken away from people in the organization without giving them anything in return, greater resistance may be expected. The ability to replace old rewards with larger new ones helps reduce resistance to change. The fact that defense appropriations were increasing at a fast rate made life much easier for Mr. McNamara. The expected objections of clientele groups, for example, were muted by the fact that defense contractors had lots of work, even if it was not exactly what they expected. Rapid organizational growth may also improve the possibilities for change. The sheer increase in organizational size means that many new people can be hired who are not tied to the old ways. And speedy promotion may help convince members that the recommended changes are desirable.

The deeper change goes into the bowels of the organization, the more difficult it is to achieve. The more change can be limited to central management, the greater the possibility for carrying it out. The changes introduced in the Defense Department did not, for the most part, require acceptance at the lower levels. Consider a proposed change in the organization of fighting units that would drastically reduce the traditional heavy support facilities for ground forces. Such a change is not easily manipulated from Washington. But the choice of one weapons system over another is much more amenable to central control. The problems for which program budgeting was most useful also turned out to be problems that could be dealt with largely at the top of the organization. The program budget group that McNamara established had to fight with generals in Washington but not with master sergeants in supply. Anyone who knows the Army knows what battle they would rather be engaged in fighting.

The ability of an organization to secure rapid change depends, of course, on the degree of its autonomy from the environment. I have argued elsewhere [4] that the President of the United States has much more control over America's foreign policy than over its domestic policy. In almost any area of domestic policy there is a well-entrenched structure of interests. In foreign and defense policy, excluding such essentially internal concerns as the National Guard, the territory within the American political system is not nearly so well defended; there are far fewer political fortifications, mines, and boobytraps.

Personnel

Experienced personnel may be a barrier to change. They know something about the consequences of what they are doing. They may have tried a variety

---

[4] Aaron Wildavsky, "The Two Presidencies," *Trans-action*, 4 (December 1966), 7–14.

of alternatives and can point to reasons why each one will not work. If I may recall my low-level Army experience (I entered as a private first class and was never once demoted), the usual reply to a question about the efficacy of present practice was, "Have you ever been in combat, son?" But the most dramatic changes introduced in the Pentagon had to do with questions of avoiding or limiting nuclear war, in which no one had a claim to experience and in which the basic purpose of analysis is to make certain that we do not have to learn from experience. If the system fails, the game is over. And since McNamara's men possessed a body of doctrines on defense policy, they had an enormous advantage over regular military who were for a long time unable to defend themselves properly in the new field.[5]

The new policy analysts did not accept the currency of military experience. In their view, naked judgment was not a satisfactory answer to why a policy should be adopted. The Army might know the fire-power of an infantry division, but fire-power was not "effectiveness." Competition among the services for appropriations, however, was favorable to PPBS. There was a defense budget that covered virtually all of the department's subject matter. There were defense missions in which trade-offs could be made between the services. Resources could actually be diverted if the analysis "proved" a particular service was right. Programs could easily be developed because of the facile identification of program with weapons systems and force units. Once the military learned the jargon, they were willing to play the game for an extra division or carrier. So long as dollar losses in one program were more than made up by gains in another, the pain of cost-effectiveness analysis was considerably eased.

BUT BACK ON THE HOME FRONT —

Favorable conditions for the limited use of program budgeting in the Department of Defense did not exist in most domestic agencies. There were no large groups of talented policy analysts expert in agency problems outside of the federal government. These nonexistent men could not, therefore, be made available to the agencies. (The time has passed when eighth-rate systems engineers in aerospace industries are expected to solve basic social problems overnight.) Most agencies had few planners and even less experience in planning. There is no body of knowledge waiting to be applied to policy areas such as welfare and crime. A basic reason for wanting more policy analysis is to help create knowledge where little now exists. There are only a few agencies in which top managers want systematic policy analysis and are able to understand quantitative studies. Goals are not easily specified for most domestic

---

[5] For further argument along these lines see my article, "The Practical Consequences of the Theoretical Study of Defense Policy." *Public Administration Review,* 25 (March 1965), 90–103.

agencies. Nor do they usually have handy equivalents for programs like expensive weapons systems. What Thomas Schelling has so pungently observed about the Department of State — it does not control a large part of the budget devoted to foreign policy — is true as well for the domestic departments and their lack of coverage.[6]

Except for a few individual programs — such as the proposals for income supplements, or assessing the desirability of a supersonic transport — the cost of most domestic policies does not rise into the billions of dollars. Congress and interested publics are not disposed to allow large margins of error. Instead of increasing, the availability of federal funds began declining soon after the introduction of program budgeting. A higher level of conflict was inevitable, especially since accepting proposed changes required the acquiescence of all sorts of people and institutions in the far-flung reaches of the bureaucracy. Social workers, city officials, police chiefs, welfare mothers, field officers, and many others were involved in the policies. Program budgeting on the domestic side takes place in a context in which there is both less autonomy from the environment and a great deal more first-hand experience by subordinates. On these grounds alone no one should have been surprised that program budgeting in the domestic agencies did not proceed as rapidly or with as much ostensible success as in the Defense Department.[7] But one is surprised to learn that with all its advantages (one could hardly imagine a more favorable environment) PPBS did not work in the Department of Defense.

So far so good. But not far or good enough. All we know is that there are any number of factors that might cause program budgeting to run into difficulty. By blaming its failures on everything, we come close to attributing them to nothing. Why does something always seem to go wrong? Why is there no set of conditions under which PPBS prospers? If one can imagine no plausible environment under which PPBS would succeed, that means its failures are built into human social life as we understand it.

---

[6] Thomas C. Schelling, "PPBS and Foreign Affairs," memorandum prepared at the request of the U.S. Senate Subcommittee on National Security and International Operations of the Committee on Government Operations, 90th Cong., 1st Sess., 1968.

[7] Dr. Alain Enthoven, who played a leading role in introducing systems analysis to the Defense Department, has observed that: "The major changes in strategy, the step-up in production of Minutemen and Polaris and the build-up in our non-nuclear forces including the increase in the Army, the tactical air forces, and the air lift . . . were being phased in at the same time that PPBS was being phased in. . . . We speeded up the Polaris and Minuteman programs because we believed that it was terribly important to have an invulnerable retaliatory force. We built up the Army Land Forces because we believed it was necessary to have more land forces for limited non-nuclear wars. We speeded up the development of anti-guerrilla forces or special forces because we believed that was necessary for counter-insurgency. Those things would have happened with or without PPBS. PPBS does not make the strategy." *Planning-Programming-Budgeting,* Hearings before the U.S. Senate Subcommittee on National Security and International Operations of the Committee on Government Operations, 90th Cong., 1st Sess., Part 2, September 27 and October 18, 1967, p. 141.

Though PPBS may fail on occasion because budgets are declining, legislatures are hostile, agencies lack sufficient authority, or whatever, it would not *always* fail unless it violated an essential condition. Underneath all the evident reasons for failure, then, lies a more basic cause, a guarantor, as it were, that if PPBS failed to fail for any number of reasons, it would always fail for THE REASON.

COGNITIVE FOUNDATIONS OF PROGRAM BUDGETING

I have previously argued that program budgeting would run up against severe political difficulties. Though most of these arguments have been conceded, I have been told that in a better world — without the vulgar intrusion of political factors such as the consent of the governed — PPBS would perform wonders as advertised. Now it is clear that for the narrow purpose of predicting why program budgeting would not work I did not have to mention political problems at all. It would have been enough to say that PPBS presented insuperable difficulties of calculation. All the obstacles previously mentioned, such as lack of talent, theory, and data, may be summed up in a single statement: *no one knows how to do program budgeting.* Another way of putting it would be to say that many know what program budgeting should be like in general, but no one knows what it should be in particular.

Program budgeting cannot be stated in operational terms. No one can agree about what the words mean, let alone show another person what to do. The reason for the difficulty is that telling an agency to adopt program budgeting means telling it to find better policies and there is no formula for doing that. One can (and should) talk about measuring effectiveness, estimating costs, and comparing alternatives — but, what a far cry from being able to take the creative leap to making a better policy.

On the basis of many talks with would-be practitioners of program budgeting at the federal level, I think I can describe the usual pattern of events. Instructions come down from the Office of Management and Budget: You must have a program budget. Agency personnel hit the panic button. They just do not know how to do what they have been asked to do. They turn, if they can, to the pitifully small band of refugees from the Pentagon who have come to light the way. But these defense intellectuals do not know much about the policy area in which they are working. That would take time. Yet something must quickly come out of all this. So they produce a vast amount of inchoate information characterized by premature quantification of irrelevant items. Its very bulk staggers the agency head and examiners in the OMB, none of whom can comprehend it. It is useless to the Director of the Budget in making his decisions. In an effort to be helpful, the program analysis unit at the OMB says something like, "Nice try, fellows; we appreciate all that effort. But you have not quite got the idea of program budgeting yet. Remember, you must clarify goals, define objectives, relate these to quantitative indicators, project costs into the future. Please send a new submission based on this understanding."

Another furious effort takes place. If they do it in Defense — it must be possible. Incredible amounts of overtime are put in. Ultimately, under severe time pressure, the mountain of data grows even higher. No one will be able to say that agency personnel did not try hard. The new presentation makes a little more sense to some people, a little less to others. But as a presentation of agency policies it just does not hang together. More encouraging words come from the OMB, along with another sermon about specifying alternative ways of meeting agency objectives — though not, of course, taking the old objectives for granted. By this time agency personnel are desperate. "We would love to do it," they say, "but we cannot figure out the right way. You experts in the OMB should show us how to do it." Silence. The word from on high is that the OMB does not interfere with agency operations; it is the agency's task to set up its own budget. After a while, cynicism reigns supreme.

The orders to expand PPBS did not say, "Let us do more and better policy analysis than we have in the past." What it said was, "Let us make believe we can do policy analysis on everything." Instead of focusing attention on areas of policy amenable to study, the PPBS apparatus demands information on *all* agency policies.

The fixation on program structure is the most pernicious aspect of PPBS. Once PPBS is adopted, it becomes necessary to have a program structure that provides a complete list of organization objectives and supplies information on the attainment of each one. In the absence of analytic studies for all or even a large part of an agency's operations, the structure turns out to be a sham that piles up meaningless data under vague categories. It suggests comparisons among categories for which there is no factual or analytical basis. Examination of a department's program structure convinces everyone acquainted with it that policy analysis is just another bad way of masquerading behind old confusions.

Even if the agency head does understand a data-reduction-summarization of the program budget, he cannot use the structure to make decisions, because it is too hard to adjust the elaborate apparatus. Although the system dredges up information under numerous headings, the materials say next to nothing about the effect of one program on another. There are data but no causal analysis. Hence the agency head is at once oversupplied with masses of numbers, undersupplied with propositions about the effect of any action he might undertake. The analyst cannot tell (because no one knows) what the marginal change he is considering would mean for the rest of his operation. At the agency level incremental changes are made in terms of the old budget categories. Since the program structure is meant to be part of the budget, however, it must be seen as a statement of current policy and it necessarily emerges as a product of organizational compromise. The program structure, therefore, fails to embody a focus on central policy concerns. More likely, it is a haphazard arrangement reflecting the desire to manipulate external support and to pursue internal power aspirations. Being neither program nor budget, program structure is useless; it is the Potemkin Village of modern administration.

Generating bits of random data for the program structures takes valuable time away from more constructive concerns; PPBS harms policy analysis. The whole point of policy analysis is to show that what had been done intuitively in the past may be done better through sustained application of intelligence. Adopting meaningless program structures, and perverting them into slogans for supporting existing policies does not — to say the least — advance the cause of policy analysis.

What, then, can PPBS do, and, what can it not do? One could hardly have a better witness on this subject than William Gorham, formerly Assistant Secretary (Program Coordination), Department of Health, Education, and Welfare, and now head of the Urban Institute — widely acknowledged to have been an outstanding practitioner of program budgeting.

At the highest level of generality, it is clear that PPBS cannot help in making choices between vast national goals such as health and defense, nor is PPBS useful in making trade-offs between more closely related areas of policy in such fields as health, education, and welfare. In his testimony before the Joint Economic Committee, Gorham put the matter bluntly:

> Let me hasten to point out that we have not attempted any grandiose cost-benefit analysis designed to reveal whether the total benefits from an additional million dollars spent on health programs would be higher or lower than that from an additional million spent on education or welfare. If I was ever naive enough to think this sort of analysis possible, I no longer am. The benefits of health, education, and welfare programs are diverse and often intangible. They affect different age groups and different regions of the population over different periods of time. No amount of analysis is going to tell us whether the Nation benefits more from sending a slum child to pre-school, providing medical care to an old man or enabling a disabled housewife to resume her normal activities. The "grand decisions" — how much health, how much education, how much welfare, and which groups in the population shall benefit — are questions of value judgments and politics. The analyst cannot make much contribution to their resolution.[8]

It turns out that it is very hard to get consensus on abstract goals within a single area of policy. As a result, analysts try to find ones that are more widely acceptable. Gorham speaks with the voice of experience when he says:

> Let me give you an example. Education. What we want our kids to be as a result of going to school is the level of objective which is the proper and

[8] *The Planning-Programming-Budgeting System: Progress and Potentials,* Hearings before the U.S. Congress Joint Subcommittee on Economy in Government of the Joint Economic Committee, 90th Cong., 1st Sess., September 1967, p. 5.

the broadest one. But we want our children to be different sorts of people. We want them to be capable of different sorts of things. We have, in other words, a plurality of opinions about what we want our schools to turn out. So you drop down a level and you talk about objectives in terms of educational attainment — years of school completed and certain objective measures of quality. Here you move in education from sort of fuzzy objectives, but very important, about what it is that you want the schools to be doing, to the more concrete, less controversial, more easily to get agreed upon objectives having to do with such things as educational attainment, percentage of children going to college, etc.

I think the same thing is true in health and in social services, that at the very highest level objective, where in theory you would really like to say something, the difficulty of getting and finding a national consensus is so great that you drop down to something which is more easily and readily accepted as objectives.[9]

What actually can be done, according to Gorham, is to make analyses of narrowly defined areas of policy. "The less grand decisions — those among alternative programs with the same or similar objectives within health — can be substantially illuminated by good analysis. It is this type of analysis which we have undertaken at the Department of Health, Education, and Welfare." [10] As examples Gorham cites disease control programs and improvements in the health of children. If this type of project analysis is what can be done under PPBS, a serious question is raised: Why go through all the rigamarole just for a few discrete studies of important problems?

A five-year budget conceived in the hodge-podge terms of the program structure serves no purpose.[11] Since actual budget decisions are made in terms of the old categories anyway, and since policy analysis may take place outside

---

[9] Ibid., pp. 80–81. One might think that a way out of the dilemma could be had by adopting a number of goals for an area of policy. When Committee Chairman William Proxmire suggested that more goals should be specified, Gorham replied, "I would like to be the one to give the first goal. The first one in is always in the best shape. The more goals you have, essentially the less useful any one is, because the conflict among them becomes so sharp" (p. 83).

[10] Ibid., p. 6.

[11] Robert N. Anthony, *Planning and Control Systems: A Framework for Analysis* (Boston: Division of Research, Graduate School of Business Administration, Harvard University, 1965), p. 16. Anthony supplies a useful comparison from private firms that makes a similar point: "An increasing number of businesses make profit and balance sheet projections for several years ahead, a process which has come to be known by the name 'long-range planning.'. . . A five-year plan usually is a projection of the costs and revenues that are anticipated under policies and programs *already approved,* rather than a device for consideration of, and decision on, new policies and programs. The five-year plan reflects strategic decisions already taken; it is not the essence of the process of making new decisions. . . . In some companies, the so-called five-year plan is nothing more than a mechanical extrapolation of current data, with no reflection of management decisions and judgment; such an exercise is virtually worthless" (pp. 57–58).

of the program structure, it is futile to institutionalize empty labels. If a policy analysis has been completed, there is no reason why it cannot be submitted as part of the justification of estimates to the OMB and to Congress. For the few program memoranda which an agency might submit, changes could be detailed in terms of traditional budget categories. Problems of program structure would be turned over to the agency's policy analysts who could experiment with different ways of lending intellectual coherence to the agency's programs without altering the old budget categories. Stability of categories in the traditional budget has real value for control,[12] whereas embodiment of contradictions in the program structure violates its essential purpose.

PPBS discredits policy analysis. To collect vast amounts of random data is hardly a serious way to analyze public policy. The obvious conclusion is for the shotgun marriage between policy analysis and budgeting to be annulled. Attempts to describe the total agency program in program memoranda should be abandoned. As most agency people now see, it is hard enough to do a good job of policy analysis without also having to meet arbitrary and fixed deadlines imposed by the budget process. There is no way to tell if an analysis will be successful. Therefore, there is no point in insisting that half-baked analyses be submitted every year because of a misguided desire to include the entire agency program. The OMB itself recognized the difficulty by requiring agencies to present extensive memoranda only when major policy issues have been identified. It is easier and more honest just to take the program structure out of the budget. And that is what happened.

But the "Death in the Bureaucracy," as Allen Schick referred to the demise of program budgeting in the federal government of the United States,[13] does not signify the end of the species, apparently, but merely the beginning. Although there are no official mortality statistics on PPBS, there have evidently been sufficient new births to keep it going for some time. Indeed, enough experience has been accumulated to permit something of a worldwide appraisal of PPBS in operation.

CONCLUSION

PPBS has failed everywhere and at all times. Nowhere has PPBS (1) been established and (2) influenced governmental decisions (3) according to its own principles. The program structures do not make sense to anyone. They

---

[12] An excellent discussion of different purposes of budgeting and stages of budgetary development is found in Allen Schick, "The Road to PPB: The Stages of Budget Reform," *Public Administration Review*, 26 (December 1966), 243–258.

[13] Allen Schick, "A Death in the Bureaucracy: The Demise of Federal PPB," *Public Administration Review*, 33 (March/April 1973), 146–146.

are not, in fact, used to make decisions of any importance. Such products of PPBS as do exist are not noticeably superior in analytic quality or social desirability to whatever was done before. These are hard words. But I believe that a theoretical appraisal of the assumptions underlying program budgeting will bear them out.

To understand how program budgeting fails everywhere and always, try to imagine what would have to be done to make success possible. Most discussion has been confined to "sufficient" conditions. The critical assumption has been that PPBS is easy to set up but difficult to practice. Presumably the problems lay in vested interests, recalcitrant politicians, and hidebound bureaucrats. It has been readily acknowledged, in addition, that implementation of PPBS has been hampered by lack of trained manpower, absence of essential data, and inadequacies in the state of the art. The point is that all these putative defects can be remedied. Politicians and bureaucrats can be got around or replaced by more receptive types. Training can be stepped up, better data can be collected, and knowledge of analysis undoubtedly will be improved. If these were the basic difficulties, it would be hard to explain why PPBS has no successes whatsoever to its credit. For surely somewhere, sometime, the right conditions for PPBS to prosper should have existed. Maybe they should have, but they don't. Why not? To answer that question we have to be prepared to accept the possibility that PPBS lacks *necessary* as well as *sufficient* conditions, that its faults are not merely those of program implementation but also of policy design — that, in a word, its defects are defects of principle, not of execution. PPBS does not work because it cannot work. Failure is built into its very nature because it demands abilities to perform cognitive operations which are beyond present human (or machine) capacities.

Program budgeting is like the simultaneous equation of governmental intervention in society. If one can state objectives precisely, find quantitative measures for them, specify alternative ways of achieving them by different inputs of resources, and rank them according to desirability, one has solved the social problems for the period. One need only bring the program budget up to date each year. Is it surprising that program budgeting does not perform this sort of miracle? Even a modified version — in which all activities are placed in programs that contribute to common objectives, but in which objectives are not ranked in order or priority — is far beyond anyone's capacity.

It is sometimes said (and more often implied) that if public officials wanted to be rational they would want to adopt program budgeting so as to relate expenditures to objectives. Thus if the world were better than it is, so that men were better than they are, program budgeting could be adopted and implemented. Is it a defect to be too good for this world? Yes, if earthly good works rather than eternal martyrdom is the goal. All mortal men live in a world made by others. To transform it (if that is their desire) they must take it from where it is with what they have, not imagine it to be a different world and they a different breed of men. Yet many defenses of PPBS, as for planning earlier, end up alleging, in effect, that the world is not good enough for PPBS. The paradox is that the world PPBS is supposed to change must first undergo that change before it can accommodate PPBS.

There is no need to blink at the inexorable conclusion: PPBS is not an embodiment of rationality; it is irrational. If the goal is to alter the allocation of resources in a more productive way, or to generate better analyses than those used, PPBS does not (because it cannot) produce these results. PPBS is not cost-effective. It produces costly rationales for inevitable failures. Put another way, PPBS sacrifices the rationality of ends to the rationality of means — seemingly rational procedures which produce irrational results.

My policy recommendations on PPBS are direct and straightforward: if you are more interested in *being* than in *appearing* rational, don't do it! Is there, then, no budgetary reform of our time that works and that can, therefore, teach us something about how to make desirable changes? Yes, there is, and its name is PESC.

It is difficult to learn entirely from failure. Normally one proceeds by trying to compare causes for success here, with failure there. This cannot be done with program budgeting, which fails everywhere. To find a major reform we must leave program budgeting in America and turn to expenditure control in Britain.

19

PESC: The Cost of Control

Most reforms fail; by now this is no news; the governmental landscape is littered with their debris. Fortunately, we can learn much from one major reform of modern times in the machinery of resource allocation, the Public Expenditure Survey Committee (PESC). Nowhere else in the world, to our knowledge, has the annual budget been replaced with an effective mechanism to control spending several years into the future. What we can learn from Great Britain's success in reform depends on understanding how and why PESC actually works.

This interdepartmental group, composed of department finance officers and Treasury officials (chaired by a Treasury deputy secretary), reports on the projection of public expenditures. The yearly PESC report seeks to show the future cost of existing government policies if these policies remain unchanged over the next five years. Its stated aim is to provide a clearer perspective so that political administrators can weigh (1) the total spending implications of present policies against the financial resources likely to be available and (2) different expenditures against each other.

The annual PESC cycle will come into sharper focus if we outline the steps involved and the approximate times of the year when each takes place. Sometime in November or December the Treasury sends the departments a statement about the economic assumptions on which to operate in preparing their spending forecasts. These operating assumptions typically will include the likely growth of productive potential, consumer expenditure, industrial production, and fixed investment. By the end of February, spending departments submit preliminary returns to the Treasury, laying out their five-year expenditure projections for existing policies. The Treasury makes a computer tabulation and sends the results to its relevant spending divisions, which figures

Most of this chapter is a revised version of material appearing in Hugh Heclo and Aaron Wildavsky, *The Private Government of Public Money: Community and Policy Inside British Political Administration* (London: Macmillan; and Berkeley: University of California Press, 1974). By permission.

Treasury divisions scrutinize and discuss with spending departments from March until May, in order to reach some agreement on statistical assumptions, on what existing policies are, and on their probable future cost. The inter-departmental PESC committee meets in May to write a report projecting the cost of present policies and specifying remaining areas of disagreement. This preliminary report then goes to the Chancellor of the Exchequer in June with copies to all departments. At this time the chancellor and top Treasury officials juxtapose the PESC report with the assessment of economic prospects and decide whether there is, in their view, room for this total of public spending within the limits of economic resources likely to be available. In June the cabinet hears what the prospects are, whether cuts are necessary, or whether there actually will be enough room for greater expenditure; usually cuts are necessary. Between June and November the cabinet makes its decisions which later appear publicly in the annual White Paper on Public Expenditure during November/December.

It is important to recognize that the yearly PESC report and the government White Paper on PESC are not the same thing: the former is the raw material for cabinet decision, the latter is the resulting product. The PESC report is a midyear costing of existing policy before ministers act. As such it is highly secret and never published, for to do so would bare the innermost compromises through which a government reconciles conflicting pressures. The PESC report is compiled by the General Expenditure Division in the Treasury. It shows: level of current expenditure; assumptions on which the projections are based; proposed expenditures over the five-year period; explanations by the departments of these figures; and percentage increases, by department. A Treasury supplement also will include a list of possible alternative reductions to keep spending at existing levels. Basically the report is a Treasury document, with an overall appraisal section written by the General Expenditure Division, edited commentaries on the figures written through the usual supply division/department negotiation, and footnotes containing any departmental objections.

The purpose of PESC is not to agree on any particular expenditure level or allocation of resources among the departments. Rather, it is supposed to produce agreement among officials on present and future costing of existing policies. The PESC interdepartmental committee therefore concentrates its efforts on the methodology of projection and presentation. The only serious arguments take place over issues in which the finance officers have a common interest apart from that of the Treasury. Thus there may be some discussion of the size of the contingency reserve to be included in the Public Expenditure Survey and on conditions for access to the sum of money involved. No serious consideration of the relative merits of departmental arguments and no bargaining take place there.

Usually all is harmonious in the Public Expenditure Survey Committee precisely because substantial disagreements are reserved for direct dealings between department and Treasury. Officials try hard to reach agreement because ministers depend on them to ascertain the overt meaning of the figures involved and what goes into them. If ministers had to debate these abstruse points, officials would be thought to be doing a poor job. Agreement on the costing of a program also is possible because it does not in any way imply that Treasury and departments agree on its desirability or relative priority.

No nation in the world can match the sophistication or thoroughness found in the British process of expenditure projection. In their offhand way, Treasury officials are more than a little proud of it. But what does it mean in practice? PESC can best be understood by examining its genesis and growth.

GENESIS, BUT NOT EXODUS

A wise man said that every constitution is written against the last usurper. The original appearance of PESC and its subsequent modifications may be traced directly to the unsatisfactory experience of Treasury officials in trying to control spending in the 1950s. To a lesser degree these officials were joined in their views by ministers who felt that the expenditure system was out of control.

After World War II the weight of the Treasury shifted into managing the national economy. The new concerns did not stress control of spending but, rather, full employment and stabilizing the trade cycle and balance of payments. Keynesian doctrine had taken hold. Under that system, however, there was no way to integrate expenditure control and macroeconomic management. For spending, the old pre-Keynesian view had been very easy to work with: you balanced the budget. If you wanted to spend more, you added 6d to the income tax. Postwar acceptance of Keynesian economics meant that expenditures were not immediately to be measured against revenues but, later, against employment. The old standards were gone and there were no ceilings to put in their place. During the 1950s, Treasury officials gradually came to see that the absence of a self-evident link between outflow and income meant that some new measure was necessary to bring expenditures into line with economic resources.

The 1950s were punctuated by economy drives, whenever financial conditions worsened. Lacking better techniques, governments periodically resorted to flat percent rate cuts, supposedly a method for sharing misery equally. But few programs had the short-term flexibility to accommodate such cuts without some distortion. Spending would build up rapidly and then have to be reduced by ham-handed methods such as percentage reductions in civil service staffs or halting construction work already under way. Departmental work was thrown out of gear and the cost of beginning again or laying off people often turned out to be greater than the so-called savings. And even then cuts did not become effective for two or three years.

A former Chancellor of the Exchequer sums up the reasons for growing disenchantment with the existing state of affairs:

The real impetus behind trying to get a longer-term control lay in the fact that several times during the 1950s and 1960s the Treasury was trapped and had to learn by bitter experience about the tendency of costs to rise in future years. The old idea was that with a new piece of legislation the Treasury had costed it when it gave the cost of the proposal in the remaining part of the existing year and added that into its cost for one full year. Increasingly in the 1950s we learned that the cost in the second or full year may not be at all related to this supposed uniform standard of "full year cost." In new weapons for defense you tended to find the cost underestimation factor something like five times what you had approved in the first instance. This was true of a great many other areas, particularly in education and in national insurance. In my day, trying to exercise control from the Treasury was, typically, trying to control things too late. We could only say you must go slower with what you are doing. Sometimes, because of this lag in the system, the only resort you had was to flat rate cuts, and this occurred both under myself, my predecessor, and my successor at the Exchequer.

Drawing together the threads of experience in the 1950s, top Treasury officials began to look for a spending system to reduce such major difficulties. Since cuts could not be made effective in a single year it would be necessary to project spending over several years. The pioneering work was done in Defense, where the need for cost projections running from five to ten years had first become obvious, and in certain "rolling" programs in roads and nationalized industries. Since the chancellor was being cut up in Cabinet, piece by piece, spending program by spending program, the expenditure system had to work by first considering the total and then making individual proposals compete for a share of it. "The purpose of PESC," as a Treasury official observed, "was to avoid this system of being nibbled to death." Thus indictments against the past and present suggested the shape of future reform: continuous, multi-year projections within a restricted total would let the government relate spending rates both to the capacity of the economy and to the willingness of political leaders to trade off one expenditure item against another. The stage was set for PESC.

The first task was to sway opinion in the Treasury itself. A participant in this campaign recalled that:

> Internally, the Treasury was constipated by the annual estimates approach and tied to the yearly cycle of Parliamentary business. It was a hard task convincing the Treasury, and I did it really by marshalling the arguments which had led me to the idea — namely, if you're going to try to control anything, you can't do it by looking at annual estimates. 98.5 percent of next year's money is already committed. The second argument was, of course, that next year's cost was no sure gauge of what the total real cost would be in the end. A third argument was that if people were anxious to reduce expenditure, then this was the way, not only to control, but to cut.

A few men with an idea can more than match a large number of men who are not sure where they have been and cannot tell you where they are going.

Concerned that an outside study committee might prove embarrassing, the Conservative Government in the summer of 1959 set up an internal Committee on the Control of Public Expenditure chaired by Lord Plowden. Three members from outside government sat with Plowden and signed the report in 1961, but they had few specific suggestions about what to do. Senior Treasury officials sat as "assessors" with the Plowden Committee, and were really the men who imported most of the key ideas — writing the substance of the report in virtually one weekend. In this way the doctrine of Treasury Deputy (now Sir) Richard Clarke — "that decisions involving substantial future expenditure should always be taken in the light of public expenditure as a whole, over a period of years, and in relation to the prospective resources" — was embedded in the core paragraph (7) of the final report.

No one, not even those in charge of making the new procedure work, could foresee precisely how it would turn out. For several years they improvised, sometimes buffeted by events, other times seizing on an unexpected opportunity. Life still had a few surprises in store for everybody.

Annual PESC exercises began under a Conservative Government in 1961. The first published version, showing expenditures for 1963–1964 and projections for 1967–1968, appeared in 1963. By that time, both parties were beginning to talk about how high rates of economic growth would make life easier all around. The Labor Party, which came into office in 1964, brought with it also a particular interest in planning, increased welfare spending, and the idea for a new, pro-growth organization separate from the Treasury — a Department of Economic Affairs (DEA).

Throughout the world, institutions that worry about running out of money and institutions that worry about increasing investment to expand the economic growth rate are found within the same governments. The one prophesies doom if expenditures exceed the total, and the other if they do not rise above it. Each one typically considers itself the representative of wisdom, the other hopelessly misguided. Because everything done by the one interferes with the other, they rarely can work out a satisfactory division of labor. The idea in Britain was that the Treasury presumably dealt with short-term affairs and the DEA with long-term planning. Yet soon it appeared that one was never out of the short term: the important was invariably compromised by the urgent. Decisions taken immediately had long-term implications, and any decision predicated on longer-term considerations had to work with the raw materials of the present. The DEA wanted to be in on the present, and the Treasury wanted to get in on the future.

For our purposes the important fact is that the Treasury became agitated by DEA targets for annual growth in Gross National Product. The original PESC exercises assumed an economic growth rate of 4 percent or more per annum, which did not materialize. The DEA might be expressing only its optimism about the future, but once a growth rate was postulated (first the 4 percent target of the National Economic Development Council in 1963 and then the DEA's 4.75 percent), the Treasury found it difficult to control public spending. What was the point? Where was the need? Everyone argued that economic growth — alchemists' gold — could accommodate their spending plans and dissolve the need for the hard choices of the past.

It was not to be so. Not only did the optimistic growth rates go unmet, but the Labor Government allowed expenditure to rise even higher than the missed economic target rate. As Figure 19.1 shows, by 1968 public spending was absorbing more of the national output than had been true during the Korean War, and committing nearly all of the growth in Gross Domestic Product. Treasury officials now are emphatic that the 1964 and 1965 PESC exercises "were vitiated by exaggerated economic targets." Yet the Treasury could not say publicly that the target was unlikely to be met: insisting on a lesser target would make it appear to be selling the country short. It would distort the Treasury position to suggest that it wanted a more accurate rate of growth in the National Plan; the Treasury saw little virtue in the entire exercise.

Figure 19.1. RATIO OF PUBLIC EXPENDITURE TO GROSS DOMESTIC PRODUCT, 1952–1971

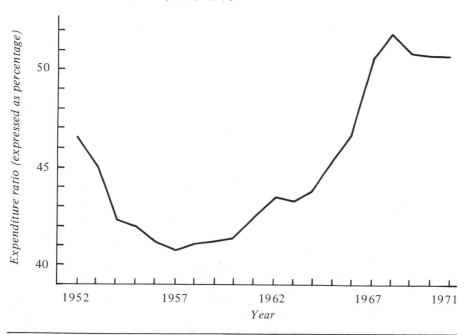

Source: Sir Richard Clarke, "Parliament and Public Expenditure," *The Political Quarterly* 44 (April–June, 1973) p. 139.

The Labor Government's original thesis, on coming into office in 1964, had been that the economy could outgrow its problems; but by 1966 it was clear that the economy was not growing fast enough. The Government was hard pressed to meet its large political commitments for social programs and PESC operations became more onerous than anyone cares to remember. Balance-of-payments crises recurred in 1966–1967 and signaled a series of ad hoc expenditure cuts completely outside the PESC timetable. PESC seemed to have failed. It had concentrated, as Plowden had suggested, on spending in the current year and on a projection five years hence, disregarding the out-turns in between. The Treasury catch-phrase for this had been "forward planning." Well before the final climax of devaluation and its vicious expenditure cuts at the end of 1967, Treasury officials had realized that "proposals from certain quarters were making a monkey out of the fifth-year target."

The inability of PESC to work adequately during the emergencies of 1966 and 1967 might have seemed enough to kill it off. Instead, these unsatisfactory experiences were interpreted to mean that PESC was essential, only more so. The financial control procedure was not good because it could not be used when it was needed most. Labor spending ministers, who had seen their gossamer plans of 1965–1966 torn to tatters when paper targets crumbled, were receptive to the idea. The Government needed more disciplines, not less. It needed not only to set total expenditure targets but also to get beneath and behind the totals to make sure that the target was hit and that, when necessary, intelligent reductions could be made. No one sat down in isolation to think up bright ideas for improving PESC. The changes flowed from practical problems of government.

For PESC to work, the projections had to be made complete. Instead of an estimate for only the first and fifth years of a program, now costs were also to be projected for the intervening second, third, and fourth years. The great symbolic phrase inside the Treasury (given official blessing in the White Paper of January 1968) became "planning the path as well as the whole." It was not a matter of recasting figures in order to make the growth rate of spending lower by the fifth year, but rather of laying down a publicly proclaimed path, year by year, for each department. Treasury officials in charge of PESC believe that to work along an expenditure path is a superior method of exercising control than to set a distant goal in the fifth year toward which to work; only if intervening years' figures are controlled can there be any meaning to the fifth-year projection. This doctrine is so well established that Treasury officials now can be found engaged in a month-by-month monitoring of each department's alignment with the proposed spending path.

Unveiled also in 1968 was the doctrine of the "focal year." Since years one and two were heavily committed, while four and five were vague, year three was chosen as the key focus for decisions. Decisions on spending would be made fairly firm for year three but only provisionally for years four and five.

Around 1970, however, the focal-year doctrine was overturned as too simple-minded. Departments were attaching unrealistic hopes to years four and five and necessarily vitiating the meaning of the total five-year target. Moreover, degrees of flexibility were found to vary with the expenditure program in question. For some, with especially large capital elements, years four and five may be largely committed; other programs may have no need to commit year three. The denouement is a current conception of PESC more in line with the way spending decisions actually are taken. The figures become more provisional the farther ahead one looks. But years four and five, although provisional, are approved and are important.

The election of a new government dedicated to further spending or suspicious of new-fangled techniques would have created havoc for PESC. An unwillingness to set ceilings or capriciously to raise them to vastly higher levels would have nullified the control aspects and reduced PESC to a worthless paper exercise. A government hostile to PESC could have abolished it. As luck (or misfortune, depending on one's preferences) would have it, the advent of the Conservative Government in 1970 proved a boon to PESC's supporters. The Government was dedicated, at least temporarily, to lowering taxes and reducing expenditures. The PESC procedure fitted well into a frame of thought determined to bring spending under control.

One important change since 1968 has been the decision to publish PESC expenditure projections in considerable detail. The information which Treasury ministers and senior officials give out springs rarely from an unadulterated desire to be informative. The publication of PESC White Papers was designed to lend more realism to the spending projections; a public document should commit the Government to what it said. The Treasury would have an anchor to restrain the tendency of spending ministers to set the figures adrift.

Despite the increasing publicity, PESC is not wholly understood in political circles. Socialists fear they suffered under it, though few can specify how or why. Some Conservative ministers have to be hand-carried through the procedure — not once, but every time it is brought up. No matter how often Treasury officials appear before the House Select Committees, patiently explaining the ABCs of PESC, they never seem quite able to overcome the puzzlement of members. Is it possible that the Treasury guards not only the purse but also the secret of understanding PESC? Or is PESC hard to fathom because it is not one, but many different things that vary with the needs and perspectives of the user?

PESC appears deceptively simple. You start from where you are and ask what it would cost to continue your present activities in the next five years. It would be easy to assume that the survey is a straightforward technical operation which produces figures on program costs within an allowable margin of error. But this is not so.

Let us go back to the simplest definition of PESC: a cost projection of existing policies. It turns out that there is often disagreement about what each element — cost, projection, and existing policy — actually means. These issues, argued out between department finance officers, Treasury principals, and assistant secretaries, of course are technical matters — or are they? Disagreements arise partly because of unresolved technical problems but also because each participant has a stake in securing a favorable outcome. The Treasury naturally projects low, whereas departments invariably project high. A large part of the PESC process involves bargaining to arrive at an agreed figure. By discussing "policy," "cost," and "projection" we can begin to understand the shadowland between technical operations and the politics of projection.

Trial by Technique

What is existing policy? Surely everyone knows. The fact is that there are continual battles in the bowels of the bureaucracy on this issue. Is existing policy that which is agreed upon, or that which is done despite the fact that no one did agree? Is the Treasury's understanding of past agreements the same as that of the department? Does agreement mean a formal concordat, or traditional acquiescence? When new circumstances arise, who shall interpret vague agreements made before any of the disputing officials were on the scene? When a policy has "existence" is a subject for profound thought; if decisions did not have to be made it could appropriately be left to metaphysical philosophers and semanticists.

In the first place there may be no present policy under which expenditures can be projected. Ministers may be undecided, contradictory, or vague. Similarly, what is casually called existing policy may be in flux. Its general outlines may be in a continual state of modification, so that it looks quite different to different viewers, depending on who does the looking. Take political promises: Suppose that a government had a target of building so many thousand houses. This target might not be met because the government did not know how to achieve it, or the private sector did not come through, or because the government later decided to use its resources elsewhere. The department can argue that it should be able to spend the housing money elsewhere, while the Treasury will say that a change in policy has occurred. In one sense "existing policy" is not to build the houses, but in another sense building them evidently is the latent policy, even if events temporarily have prevented it from happening.

It is hard also to distinguish "natural" increases from policy changes. Does existing policy mean only what was done last year, or did it always anticipate a gradual increase in the quality of the services or facilities provided? The PESC projection can include both maintenance and improvement of existing standards (such as pupil-teacher or doctor-patient ratios, space per classroom, or hospital beds).

The department will insist that existing policy covers the standards and can usually prevent their deterioration. But departments will insist also that an improvement factor is built into current policy. It was assumed, the department will argue, that standards would alter with the general expectation of the citizenry for a higher level of performance. The Treasury may say that an improvement factor was not agreed on or has lapsed and that the proper level of projection is whatever the department bought in the first year.

Or again, suppose that for some reason a program which cost so many million pounds a year has suddenly shot up to twice that amount. The Treasury will claim the increased cost came from special circumstances and that "existing policy" dictates that the program return to its original level. The department will argue that the proper base for projecting its future expenditures should be the higher total or at least some amount between the lower and higher figures. The end result is less likely to be agreement on some supposedly "correct" figure than a deal on an in-between amount with which both parties believe they can live.

One can see that the precise detail of existing policy is unclear. But surely its general outlines and configuration are understood and agreed on. Is this not another example of pettifogging bureaucracy? Not at all. In spending, one man's margin is another man's profit, and what may seem unworthy of argument can yield the little extras that make life worth living. Policies are bargained out precisely on these margins. A few percent on hundreds of millions of pounds may make the difference between sufficiency and stringency, contentment and dissatisfaction, elbow room and the straitjacket.

A strength of the PESC exercise is that it goes on year after year. Eventually most initial disagreements are negotiated, and differences between the Treasury and departments narrowed down to more manageable proportions. To be sure, new disagreements surface continually but they are more readily resolved in the context of a pattern of past settlements. A record of understandings about the meaning of existing policy is built up over the years. For the departments, this record protects them against cuts in their accustomed income. The Treasury also can be more confident about the foundations of the five-year projections on which it has staked so much. For each participant, uncertainty is reduced and security is increased.

A second large area of technical-political argument is the price basis for costing, whatever definition of existing policy is agreed on. The prevailing view that spending forecasts should be based on constant pounds has considerable intuitive and political appeal. How can any comparisons be made unless the objects compared — expenditures — are placed on the same basis? But PESC is also a five-year projection rolling forward each year; constant prices of one year are in no way directly comparable with the constant prices used next year. Comparing current prices would not take account of price changes and could exaggerate the rate of "real" increase. But a succession of yearly projections — each on its own particular constant price basis, with no clear method of translation between the current and previous years — means that it is very hard to monitor and verify past projections.[1]

In the ongoing debate with departments, there is a vast field for squabbling about "true" costs and price changes. Each program has its own distinctive set of component prices. To compare a change between only two years, moreover, can involve looking at prices at the beginning of year one's projection, or its outturn, at the time of year two's projection, or at any time in between, and in any combination thereof. Every department will make a strong case for a generous updating and recosting of its existing policy and deny that any new policy is involved. The department that wins a higher price adjustment gets more money — without a change in the PESC figures which could alert others to its recent largesse. After all, the difference between underspending, overspending, and coming out right depends heavily on the prices at which one chooses to look.

If there is disagreement over what constitutes, first, existing policy and, second, its cost, there can scarcely be agreement on any projections which come out of these disputed premises. Projections require either (1) theories accounting for the growth rate of certain expenditures — in scarce supply, to say the least; or (2) extrapolations from past trends, which may prove fallacious under future conditions; or (3) conventions about costing that have little but convenience to recommend them. Projection may be better than untutored judgment, but it is still more art than science.

The difficulties of projection vary with the kind of program involved. In some, all governmental priorities, past trends in expenditures, and the important variables determining future costs are known. The expenditure projection takes the form of a forecast, i.e., what the government thinks will happen. Occasionally the facts are sufficiently clear for the forecast to be a firm postulation of how spending will develop. Possibly a deal between Treasury and department on the growth of capital expenditures has settled the major issue and the remaining variables are open to little question. Given a few demographic facts, such as student enrollments, and assuming a few bargains on the improvement factor involved, educational expenditures generally fall into this class. Projection is easier when the amount of business involved remains fairly constant so that the cost associated with it in earlier years may be confidently extrapolated into later ones. Where social services (or other

---

[1] In this respect, PESC in its early stages has taken a step backward from the much-maligned annual estimates procedure. When control was exercised through estimates prepared for Parliament, there was a kind of inherent monitoring process. Since staying within the estimates was important, and since the accounting system was geared to that end, there was a tendency to look at what actually had happened in the past year or two. Departments that deviated markedly from their proposed estimates could be held to account. As the Treasury began to tell departments that they no longer needed to pay so much attention to the estimates, that one meager feedback operation fell into disuse. In PESC now there is more forecasting and less monitoring.

programs relying on public applications) are involved, predicting future costs depends on being able to assess future demand. The number of people applying for hospital care, for example, will depend on factors — the economy and employment, climatic conditions, appearance of new diseases or new treatments for old ones, and the general state of society — which no one knows how to predict. Such projections are not estimates so much as "guesstimates."

In a second type of program, conditions are so uncertain that there is really no attempt at forecasting. The projection becomes an arbitrary *convention.* In agricultural supports, for example, PESC does not try to anticipate annual farm price reviews or market prices; it merely projects the level of support agreed at the last price review. The cost to the government of debt interest similarly is projected on the assumption of fixed interest rates. Staff ceilings certainly are not known five years ahead. The largest of all public expenditure programs, social security cash benefits, also rely heavily on such conventional projections.

A third category of projections, a hybrid of forecasts and conventions, is based on a purely hypothetical government hope or *target,* and spells out some particular desideratum. The five-year cost projection of unemployment and redundancy benefits from 1970–1971, for example, showed a decline and was based on a statistical-political assumption about unemployment. This assumption was made consistent with the government's view that the present level of unemployment was too high.

These "technical" difficulties could be multiplied at length. Clearly PESC figures do not add up automatically to a total; the projection is neither a simple forecast, convention, or target but some indeterminate combination of all three. But in all of this area, we are speaking only of the supposedly "technical" issues. Political bargaining is far more overt in the substance of the PESC process itself.

Payoffs and Punishments

A finance officer recalled to us that in 1967 his predecessor had briefed him with a long description of the annual estimates cycle. "To my successor now, I would say nothing of the estimates and speak only of PESC." This reorientation is significant and representative. PESC has become an integral part of the process through which government funds are allocated in Great Britain. Those who feel they benefit by it try to make it work; those who feel they lose out try to cushion its effect. All those who take part in the PESC procedure know that the politics of public policy is being played out under their eyes and that they had better do the best they can. PESC is not only a way of helping some participants make better decisions, it is an arena for decision in which strategy is more important than an elegant report.

This is not to say that PESC has worked out as intended by its Treasury founders and as proposed in the Plowden report over a decade ago. Nowhere has the original rationale for PESC been more confounded than in its efforts to weigh particular expenditures against each other. Experiments with Cabinet committees of nonspending ministers consistently have failed. Ministers and officials use the last or the next PESC exercise as a launching platform for their particular spending plans. It is just one more move along the long road toward getting one's way in Cabinet. PESC, with its once yearly overview, may initiate or record the results of Cabinet bargaining but it is not that bargaining itself.

Outside pressures, departmental strategy, or ministerial forcefulness can result in a Cabinet decision and preemptive strike on resources at any time. Instead of comparing alternative uses of resources, the Cabinet decides something on health in June, and on roads in December. There is no reason whatsoever to believe that this process will change unless one is also prepared to believe that emergencies (real or apparent) will disappear in the future and not play havoc in Cabinet as they have in the past. Every government has things that matter to it at the moment. Indeed, flexibility of response to emerging conditions is supposed to be one of the hallmarks of a successful government. But adaptability means also that spending decisions are not made comparatively and finally at any single time in any year.

The Treasury itself has mixed feelings about the value of PESC for its everyday work of expenditure control. PESC, strictly conceived, is only a set of figures — and aggregate figures at that. Few things are more likely to arouse the practiced skepticism of Treasury men who have already spent much of their adult lives looking for substance behind such superficial totals. To them totals without the details are practically meaningless. That is why Treasury division heads are encouraged to live in close association with the departments. It is there, between Treasury and department, that substantive meaning is given to existing policy, projections, improvement factors — in short, to the whole panoply of considerations involved in the department's spending proposal and the Treasury view on the subject.

If PESC is not a scale, is it nevertheless effective as a ceiling? If it cannot count on weighing expenditure decisions against each other, can PESC still be rated a success in holding individual spending programs down to a prearranged and fixed total? There is, alas, no simple answer. But unraveling some of its complexities can help us understand more about spending. Few programs are subject to control in the narrow sense of a "ceiling," i.e., a fixed sum projected ahead and under which the program must at all costs stay. Rigid ceilings have been found practical only in those few programs where the central government has complete control over both the finances and the determinants of the expenditure. In both research councils and overseas aid, for example, money is allocated largely at the government's will (though not entirely without pressure by beneficiaries and their friends). But in a great many other areas an absolute PESC ceiling is impossible. Local authority and agricultural spending are tied to their own external determinants — from changes in the political winds to sun and rain that affect crops. Social security expenditures are based on statutory entitlements and depend on numbers of beneficiaries, rates, and conditions. Housing subsidies and improvement grants follow automatically from the number of accommodations meeting fixed requirements; control consists in assessing the accuracy of building forecasts, not of financial limits. There is also a vast range of individually small, but collectively large, programs for which strict individual ceilings would require far finer tuning than PESC can perform.

The fact that so few programs have absolutely fixed ceilings, however, scarcely ends the matter. PESC's origins clearly show that its founders intended to introduce, if not an oak-beamed ceiling, at least a springtop lid on expenditures. The spending implications of individual decisions had to be spelled out for the future and related *in toto* to likely resources, an area in which the Treasury has been moderately successful.

In essence, PESC has made it much more difficult, if not impossible, for departments to argue the merits of their position to the Treasury without considering the implications for total spending and the costs five years ahead. PESC mechanics may be a bookkeeping exercise but now the figures are kept in one book, and for five years. The strategic environment for bargaining has thereby been subtly but significantly altered. Although it is true that PESC is essentially a reporting exercise which represents a cumulative result of continuous haggling, neither this nor other difficulties make it ineffective. Experienced Treasury men are willing to trade statistical exactitude for shaping the argument in their own terms. All agree that spending debates now take place in the Treasury terms of agreed expenditure paths and a view of the resulting totals. Treasury reformers of the 1950s and 1960s may feel some just satisfaction.

But every innovation also has unintended effects and new strategic possibilities. PESC is no exception; it is meant to control spending and is thus peculiarly vulnerable to tactics that claim alleged savings. Treasury doctrine, accepted by recent governments, is that if you want to do X you must save in Y. But interesting forms of bargaining still are possible. Under the old system, departments knew they would have to fight and would end up with a certain figure for the year immediately ahead; the Treasury might demand offsetting savings, but these were always "real" savings to materialize in next year's outturn. With PESC, departments are tempted to use larger amounts in the first of the five years and promise to be good boys later on. Departments may readily accept "shadow cuts" for years four and five so they can get more earlier on. Sufficient unto the day is the increase thereof, is their motto. The reader must try to imagine the fanciful possibilities involved in sacrificing a set sum of money (called "fairy gold" in some Whitehall circles) in year two for one in year three, about which little is known, or for another in year five, about which virtually nothing is known.

Most important, PESC has enshrined incrementalism with a vengeance.

It is incrementalism to the nth power. If PESC helps prevent departments from going beyond established bounds, it also commits the Treasury in public to keeping their expenditures going at the projected rate. Both sides find it harder to depart from the historical base. If PESC makes it less likely for new monetary programs with large spending implications to be introduced inadvertently, it also helps to assure departments that ongoing programs will not suddenly be disrupted. PESC may make it harder to get money, but it makes it easier to keep what has been given. Like a fast merry-go-round, PESC makes it hard to jump on, but once there, equally difficult to get pushed or pulled off.

Incrementalism has been reinforced through PESC by making each department more conscious of its own fair share of the total and more aware of other departments' departures from the expected rate of increase. In this sense, PESC has increased openness by reducing the scope for backstairs deals between Treasury and spending ministers. But equal treatment easily can come to mean a standard of equal marginal changes. A contemporary and critical Treasury view is that "PESC has simply enforced an earlier tendency for each dog to get its share."

By this time it should be clear that the diverse meanings and effects attributed to PESC are a product not merely of disagreement about its consequences but also of the different functions it performs for different people. The actual use made of PESC also helps explain why this device for supposedly increasing Treasury spending control has been so readily accepted and implemented by the spending departments. The Treasury's desire for increased control and the department's desire for increased security were a powerful parlay backing PESC.

Treasury proponents of PESC know its weaknesses full well. Has security in expenditure planning and all-round marginal increases overbalanced the need for asking fundamental questions and staying in touch with policy? Are not the virtues which departments find in PESC also its vices? So Treasury men hope that Program Analysis and Review (PAR)[2] — discrete analyses of individual programs within departments which they helped establish — will create impetus for change within agreed ceilings.

The founders of PESC were lucky. Their innovation might have died in the cradle had it not been rescued by that period's need for severe financial stringency. But it was more than luck. The men behind PESC had an idea that could be put into practice. They could teach others how to do it and they could check to see whether it had been done. This operational quality is nonexistent in program budgeting, which fails the world over when political currents run against it, and does not succeed even in favorable times because no one knows how to implement it.

---

[2] See Heclo and Wildavsky, *The Private Government of Public Money,* for description and analysis of PAR.

PESC works with men and machinery as they are — no need to postulate a new type of administrative animal. Readily grafted onto the existing public expenditure group in the Treasury, PESC could place its modest apparatus in a well-established home.

Not that it was easy to establish. It took years of patient effort to improve procedures and gain cooperation. Treasury men never forgot that if it were to last PESC had to serve the purposes of other departments than their own. So they set out to create a nexus of common interest. All was not sweetness and light, but many a detour was allowed and many bits of nonsense tolerated, so as to create a feeling of mutual responsibility for a joint enterprise. Yet, in the end, PESC had to have an ultimate client whose interests were vitally connected with its survival. It proved useful to chancellors of the exchequer, chief secretaries, and the public expenditures group as a whole. Since it helped them, they protected it.

The Treasury's achievement in establishing and making PESC work is substantial. It has been accomplished, not because the Treasury can manage public money better than anyone else, but because it is so much more skilled at managing men and their community relationships. Adaptability to expenditure problems, appreciation for departments' needs, strategic prudence in aiming to create habits of mind rather than lock-step obedience — all these features say much for the sensitivity of the men involved.

PAR is one of the prices to be paid for PESC. The cost of agreeing to spending limitations was enhanced protection for items already safely ensconced. Each reform not only compensates for old defects but creates new faults to be resolved by future efforts. That is why the work of perfecting social arrangements, which cannot wait for history to unfold all its secrets, is never finished.

20

What Good Is It?
Two Reforms

What good is all this? Having learned what is known about budgeting, what use can we make of our understanding? I would not put down those who are interested in knowledge for its own sake. No one would work on a subject for as long as I have without developing a lot of curiosity. It would be easy to fob off the reader by saying that resource allocation is everywhere acknowledged as an important subject, and it is obviously good to know more about important things. But how, specifically, could we use this knowledge? The test of social theory is social action. The knowledge now at our disposal, a reasonable man might well argue, should lead to better proposals for reform than those experience has shown wanting. One way, then, of finding out whether we have learned anything useful is to employ that knowledge to suggest reform, that is, changes in the process of budgeting. The reader should then be in a better position to decide whether this trip has been necessary.

Reform is hard. Most do not work and are soon discarded. Look at it another way: most of what we object to now was once someone's favorite reform. I shall content myself with two proposed reforms — one for poor-country budgeting as a whole and one for increasing the budgetary power and effectiveness of the United States Congress — to illustrate the connections between knowledge and change. The idea is to have reforms flow from our understanding of budgetary theory in the context of the specific conditions in these vastly different environments.

The material in this chapter has been adapted, by permission, from Naomi Caiden and Aaron Wildavsky, *Planning and Budgeting in Poor Countries* (New York: Wiley, 1974), © 1974 by John Wiley and Sons and Aaron Wildavsky, "The Annual Expenditure Increment — or How Congress Can Regain Control of the Budget," *The Public Interest,* 33 (Fall 1973), 84–108. Copyright © 1974 by National Affairs, Inc.

REFORM ONE: CONTINUOUS BUDGETING
IN POOR COUNTRIES

Budgeting broadcasts. To the extent that a budget is meaningful, it communicates information about the real priorities of government. Each act in the process is important, not only for specific decisions (so much for this, less for that), but also for information conveyed to others who alter their activities accordingly. The initial budget decision sets off a train of responses as each participant reacts to what others are doing in the new situation. Informal coordination takes place through mutual adjustment.

The closest analogy to budgeting in the political arena is pricing in the economic marketplace. Prices are the major signals to which people adapt in choosing what to buy and sell, produce and consume, undertake or abandon. These signals communicate more about what is valued than any other kind of economic decision. Prices are beacons through which a society, whether intentionally or not, signals its preferences to the vast complex of individual's who make daily choices with regard to their own advantage in economic affairs.

Prices receive unstinting attention from economists; but budgets, despite comparable importance, languish in relative neglect by political scientists. Yet they are important; what profit will there be in improving prices if the state dissipates its resources through faulty budgeting so that little or nothing is left to distribute? These goals must be reflected in budgets and prices or they are unlikely to be accomplished. If society can be said to have an operational plan, prices and budgets are the future writ in the present.

The major source of investment in many poor countries is the government budget which must accumulate surpluses for investment, because they are unlikely to be gathered in large amounts elsewhere. Now economists may and do disagree about how high the level of investment should be, partly because they disagree about what constitutes an investment, and partly because their theory is inadequate for the purposes; but they do agree that without significant amounts of investment growth cannot take place. There is a moral to this story: virtually all other goals, from redistribution of income toward the poor to concentration of capital among the rich, depend on budgeting. That is why it is so important for us to stress reform.

If the budgetary process in poor countries is controlled by poverty and uncertainty, positive change must focus precisely on those variables. The first can be ruled out on various grounds: no one knows how to get rich quick and, besides, eliminating poverty would assume out of existence the main condition that better budgeting is supposed to help alleviate. That leaves uncertainty. We cannot eliminate it but perhaps we can learn better how to live with it.

The weakness of government in poor countries lies at the heart of their budgetary troubles. The uncertainties stemming from poverty are intensified by frequent changes of regimes that lack sufficient strength to mobilize resources or direct those they do have. Unable to collect enough taxes and without control over a significant proportion of the resources they do collect, these governments work in a perpetual aura of financial crisis. Finance ministries usually bear the burden of decision. Fearful of being blamed when the money runs out and anxious to respond to what they see as real priorities for existing governments, finance ministries desperately seek protection against the unexpected. Maintaining liquidity becomes the crucial objective. Under normal conditions of extreme uncertainty (if not plain ignorance), this understandable desire leads to the sequence of conservative estimating devices, repetitive budgeting, delays in releasing funds, and inordinate amounts of paperwork that we have already described. At first these procedures accomplish their purposes; a surplus is protected for the time being, the finance ministry is able to adapt to changing circumstances by delaying decision, and the causes of uncertainty are pushed onto the operating departments. They respond, in turn, by trying to stabilize their own environments. Departments withhold information on unexpended balances, thus increasing underspending, in order to retain some flexibility. They become more political because they must engage in ceaseless efforts to hold on to the money ostensibly allocated to them, lest the finance ministry claw it back. Ultimately they seek their own form of financing through earmarked taxes, or they break off to form autonomous organizations — a sequence of events encouraged by foreign donors seeking stability through creating recipient organizations with whom they can have more predictable relations. Because the official budget is not a reliable guide to what they actually can spend, departments are not motivated to take it seriously. There is a huge amount of padding which reinforces the tendencies of the finance ministry to mistrust departments and to put them in a variety of straitjackets.

To reform budgeting it would be necessary to break into this cycle of mutually reinforcing behavior. How can this be done? What incentives can replace those which now convert organizational rationality to societal irrationality?

From a financial standpoint, the dimension of predictability is of critical importance. If governments knew how much they had to spend now and for a few years into the future, they would not feel obliged to follow deleterious financial procedures. Though they would still be poor, they could allocate expected funds with greater confidence. The multiple hedges against uncertainty could be relaxed and the strategic maneuvers of the spending department could be reduced in scope and amplitude. The more meaningful the annual budget, the greater incentive there is to prepare it carefully. The greater the ability to reward those who conform to the budget with actual funds, the more incentive they have to make it good. If each participant sticks close to initial agreements there is less call for constant renegotiation. Trust increases as reciprocal expectations are more nearly met. Paperwork declines in magnitude with the decreased need for building in delay and hiding money. The inevitable political struggle over resource allocation will take place within more clearly defined boundaries.

Though what everyone wants is unchanged, the more debilitating strategies will fall into misuse, either because they are unnecessary or because everyone has somewhat more reassuring information about what others are getting and giving.

Would not this happy chain of circumstances depend on things, especially uncertainty, being other than they are? Perhaps there are internal mechanisms for creating instability so that temporary gains in certainty will be wiped out by counteractions. A new financial surplus, for instance, might set off efforts to use it up so that the finance ministry would again find itself in danger of falling below an acceptable margin of safety. Why bother to raise revenues if, after accepting the political costs, there is no more room for maneuver at the end than at the beginning? The inescapable conclusion would be that nothing can be done unless everything can be done at once.

Such hopelessness might, however, give way to moderate pessimism. Possibly the system of relationships in budgeting is not wholly determined or limited by inescapable forces. Although trust among people may be partly determined by past history, surely present experience matters also. The question is whether their distrust makes it impossible for them to have new experiences. Might there not be more trust if there were a few experiences that showed it paid off? Once a financial margin becomes part of the environment to which others react, for instance, the easier release of funds may encourage meeting deadlines; this could mean a further decrease in paperwork, which in itself would be a significant advance. We shall begin by talking about ways to mitigate uncertainty and then go on to discuss how to live with it if it cannot be diminished.

One reason to concentrate on uncertainty is its readily apparent international implications. Up to now, like poor countries themselves, we have taken international economic arrangements as fixed in the short run. Poor countries, which can do little to alter them, must adjust to them as best they can. Obviously, anything that stabilizes commodity prices will increase certainty in the poor countries dependent on them for so much of their income. But our research does not bear on this issue; our major emphasis must be in the area of foreign aid on which our investigation has an indirect but important bearing.

According to our theory of budgeting in poor countries, the most important changes in behavior would come about with increased financial certainty for the central government. Uncertainty comes from two sides: unexpected increases in spending and sudden decreases in revenue. Foreign aid could work directly on the income side, though to be effective the expenditure level would also have to be involved.

The most significant way foreign aid could improve the quality of daily decisions would be direct budgetary support. Rather than paying for individaul projects, foreign donors would provide a stipulated amount for several years at least. That sum would provide part of the poor country's budget or it could be treated as part of its reserve to be drawn on in time of need.

Clearly success depends on using the reserve, as intended, to strengthen budgetary decisions. Governments bent on (or unable to avoid) dissipating their resources, as they already do, will always find ways to get around restrictions imposed by the project approach. For them, budget support would be no better, but also no worse, than money for projects. But those governments willing and able to make their resources grow will be helped most by direct budgetary support that decreases their financial uncertainty. Policy should be based on helping the best rather than restraining the worst. Besides, rich nations should do more to help poor ones, and direct budget support is the most palatable form of aid. To us the risk seems worthwhile.

We have now gone as far as we can without coming to grips with what a poor country can do on its own to deal with budgetary problems. After all, budgetary support through foreign aid may not be available and, in any event, could not work without support from inside. Rich nations may have their own reasons — pressure from exporters, desire to gain credit or exert control through individual projects — for preferring not to try the direct budget-support idea. And, no doubt poor countries that depend on their own resources and capabilities are less likely to be disappointed than those who wait for help from a capricious world.

So let us go back to where we began, with the conditions of the poor countries themselves. What approach to governmental decision-making would be appropriate for a society best characterized as poor and uncertain? Since we can't wish these conditions away, we must learn how to work with and through them.

How do you plan for contingencies? How do you take the unexpected into account on a regular basis? The terms seem incompatible. If you don't know what is going to happen or when, how can you anticipate unknown and spasmodic occurrences? You do know that you won't know what is coming. You realize you will have to adapt to rapidly changing conditions with poor data, missing theory, unskilled manpower, and few resources. Naturally, you can try to better these conditions — to train manpower, to increase the reliability and accuracy of your data, and to enhance your resources position. Experience teaches, however, that such efforts are likely to produce only slow rates of improvement. It is one thing to provide training and to collect data; it is another to use this information and exploit these skills. That requires organizational ability and social incentives that are often lacking. So what should be done?

Instead of seeking premature escape from the constraints that bind them, poor countries need to learn how to cope with and actually take advantage of them. Poor countries cannot and should not attempt to follow a fixed path. Just the opposite. They should enhance their ability to change course at short notice. They cannot avoid error but perhaps they can reduce the cost of making mistakes.

The immediate problem in most poor countries is the extreme difficulty of allocating resources at yearly intervals. The familiar air of unreality which pervades the annual budget is ample testimony to that. Often the budget provides no reasonable clues as to which agencies will actually spend how much money for what purposes. The fact that budget allocations are being constantly reconsidered means that the financial environment is too turbulent to be tamed by an annual budget. How, then, can budgeting be improved?

All previous suggestions take for granted an annual spending budget which in its existing form is a comprehensive statement of governmental intentions for the following year — such an accepted fact that many people find it hard to picture governmental administration without it. Yet in practice it does not work, for the reasons given. Questioning the validity of the annual budget, however strange this may appear, leads us to ask again about what would be appropriate for poor and uncertain nations. Suppose we consider accommodating to the idea of continuous adaptation rather than fighting it. Less might be promised, but more might be done.

Can participants in poor countries take advantage of that constant remaking of the budget called repetitive budgeting? If the budget is conceived as a best estimate of minimum amounts that must be spent to carry out existing activities, then let the budget process be explicitly geared to making ad hoc decisions on resource allocation against a background of what is known about current revenue and spending. The annual budget becomes a statement of what each agency spent in the previous year as nearly as can be determined. The best (though not necessarily a good) guide to the year ahead is the one that has just ended. Only three basic questions should be considered in compiling the budget. What did each agency spend last year? Are there built-in increases such as a rise in salaries that should be added to the total? Are there expenditures that should and could be eliminated? Departments that want additions to this budgetary base can come in at any time during the year with their justifications. They would have to convince the finance ministry that there were significant advantages in proposed expenditures, and Finance, in turn, would have a current notion of available resources and competing demands. Departments would know that a request for an increase carried with it the possibility that Finance might instead suggest cuts. Finance could, if it wished, ask that new bids be submitted on a quarterly or bimonthly basis so that it would be able to space out these requests and devote as much analytical attention to them as possible.

Departments would be more sure of the base amount but less so about increases. They could program existing activities with greater assurance, but would have to worry more about getting new money. This, we believe, increases certainty where it is most desirable and lets uncertainty remain where that would be advantageous. With greater control over new spending, the finance ministry could increase its ability to hold a surplus against contingencies at the cost of providing a floor for departmental expenditures below which it would be reluctant to go.

Under this scheme departments would have a tangible incentive to provide timely and accurate cost estimation. If they delayed, Finance would have to make the estimates for them, undoubtedly biased in a lower direction. If they systematically overestimated, Finance would learn to discount their requests and might cut them still lower. At the same time, departments would see the value of preparing proposals for new spending and keeping on hand a reservoir of projects that could be called up when the finance ministry sent out the word. After all, there are times when, through underspending or foreign aid or other circumstances, new funds do become available; departments will want to take advantage of those situations. If a call from the finance ministry means that money is actually available at that time, it should lend to the enterprise a sense of importance that is often lacking. For it is well and good to recommend keeping a supply of projects on the shelf, but if there is little or no chance for adoption so they only gather dust, the desire to produce them will rapidly decrease.

No one can guarantee that projects will be selected on their technical or economic merits. There must and should be times when political considerations prevail. Memories of the third London Airport in England or the supersonic transport in America do not suggest that unvarnished economic rationality prevails even in richer environments. Continuous budgeting would, however, allow those in charge of project approval to be as wise as their circumstances and talent permit. Perhaps that is all a budget procedure can do.

A basic purpose of continuous budgeting is to facilitate adapting to emergent problems. Some programs may remain in a steady state; others can be reviewed as often as any participant deems it necessary. Demands can be dealt with as they arise. If the latest move suggests a new step calling for changes in appropriations, a decision could be made right then and there. The tyranny of the annual budget — demanding formal review of programs of little immediate interest, and inhibiting action on programs that need immediate attention — would be ended.

A nagging doubt remains. Does not rationality require simultaneous consideration of all competing claims for resources? Not if it can't be done. If there is no way to compare each item against the others, if information is inadequate to support that effort, and if capacity to implement is lacking, rationality rules against pretending to do it. Putting book covers around the proposed allocation and calling it a budget does not mean that comparisons among programs have been made and used.

One objection to continuous budgeting might be that certain programs could escape investigation for several years. This potential problem might be solved by periodically appointing people to review programs or activities that do not change very much from year to year and would, therefore, tend to escape frequent scrutiny. A thorough going-over every few years or so would suffice. Chances are, however, that most programs would be evaluated in the normal course of requesting increases or trying to hold them down.

At first glance it might appear that continuous budgeting would make problems of coordination more difficult than they are today. We think not, unless, of course, one is prepared to define coordination as placing all appropriations on papers that lie side by side. Nor does it make much sense to define coordination as a central review, since this begs the question of whether policies have actually been related to one another in a reasonable way. It is a lot easier to talk about central coordination than to practice it. Continuous budgeting, however, can be practiced. Each small part of the budget can be considered as it comes up. Attempts can be made to adapt the new policy, through successive approximation, to major features of the environment as revealed by experience. Under continuous budgeting adaptation can be undertaken with greater intelligence because (1) the action is close in time to the awareness of the problem, (2) changes are limited in scope and therefore more easily made, (3) decision-makers can have a better grasp of where they are in relation to where they want to be, (4) each change can be separately evaluated against a general picture of the most relevant programs then in operation instead of (an immensely more complicated task) multitudes of suggested changes pitted against each other simultaneously, and (5) every change is always important if a major participant in the system wants it. Information can be marshaled when it is needed, not merely to fulfill an annual deadline.

Continuous budgeting might increase the power of finance ministries vis-à-vis spending departments. That is all right. We need not be overly concerned with the specter of all too powerful finance ministers. Nothing here would give them political advantages they did not have before. Finance was already powerful under the old system of repetitive budgeting, but not always in ways that contributed to governmental effectiveness. To the extent that continuous budgeting makes governments more effective in allocating resources, the desired objective has been achieved. Departments may have to defer more to finance ministries; yet they will find that the flow of funds on which they depend has been markedly improved. Not one but two notions of power are involved: departmental versus financial, and governmental versus environmental. The first is finite — more for one means less for the other — but the second is infinite; there is scarcely a limit to how much governments can improve their ability to deal with problems. Thus departments may be weak compared to Finance but strong in relation to the social problems within their jurisdiction. The idea is to get away from the cycle of irrationality — in which certainty for one side can be won only through uncertainty for the other — by expanding the amount of security within which both can work in mutually supportive ways.

The ultimate objection is that our proposal for continuous budgeting is a cloak for perpetuation of the costly and confusing pattern of repetitive budgeting. Being forced into error is bad enough, but legitimizing it is worse. What are the alternatives? There is no real choice between repetitive budgeting and a meaningful annual budget. If there were, if poor countries *could* make budgets that would predict well a year in advance, there would be no need for our recommendations. Since they can't, they would be better off counting on remaking the budget continuously than being forced to repeat their work at unpredictable intervals.

Our objective is to make budgets more meaningful. If they cannot last a year, then the allocations in them should correspond to what *will* happen for a shorter time. If all expenditures cannot assuredly be included, then a lesser proportion will have to do. Continuous budgeting would include less but give respect to more, and that is better than pretending the document is authoritative when everyone knows it is not.

REFORM TWO: THE ANNUAL EXPENDITURE INCREMENT; OR, HOW CAN CONGRESS REGAIN CONTROL OF THE BUDGET?

To suggest reforms for poor and uncertain countries is quite different from devising proposals for the rich and certain ones, who already have what poor nations want most — a meaningful budget. Reform among the rich is more likely to be a question of power: What institutions, responsive to which interests, are more likely to exercise power over a budget that is already worth making? A prime motivation behind PESC, for example, was to shore up the power of the Treasury (and hence the Chancellor of the Exchequer) over the departments (and hence the spending ministers). The Central Policy Review Staff, in turn, was supposed to redress the balance in favor of the prime minister against his Cabinet colleagues, and all ministers versus civil servants.

So, too, in the United States: the current question of reform sets Congress against the president. My personal preference, which I shall not seek to justify here, is for a government based on a sharing of powers, rather than an executive hegemony. So I have set myself the task of devising budgetary mechanisms that would allow Congress to compete more effectively for control of spending with the chief executive and his assistants.

Why does a president whose administration is responsible for a deficit of over $30 billion in the last fiscal year appear suddenly to be a protector of the purse? Why do congressmen, who vote for their share of spending increases, express unhappiness with the collective results of their individual actions? How can a president get away with impounding funds when Congress has the power of the purse? The answer to all these questions is the same: because Congress is losing faith in its appropriations process. If congressmen believed in what they were doing, they would support each other enough to get their way. The president prevails because secretly congressmen think he is right. Since they do not believe in themselves, they espouse the heresy that the president knows best.

It is true that former President Nixon forced the issue by insisting that he need not spend even after Congress passed bills over his vetoes. In this he was, as he should have been, beaten back. But if the congressional response is confined to that level, the same pattern will recur as soon as the issue leaves the headlines: congressmen again will vote for appropriations one day, knowing the president will impound them the next. Feeling that the financial situation has got out of control, they will give the president far more of their power than he is capable of wresting from them. Yet the belief that the presidency is a better institution to do budgeting than Congress, that somehow it knows more or acts more rationally, is just what I said it was — a heresy. What is more, it is an illusion, created with mirrors; it is produced by sleight of hand or, to be more precise, by sleight of mind.

The Magic of Totals

Why does the president, who spends perhaps 20 hours a year on the annual budget, seem more rational than the Chairman of the House Appropriations Committee, who must spend 2,000 hours on it? It is simply because the former announces himself with trumpet blasts from on high, whereas the latter sounds more like the Tower of Babel than the Heavenly Chorus. The president's budget is made in private, the congressional budget in public. Congressmen see how their budget is made; knowing what went into it they are, like sausage makers, leery of what will come out of it. Unaware of what has been going on in the executive office of the president, they respect its products more because they know the ingredients less. Thus congressmen have come to prefer other people's errors to their own.

The magic is in the totals. If the president seems more rational, if he somehow appears to be in control and to know what he is doing, it is because he announces his government spending totals with an air of conviction. Presidents naturally make up in assurance what they lack in knowledge. Although the executive's total is not entirely plucked out of the air, neither is it turned out down to the last decimal by some infallible sausage machine of modern economic science. The total so authoritatively proclaimed by one man is in fact a product of the fair guesses and wild surmises of many within the executive branch.

What is in a total? For spending, it is "a thing of shreds and patches." Ability to project or predict federal expenditures is poor. Estimates can easily be off by $5 or $10 billion. Underspending usually runs a good 2–3 percent, creating the possibility of an additional error of $4 to $6 billion. More than half of the total is left over from previous years in the form of unobligated balances, and no one is quite certain how large they are or how soon they will be liquidated. Afficionados of the craft also recognize that exactly what is included in the budget as an expenditure is, at the all-important margin, a matter of convenience rather than of necessity: Give me my way or give them theirs, and any of us will be able to make that budget larger or smaller by anything from $10 to $50 billion with just a flick of the projection or a twist of the definition.

Nowadays it seems that an allowable total spending figure is born from economic theory untouched by human hands. Keynesian doctrine is universally popular because the instructions it conveys — spend when underemployed, save when overemployed — are simple enough for all of us to pretend we understand the economy. But the argument for impounding goes beyond this maxim by making the further suggestion that there is a direct and immediate connection between expenditures not made and the health of the economy. Yet spending changes, unlike variations in tax rates, make awkward tools for short-term economic management. Often no one knows what the employment or inflationary effect of an expenditure will be. It is quite possible for a short-term cut in authorization to lead to a middle-term increase in spending because closing costs have to be paid and permanent leave has to be given to workers that are laid off. By the time the effects of expenditure cuts are felt, the chances are that the economic circumstances at which they were aimed will have changed. No one can be certain that presidential spending targets are correct for economic spending purposes; or, if they are, that the limits proposed will come near to meeting them; or if they do, that the contrary effect will not occur. The totals are hunches, on top of guesses, wrapped in conjectures.

Because the president announces his preferred total only once, the impression grows that it is the total he has always had in mind. Nothing could be further from the truth. The most obvious feature of the presidential total is never mentioned, no doubt because it appears self-evident: He announces it at the end — not the beginning — of his consideration of the budget. The total can change up to late December, when the government printer imposes the final deadline. True, there is a planning figure bandied about within the OMB during the spring. This preliminary total is not necessarily devoid of meaning, but neither is it binding. Everyone knows it is subject to change, not only in response to events, but also as the actual decision process further reveals their preferences to participants. In the last month, week, or day, the president must weigh his expenditure desires on, say, six to ten major programs against the prospect of raising or lowering taxes within the context of the economic situation. If he changes his total a dozen times, only his budget director will know.

Just because the importance of budgetary totals has been exaggerated does not mean that Congress should not be interested in them. If congressmen will not think well of themselves (or outsiders think well of congressmen) unless they come up with a total, then Congress must equip itself to produce a magic number. If many Americans, including congressmen, believe the nation is spending too much and want to return more purchasing power to individuals, that is another and better reason for being interested in the totals. Indeed, the widespread feeling that Congress is indifferent to the total explains its vulnerability to presidential impounding.

Imperfect Budgets and Negligent Guardians

The last decade has revealed certain imperfections in the congressional political arena. Members of Congress who vote for spending proposals find themselves unhappy with the resulting totals or the tax rates related to them. It appears undesirable either to turn down spending bids or to raise taxes to accommodate totals. The president accuses Congress of wanting the credit for spending but not the blame for taxing. Impoundment is his challenging response: either take the onus for raising taxes or allow me to make my limits stick by refusing to spend beyond them.

Power and responsibility go together: irresponsibility equals impotence. Legislatures in a democracy are often enfeebled by making unreal decisions. When legislatures typically authorize several times the amount of expenditure that is available to the national treasury, as happens, for instance, in the Philippines, the actual allocation of money is necessarily transfered to the executive. The price of depriving no one is inability to indulge anyone.

In the past, Congress maintained the power of the purse because it played the role of guardian of the treasury. Usually it cut requests the president made on behalf of the spending agencies. Although Congress did not formally set a total, expenditures as a whole were kept within tacit boundaries acceptable to most legislators. Today guardianship still exists but it has declined. Congress still cuts more than it increases, but not by much nor with the regularity for which it was once (in)famous, and the appropriations subcommittees are more likely to try to hold the line at the president's request than they are to assume it will be cut.

If Congress goes all the way in abandoning guardianship, the show will still go on, but the president's men will have to act as guardians. The role of advocacy already is built into the system through the spending agencies. Congress cannot do better than the original cast in crying, "More, more!" Left unchecked, the agencies' desires would know few bounds. So there must be guardians. What is now being decided is whether Congress will continue to play the role of guardian effectively or will see another actor take over its role, and so its power.

The decline of guardianship as a congressional role has been accompanied by the erosion of reciprocity as a congressional norm. No large body of men can make as many decisions as an annual budget requires without breaking up into specialized groups and then deferring to the judgments of these groups. Reciprocity has been attacked from two separate directions with a single result — higher appropriations. Recommendations of appropriations subcommittees are being overturned on the floor more frequently than in the past, usually to increase the amount appropriated. Legislative committees have begun to rail against their opposite numbers on the appropriations side for exercising more power with less information, usually on the ground that expenditures should be greater than they are, even if that means getting around the annual appropriations process through direct (backdoor spending) or indirect (tax subsidies) access to the treasury. The displeasure of the legislative committees is evident in the growth of annual authorizations which gives them grounds for challenging the expertise of the appropriations committees and a platform for advocating higher appropriations. Being the adaptive creatures they are, members of appropriations subcommittees have tried to reestablish the deference customarily shown to them by raising the price they are prepared to pay. Yet few like the total cost.

What is to be done? When we say that economic markets are imperfect, we mean they do not produce essential information for buyers and sellers, with the result that optimal decisions are unlikely to be made. The solution is to "rig" the market by changing the rules governing permissible exchanges. When the budgetary process produces imperfections in the form of discrepancies between preferences on specific programs and the overall expenditure total, comparable steps have to be taken. Now it may be that rules which would make it easier to reconcile desired totals with programatic preferences are the last thing congressmen want to see. Maybe congressmen do not wish to face the totals arising from individual spending actions. Perhaps they would rather avoid confrontation between desirable expenditures and unavoidable taxes. Then, impounding would be not the abominable action of a pugnacious president but instead the routine undertaking of a conscientious chief executive. It would represent a systemic adaptation to the decline in congressional guardianship. Congress would still be allowed to act as if it were budgeting, with the understanding that the president would cut back the total when he deemed it advisable. As a result, congressmen would stand to lose not only the power over totals they conveniently wish to give up, but the power over spending they still want to retain. My own view is that it is both desirable and possible to maintain — and even enhance — the congressional power of the purse.

In making recommendations for Congress, I shall draw on the lessons to be learned from other nations' budgetary practices, but there can be no thought of directly imitating them. Congress is not like the parliaments in these other countries: Congress is still powerful. Legislatures that actually exercise power independently of the executive over a wide range of activities are rare in the contemporary world. Members of the Japanese Diet act on the budget not as members of the legislature, or even as adherents of the party in parliament, but by virtue of their association with the extraparliamentary Liberal Democratic Party. Members of the House of Commons have little influence over expenditures in any capacity, and most of what little they do have comes from being back-benchers in the majority party. Deputies and senators in France may trade on their extraparliamentary positions as civil servants or mayors to importune for favors before the executive budget is made up. What is required to convince the executive to accede on one program or another is so involved that few try and fewer still succeed. It is important, then, that in appraising recommendations for change we take account of Congress' special characteristics.

Congressional Realities

Past proposals to reform congressional procedures for budget review failed because they did not take into sufficient account the realities of decision-making under congressional conditions. Whatever is recommended must be workable in a large, heterogeneous, and independent body operating within an environment of fragmented and dispersed power. There is no sense in treating Congress as if it were led by a small, cohesive group easily able to agree or to impose their will on others. To avoid these traps, it may be helpful to state the characteristics of the congressional environment in the form of criteria for evaluating alternative budgetary procedures.

1. *Many committees, not one.* If you have a committee that makes a budget which is not then altered by other committees — a committee without rivals, a steering committee of the legislature — it can be called a Cabinet on the British model. Congress is a pluralistic institution; it has many centers of power, depending on the time and the issue. To be effective, Congress must exploit rather than fight against its dispersed, fragmented, and pluralistic nature. A good way to use pluralism is to embrace specialization.

2. *More specialization, not less.* Without specialization, there is no knowledge, and without knowledge there is no power. When executives wish to emasculate legislatures, they break up existing committees and prevent formation of new ones specialized enough to look into specific areas of policy and small enough to act with dispatch. It is no good railing at last year's failures or the previous decade's disasters. Unless the legislature can keep up with the executive, it will become an auditor after the fact rather than the budgeter ahead of time. To keep up means to lead with one's strength, which in a legislature means its strongest committees.

3. *Revitalize old committees rather than create new ones.* The budget must be passed every year. There is no time for a new committee to learn; it must perform well the first time or its activity will be held in disrepute. Old committees have the virtue of age; they have long been there and legislators expect them to stay around. Because they perform other essential purposes (appropriations and finance), they can survive initial disappointments of failing to set a total or having it exceeded. Since they cannot compel other legislators to follow their lead, they also need the advantages of existing power levers. Putting the matter another way, it is too much to ask a new committee to take on a new function; in this case new wine will age better in old bottles. But will old committees agree to learn new budgetary tricks? That depends on being able to answer the always relevant political question of incentives.

4. *Something for all, not nothing for most.* If budgeting is a game, all

players must have a chance to score. There has to be something in it for all —
bureaucrats, executives, central control organs, legislators — or they will refuse
to play seriously. (Finance Ministries could not enhance their control, for
instance, unless they were prepared to concede enhanced discretion over allocations within those amounts to spending departments and their ministers. The
five-year PESC projections would not have worked unless the spending departments got enhanced security for vulnerable old programs as the price of lesser
security for attractive new ones.) So, too, congressional committees, the House
and Senate as separate chambers, the leadership of both houses, the president,
and departments must all have something to gain from playing the expenditure
game under new rules.

5. *Representation, not bureaucratization.* Congressmen are chosen to
provide representation. They are originators, purveyors, and mediators of
preferences. Their preferences need to be open to living facts, not buried under
layers of bureaucracy. Congressmen should not spend their time managing a
legislative bureaucracy that is supposed to help them deal with the presidential
bureaucracy, which itself threatens to immobilize the presidency under the
guise of helping presidents cope with the executive bureaucracy. The natural
defensive posture of bureaucracies is to bury outsiders in mountains of paper.
If legislators also are managers, and managers are bureaucrats, the advantages
of differences in role are being lost. Better a lousy legislator than a beautiful
bureaucrat.

6. *Simplification, not mystification.* Rationality is supposed to mean
effective action, not pretentious inaction. The rationality of results must prevail
over the rationality of form. The rational man is not the one who makes believe
he compares everything to everything else; the rational person is the one who
manipulates the few variables under his control to good effect. If attention is
focused on all or most possible relationships, it will be impossible to single out
those most in need of change. However badly the chief executive confuses
himself, he can always produce a last-minute decision with a gloss of justification. If congressmen confuse themselves, they will not be able to act at all. They
need mechanisms to reduce the number of decisions up for consideration at
any one time; they need ways of structuring a series of votes so that these are
both meaningful and manageable. Before a legislature can act wisely, first it
must be able to act. If congressmen do not use aids to calculation, they will be
unable either to arrive at their own preferences or to settle their differences with
others. Making calculations manageable is essential to effective legislative
decision-making.

What Should Not Be Done

Criteria for congressional choice cut two ways: They help determine what
should not be done as well as what might be attempted. To clear the way for my

positive recommendations, let me begin by explaining why I have rejected a number of frequently proposed reforms.

1. *The president should not be given power to make cuts from a congressionally established ceiling through proportionate reductions.* This proposal would have the unfortunate effect of encouraging spending departments and appropriations subcommittees to inflate their recommendations in order to emerge with more after across-the-board cuts have been made. Moreover, this device creates the unfortunate impression that Congress is not able to handle its own affairs by disciplining itself. In the concluding section I shall try to show that Congress can convey a far more favorable impression by actually keeping budgetary outlays within boundaries it considers reasonable.

2. *For most programs, five-year projections of governmental expenditures should not be mandated.* A formal requirement to this effect already exists but produces no useful results. There is no need to create make-work in an already overburdened federal government. Such projections make sense only if the participants are willing to make commitments for that long a period. Experience with five-year projections under the British Public Expenditure Survey reveals that spending departments get an implied commitment for continuation of expenditures on existing policies as the price of their cooperation. I do not believe that either the president or Congress is willing to go this far in reducing its already small degree of budgetary discretion, and I do not believe they should. The extreme incrementalism produced by the British procedure may not be desirable and, in any event, requires the existence of a central budget organ like the Treasury with the power to make commitments that for the most part will be followed by government. The essence of American government is that no one actor has (or is supposed to have) this authority.

3. *We should reject also the variety of proposals calling for huge amounts of vaguely specified data on the theory that more data would somehow improve the budgetary process.* These requests range from pilot trials of each new proposal (thus guaranteeing that Congress would be unable to respond to emerging conditions) to cost-benefit analysis before (and evaluation after) the establishment of programs. Part of the difficulty here stems from the failure to distinguish between *data* — anything that can be collected, ranging from laundry lists to telephone directories — and *information,* which is data collected according to a theory which relates inputs to outputs, and means to ends in a particular policy area. Congress is already inundated with data; what it lacks, and needs, is information. Unfortunately, creativity is scarce throughout the country; theories telling us how to make effective decisions in education, welfare, and many other areas are hard to find. Congress might well support social research to provide such theories, but there is no point in demanding information that cannot be produced without this knowledge. It is all too easy to suppose that if there were more data, there would be more understanding. But random data make barriers, not gates, to informed decision. The surest way for

Congress to stultify itself is to collect more data than either Congress or anyone else can handle. As a general rule, no data should be produced unless there is a client who can specify the bit relevant to the particular theory related to the specific decision he is prepared to make.

4. *The numerous proposals calling for a joint committee on the budget are unwise.* The effect of the proposals would be to transfer congressional power over the budget from the House Appropriations Committee to the joint committee staff without substantially benefiting senators. Senators are few in number; their time and talents are necessarily spread thin. They command a wide audience but have trouble keeping up with the many subjects that come before them. So it is natural for them to rely more on staff work than do most representatives, with enough time to specialize in the narrower jurisdictions that are their lot. The power of a member of the House Appropriations Committee is tied to his place on this committee far more than is the power of his opposite number in the Senate, who serves on numerous committees and whose role in securing public attention for issues and causes often absorbs a considerable part of his attention. A joint committee, then, would mean a further over-shadowing of representatives by senators. It means giving senators the benefit of the hard work done by representatives, without corresponding return. It means that senators will use staff to counter the expertise of House members. The voice may be the voice of the Senate, but the guiding hand will come from the staff.

The worst feature of the joint committee idea is how easily it slides over into a cabinet model without anyone quite realizing what has happened. The result, as the report of the Joint Study Committee on the Budget shows, is to replace an unsatisfactory executive budget bureaucracy with an even less desirable legislative bureaucracy. Their idea is that a committee in each house will fix a budget total, allocate amounts for major categories, and adjust taxes accordingly. Their assumption is that orders will go down and obedience will come up. That doesn't sound much like the Congress of our common despair and mutual affection — the Board of Estimate in New York City maybe, or possibly even the Bundestag, but not the U.S. Congress. Reforms that require Congress to be something other than it is or, worse, that would transform it into something not worth having, are somewhat less than compelling. The virtue of Congress is that its vices are exposed. Can't we keep our Congress and (some of) our money too? I think we can.

The Annual Expenditure Increment

Despite all the difficulties, there *is* a way in which congressmen can reconcile their desires on individual expenditures with their feelings about the total, and in which Congress can coordinate expenditures and revenues with the economic situation, even in the absence of a central leadership capable of compelling obedience. The procedure would work roughly like this: The president submits his budget. The small and capable staff of the Joint Committee on Internal Revenue Taxation makes its own estimates of income. A similar small staff is created on the expenditure side to estimate likely outlays and to check on what really was spent in the past year. To these actual expenditures for each agency the expenditure staff adds an estimate of what is essentially a cost-of-living increase based on salary raises, price changes, and population movements. The starting figure of the appropriations process in the House of Representatives, then, would be made up of the previous year's spending plus an estimate of what it would take to keep the same activities going in the coming year.

This base expenditure would be calculated in total and for the agencies under the jurisdiction of the dozen or so appropriations subcommittees. These subcommittees would hold hearings and report out bills as they do now,. with the important proviso — which would have to be embedded in House rules — that the total could not exceed a previously determined base expenditure. Within that initial total, agencies could suggest changes and subcommittees could reallocate as they wished. When the bill came to the floor, members of the House would have the same rights and obligations; they could decrease the base expenditure or propose reallocations, but could not move to increase it. A similar procedure would be followed in the Senate, which would have to reorganize its Finance subcommittees so that they corresponded to those of the House. The Senate could continue to serve as an appeals court in the sense of considering requests from agencies to have their monies raised to the base expenditure or to have a different allocation made. Once an appropriations bill was on the floor, Senate appropriations subcommittees (and senators themselves) would have to adopt rules forbidding increases above base expenditures; the Conference Committee would be bound by the same rules. Thus both houses of Congress, at this initial stage, would concentrate essentially on how to do better what had been done before, or (no doubt less frequently) on whether what had been done ought to continue to be done at all.

Let us suppose that the annual spending increment would approximate 3 percent of the total. Indeed, in the absence of compelling macroeconomic considerations to the contrary, a 3 percent real increase in expenditures per year seems reasonable, producing a yearly increase of approximately $8 to $10 billion as spending approaches $300 billion. The key to my expenditure proposals lies in how this annual increment would be treated.

Just as the base expenditure budget is, in reality, a series of subcommittee budgets, the annual increment is meant to be a budget of the entire committee. Agencies would make their spending bids for a part of the annual increment. Each subcommittee would hold hearings and then make recommendations to the committee as a whole. No doubt the bids would add up to more than the available amount. The appropriations committee's task would be to establish an order of priority among them so that they could be made to fit within the total.

Possibly the appropriations committee would become so convinced of the desirability of the spending proposals that it would wish to raise its working total. This should not necessarily be condemned. There is no reason for congressmen to impose on themselves a task — fixing an inflexible total at the beginning of the budget process and sticking to it come what may — that no president could (or has even tried to) accomplish. Circumstances may change from the time the original working total is established; committee members may learn more about their own preferences in the process of considering each request. What they must then do is negotiate with the House Ways and Means Committee, through its leaders, for a new package of revenues and expenditures. The point is not that Congress should always stick to some arbitrary total, but that it should always act (and equally important, that it should appear to act) responsibly in relation to the nation's finances.

The annual increment would be reported as a single bill to the House of Representatives. The answer to what the total should be would equal the base plus the increment.

At this point I do not believe there should be a rule prohibiting increases in the increment. The House should be allowed to work its will. There seems little point in tying its hands because, when sufficiently determined, that body will find a way to do what it wants. If the problem is that congressmen fear they will act unwisely under pressure, the House itself may wish to adopt the suggestion of William Niskanen who proposes that increases above the annual increment should trigger automatic tax hikes.

The Senate Appropriations Committee would receive the annual increment and proceed to hold hearings on appeals to increase the total or to alter the composition of expenditures within it. Then the Senate as a whole would have the opportunity to alter the annual increment bill and the tax package with which it would be associated. The final total, as before, would be the increment that Congress actually votes, added to the previous base.

Suppose legislators with a spending mentality deliberately estimate spending low and revenues high? Precisely this happened with the legislative budget proposal after the Second World War and is a frequent practice of planning commissions in poor countries wishing to encourage higher levels of investment. Suppose legislators with a saving mentality estimate expenditures high and revenues low? This happens all the time in American cities and is practiced by finance ministries in poor countries around the world. People can learn to play any game. It is easy to bring legislators in touch with procedures that will let them mix revenues and expenditures, but you can't force them to produce a brew you will like.

Why Almost Everyone Stands to Benefit

The effect of the annual expenditure increment would be to focus congressional attention on important choices at the margin — a huge margin, it is true, but a margin of the total nonetheless. Having previously decided which existing programs it would like to rearrange and which it could do without, Congress would be choosing among new ventures and expansions of old ones. By a process of sequential reduction, through successive iterations, Congress would have refined its preferences on spending and related them to notions of desirable tax and economic policy.

Why should anyone want to do this? What's in it for them? What incentives are there for those participants in the budgetary process whose cooperation is essential if anything is to happen at all? Let us start with the House Committee on Appropriations. By dividing itself into subcommittees that are careful of each other's prerogatives, it not only gets the power that goes with expertise, but avoids the conflicts that come from people minding other people's business. Yet minding other people's business is exactly what the committee members must do if the base expenditure and annual increment proposal is to have a chance. Why should they want to? Because by doing so they can hold on to and even enhance their power as congressmen. If they do not, they will lose their power to the president, who will be doing the real budgeting at the margins; this will force them into ruinous experiments with joint committees in which staff and Senate will nibble away at what little importance they have left. It is the old story again: "Harry, how's your wife?" "Compared to what?" he replies. The outcry over impounding is symptomatic of the general disintegration of the congressional appropriations process. Compared to the alternatives, I think members will support a stronger voice for the entire appropriations committee.

The Senate is asked to choose between expanding its influence over an (increasingly unimportant) appropriations process through a joint committee with large staff, and exercising more strategic control at the margin of the base expenditure and annual increment. Moreover, given the national prominence of economic management issues and the natural interest of senators in prominent national concerns, senators would be able to use their positions on the Finance and Appropriations committees, and their role in relating revenues and spending, to enter one of the most important realms of national policy. They would not be giving up any control over appropriations they could actually exercise; in fact, they would be gaining access to issues of broader national scope.

Through base expenditures spending agencies would both enjoy increased stability in their existing programs and suffer more tightly constrained competition for the annual increment. It seems like a fair exchange. Agency opinion will probably be divided: Some will want to protect what they have, whereas others will prefer to take a chance on getting more. Yet on balance I believe administrative agencies will find this procedure more helpful than not, especially since it guarantees that at least they will know about their base expenditure far earlier than is now true.

Despite surface noise to the contrary, I do not believe that presidents will find impounding a satisfactory way of life. It gives them greater power over the budget at the cost of enhanced responsibility for everything that happens. Since no one person possibly can do all the work involved, power, in effect, would be transferred to the White House staff and the OMB. And, indeed, there are signs of increasing presidential interest in economic management and decreasing interest in the details of expenditure. Why, otherwise, would the president increasingly relegate the solution of social problems to state and local governments through revenue sharing? But in trying to manage the economy, he will find that it is hard to gather all the threads in his hands unless there is somebody in each house of Congress with whom he can deal. The more Congress does to develop a mechanism for relating outflow and income, the greater the input the president can make to it. If Congress agrees to take some of the heat, presidents will find it both proper and necessary to make room in the kitchen and share their recipe for making the annual budget. The new Congressional budget committees and the President will be natural allies because their main task will be to impose limits.

Now appropriations committees are not the only committees that create expenditures. They control only 45 percent of the total. True, these are the most flexible funds, but being less than half, they now bear a disproportionate share of the pressure when spending is thought to be too high. Clearly, the committees that cover revenue sharing, tax subsidies, price supports, housing loans, and the like — the committees that do their financing by the back door, so to speak — must play their part, and it is true they will have less reason to support this proposal. The Ways and Means Committee has the least incentive; in its new power to agree on totals with Appropriations, it may find slender compensation for having to give others a voice in revenue sharing and tax subsidies. Yet even these congressmen may come to see the advantage for them in the annual expenditure increment. They know that Congress lives or dies in its committees. If Congress loses power, it will happen because of failure to work out appropriate relationships among its many committees. As is true for the rest of us, the harm others can do to Congress is vastly exceeded by the damage it can do to itself.

Regaining Control of the Budget

If Congress is willing to accept the responsibility that goes with power, it can relate its preferences on expenditure with those on taxation and economic management. The trick is to break down the budget so that it can be handled by a large number of independent and diverse legislators who must coordinate their activities without central control. What must be done is to take advantage of precisely those most characteristic features of the congressional system: independence, diversity, large size, capacity for specialization, and representation and brokerage of preferences. The annual expenditure increment is designed to do this job. Congress first decides whether it wants to reallocate funds for existing programs in around a dozen major areas of policy. Then it relates the last $10 billion or so to its desire for new expenditures, together with its preferences on taxation. Congress thus has a chance to work its will; no more than this can be done.

AFTERWORD

How do I know these reforms will prove successful? I don't. More can happen than I can imagine. The fourfold increase in the price of oil is a striking example. A few poor countries — Iran, Nigeria, Venezuela, etc. — are now richer than anyone predicted. What to do with their money, rather than how to acquire it, is their main problem. Because their capacity to spend is likely to lag behind their ability to receive, they will have large surpluses for at least a decade. The other poor countries — India, Ghana, Colombia, etc. — are poorer than ever. They can afford neither to buy the oil-based fertilizer they need to increase food production nor pay the costs of importing food on ships run on oil. The rich are also rueful. Their balance of payments is shot and their efficiency is down because the price of energy has increased much faster than their productivity. Fixed costs are rising, social demands increasing, revenues falling in relation to the burden placed on them. How, then, can the budgetary reforms advanced here stand up under these much-changed conditions? Are they relics of a bygone era, a memorial to the super sixties instead of the sorry seventies?

I think not. The theory in this book attempts to state how and why budgetary processes will operate under various conditions, not what those conditions will be. A book of pure prediction would not be a theory of budgetary subsystems but a general theory of political systems or, indeed, of universal history. Nothing herein says the rich will not become poor, the poor rich, the rich richer, or the poor poorer. If some of the past poor become the future rich, they can be expected to behave like the rich they are instead of the poor they were.

The poor who are poorer than they were should find the theory still applicable. If external aid from the old rich is not replaced by aid from the new rich, they should try to mitigate budgetary uncertainties by internal devices. I am not saying that their total position may not be worse — that depends on a lot more than budgeting — but that they can help themselves, wherever they are, by gearing budgeting to their condition.

The rich countries with whom we have been concerned will not be made poor but merely less wealthy than they were. Certainly this is true of the United States. The calculating mechanisms in its new congressional budget reform look remarkably like the annual expenditure increment. The staffing arrangements, however, are far more ample than I thought appropriate for a legislative body, and the new budget committees are less connected to the old appropriations and finance committees than I thought advisable. If the budget committees give in to the temptation to act like steering committees of the legislature, which would be out of keeping with American political conditions, they will not prosper. The desire of Democratic Party majorities for social programs will undoubtedly strain their willingness to keep the budget within bounds. Other more favorable circumstances could also be imagined. No matter. I believe that any successful reform, whether it occurs now or later, must conform with American conditions. Connecting contemplated reforms with actual conditions, making the *is* serve the *ought,* has been my purpose.

Bibliography

Almond, Gabriel, and Sidney Verba. *The Civic Culture; Political Attitudes and Democracy in Five Nations.* Princeton: Princeton University Press, 1963.

Anthony, Robert N. *Planning and Control Systems: A Framework for Analysis.* Boston: Division of Research, Graduate School of Business Administration, Harvard University, 1965.

Anton, Thomas J. *Budgeting in Three Illinois Cities.* Urbana: Institute of Government and Public Affairs, University of Illinois, 1964.

————. *The Politics of State Expenditure in Illinois.* Urbana: University of Illinois Press, 1966.

————. "Roles and Symbols in the Determination of State Expenditures," in *Policy Analysis in Political Science,* ed. by Ira Sharkansky. Chicago: Markham, 1970.

Argyris, Chris. *The Impact of Budgets on People.* New York: Controllership Foundation, 1952.

Armstrong, K. G. "Programme Budgeting: Its Meaning and Uses" (New Zealand). *An Introduction to Program Budgeting.* Papers presented to the Symposium on Program Budgeting held at Melbourne University, November 20, 1968. 48 pp.

Art, Robert J. "Why We Overspend and Underaccomplish." *Foreign Policy,* Spring 1972, pp. 95–114.

Axelrod, Donald. "Post-Burkhead: The State of the Art or Science of Budgeting." *Public Administration Review,* 33 (November/December 1973), 576–586.

Axelson, Charles F. "What Makes Budgeting So Obnoxious?" *Business Budgeting,* 11 (May 1963), 22–27.

Bahl, Roy W. *Metropolitan City Expenditures; A Comparative Analysis.* Lexington: University of Kentucky Press, 1969. 140 pp.

Banfield, Edward. "Congress and the Budget: A Planner's Criticism." *American Political Science Review,* 43 (December 1949), 1217–1228.

Barber, James D. *Power in Committees: An Experiment in the Government Process.* American Politics Research Series. Chicago: Rand McNally, 1966.

Baumol, W. J. *Welfare Economics and the Theory of the State*. Cambridge: Harvard University Press, 1952.

Berliner, Joseph. *Factory and Manager in the USSR*. Russian Research Center Studies, no. 27. Cambridge: Harvard University Press, 1957.

"Big Turnabout for the States — Now the Money Is Rolling In." *U.S. News and World Report*, 75 (June 18, 1973), 22–23.

Black, Guy. "Externalities and Structure in PPB." *Public Administration Review*, 31 (November/December 1971), 637–643.

Boekh, Augustus. *The Public Economy of the Athenians*. London: John Murray, 1828, vol. II.

Boggs, Hale. "Executive Impoundment of Congressionally Appropriated Funds." *University of Florida Law Review*, 24 (Fall 1971), 221–229.

The Book of the States, 1972–1973. Lexington, Ky.: Council of State Governments, 1973.

Bordua, David J., and Edward W. Haurek. "The Police Budget's Lot: Components of the Increase in Local Police Expenditures, 1902–1960." *American Behavioral Scientist*, 13 (November/December 1969) 667–680.

Bosher, J. P. "Chambres de Justice in the French Monarchy," in J. P. Bosher, ed., *French Government and Society, 1500–1850, Essays in Memory of Alfred Cobban*. London: Athelone Press, 1973.

Braybrooke, David, and Charles E. Lindblom. *A Strategy of Decisions; Policy Evaluation as a Social Process*. New York: Free Press of Glencoe, 1963.

Breasted, James. *A History of Egypt from the Earliest Times to the Persian Conquest*. New York: Scribners, 1916.

Bridges, Sir Edward. *Treasury Control*. Oxford: Clarendon Press, 1957.

Bridges, Lord. "The Treasury as the Most Political of Departments." Pollack Lecture delivered at Harvard University, November 1961.

Brittain, Herbert. *The British Budgetary System*. New York: Macmillan, 1959.

Brown, Vincent J. *Control of the Public Budget*. Washington, D.C.: Public Affairs Press, 1949.

Brown, William H., Jr., and Charles E. Gilbert. "Capital Programming in Philadelphia: A Study of Long-Range Planning." *American Political Science Review*. 54 (September 1960), 659–668.

———. *Planning and Municipal Investment: A Case Study of Philadelphia*. Philadelphia: University of Pennsylvania Press, 1961.

Brundage, Percival Flack. *Bureau of the Budget*. Praeger Library of U.S. Government Departments and Agencies, no. 20. New York: Praeger Publications, 1970. 327 pp.

Buchanan, James M., and Gordon Tullock. *The Calculus of Consent; Logical Foundations of Constitutional Democracy*. Ann Arbor: University of Michigan Press, 1962.

Buck, Arthur E. *Public Budgeting; A Discussion of Budgetary Practice in the National, State and Local Governments of the U.S.* New York: Harper, 1929.

———. *The Budget in Governments of Today*. New York: Macmillan, 1934.

Burk-Bergson, Abram. "A Reformation of Certain Aspects of Welfare Economics." *Quarterly Journal of Economics*, 51 (February 1938).

Burkhead, Jesse. "Budget Classification and Fiscal Planning." *Public Administration Review*, 7 (Autumn 1947), 228–235.

————. *Government Bugeting.* New York: Wiley, 1956.

Burkhead, Jesse, and Jerry Miner. *Public Expenditure.* Chicago: Aldine-Atherton, 1971.

Burton, Ann M. "Treasury Control and Colonial Policy in the Late Nineteenth Century." *Public Administration* (London), 44 (Summer 1966), 169–192.

Caiden, Naomi, and Aaron Wildavsky. *Planning and Budgeting in Poor Countries.* New York: Wiley, 1974.

Cairncross, Alexander K. "The Short Term and the Long in Economic Planning." Tenth Anniversary Lecture, Economic Development Institute, Washington, D.C., January 6, 1966. 30 pp.

California. Assembly. Committee on Efficiency and Cost Control. *A Review of Program Budgeting in California, Part I.* Sacramento, 1971. 60 pp.

Campbell, John Creighton. "How Powerful Is the Ministry of Finance?" (Japan). University Seminar on Modern East Asia, Columbia University, December 10, 1971. 20 pp.

————. "Contemporary Japanese Budget Politics." Unpublished Ph.D. dissertation, Columbia University, 1973.

————. "Japanese Balanced Budgeting." Prepared for the Research Conference on Japanese Organization and Decision-Making, Maui, Hawaii, January 5–10, 1973. 55 pp.

Campbell, W. J. *Australian State Public Finance.* Sydney: Law Book Co., 1954.

Canada. Royal Commission on Government Organization. *Management of the Public Service,* vol. I: section III, "Financial Management," pp. 93–230. Ottawa: The Queen's Printer, 1962.

————. Treasury Board. *Financial Management in Departments and Agencies of the Government of Canada.* 1966.

Cannon, Joseph G. "The National Budget." *Harper's Magazine,* 139 (October 1919), 617–628.

Carey, William D., and Abram M. Vermeulen. "Intergovernmental Co-operation through Budget Channels." *State Government* 36 (Summer 1963), 166–171.

Chase, Samuel B., ed. *Problems in Public Expenditure Analysis. Papers Presented at a Conference of Experts Held September 15–16, 1966.* Studies of Government Finance. Washington, D.C.: Brookings Institution, 1968. 269 pp.

Chermak, Lawrence E. "Planning, Programming, and Budgeting-Accounting." *Armed Forces Comptroller,* 8 (June 1963), 3–8.

Chester, Daniel N. "The Central Machinery for Economic Policy." *Lessons of the British War Economy.* Edited by Daniel N. Chester. Cambridge: Cambridge University Press, 1951.

————. "The Treasury 1956." *Public Administration* (London), 35 (Spring 1957), 15–23.

Chie, Nakane. *Japanese Society.* Berkeley: University of California Press, 1970.

Chow, G. C. "Tests of Equality between Sets of Coefficients in Two Linear Regressions." *Econometrica,* 28 (July 1960), 591–605.

Church, Frank. "Impoundment of Appropriated Funds: The Decline of Congressional Control over Executive Discretion." *Stanford Law Review,* 22 (June 1970), 1240–1253.

Clark, Terry N. "Community Structure, Decision-Making, Budget Expenditures, and Urban Renewal in 51 American Communities." *American Sociological Review*, 33 (August 1968), 576–593.

Clarke, John Maurice. "The Process of Formulating and Authorizing the Budget of the Commonwealth Government of Australia." Unpublished Ph.D. dissertation, American University, 1960.

Clarke, Sir Richard. *New Trends in Government*. Lectures delivered by Sir Richard Clarke at the Civil Service College between March 1 and April 5, 1971. London: Her Majesty's Stationery Office, 1971.

————. "Parliament and Public Expenditure." *Political Quarterly*, 44 (April/June 1973), 137–153.

Cleveland, Frederick A. "Evolution of the Budget Idea in the United States." *Annals of the American Academy of Political and Social Science*, 62 (November 1915), 15–35.

Cohen, Stephen. *Modern Capitalistic Planning; the French Model*. Cambridge: Harvard University Press, 1969.

Cohn, Samuel M. "Economic Policy and the Federal Budget." *Federal Accountant*, 9 (September 1959), 19–30.

Colbs, Marvin. "The Tangled Purse Strings." *GAO Review*, Winter 1970, pp. 11–18.

Commission on the Organization of the Executive Branch of the Government (1947–1949). *Budgeting and Accounting*. Washington, D.C.: Government Printing Office, 1949.

Comptroller General of the United States. Report to Congress. "Survey of Progress in Implementing the Planning-Programming-Budgeting System in Executive Agencies," July 29, 1969, 103 pp.

Cookingham, L. P. "Make Performance Budgeting Practical." *American City*, 72 (May 1957), 141–142.

Cooper, Richard N. "Report of the Provost on the Budget Discrepancy." *Yale Alumni Magazine*, 36 (November 1972), 59–68.

Coskun, Gulay. "Budget Reform in the Republican Government of Turkey." *International Review of Administrative Sciences*, 37 (1971), 330–336.

Cotten, Jonathan. "Campaign 1972 Report: O'Brien Presses for Unity; Democrats Prepare for 1972 Convention." *National Journal*, 3 (October 16, 1971), 2092–2100.

Cowart, Andrew T.; Tore Hansen; and Karl-Erik Brofoss. "Budgetary Strategies and Success at Multiple Decision Levels in the Norwegian Urban Setting." Institute for Political Science, University of Oslo [Norway], January 15, 1974. 50 pp.

Crecine, John P. "Defense Budgeting: Constraints and Organizational Adaptation." Discussion Paper no. 6, Institute of Public Policy Studies, University of Michigan, July 1969, 61 pp. Xerox.

————. *Governmental Problem-Solving: A Computer Simulation of Municipal Budgeting*. American Political Science Research Series. Chicago: Rand McNally, 1969.

Crecine, John P., and Gregory Fischer. "On Resource Allocation Processes in the U.S. Department of Defense." Discussion Paper, Institute of Public Policy Studies, University of Michigan, October 1971.

Crozier, Michel. *The Bureaucratic Phenomenon*. Chicago: University of Chicago Press, 1964.

Culyer, A. J., and P. Jacobs. "The War and Public Expenditure on Mental Health Care in England and Wales — The Postponement Effect." *Social Science and Medicine*, 6 (February 1972), 35–56.

Dahl, Robert. "Power." *International Encyclopedia of the Social Sciences*. New York: Macmillan and Free Press, 1968.

Davies, Robert William. *The Development of the Soviet Budgetary System*. Cambridge: Cambridge University Press, 1958.

Davis, David Howard. "The Price of Power: The Appropriations Process for Seventeen Foreign Affairs Agencies." *Public Policy*, Spring 1970, pp. 355–381.

Davis, Gerald W. "Congressional Power to Require Defense Expenditures." *Fordham Law Review*, 33 (1964/1965), 39–60.

Davis, James W., and Randall B. Ripley. "The Bureau of the Budget and Executive Branch Agencies: Notes on Their Interaction." *Journal of Politics*. 29 (November 1967), 749–769.

Davis, Otto A., and George H. Haines. "A Political Approach to a Theory of Public Expenditure: The Case of Municipalities." *National Tax Journal*, 19 (September 1966), 259–275.

Davis, Otto A.; M. A. H. Dempster; and Aaron Wildavsky. "A Theory of the Budgetary Process." *American Political Science Review*, 60 (September 1966), 529–547.

———. "On the Process of Budgeting II: An Empirical Study of Congressional Appropriations." *Studies in Budgeting*. Edited by Byrne, et al. Amsterdam and London: North Holland Publishers, 1971.

———. "Toward a Predictive Theory of the Federal Budgetary Process." Paper delivered at the Annual Meeting of the American Political Science Association, September 1973.

———. "Towards a Predictive Theory of Government Expenditure: U.S. Domestic Appropriations." *British Journal of Political Science*, vol. 4, part 4 (October 1974), 419–452.

Dean, Alan, as quoted by George A. Steiner. "Problems in Implementing Program Budgeting." *Program Budgeting: Program Analysis and the Federal Budget*, ed. by David Novick. Cambridge: Harvard University Press, 1965.

Dent, Julian. *Crisis in Finance, Crown, Financiers and Society in Seventeenth Century France*. Newton Abbot: Davis and Charles, 1973.

Dhrymes, P. J., et al. "Criteria for Evaluation of Econometric Models." Discussion paper No. 173, Wharton School, Department of Economics, University of Pennsylvania, 1970.

Diesing, Paul. *Reason in Society; Five Types of Decisions and Their Social Conditions*. Urbana: University of Illinois Press, 1962.

Dore, Ronald P., ed. *Aspects of Social Change in Modern Japan*. Princeton: Princeton University Press, 1967.

Doubleday, D. Jay. *Legislative Review of the Budget in California*. Berkeley: Institute of Governmental Studies, University of California, 1967.

Downs, Anthony. "Why the Government Budget is Too Small in a Democracy." *World Politics*, 12 (July 1960), 541–563.

Drees, Willem, Jr. *On the Level of Government Expenditure in the Netherlands After the War.* New York: H. E. Stenfert, 1955.

Dye, Thomas R. *Politics in States and Communities.* Englewood Cliffs, N.J.: Prentice-Hall, 1969.

Earley, James S. "Business Budgeting and the Theory of the Firm." *Journal of Industrial Economics,* 9 (November 1960), 23–42.

Easton, David, ed. *Varieties of Political Theory.* Englewood Cliffs, N.J.: Prentice-Hall, 1966.

Eckstein, Harry. "The Evaluation of Political Performance: Problems and Dilemmas." Sage Professional Papers in Comparative Politics, Series 01–017, vol. 2. Beverly Hills, Calif.: Sage Publications, 1971.

Eckstein, Otto. "A Survey of the Theory of Public Expenditure Criteria." *Public Finances: Needs, Sources, and Utilization; A Conference of the Universities.* National Bureau of Economic Research Special Conference Series 12. Princeton: Princeton University Press, 1961.

"Economics and Operations Research: A Symposium." *Review of Economics and Statistics,* 40 (August 1958).

Fabella, A. V. *An Introduction to Economic Policy.* Manila: University of the Philippines, 1968.

Fellowes, Sir Edward. "Parliament and the Executive: Financial Control of the House of Commons." *Journal of the Parliaments of the Commonwealth,* 43 (July 1962), 223–231.

Fenno, Richard F., Jr. "The House Appropriations Committee as a Political System: The Problem of Integration." *American Political Science Review,* 56 (June 1962), 310–324.

———. Review of *Congressional Control of Administration* by Joseph P. Harris, *American Political Science Review,* 58 (September 1964), 674.

———. *The Power of the Purse; Appropriations Politics in Congress.* Boston: Little, Brown, 1966.

———. "The Impact of PPBS on the Congressional Appropriations Process." *Information Support, Program Budgeting and the Congress.* Edited by Robert Chartrand, Kenneth Janda and Michael Hugo. New York: Spartan Books, 1968.

Fisher, Glenn W., and Robert P. Fairbanks. *Illinois Municipal Finance; A Political and Economic Analysis.* Urbana: University of Illinois Press, 1968.

Fisher, Louis. "Funds Impounded by the President: The Constitutional Issue." *George Washington Law Review,* 38 (October 1969), 124–137.

———. "The Politics of Impounded Funds." *Administrative Science Quarterly,* 15 (September 1970), 361–377.

———. "Presidential Spending Discretion and Congressional Controls." *Law and Contemporary Problems,* 37 (Winter 1972), 135–172.

———. "Impoundment of Funds: Uses and Abuses." *Buffalo Law Review,* 23 (Fall 1973), 141–200.

———. Reprogramming of Funds by the Defense Department." *Journal of Politics,* 36 (February 1974), 77–102.

Flinn, Thomas. *Governor Freeman and the Minnesota Budget.* Inter-University Case Program, no. 60. University of Alabama Press, 1961.

Fox, Douglas M. "Congress and U.S. Military Service Budgets in the Post-War Period: A Research Note." *Midwest Journal of Political Science,* 15 (May 1971), 382–393.

Fox, Irving K., and Orris C. Herfindahl. "Attainment of Efficiency in Satisfying Demands for Water Resources." *American Economic Review,* 54 (May 1964), 198–206.

Fried, Robert C. "Communism, Urban Budgets, and the Two Italies: A Case Study in Comparative Urban Government." *Journal of Politics,* 33 (November 1971), 1008–1051.

Gabis, Stanley T. *Mental Health and Financial Management: Some Dilemmas of Program Budgeting.* Bureau of Social and Political Research, College of Business and Public Service, Michigan State University, 1960. 68 pp.

Galper, Harvey, and Helmut F. Wendell. "Progress in Forecasting the Federal Budget." *American Statistical Association, Proceedings of the Economics and Business Statistics Section* (1968), 86–98.

―――. "Time Lags in the Federal Expenditure Process and Their Stabilization Implications." *Public Finance Quarterly,* 1 (April 1973), 123–146.

Gerwin, Donald. *Budgeting Public Funds; the Decision Process in an Urban School District.* Madison: University of Wisconsin Press, 1969.

Gilmour, Robert. "Central Legislative Clearance: A Revised Perspective." *Public Administration Review,* 31 (March/April 1971), 150–158.

Goodnow, Frank J. "The Limit of Budgetary Control." *Proceedings of the American Political Science Association.* Ninth Annual Meeting, Boston, December 28–31, 1912 (Baltimore: Waverly Press, 1913), pp. 68–77.

Graham, Cole Blease, Jr. *Budgetary Change in South Carolina, 1945–1970.* Unpublished Ph.D. dissertation, University of South Carolina, 1971.

Granick, David. *Management of the Industrial Firm in the USSR: A Study in Soviet Economic Planning.* Studies of the Russian Institute, Columbia University. New York: Columbia University Press, 1959.

Greaney, Walter T., Jr. *The Massachusetts Budget Process.* Bureau of Government Research Public Information Series No. 3. Amherst: University of Massachusetts, 1962.

Groenewegen, P. D. "The Australian Budget Process." *Public Administration* (London), 32 (September 1973), 251–267.

Groves, Harold M. *Financing Government.* Revised edition. New York: Henry Holt, 1945.

Gulick, Luther, et al. *Papers on the Science of Administration.* New York: Columbia University Press, 1937.

Hammond, Arthur, and Aaron Wildavsky. "Comprehensive Versus Incremental Budgeting in the Department of Agriculture." *Administrative Science Quarterly,* 10 (December 1965), 321–346.

Harper, Edwin; Fred A. Kramer; and Andrew M. Rouse. "Implementation and the Use of PPB in Sixteen Federal Agencies." *Public Administration Review,* 29 (November/December 1969), 623–632.

Harsanyi, John. "Measurement of Social Power, Opportunity Costs, and the

Theory of Two-Person Bargaining Games." *Behavioral Sciences.* 7 (January 1962).

Haveman, Robert H., and Julius Margolis, eds. *Public Policy Expenditures and Policy Analysis.* Chicago: Markham, 1970.

Heard, Alexander, ed. *State Legislatures in American Politics.* Englewood Cliffs, N.J.: Prentice-Hall, 1966.

Heckert, Josiah B. *Business Budgeting and Control.* New York: Ronald Press, 1946.

Heclo, Hugh. *Modern Social Policy.* New Haven: Yale, 1974.

Heclo, Hugh, and Aaron Wildavsky. *The Private Government of Public Money: Community and Policy inside British Political Administration.* London: Macmillan; Berkeley: University of California Press, 1974.

The Helpless Giant: A Metaportrait of the Defense Budget. With an essay by Andrew Hamilton and an introduction by Congressman Les Aspin. New York: Schocken Books, 1972.

Hicks, J. R. "The Valuation of Social Income." *Economica,* 7 (May 1940), 105–124.

Higgs, Henry. *The Financial System of the United Kingdom.* London: Macmillan, 1914.

———. "Treasury Control." *Journal of Public Administration* (London), 2 (April 1924), 122–130.

Hitch, Charles J. "Economics and Military Operations Research" in "Economics and Operations Research: A Symposium, II. *Review of Economics and Statistics,* 40 (August 1958).

———. *On the Choice of Objectives in Systems Studies.* Santa Monica, Calif.: The RAND Corp., 1960.

Hitch, Charles J., and Roland N. McKean. *The Economics of Defense in the Nuclear Age.* Cambridge: Harvard University Press, 1963.

Hofferbert, Richard I., and Ira Sharkansky, eds. *State and Urban Politics.* Boston: Little, Brown, 1971.

Hofstede, Geert H. *The Game of Budget Control; How to Live with Budgetary Standards and Yet be Motivated by Them.* New York: Humanities Press, 1968.

Horn, Stephen. *Unused Power: The Work of the Senate Committee on Appropriations.* Washington, D.C.: The Brookings Institution, 1970.

Howard, S. Kenneth. *Changing State Budgeting.* Lexington, Ky.: Council of State Governments, 1973.

Howard, S. Kenneth, and Gloria A. Grizzle. *Whatever Happened to State Budgeting?* Lexington, Ky.: Council of State Governments, 1972.

Howrey, E. P.; L. R. Klein; and M. D. McCarthy. "Notes on Testing the Predictive Performance of Econometric Models." Discussion Paper No. 173, Wharton School, Department of Economics, University of Pennsylvania, 1970.

Huitt, Ralph K. "Congressional Organization and Operations in the Field of Money and Credit." *Fiscal and Debt Management Policies,* a series of research studies. Commission on Money and Credit. Englewood Cliffs, N.J.: Prentice-Hall, 1963.

Improving Congressional Control Over the Budget, A Compendium of Materials. Prepared for the U.S. Senate Subcommittee on Budgeting, Management, and

Expenditure of the Committee on Government Operations, 93rd Cong., 1st Sess., 1973.

International Institute of Administrative Sciences. Report of the Israel National Section, Jerusalem. *New Techniques of Budget Preparation and Management.* Warsaw, 1964. 32 pp.

Ivarsson, Sven Ivar. "Program Budgeting in Sweden." Reprint. Riskrevisionsverket, Fack, 100 26 Stockholm 34, Sweden, June 1969. 23 pp.

Jackson, John E. "Politics and the Budgetary Process." *Social Science Research,* 1 (1972), 35–60.

Jacob, Herbert, and Kenneth Vines, eds. *Politics in the American States: A Comparative Analysis.* Boston: Little, Brown, 1965.

Jacqmotte, J. P. "Tentative Comparative Study of RCB in France and PPBS in Belgium." *International Review of Administrative Sciences,* 36 (1970), 47–55.

Jasinsky, Frank. "Use and Misuse of Efficiency Controls." *Harvard Business Review,* 34 (July/August 1956), 105–112.

Jay, Peter. *The Budget.* Jackdaw no. 125. London: Jackdaw Publications, 1972.

Jewell, Malcolm E. "State Decision Making: The Governor Revisited." *American Governmental Institutions,* ed. by Nelson Polsby and Aaron Wildavsky. Chicago: Rand McNally, 1968.

Jewell, Malcolm E., and Samuel C. Patterson. *The Legislative Process in the United States.* New York: Random House, 1966.

Jones, A. H. M. *A History of Rome Through the Fifth Century, Vol. 1, The Republic.* New York: Walker & Company, 1968.

Johnson, A. W. "Planning, Programming, and Budgeting in Canada." *Public Administration Review,* 33 (January/February 1973), 23–31.

Johnson, Lyndon B. "Transcript of the President's News Conference on Foreign and Domestic Matters, Thursday, August 26, 1965." Quoted in *Program Budgeting,* ed. by David Novick. Cambridge: Harvard University Press, 1965.

Kahn, Herman, and Irwin Mann. *Techniques of Systems Analysis.* Santa Monica, Calif.: The RAND Corp., 1957.

Kaldor, N. "Welfare Propositions of Economics and Interpersonal Comparisons of Utility." *Economic Journal,* 49 (September 1939), 549–552.

Kammerer, Gladys. *Program Budgeting: An Aid to Understanding.* Gainesville: Public Administration Clearing Service, University of Florida, 1959.

Kane, Douglas. "Our Streamrollered Assembly." *Courier-Journal Magazine,* February 20, 1966.

Katzenbach, Edward L., Jr. "How Congress Strains at Gnats, Then Swallows Military Budgets." *Reporter,* 11 (July 20, 1954), 31–35. Mimeographed.

Key, V. O., Jr. "The Lack of a Budgetary Theory." *American Political Science Review,* 34 (December 1940), 1137–1144.

Kim, Sun Kil. "The Politics of a Congressional Budgetary Process: 'Backdoor Spending.' " *Western Political Quarterly,* 21 (December 1968), 606–623.

Kimmel, Lewis H. *Federal Budget and Fiscal Policy 1789–1958.* Washington, D.C.: Brookings Institution, 1959.

Knight, Jonathan. "The State Department Budget, 1933–1965: A Research Note." *Midwest Journal of Political Science,* 12 (November 1968), 587–598.

Knight, Kenneth W. "Formulating the New South Wales Budget." *Public Administration* (Australia), 18 (September 1959), 238–253.

———. *The Literature of State Budgeting in Australia, Canada, and the United States of America: A Survey and Select Bibliography.* Queensland: University of Queensland Press, 1970.

Kolodziej, Edward A. "Congressional Responsibility for the Common Defense: The Money Problem." *Western Political Quarterly,* 16 (March 1963), 149–160.

Kressbach, Thomas W. *The Michigan City Manager in Budgetary Proceedings.* Ann Arbor: Michigan Municipal League. Institute of Public Administration, University of Michigan, 1962. 51 pp.

Krutilla, John V. "Is Public Intervention in Water Resources Development Conducive to Economic Efficiency?" *Natural Resources Journal,* January 1966, pp. 60–75.

Krutilla, John V., and Otto Eckstein. *Multiple Purpose River Development.* Studies in Applied Economic Analysis. Baltimore: Johns Hopkins Press, 1958.

LaFaver, John D. "Zero-Base Budgeting in New Mexico." *State Government* XLVII:2 (Spring 1974).

Landau, Martin. "Redundancy, Rationality and the Problem of Overlap and Duplication." *Public Administration Review,* 29 (July/August 1969), 346–358.

Lawton, Frederick J. "Legislative-Executive Relationships in Budgeting as Viewed by the Executive." *Public Administration Review,* 13 (Summer 1953), 169–176.

Lazarsfeld, P. F., and Morris Rosenberg, eds. *The Language of Social Research.* Glencoe, Ill.: Free Press, 1955.

Lee Hahn-Been. "The Korean Budget Reform 1955–1961: A Reformer's Self-Evaluation." Prepared for presentation to the Development Administration Group Research Seminar held in Bangkok, Thailand, March 18–23, 1968.

Leiserson, Avery. "Coordination of Federal Budgetary and Appropriations Procedures under the Legislative Reorganization Act of 1946." *National Tax Journal,* I (June 1948), 118–126.

Leppo, Matti. "The Double-Budget System in the Scandinavian Countries." *Public Finance,* 5 (1950), 137–147.

Levy, Frank; Arnold Meltsner; and Aaron Wildavsky. *Urban Outcomes.* Berkeley: University of California Press, 1974.

Lewis, Verne B. "Toward a Theory of Budgeting." *Public Administration Review,* 12 (Winter 1952), 42–54.

Lindblom, C. E. "Decision-Making in Taxation and Expenditure." *Public Finances: Needs, Sources, Utilization; A Conference of the Universities — National Bureau Committee for Economic Research.* National Bureau for Economic Research Special Conference Series, 12. Princeton: Princeton University Press, 1961.

Lipset, Seymour, et al. *Union Democracy: The Internal Politics of the International Typographical Union.* Glencoe, Ill.: Free Press, 1956.

Little, I. M. D. *A Critique of Welfare Economics.* Oxford: Clarendon Press, 1950.

Loarie, Don. "Budgeting in the California Department of Public Health." Unpublished paper, University of California, Berkeley, 1969.

Loeffler, Herman C. "Alice in Budget-Land," *National Tax Journal,* 4 (March 1951), 54–64.

Lord, Guy. *The French Budgetary Process*. Berkeley: University of California Press, 1973.

Maas, Arthur. "In Accord with the Program of the President?" *Public Policy: A Yearbook of the Graduate School of Public Administration,* Harvard University, Vol. IV. Edited by Carl J. Friedrich and John K. Galbraith. Cambridge: Harvard University Press, 1953.

McCorry, Jesse J. Unpublished paper on Oakland budgeting submitted to Aaron Wildavsky's course on Budgeting.

McKean, Ronald N. *Efficiency in Government Through Systems Analysis with Emphasis on Water Resources Development*. New York: Wiley, 1958.

McLeod, T. H. "Budgeting Provincial Expenditure." *Proceedings of the Fifth Annual Conference of the Institute of Public Administration of Canada, September 9–12, 1953*. Edited by Philip T. Clark. Toronto: The Institute, 1953.

March, James. "The Power of Power." *Varieties of Political Theory,* ed. by David Easton. Englewood Cliffs, N.J: Prentice-Hall, 1966.

Marre, A. S. "Departmental Financial Control." *Public Administration,* 35 (Summer 1957), 169–178.

Martin, James W., ed. *Management Analysis for State Budget Offices*. Lexington, Ky.: MASBO, Council of State Governments, 1969.

Marx, Fritz M. "The Bureau of the Budget; Its Evolution and Current Role, I." *American Political Science Review,* 39 (August 1945), 653–684; II: *American Political Science Review,* 39 (October 1945), 869–898.

Masotti, Louis H., and Don R. Bowen. "Communities and Budgets: The Sociology of Municipal Expenditures." *Urban Affairs Quarterly,* I (December 1965), 39–58.

May, Ronald James. *Financing the Small States in Australian Federalism*. Melbourne: Oxford University Press, 1971.

Mayo, Elton. *The Social Problems of an Industrial Civilization*. Cambridge: Graduate School of Business Administration, Harvard University, 1945.

Meade, J. E. *The Theory of International Economic Policy*. Vol. II: *Trade and Welfare*. New York: Oxford University Press, 1955.

Meltsner, Arnold J. *The Politics of City Revenue*. Berkeley: University of California Press, 1971.

Meltsner, Arnold J., and Aaron Wildavsky. "Leave City Budgeting Alone!: A Survey, Case Study and Recommendations for Reform." *Financing the Metropolis: Public Policy in Urban Economies*. Edited by John P. Crecine. Urban Affairs Annual Reviews, IV, Beverly Hills, Calif.: Sage Publications, 1970.

Merewitz, Leonard, and Stephen H. Sosnick. *The Budget's New Clothes: A Critique of Planning-Programming-Budgeting and Benefit-Cost Analysis*. Series in Public Policy Analysis. Chicago: Markham, 1971.

Merton, Robert K. *Social Theory and Social Structure*. Glencoe, Ill.: Free Press, 1957.

Miyamoto, M.; Y. Sakudo; and Y. Yasuba. "Economic Development in Preindustrial Japan, 1859–1914." *The Journal of Economic History,* vol. 25, no. 4 (December 1965).

Mosher, Frederick C. "The Executive Budget, Empire State Style." *Public Administration Review,* 12 (1952), 73–84.

————. *Program Budgeting: Theory and Practice; with particular reference to the U.S. Department of the Army.* Chicago: Public Administration Service, 1954.

————. "Limitations and Problems of PPBS in the States." *Public Administration Review,* 29 (March/April 1969), 160–167.

Mosher, Frederick C., and John E. Harr. *Programming Systems and Foreign Affairs Leadership; An Attempted Innovation.* Inter-University Case Program. New York: Oxford University Press, 1970.

Mueller, Eva. "Public Attitudes Toward Fiscal Program." *Quarterly Journal of Economics,* 77 (May 1963), 210–235.

The Municipal Yearbook, 1973. Washington, D.C.: International City Management Association, 1973.

Musgrave, Richard Abel. *Fiscal Systems.* Studies in Comparative Economics, 10. New Haven: Yale University Press, 1969.

Mushkin, Selma J., et al. *Implementing PPB in State, City, and County; A Report on the 5-5-5 Project.* Washington, D.C.: State-Local Finances Project, George Washington University, 1969.

Natchez, Peter B., and Irvin C. Bupp. "Policy and Priority in the Budgetary Process." *American Political Science Review,* 67 (September 1973), 951–963.

National Bureau of Economic Research. *Public Finances: Needs, Sources, Utilization; A Conference of the Universities — National Bureau Committee for Economic Research.* National Bureau of Economic Research Special Conference Series, 12. Princeton: Princeton University Press, 1961.

National Journal, 3 (October 16, 1971) 2092.

Neher, Clark D. *Rural Thai Government: The Politics of the Budgetary Process.* Special Report Series, no. 4. Center for Southeast Asian Studies, Northern Illinois University, DeKalb, January 1972. 63 pp.

Nelson, Dalmas H. "The Omnibus Appropriations Act of 1950." *Journal of Politics,* 15 (May 1953), 274–288.

Neumann, Rudiger W. "Introducing Programme Budgeting in Norway." *International Review of Administrative Sciences,* 37 (1971), 403–409.

————. "Structural Reform of the Federal Budget Process." Domestic Affairs Study, no. 12. Washington, D.C.: American Enterprise Institute for Public Policy Research, 1973. 58 pp.

Neustadt, Richard. "Presidency and Legislation: The Growth of Central Clearance." *American Political Science Review,* 48 (September 1954), 641–671.

————. "Presidency and Legislation: Planning the President's Program." *American Political Science Review,* 49 (December 1955), 980–1021.

New York (State). Division of the Budget. *Guidelines for Program Analysis and Review.* 1970.

Nienaber, Jeanne, and Aaron Wildavsky. *The Budgeting and Evaluation of Federal Recreation Programs, or Money Doesn't Grow on Trees.* New York: Basic Books, 1973.

Niskanen, William A. *Controllability of the Fiscal Variables.* Evaluation Division Report, OMB, 1971.

Novick, David. *Origin and History of Program Budgeting.* Santa Monica, Calif.: RAND Corp., October 1966. 11 pp.

Novick, David, ed. *Program Budgeting: Program Analysis and the Federal Budget.* Rand Series. Cambridge: Harvard University Press, 1965.

Olsen, Johna P. "Local Budgeting, Decision-Making or a Ritual Act?" Unpublished draft. Institute of Sociology, University of Bergen, Norway. Date unknown. 45 pp.

O'R. Hayes, Frederick. "Creative Budgeting in New York City: An Interview with Former Budget Director Frederick O'R. Hayes." Washington, D.C.: Urban Institute, June 1971.

Organizing for National Security: The Budget and the Policy Process. Hearings before the U.S. Senate Subcommittee on National Policy Machinery of the Government Operations Committee, 87th Cong., 1st Sess., Part VIII, 1961.

Ott, David J., and Attiat Ott. *Federal Budget Policy.* Rev. ed. Washington: Brookings Institution, 1969.

Otto, Eberhard. *Aegypten, Der Weg des Pharaonenreiches,* 3rd ed. Stuttgart: W. Kohlhammer (Urban), 1968.

Ouchi, Hyoye. "The Japanese Financial Department." *Municipal Research,* no. 83 (March 1917), 45–56.

Palmer, Robert S. "An Administrative Board's Response to Statutory Control: A Review of the Budgetary Process in the ——— Water Conservation District." (December 1965).

Patton, Carl V. "Budgeting Under Crisis: The Budgetary Process of the Confederate States of America." Paper submitted to Aaron Wildavsky's seminar on Budgets as Political Instruments, 1974.

Paulson, Robert I. "Poverty, Uncertainty and Goal Dissensus: The Causes of Underspending in the Model Cities Program." Paper submitted to Wildavsky's seminar on Budgeting as Political Instruments, University of California, Berkeley, 1973.

Phillips, John. "The Hadacol of the Budget Makers." *National Tax Journal,* 4 (September 1951), 255–268.

Pierce, Lawrence. *The Politics of Fiscal Policy Formation.* Pacific Palisades, Calif.: Goodyear, 1971.

Pine, Norman. "The Impoundment Dilemma: Crisis in Constitutional Government." *Yale Review of Law and Social Action,* 3 (Winter 1973), 99–143.

Planning-Programming-Budgeting. Hearings before the U.S. Senate Subcommittee on National Security and International Operations of the Committee on Government Operations, 90th Cong., 1st Sess., 1967.

Planning-Programming-Budgeting System: Progress and Potentials. Hearings before the U.S. Congress Joint Subcommittee on Economy in Government of the Joint Economic Committee, 90th Cong., 1st Sess., 1967.

Pressman Jeffrey L. "Political Implications of the New Federalism." Paper submitted for a meeting of the Metropolitan Governance Research Committee, Columbus, Ohio. May 17, 1974.

Pressman, Jeffrey, and Aaron Wildavsky. *Implementation.* Berkeley: University of California Press, 1973.

Prest, A. R., and R. Turvey. "Cost-Benefit Analysis: A Survey." *Economic Journal,* 75 (December 1965), 683–735.

Priestley, Margaret. "The Gold Coast Select Committee on Estimates: 1913–1950." *The International Journal of African Historical Studies,* 6 (1973), 543–564.

Proxmire, William. *Uncle Sam — The Last of the Bigtime Spenders.* New York: Simon & Schuster, 1972.

Pryor, Frederic. *Public Expenditures in Communist and Capitalist Nations.* London: Allen & Unwin, 1968.

Putnam, Robert D. *The Beliefs of Politicians: Ideology, Conflict, and Democracy in Italy and Britain.* Yale Studies in Political Science, 24. New Haven: Yale University Press, 1973.

Pyhrr, Peter A. *Zero-Base Budgeting: A Practical Management Tool Evaluating Expenses.* New York: John Wiley & Sons, 1973.

Quade, E. S., ed. *Analysis for Military Decisions.* Amsterdam: North Holland Pub., 1970.

Rae, Douglas W. *Political Consequences of Electoral Laws.* Rev. ed. New Haven: Yale University Press, 1971.

Ranney, Austin. "Parties in State Politics." *Politics in the American States.* Edited by Herbert Jacob and Kenneth W. Vines. Boston: Little, Brown, 1965.

Ranum, O. A. *Richlieu and the Councillors of Louis XIII.* Oxford: Clarendon Press, 1963.

Reagan, Michael D. "Congress Meets Science: The Appropriations Process." *Science,* 164 (May 23, 1969), 926–931.

Redford, Emmette S., et al. *Politics and Government in the United States.* Coordinating editor Alan F. Westin. New York: Harcourt Brace and World, 1965.

Rivlin, Alice. "The Planning, Programming, and Budgeting System in the Department of Health, Education, and Welfare: Some Lessons in Expertise." *Public Policy Expenditures and Policy Analysis.* Edited by Robert H. Haverman and Julius Margolis. Chicago: Markham Press, 1970.

———. "Improving the Congressional Budget Process." U.S. House Select Committee on Committees, *Working Papers on House Committee Organization and Operation,* 93rd Cong., 1973. 5 pp.

Roberts, Ralph S. "USDA's Pioneering Performance Budget." *Public Administration Review,* 20 (Spring 1960), 74–78.

Roethlisberger, Fritz. *Management and Morale.* Cambridge: Harvard University Press, 1941.

Roskamp, Karl W., and Gordon C. McMeekin. "The Symmetry Approach to Committee Decisions: An Empirical Study of a Local Government Budget Committee." *Zeitschrift Fur Die Gesamte Staatswissenschaft,* Band 126, Heft 1 (January 1970), 75–96.

Ross, Lillian. "$1,031,961,754.73." *New Yorker,* 28 (July 12, 1947), 27–36.

Rostovtseff, Mikhail. *The Social and Economic History of the Roman Empire.* Oxford: Clarendon Press, 1926.

Royal Institute of Public Administration, Chairman: R. S. Edwards, Research Officer: J. S. Hines. *Budgeting in Public Authorities.* New York: Macmillan, 1959.

Sacks, Seymour, and William F. Hellmuth, Jr. *Financing Government in a Metro-*

politan Area; The Cleveland Experience. New York: Free Press of Glencoe, 1961.

Sakatani, Y., Baron. "Government of the City of Tokyo." *Municipal Research,* no. 83 (March 1917), 57–72.

Saloma, John S., III. *The Responsible Use of Power; A Critical Analysis of the Congressional Budget Process.* Washington, D.C.: American Enterprise Institute for Public Policy Research, 1964.

Sansome, George. *A History of Japan, 1615–1867.* Stanford: Stanford University Press, 1963.

Sapolsky, Harvey M. *The Polaris System Development; Bureaucratic and Pragmatic Success in Government.* Cambridge: Harvard University Press, 1972.

Schelling, Thomas C. "PPBS and Foreign Affairs." Memorandum prepared at the request of the U.S. Senate Subcommittee on National Security and International Operations of the Committee on Government Operations, 90th Cong., 1st Sess., 1968.

Schick, Allen. "Control Patterns in State Budget Execution." *Public Administration Review,* 24 (June 1964), 97–106.

———. "The Road to PPB: The Stages of Budget Reform." *Public Administration Review,* 26 (December 1966), 243–258.

———. "Systems Politics and Systems Budgeting." *Public Administration Review,* 29 (March/April 1969), 137–151.

———. "The Budget Bureau that Was: Thoughts on the Rise, Decline and Future of a Presidential Agency." *Law and Contemporary Problems,* 35 (Summer 1970), 519–539.

———. *Budget Innovation in the States.* Washington, D.C.: Brookings Institution, 1971.

———. "Congress v. the Budget." U.S. House Select Committee on Committees, *Working Papers on House Committees Organization and Operation,* 93rd Cong., 1973. 11 pp.

———. "A Death in the Bureaucracy: The Demise of Federal PPB." *Public Administration Review,* 33 (March/April 1973), 146–156.

Schubert, Glendon A., Jr., and Donald F. McIntyre. "Preparing the Michigan State Budget." *Public Administration Review,* 13 (Autumn 1953), 237–246.

Schulsinger, Gerald G. *The General Accounting Office: Two Glimpses.* Inter-University Case Program, no. 35. University of Alabama Press, 1956.

Schultze, Charles L. *The Politics and Economics of Public Spending.* The H. Rowan Gaither Lectures in Systems Science. Washington, D.C.: Brookings Institution, 1968.

Scitovsky, T. "A Note on Welfare Propositions in Economics." *Review of Economic Studies,* 9 (1941), 77–88.

Scott, Robert E. "Budget Making in Mexico." *Inter-American Economic Affairs,* 9 (1955), 3–20.

Scott, W. R. *The Constitution and Finance of English, Scottish and Irish Joint-Stock Companies to 1720,* Vol. 1. Cambridge: University Press, 1912.

Segsworth, R. V. "PPBS and Policy Analysis: The Canadian Experience." *International Review of Administrative Sciences,* 38 (1972), 419–425.

Setting National Priorities: The Budget. 1971. Prepared by Charles L. Schultze and others. Washington, D.C.: Brookings Institution.

Shadoan, Arlene Theurer. *Organization, Role, and Staffing of State Budget Offices.* Lexington: University of Kentucky, 1961.

————. *Preparation, Review and Execution of the State Operating Budget.* Lexington: Bureau of Business Research, College of Commerce, University of Kentucky, 1963.

Sharkansky, Ira. "Four Agencies and an Appropriations Subcommittee: A Comparative Study of Budget Strategies." *Midwest Journal of Political Science,* 9 (August 1965), 254–281.

————. "Agency Requests, Gubernatorial Support and Budget Success in State Legislatures." *American Political Science Review,* 62 (December 1968), 1220–1231.

————. *The Politics of Taxing and Spending.* Indianapolis: Bobbs-Merrill, 1969.

Sharkansky, Ira, ed. *Policy Analysis in Political Science.* Chicago: Markham, 1970.

Shipp, G. W. "Program Budgeting in the Defense Department: A Small Change." Unpublished paper, University of California, Berkeley, 1966.

Simon, Herbert A. "The Birth of an Organization: The Economic Cooperation Administration." *Public Administration Review,* 13 (Autumn 1953), 227–236.

————. *Models of Man.* New York: Wiley, 1957.

Smith, Napier V. "Budgeting on the ———— Deficit." Unpublished paper submitted for Aaron Wildavsky's course on Budgeting, December 1969.

Smith, T. M. "County Budgeting in a Rural Small Town Setting." Unpublished paper submitted for Aaron Wildavsky's course on Budgeting, January 1965.

Smith, William O. *Atlanta Journal–Atlanta Constitution.* February 6, 1969.

Smithies, Arthur. *The Budgetary Process in the United States.* New York: McGraw-Hill, 1955.

Spigelman, James. "Program Budgeting for New South Wales." *Public Administration* (Australia), 26 (December 1967), 348–367.

Stedry, Andrew C. *Budget Control and Cost Behavior.* Ford Foundation doctoral dissertation series. Englewood Cliffs, N.J.: Prentice-Hall, 1960.

Steiss, Alan Walter. *Public Budgeting and Management.* Lexington, Mass.: Lexington Books, 1972.

Stourm, René. *The Budget.* Translated by Thaddeus Plazinski from the 7th ed. of *Le Budget,* Paris, 1913. New York: D. Appleton, 1971.

Sturm, Albert L. "Structural Factors in Management Analysis." *Management Analysis for State Budget Offices,* ed. by James W. Martin. Lexington, Ky.: MASBO, Council of State Governments, 1969.

Sundleson, Jacob Wilner. *Budgetary Methods in National and State Governments.* New York State Tax Commission Special Report no. 14. Albany, N.Y.: J. B. Lyon, 1938.

Surrey, Stanley S. "Tax Expenditures in Relation to Congressional Control over Budgetary Outlay and Receipt Totals." U.S. House Select Committee on Committees, *Working Papers on House Committees Organization and Operation,* 93rd Cong., 1973. 5 pp.

"Symposium on Budgetary Theory." *Public Administration Review,* 10 (Winter 1950), 20–31.

"Symposium on Performance Budgeting: Has the Theory Worked?" *Public Administration Review,* 20 (Spring 1960), 63–85.

Thayer, Nathaniel B. *How the Conservatives Rule in Japan.* Princeton: Princeton University Press, 1969.

Toward Better Budgeting. Detroit: Governmental Research Association, 1941.

Trend, B. St. J. "Great Britain." *International Social Science Bulletin,* 8 (1956), 239–252.

Trever, Albert E. *History of Ancient Civilization,* Vol. II, *The Roman World.* New York: Harcourt Brace, 1939.

Turnbull, Augustus B., III. *Politics in the Budgetary Process: The Case of Georgia.* Unpublished Ph.D. dissertation, University of Georgia, Athens, Georgia, 1967.

U.S. Congress. Joint Study Committee on Budget Control. "Recommendations for Improving Congressional Control over Budgetary Outlay and Receipt Totals." Washington, D.C.: Government Printing Office, 1973. 50 pp.

U.S. News and World Report. "Big Turnabout for the States — Now the Money is Rolling In." June 18, 1973.

U.S. Senate, Committee on Government Operations, Subcommittee on National Policy Machinery. *Organizing for National Security; The Budget and the Policy Process.* 87th Cong., 1st Sess., 1961.

Van Gunsteren, Herman R. *The Quest for Control.* New York: Wiley, in press.

Walinsky, Louis J. *Economic Development in Burma, 1951–1960.* New York: Twentieth Century Fund, 1962.

Wallace, Robert A. "Congressional Control of the Budget." *Midwest Journal of Political Science,* 3 (May 1959), 151–167.

Wallin, Bruce. "The Impact of Revenue Sharing on Urban Areas: California and New Jersey." Unpublished master's thesis, University of California, Berkeley, March 1973.

Wann, A. J. "Franklin D. Roosevelt and the Bureau of the Budget." *Business and Government Review,* 9 (March/April 1968), 32–41.

Ward, Norman. *Public Purse: A Study in Canadian Democracy.* Toronto: University of Toronto Press, 1962.

Washington, D.C. *The Fiscal Year 1971 Program Budget for the City of Washington, D.C.* 1971.

Waterston, Albert. *Planning in Pakistan; Organization and Implementation.* Baltimore: Johns Hopkins Press, 1963.

———. *Development Planning: Lessons of Experience.* Baltimore: Johns Hopkins Press, 1965.

———. *Practical Program of Planning for Ghana.* Washington, D.C.: International Bank for Reconstruction and Development, 1968.

Weidenbaum, Murray L.; Dan Larkins; and Philip N. Marcus. *Matching Needs and Resources: Reforming the Federal Budget.* Washington, D.C.: American Enterprise Institute for Public Policy Research, 1973.

Wetlesen, Tone Schou. "University Budgeting. A Study in Administrative Behavior." Abstract of Magister Dissertation, Oslo, 1967. Unpublished draft. Berkeley, Calif., February 1968.

White, Michael J. "The Impact of Management Science on Political Decision

Making." *Planning Programming Budgeting; A Systems Approach to Management.* Edited by Fremont J. Lyden and Ernest G. Miller. 2nd ed. Chicago: Markham, 1971.

Wildavsky, Aaron. "Political Implications of Budgetary Reform." *Public Administration Review,* 21 (Autumn 1961), 183–190.

——. *The Politics of the Budgetary Process.* Boston: Little, Brown, 1964.

——. "The Practical Consequences of the Theoretical Study of Defense Policy." *Public Administration Review,* 25 (March 1965), 90–103.

——. "Toward a Radical Incrementalism; A Proposal to Aid Congress in Reform of the Budgetary Process." *Congress: The First Branch of Government.* Washington, D.C.: American Enterprise Institute for Public Policy Research, 1965.

——. "The Political Economy of Efficiency: Cost-Benefit Analysis, Systems Analysis, and Program Budgeting." *Public Administration Review,* 26 (December 1966), 292–310.

——. "The Two Presidencies." *Trans-action.* 4 (December 1966).

——. "Budgeting as a Political Process." *International Encyclopedia of the Social Sciences,* II. New York: Macmillan and Free Press, 1968.

——. "Rescuing Policy Analysis from PPBS." *Public Administration Review,* 29 (March/April 1969), 189–202.

——. "Does Planning Work?" *The Public Interest,* 24 (Summer 1971), 95–104.

——. "The Self-Evaluating Organization." *Public Administration Review,* 32 (September/October 1972), 509–520.

——. "The Annual Expenditure Increment — or How Can Congress Regain Control of the Budget?" *The Public Interest,* 33 (Fall 1973), 84–108.

——. *The Politics of the Budgetary Process.* 2nd ed. Boston: Little, Brown, 1974.

Wildavsky, Aaron, and Arthur Hammond. "Comprehensive Versus Incremental Budgeting in the Department of Agriculture." *Administrative Science Quarterly,* 10 (December 1965), 321–346.

Wildavsky, Aaron, and Jeanne Nienaber. *The Budgeting and Evaluation of Federal Recreation Programs, or Money Doesn't Grow on Trees.* New York: Basic Books, 1973.

Wildavsky, Aaron, and Nelson Polsby, ed. *American Governmental Institutions.* Chicago: Rand McNally, 1968.

Williams, J. D. "Impounding of Funds by the Bureau of the Budget." Inter-University Case Program no. 28. University of Alabama Press, 1955.

Williams, Philip. *Crisis and Compromise: Politics in the Fourth Republic.* 3rd ed. Previous ed. published under *Politics in Post-War France.* Hamden, Conn.: Anchor Books, 1964.

Williamson, Oliver E. "A Rational Theory of the Federal Budgeting Process." *Papers on Non-Market Decision Making,* II. Edited by Gordon Tullock. Charlottesville: Thomas Jefferson Center for Political Economy, University of Virginia, 1967.

Willoughby, William Franklin. *The Movement for Budgetary Reform in the States.* New York: D. Appleton, 1918.

——. *The Problem of a National Budget.* New York: D. Appleton, 1918.

————. *The National Budget System; With Suggestions for Its Improvement.* Baltimore: Johns Hopkins Press, 1927.

Winnie, Richard W. "The City of ———— Deficit." Unpublished paper; University of California, submitted for Aaron Wildavsky's course on Budgeting, December 1969.

Wohlstetter, Albert. "Analysis and Design of Conflict Systems." *Analysis for Military Decisions,* ed. by E. S. Quade. Amsterdam: North Holland Publishing, 1970.

Wolfson, Stanley M. "Economic Characteristics and Trends in Municipal Finances." *Municipal Year Book, 1973.* Washington, D.C.: International City Management Association, 1973.

Woolsey, Robert James, Jr. "Program Budgeting for Police Departments." *Yale Law Journal,* 76 (March 1967), 822–828.

Wright, Deil S. "Trends in Municipal Expenditures and Taxes in Iowa." Parts I and II. *Iowa Municipalities,* 17 (January/February 1963).

————. "The Dynamics of Budgeting — Large Council Manager Cities." Unpublished draft. Department of Political Science. Institute for Research in Social Science, University of North Carolina, 1969.

Wright, Deil S.; Robert W. Marker; and Garlyn H. Wessel. *A Half-Century of Local Governmental Finances: The Case of Iowa — 1910–1960.* Institute of Public Affairs, Iowa Center for Research in School Administration, 1963.

BUDGET BIBLIOGRAPHIES

Doh, Joon Chien. *Planning-Programming-Budgeting System in Three Federal Agencies.* New York: Praeger, 1971. Bibliography pp. 185–190.

Hawaii State Library. *PPB Bibliography.* 1970. 53 pp.

Honey, Harold A. *Planning-Programming-Budgeting Approach to Government Decision-Making.* New York: Praeger, 1968. Annotated bibliography pp. 255–264.

Jacobson, S. "Bibliography on Planning-Programming-Budgeting." *Municipal Reference Library Notes,* 43 (January 1969), 1–3.

Tolmachev, Mirjana. *Planning-Programming-Budgeting System; A Selected Bibliography of Recent Materials.* Pennsylvania State Library. General Library Bureau. July 1970. 5 pp.

Tudor, Dean. *Planning-Programming-Budgeting Systems.* Rev. ed. including Exchange Bibliographies nos. 121 and 183. Council of Planning Librarians (Exchange Bibliography no. 289), 1972. 28 pp.

U.S. Bureau of the Budget. Library. *House Committee on Appropriations and the Budget Process: Selected References.* 1963. 5 pp.

U.S. Library of Congress. *The Appropriations Process and Committees in Congress, A Selected Bibliography.* Legislative Reference Service, 1965.

U.S. Library of Congress. Legislative Reference Service. *The Planning-Programming-Budgeting System: An Annotated Bibliography.* By Robert L. Chartrand and Dennis W. Brezene. 1967. 23 pp.

Washington State Library, Olympia. *Performance Budgeting Bibliography.* 1969. 6 pp.

Young, H. "Performance and Program Budgeting; An Annotated Bibliography." *American Libraries,* 61 (January 1967), 63–67.

Index

Accounting, shifts caused by changes in, 42–43

Advocates (spenders): impact of absence of, 15, 187–188, 191–193, 198; impact of absence of both guardians and, 194–198, 198–199; role of, in process of budgeting, 7, 8–9; in United States federal government budgeting, 24–26

Agencies: exploring environmental influences on, 65–68; and OMB decision rules, equations for, 33–35, 38–39

Agency for Legislative Fiscal Analysis (California), 183

Agricultural Marketing Service, 46

Alternating incremental and repetitive budgeting, in wealthy and uncertain environments, 12, 16

Annual expenditure increment, 398–400; impact of, 400–402

Anshen, Melvin, 326, 327, 328, 331

Anton, Thomas J.: on city budgeting, 129, 130–131; *The Politics of State Expenditure in Illinois,* 171; on role of legislatures in state budgets, 180–181, 182; on state budgeting, 168, 173, 177

Appropriations Committee, House, 25–26, 50, 184, 398; and annual expenditure increment, 401; on appropriations for soil and water conservation activities, 43; on budget cuts, 44–45; and Congress, 210; and percentage cuts, 31; and program budgeting, 311, 313, 329; role of, in guarding Treasury, 28–29; role of politics in reshaping agency budgeting

by, 133; time spent by chairman of, on budget, 211

Appropriations Committee, Senate, 25–26, 184, 398; and annual expenditure increment, 400; on Bureau of Internal Revenue's budget cut, 43; and percentage cuts, 31

Appropriations committees, 43; congressional power and, 29–30; coordination within, 27–28; power of, 24, 30

Appropriations policy, changes in, causing shifts, 43–44, 46

Arbitration (*arbitrage*), prevalence of, as norm in French budgeting, 98, 227

Argentina, 158, 159; expenditure constraints in, 148, 149; program budgeting in, 349, 350; repetitive budgeting in, 144–145; revenue constraints in, 143

Army Corps of Engineers, 62

Atomic Energy Commission, 62

Australia, 336

Austria, 337

Axelrod, Donald, 295–296

Balance (*baransū*), emphasis of, in Japanese budgeting, 104–105, 217, 227

Bankhead-Jones Farm Tenant Act, 43, 45

Base, budgetary, 6, 24–25, 222–223

Belgium, 337

Bell, David, 281

Bell, George A., 180

Bentley, Eric, 332

Biser, Benton, 279

Board of Education, 132

Transportation, program budgeting and, 326–327

Treasury (Great Britain), 73–75, 87, 91; ministers, 81–86; PESC and, 366–381 *passim;* and program budgeting, 335–336; relations between departments and, 75–80

Treasury (United States), 207, 218

Truman, Harry, 56, 333

Trust, as feature in British government, 69, 70–71, 227

Turnbull, Augustus B., III, 178, 180, 181, 184–185, 295

Turvey, R., 319

TVA, 67

"Twelfths," French practice of, 12, 93

Uncertainty, budgetary, 10–12, 139–142, 383–385

Underspending, problem of, in low-income countries, 150

United Nations Budgeting and Planning Workshops, 255

United States, 18; absence of finance ministry in, 207; containment of conflict (COC) in, 243–247, 248, 266; effect of political structure and elite culture on budgetary process in, 12–15; incrementalism in, 216; levels of budgetary decision to cope with conflict in, 225–231 *passim;* measures of incrementalism and proportionality in, 239–243; program budgeting in, 337–348; support-on-spending (SOS) ratio for, 239, 240, 248, 266; taxation in, 235–236; visibility-of-tax-increase index for, 238–239; wealth (GNP) of, 233; wealth-growth index for, 236–238, 239

University of California at Berkeley, 164–165

Venezuela, 403

Verres, Gaius, 271

Visibility-of-tax-increase index, 238–239, 265

Walinsky, Louis J., 146

Washington, D.C., program budgeting in, 340

Waterston, Albert, 146–147, 154, 156

Ways and Means Committee, 400, 402

Wealth, budgeting in environments of, 10–13, 16, 19

Wealth-growth index, 236–238, 239, 265

Wealthy countries, program budgeting in, 335–337

Williams, Mennen, 171

Wilson, Harold, 205

Wisconsin, PPBS in, 345, 346

Wohlstetter, Albert, 322, 323, 324

Wright, Deil S., 130

x_t, 33–38

y_t, 33–38

Young, E. Hilton, 279

Zero-base budget, 221, 276, 341; adoption of, 281–282; application of concept of, 282–285; attitude toward annual, 293–294; comprehensiveness of, 285–286; defined, 280; institution of, in Georgia and New Mexico, 294–296; objectives of, 287–290; political use of, 293; staff on, 287; unanticipated consequences of preparing, 290–293